Islam, Secularism, and Liberal Democracy

Islam, Secularism, and Liberal Democracy

Toward a Democratic Theory for Muslim Societies

NADER HASHEMI

OXFORD
UNIVERSITY PRESS

OXFORD
UNIVERSITY PRESS

Oxford University Press is a department of the University of Oxford.
It furthers the University's objective of excellence in research, scholarship,
and education by publishing worldwide.

Oxford   New York
Auckland   Cape Town   Dar es Salaam   Hong Kong   Karachi
Kuala Lumpur   Madrid   Melbourne   Mexico City   Nairobi
New Delhi   Shanghai   Taipei   Toronto

With offices in
Argentina   Austria   Brazil   Chile   Czech Republic   France   Greece
Guatemala   Hungary   Italy   Japan   Poland   Portugal   Singapore
South Korea   Switzerland   Thailand   Turkey   Ukraine   Vietnam

Oxford is a registered trade mark of Oxford University Press
in the UK and certain other countries.

Published in the United States of America by
Oxford University Press
198 Madison Avenue, New York, NY 10016

Library of Congress Cataloging-in-Publication Data
Hashemi, Nader, 1966–
Islam, secularism, and liberal democracy / Nader Hashemi.
  p. cm.
Includes bibliographical references and index.
ISBN 978-0-19-532124-1 (hardcover); 978-0-19-992907-8 (paperback)
1. Islam and secularism.   2. Democracy—Religious aspects—Islam.   3. Secularism—
Islamic countries.   4. Democracy—Islamic countries.   5. Islam and politics—Islamic
countries.   6. Islamic countries—Politics and government—20th century.   I. Title.
BP190.5.S35H38 2009
297.2'72—dc22   2008026682

9 8 7 6 5 4 3 2 1

Printed in the United States of America
on acid-free paper

To My Parents; for All Their Sacrifices

We should not . . . conclude from this that politics and religion have a common object among us, but that in the beginning stages of nations the one serves as an instrument of the other.

—Jean-Jacques Rousseau

Men make their own history, but they do not make it just as they please; they do not make it under circumstances chosen by themselves, but under circumstances directly found, given and transmitted from the past.

—Karl Marx

And, topping democracy, this most alluring record, that it alone can bind, and ever seeks to bind, all nations, all men, of however various and distant lands, into a brotherhood, a family. It is the old, yet ever-modern dream of earth, out of her eldest and her youngest, her fond philosophers and poets. . . . For I say at the core of democracy, finally, is the religious element. All the religions, old and new, are there.

—Walt Whitman

Christianity has functioned for the normative self-understanding of modernity as more than a mere precursor or a catalyst. Egalitarian universalism, from which sprang the ideas of freedom and social solidarity, of an autonomous conduct of life and emancipation, of the individual morality of conscience, human rights, and democracy, is the direct heir to the Judaic ethic of justice and the Christian ethic of love. This legacy, substantially unchanged, has been the object of continual critical appropriation and reinterpretation. To this day, there is no alternative to it. And in light of the current challenges of a postnational constellation, we continue to draw on the substance of this heritage. Everything else is just idle postmodern talk.

—Jürgen Habermas

Throughout the nineteenth century, theorists of democracy found it quite natural to discuss whether one country or another was "fit for democracy." This thinking changed only in the twentieth century, with the recognition that the question itself was wrong: A country does not have to be deemed fit *for* democracy; rather, it has to become fit *through* democracy.

—Amartya Sen

Secularists are wrong when they ask believers to leave their religion at the door before entering into the public square. Frederick Douglass, Abraham Lincoln, William Jennings Bryan, Dorothy Day, Martin Luther King—indeed, the majority of great reformers in American history—were not only motivated by faith, but repeatedly used religious language to argue for their cause. So to say that men and women should not inject their "personal morality" into public policy debates is a practical absurdity. Our law is by definition a codification of morality, much of it grounded in the Judeo-Christian tradition.

—Barack Hussein Obama

Preface to Paperback Edition

The Arab Spring of 2011 has given this book a pressing new relevance. While most of the research and writing took place between 2004 and 2007, well before there was any hint of a democratic tumult on the horizon, the arguments, theories and recommendations found in these pages prefigure and directly apply to recent developments in North Africa and the Arab Middle East.

Given the prominent role played by the Islamist Ennahdha party in leading Tunisia's democratic transition, one of the central claims of this book has been confirmed, namely that forms of religious politics and liberal-democratic development are indeed compatible. While the case of Egypt and religious-based parties is more complex, one of the clear lessons of the Arab Spring is that the key question is not whether Islam is compatible with democracy but whether ruling elites and the military are willing to give up power and accept popular sovereignty[1].

A central objective of this book was to advance new thinking on the relationship between Islam and secularism. I argued that the consolidation of liberal democracy in Muslim societies would be deeply intertwined with the ability of religious-oriented political actors to develop and indigenize a form of political secularism that approximates what Alfred Stepan has called the "Twin Toleration."[2] Achieving this will be difficult, partly because this process is inherently conflict-ridden but also due to the negative legacy of the post-colonial secular state and the secular nationalist ideologies that bolstered it. In Syria today, for example, the ruling regime justifies its rule in large part in the name of secularism.[3] At the same time it has responded to pro-democracy protests with such extreme brutality that Amnesty International, Human Rights Watch, and the UN Human Rights Council have all characterized the Syrian regime's behavior as "crimes against humanity."[4] As a consequence, the challenges facing democrats in Syria in the likely aftermath of the demise of the secular dictatorship in Damascus will be formidable, especially in terms of reconstituting an authentic form of political secularism on the ruins of rapacious secular post-colonial state.

Furthermore, the challenges facing the Arab-Islamic world with respect to political secularism were on display in September 2011 when Turkish Prime Minister Recep Tayip Erdoğan, whose country is viewed by mainstream Islamists as a political model that they seek to emulate, travelled to Egypt and was hailed as a hero. Thousands of people, mostly supporters of the Muslim Brotherhood, came out to catch a glimpse of the Turkish leader. When they saw him they cheered: "Erdoğan! Erdoğan! A real Muslim and not a coward," and "Turkey and Egypt, a single fist. The blockade [of Gaza] will be broken."[5]

As part of his media blitz Erdoğan was interviewed on the popular Egyptian talk show *10 O'clock*, where he defended the concept of secularism. "Don't be wary of secularism. I hope there will be a secular state in Egypt," he stated. He went on to clarify that to "Egyptians who view secularism as removing religion from the state, or as an infidel state, I say you are mistaken. It means respect to all religions. . . . If this is implemented, the entire society will live in safety."[6]

The reaction to these comments from the Muslim Brotherhood was revealing. Their passion and enthusiasm for the Turkish Prime Minister quickly soured. He was suddenly accused of interfering in Egypt's internal affairs and seeking to dominate the region.[7] New questions were raised about Erdoğan's status as a hero and to what extent Turkey could be a role model for the Arab world. The political explanations for this episode can be found in the pages of this book.

They are rooted in the different legacies of modernization that Muslim societies experienced during the 20th century. The Turkish experience with secularism and democracy has been qualitatively unique and distinct from that of the Arab world, where the word secularism is a conversation stopper. The neologism that seems to be emerging, which is conceptually distinct from both a secular state and an Islamic state, is *al-dawla al-madaniya* (civil state). This is what mainstream Islamist parties claim to aspire to. A consensus on the meaning of this term, especially as it relates to key issues such as minorities rights, gender, the nature of the legal system and the separation of powers, is currently being developed and debated in the Arab world. The opening of political space and the flourishing of multi-party politics will inevitably provide clarity on these issues. To the extent that Tunisia is a harbinger of what an Islamist-led "civil state" might look like, there is room for optimism.

In many ways Tunisia represents a bright spot in the Arab Spring, particularly in terms of reconciling the tensions between Islam, secularism, and democracy. Rached Ghannouchi, the intellectual leader and founder of Ennahdha, has been leading the way. Through a series of interviews and lectures he has begun the process of reconciling the tensions between secularism and Islamic political thought on a mass level. The way he has proceeded to do so is revealing.

In a visit to Turkey in December 2011, Ghannouchi gave an interview in which he stated that we "need democracy and development in Tunisia and we strongly believe in the compatibility between Islam and democracy, between Islam and modernity. So we do not need secularism in Tunisia."[8] He has repeatedly rejected and condemned the application of secularism to Tunisia, but in the same breath he has also stated that "we provide guarantees for all Tunisians whether secular or Islamic. We believe the state is based on the principle of citizenship. People despite their differences and attitudes, men and women, should enjoy equal rights in Tunisia. All are equal before the law regardless of their beliefs."[9] How to make sense of this formulation?

What Ghannouchi seems to be saying is that he accepts the important values that flow from political secularism (as understood in the Western tradition) and which modern democracies require (popular sovereignty and equality of citizenship), yet he rejects the word secularism because of its negative association with the ravages of the post-colonial state in the Islamic world. In other words, political secularism is fine as long as we call it by another name and don't invoke the dirty "s" word.

In a more detailed treatment of the topic, Ghannouchi delivered an important lecture on Islam and secularism in March 2012, where he provided a highly nuanced, historically-rooted comparative analysis that amounts to a political theory for Muslim secularism. The influence of the religious-friendly American version of secularism on Ghannouchi's thinking is clearly evident in his thoughtful treatment of the topic. The two key passages are the following:

> The issue of the state's neutrality involves a great deal of risk and
> adventure. If what is meant by the separation between religion and
> state is that the state is a human product and religion a divine
> revelation, as the distinction was made clear [earlier] in the context of
> the early Muslims between the realm of revelation (*wahy*) and what
> was the realm of the political, then it is ok. But if what is meant is the

separation in the French sense or in accordance with the Marxist experience then we may engage in a dangerous adventure that may harm both religion and state.

Echoing John Locke he concluded:

The primary orbit for religion is not the state's apparatuses, but rather personal/individual convictions. The state's duty, however, is to provide services to people before anything else, to create job opportunities, and to provide good health and education not to control people's hearts and minds.[10]

Over a decade ago the sociologist Shmuel Eisenstadt coined the term "multiple modernities."[11] He argued that the cultural program of transformation and the basic institutional constellations that emerged in Europe are not the only path to modernity. Other cultures and regions will travel diverse pathways and will have varied experiences in their modernization processes. In other words, one model does not fit the entire world, especially when it comes to reconciling the deep tensions and contractions between religion, secularism, and democracy. This observation has special relevance to the case of the contemporary Arab-Islamic world and it should be kept in mind as we attempt to understand the unfolding events of the Arab Spring and the unique path of democratic development that Muslim societies are currently traversing.

Nader Hashemi
April 2012

Preface

This book was written during difficult times. While the basic parameters and arguments were first conceived in the aftermath of 11 September 2001, the critical questions that spawned my interest in this topic have been percolating in my mind for most of my adult life. They were given greater impetus in the lead up to and aftermath of the United States-led invasion and occupation of Iraq and Afghanistan. The new American foreign policy thrust to promote, at least rhetorically, liberal democracy in the Muslim world also gave this project a pressing new relevance.

Fundamentally, this is a study about the relationship between religion and democracy. The principal goal is to promote a rethinking of this relationship by challenging long-standing premises, paradigms, and conceptual models against the backdrop of what Fernand Braudel called the *longue durée* (the study of history as a long duration). The focus, therefore, is not on the immediate social conditions that can generate reconciliation between the claims of religion and the demands of liberal democracy but on the connection and the coherence of a set of ideas—specifically, how we can study the connection between religion and democracy with fresh eyes, with a sense of history and free from the unexamined assumptions that have often clouded an understanding of this subject.

In pursuit of the same objective, Fred Dallmayr has observed that one of the main goals of comparative political theory is to "rekindle the critical élan endemic to political philosophy since the

time of Socrates and Plato but likely to be extinguished by canonization."
Challenging the received wisdom on any subject, Dallmayr suggests, can
"help restore the sense of 'wondering' (*thaumazein*) that the ancients extolled
as pivotal to philosophizing."[1] One of my key objectives, therefore, in writing
this book is to challenge the received wisdom on the relationship between
religion and democracy—especially in the context of Muslim societies—that
dominates the scholarly and public debate on this topic in the West. A new
paradigm is urgently needed today that is firmly rooted in the comparative
study of history, religion, and political theory.

While writing this book, I had several audiences in mind. First, this study
has been significantly shaped by many conversations and (often heated) debates with close friends and colleagues who consider themselves part of the
"political left." From the moment I began to think seriously about the relationship between religion and politics, it struck me that much (but not all) of this
commentary and analysis—while rightfully critical of religion and laudatory of
secularism—was ahistorical, unnuanced, and elitist. This contrasted quite
sharply with my own study of history. It also clashed with my personal
observations on the sociological aspects of religion based on time spent living
and teaching in the Middle East and several field trips to Egypt, Turkey, Iran,
Lebanon, Israel/Palestine, and Indonesia, where I interviewed human rights
activists, students, feminists, religious leaders, reformist thinkers, political
dissidents, and—most important—ordinary people.

The political analysis of my left-of-center friends was particularly unhelpful in understanding the complicated politics of Muslim societies where today
religion is a key marker of identity, secularism has few supporters, and social
movements whose participants self-identify with Islam are gaining in popularity and are important players in emerging social and political debates. As
events over the past decade in Turkey have demonstrated, the binary division
between secularists-equals-good guys and Islamists-equals-bad guys is simplis-
tic and distorting. While it may be intellectually soothing and familiar to us to
think in these terms, it fundamentally fails to contribute to a deeper understanding of the complex role religion plays in emerging democracies within
the Muslim world. Such labels and categories also fail to provide any illumina-
tion on the important moral and political questions facing Muslims at the
dawn of the twenty-first century. A more nuanced, historically rooted, and
comparative perspective is needed to arrive at a more balanced comprehension
of the multifaceted, complex, and interweaving relationship between religion
and politics both within the Muslim world and beyond.

Part of this analytical failure is due to an intellectual framework that has
been demarcated on the one side by Karl Marx and his ideological successors in

terms of social theory and on the other side by the French Revolution as a paradigmatic political event that shapes an understanding of the role of religion in society. As an alternative, as I argue in this book, if one wanted to look to Western political theory and history to shed light on the contemporary politics of Muslim societies, the seventeenth century is a better place to turn, where the political ideas of Thomas Hobbes, Baruch Spinoza, and John Locke are particularly relevant. As a seminal event, the English Revolution (1640–1660) not the French Revolution provides a more useful reference point for comparative historical analysis than my friends and colleagues on the political left have generally appreciated.

Second, this book is a partial response to a group of writers who believe in the "Islamic exceptionalism" thesis. Often identified as Orientalist scholars they subscribe to an essentialized conception of Muslim politics and history and have long argued that Muslims societies are uniquely resistant to secularism and liberal democracy due to an inner antimodern, religiocultural dynamic that has few parallels with other religious traditions or civilizations. Their writings attracted a larger audience in the early 1980s after Ayatollah Khomeini and his Islamist followers seized the Iranian state. Not only did this event represent a dramatic sea change in modern Middle East politics but it also signified a renewed interest among social scientists more broadly in the general theme of the resurgence of religion in politics. Existing social science theory was at a loss to explain the Iranian revolution and the concomitant rise of political Islam across the Muslim world. The confident predictions of modernization theorists and the assumptions of liberal philosophers and dependency theorists with respect to secularization failed to predict the vitality and popularity of the religious opposition in Iran.[2]

The most plausible explanation came from the pens of Orientalist scholars. Their emphasis on Islam's inner problem with modernity, and on secularism in particular, seemed like a perfectly rational explanation for the rise of Islamist politics, in part because it confirmed long-standing Western prejudices and stereotypes about Muslim societies. According to Bernard Lewis, the 1979 Iranian revolution could be explained by "Islamic history [which] provides its own models of revolution; its own prescriptions on the theory and practice of dissent, disobedience, resistance, and revolt." He added in the same essay that it is "now a truism that in Islam there is no distinction between church and state," unlike "Christendom [where] the existence of two authorities goes back to the founder of Christianity, who enjoined his followers to render to Caesar that which is Caesar's and to God that which is God's."[3]

Ernest Gellner advanced a similar but more sophisticated thesis about Islam and modernity. He drew a distinction between the "high culture" of the urban clergy, which was characterized as scriptural and puritanical and which Gellner claimed was normative for the urban life of the entire Islamic world, versus the "low culture" of the tribe and village life where folk Islam was practiced. Under modern conditions, Gellner argued, the puritanical Islam of the urban clergy is appropriated at the mass level due to political centralization, urbanization and the development of mass communications and education. The rise and appeal of Islamic fundamentalism is thus an attempt to realize the norm of the "high culture" among the new urbanized masses.[4] This explanation of Muslim politics, argued Gellner, is compatible with the require-ments of political modernity where contrary to the previously dominant as-sumptions of social theory modernity required secularization. Thus, Islam's relationship to modernity is unique in that modernity strengthens religion's hold over society, and this explains why secularism has not flourished in Muslim societies. In his last lecture before his untimely death in 1995, Gellner reaffirmed this perspective.[5]

While this book is not a comprehensive response to this body of scholar-ship, it does seek to provide an alternative to this widely influential perspective. I suspect that this narrative will gain new adherents in the coming years as the situation in Iraq and Afghanistan continues to implode and a search will begin for easy answers as to why Iraqis/Afghans could not seize the gift of freedom we so generously bestowed on them.

The final audience I have in mind are Muslim democrats. These are difficult days for democracy and human rights activists in the Muslim world. I think many of them would agree that the policies pursued by the great powers since 11 September 2001 have made their struggle more difficult. It is hoped, however, that notwithstanding the difficult environment in which they must operate and the many challenges that lie ahead, these individuals may derive some benefit from the arguments in this book, especially in making sense of the problem of Islamic fundamentalism, the question of secularism and its discontents in Muslim societies, and its relationship to democratic governance.

The topic of secularism has long been a fascination of mine for both political and personal reasons. Politically, it slowly became apparent that with rare exceptions, secularism was extolled in the West in an almost inverse proportion to how much it was disdained in Muslim societies. Trying to explicate this phenomenon has been a long-standing obsession of mine, and this book is a by-product of this fixation. Furthermore, as Abdelwahab El-Affendi has noted, "the tension between democracy and secularism . . . re-mains the dominant feature of Muslim politics to this day."[6] Reconciling this tension is vital to advancing a democratic theory for Muslim societies. I seek to contribute to this endeavor via a critical reading of key moments in the history of Western political thought, with an eye to the lessons to be learned for the political development of Muslim societies. This analytical approach underpins and informs this study.

Finally, the work of C. Wright Mills is germane to this book. Critical of the prevailing modes of social inquiry that dominated early post–World War II American social science, Mills called for the revival of the "classic" tradition of social analysis. This form of analysis "stands opposed to social science as a set of bureaucratic techniques which inhibit social inquiry by 'methodological pretensions,' which congest such work by obscurantist conceptions, or which trivialize it by concern with minor problems unconnected with publicly relevant issues."[7]

Mills viewed social science as a critical and historically rooted endeavor. He encouraged scholars to "use historical evidence and comparative reasoning to explore power relations and processes of social change. Scholars should debate hypotheses, theories and techniques, not for their own sake, but in close relation to important substantive inquiries." The main audience for such a sociological inquiry should be "students and the thinking public, not managers seeking merely to make the status quo more efficient." He was critical of research that was guided more by the requirements of administrative than intellectual concerns. Thus, his advice to future scholars was to pursue research and take up questions that were both morally compelling and relevant to the human condition, both past and present.[8]

This book seeks to live up to the intellectual standards Mills set out. For these reasons I have chosen to write about the theoretical and practical relationship between religion, secularism, and liberal democracy. Doing so, of course, has its pitfalls, especially during this polarizing moment in global politics where terms such as "Islam," "Muslims," "secularism," "religion," and "liberal democracy" are emotionally charged topics deeply embedded in a set of identities that are championed by individuals and groups on both sides of the Islam-West divide who sometimes are more interested in affirming an ideological position than in advancing human understanding. Nonetheless, it would be a betrayal of my own intellectual vocation to shy away from what Alexis de Tocqueville called the "great problem of our time" (i.e. the relationship between religion and democracy) and not engage it with as much intellectual rigor and stamina as I could muster. In the end, to borrow from Robert Frost, I took the road "less traveled by." I hope it makes a modest difference.

Acknowledgments

Writing acknowledgments for a book is always a risky endeavor. After it is too late one is bound to remember the name of a friend or colleague who deserves recognition but whose name does not appear on these pages. Let me begin, therefore, by apologizing in advance to those people whose names I should have listed but due to my own absentmindedness I have embarrassingly omitted. This book is a revised version of my doctoral dissertation, which I researched, wrote, and successfully defended while a graduate student in the Department of Political Science at the University of Toronto. As a result, I am indebted to Frank Cunningham for his unflinching intellectual support and for his excellent supervision of my work. He helped me narrow a very broad dissertation topic into a concrete one and helped crystalize my thinking on various aspects of democratic theory that pertained to the relationship between religion and liberal democracy. His graduate course on democratic theory, I fondly remember, was one of the most intellectually stimulating courses I took as a graduate student. It allowed me to both deepen my grasp of democratic theory as well as explore new ideas that eventually formed the foundation of this book. I would also like to thank the other members of my committee for their support and constructive criticisms: James Reilly, Paul Kingston, and Ronald Beiner.

Much of the rewriting of my dissertation took place during my stay at Northwestern University, where I was an Andrew W. Mellon Postdoctoral Fellow in the Department of Political Science. I am indebted to Marie Jones, Hendrick Spruyt, and Elizabeth Hurd for their support and interest in my work. I would also like to thank the students at Northwestern who took my "Introduction to Middle East Politics" course and my seminar on "Islam and Democracy in the Middle East." They were the most impressive group of students I have taught. Their feedback and comments on my course material, much of it drawn from my doctoral research, assisted me in revising and rewriting this manuscript.

While teaching at Northwestern, I had the opportunity to live at the Northshore Retirement Hotel in Evanston, Illinois, where I delivered a weekly lecture on religion and democracy and sometimes on the politics and history of the modern Middle East. I am grateful for the residential scholarship I was awarded that facilitated the revising of this manuscript. I would like to thank all the wonderful people who attended my Thursday evening lectures; their enthusiasm for my ideas and their interest in my work helped in the refinement and completion of this book project. I would like to single out for special recognition Margaret Gergen, Phyllis Adams, Eduardo Shua, Mary Sorin, Addie Katz, Sid Cohen, Leslie Rubin, Sherwin Gaines, Sylvia Letterman, Goldye Rosenberg, Rita Stevens, Geraldine Freedman, and Evelyn Orsor.

During my stay in Chicago, I benefited immensely from Danny Postel's friendship and intellectual support. He is a gifted writer, a dedicated human rights activist, and a committed cosmopolitan public intellectual. In a truly just world, he would be teaching philosophy at a prestigious institution of higher learning. I have learnt much from him and deeply appreciate his solidarity and camaraderie. I look forward to future collaboration with him on projects of mutual interest.

Very few people can claim authorship of a truly original idea. I want to single out for special recognition, therefore, the work of Alfred Stepan, in particular his magisterial thesis, "The World's Religious Systems and Democracy: Crafting the 'Twin Tolerations,'" which inspired this book. On reading it, many scattered thoughts I had been struggling with on the relationship between religion and democracy began to make sense, and this book's broad outline started to take shape. On a related note, it was a huge honor for me to meet Professor Stepan in person and an even greater honor to be invited to Columbia University to present some of my work at his seminar series on religion and democracy.

I am also indebted to the work of Stathis Kalyvas. His scholarship on religion and democracy is a must read for any serious student of this topic. I draw on his idea that some forms of unsecular politics and democratic development, contrary to the dominant view in the social sciences, are indeed compatible. I thank him for his prompt replies to my emails and for sharing with me some of his unpublished essays.

In the field of political theory, as readers of this book will discover, I draw on the work of Charles Taylor and Fred Dallmayr. In recent years, both have produced important new scholarship on the relationship between religion and politics that I eagerly consumed and significantly shaped my thinking on the topic. In November 2004, Professor Taylor taught an intensive course on secularization at the University of Toronto, which I managed to audit, and which formed the foundation of his massive work *A Secular Age* (Harvard University Press, 2007). I am grateful to him for reading an early draft of chapter 4 and for his constructive feedback. Professor Dallmayr's writings on political philosophy have made a lasting impression on me. He has been the chief theoretician of the emerging field of comparative political theory. I hope he will accept this volume as a small contribution to this new subdiscipline of political science. I have been especially drawn to and inspired by his more recent work on non-Western societies, India and the Middle East in particular. I am indebted to him for his interest in my work and his ongoing intellectual support. I hope to emulate in my own career the high intellectual standards that inform his writings. More important, however, what has greatly impressed me is the spirit of crosscultural understanding cosmopolitanism and ecumenism that underpins his scholarship. He is a true citizen of the globe and an important moral voice that our planet desperately needs during these difficult and trying times.

In the area of Middle East history, politics and Islamic studies, I draw on the scholarship of Khaled Abou El Fadl, Nikki Keddie, and Vali Nasr. These scholars have written insightfully and influentially in their respective areas of specialization. I thank them for their interest in my work, their time, and the feedback they have given me. The standards of academic excellence they have demonstrated in their careers serve as an excellent model to many younger academics just entering the field.

A project of this magnitude accrues many intellectual debts over the years. I would like to thank Salim Mansur for nurturing my interest in this general area of study. As a young undergraduate student at the University of Western Ontario without any direction or focus he took me under his wing and provided me with the first real intellectual mentorship that I yearned for. I remember his insistence that the study of history was much more important than political science, as a way of making sense of the human condition. The heavy dose of history in this book is in large part due to his influence. While our political views have diverged over time, my debt to him is in no way diminished.

John Sigler at Carleton University was my teacher and mentor during my formative years in Ottawa. His deeply ethical and ecumenical approach to the study of global politics, in particular to the problems and challenges facing Arab and Islamic societies, left a huge mark on my intellectual development. I recall fondly the many occasions I lined up outside of his door during his office hours. After consulting with him I always left his office with my intellectual batteries recharged. He had the unique ability to both inspire his students in their ability to change the world and to push them to reach their full intellectual potential. He is a gifted scholar and teacher and his example is with me every time I step into the classroom. Dr. Sigler's influence can be felt throughout the pages of this book, especially in Chapter 1. I am a better political scientist and person for having studied with him.

I interviewed many other scholars during the course of my research. Some of them were generous enough to read and comment on various chapters in draft form; others simply shaped my thinking during the course of our conversations and correspondence on the relationship between religion and politics in a myriad different ways. I am indebted to all of them, but in particular I would like to thank Seyla Benhabib, William Shepard, Michael Sells, Richard Bond, Shabbir Akhtar, Farid Esack, Ebrahim Moosa, Abdullahi An-Na'im, Azyumardi Azra, Amien Rais, Robert Hefner, Dadi Darmadi, Ulil Abshar-Abdullah, Sukidi, Fajar Riza Ul Haq, Raja Juli Antoni, Recep Sentürk, Nur Yalman, Mujeeb Khan, Ahmet Kuru, John Esposito, Haroon Siddiqui, Jareer Khouri, Richard Bulliet, John Keane, Eric Hooglund, Richard Falk, Noam Chomsky, Norman Finkelstein, Eqbal Ahmad, Gulzar Haider, Ramin Jahanbegloo, Houchang Chehabi, Ahmad Sadri, Farhang Rajaee, Abdulaziz Sachedina, Duncan Ivison, James Tully, and John Dunn.

Two research trips to Indonesia and Turkey helped solidify my understanding of these countries. I would like to thank the United States-Indonesia Society and the Andrew W. Mellon Foundation for their financial support of my work.

My parents, Esmat Hashemi and Mehdi Hashemi, deserve special recognition and praise. I am grateful to them for many things (the list is too long to give here), but in this context I want to especially thank them for instilling in me a love of education. This book is dedicated to them, for all their sacrifices, for putting up with their rebellious son and for their ongoing and unconditional love.

I would also like to single out my siblings, their spouses, and my nephews and nieces for their encouragement and love. They all deserve to be recognized by name: Fereshteh, Shahid, Noor, Ameer, Naseem, Firoozeh, Mehdi, Negean, Ameen, Namjoo, Armita, and Iman.

Many of the ideas that appear in this book were tested and first debated in front of a close group of friends affiliated with the Ottawa-based Second Generation Muslim Discussion Group (affectionately known as the "2nd gen"). The intellectual stimulation, laughter, and companionship they have provided me with over the years have been invaluable, and our email listserver has acted as an important sounding board for many of my thoughts and frustrations with the state of the world—the Muslim world in particular. I want to thank this group of people for their friendship, religiosity, solidarity, and camaraderie. Several people deserve special recognition.

Emran Qureshi has been my best friend for most of the past decade. He has been an important resource person for me over the years, keeping me on my toes intellectually and abreast of unfolding debates that are/were germane to this book. A subtext to our friendship has been the tension between secularism and religion. We have argued about this topic on many different occasions and in countless diverse political contexts, both in person and via email, to the extent that this book bears his imprint.

I would also like to thank Andaleeb Qayyum and Soraya Moghadam for their friendship, laughter, and the many camping trips, debates, and arguments over the years that indirectly contributed to my intellectual development. Over the years their solidarity, camaraderie, and religiosity has meant a lot to me. Afra Jalabi deserves to have a Ph.D. already. I have learned much from her and especially benefited from her moral reading of the Qur'an and early Muslim history and her ruminations on the philosophy and merits of nonviolence. I hope this book will inspire her to begin work on the twenty books I've been encouraging her to write since we first met. Alim Elliot Khan has been a loyal friend for the past fifteen years. I deeply appreciate his support and solidarity over the years. Other members of the larger 2nd gen family I would like to acknowledge are Nelofer Pazira, Alim Khan, Rafi Khan, Akram Bhatti, Majid Moghadam, Saied Moghadam, Alireza Rahbar Shamskar, Rahat Kurd, Yasmine Abou El Kheir, Noreen Majeed, Adnan Qayyum, Humera Ibrahim, Faisal Bhabha, Kim Elliott, Ayman Hassan, and, last but not least, the godparents of the 2nd gen, Uncle Murray and Alia Hogben. May they live long and prosper.

Other friends who contributed to this book include John Trumpbour, for his scholarly references on Puritanism and early modern English history, Andras Riedlmayer, for his prompt and thorough replies to my numerous research questions, and Hakan Yavuz, for his interest in my work and strong intellectual support; my sincere thanks to all of them. Last but not least, I am deeply indebted to Ausma Khan for her editorial support and for reading most of the revised version of this manuscript. Without her love, patience, and understanding this book could not have been written.

Contents

Islam, Secularism, and Liberal Democracy

Introduction

This book analyzes the theoretical relationship between religion and democracy, specifically Islam's relationship with liberal democracy. The intent is to discuss the relationship between Islam, Muslim-majority societies, and liberal democracy in a way that will advance theory and practice regarding their relations. Though this relationship is the immediate focus of this study, the conclusions of this book have a much broader applicability in illuminating the theoretical relationship between religion, secularism, and democracy in general, and in contributing to the development of a liberal-democratic theory for Muslim societies in particular.

The central problematic this inquiry seeks to resolve is the following. Liberal democracy requires a form of secularism to sustain itself, yet simultaneously the main political, cultural, and intellectual resources at the disposal of Muslim democrats today are theological. A paradox thus confronts the democratic theorist. This study seeks to unravel this paradox. In the course of doing so, this book challenges the widely held assumption in the social sciences that religious politics and liberal-democratic development are incompatible.[1] Three key arguments are advanced:

(1) Liberal democracy requires secularism (properly understood). While this equation is not in dispute, two caveats are in order. First, religious traditions are not born with an inherent democratic and

secular conception of politics. These ideas must be socially constructed. In the context of an emerging liberal democracy, *how* secularism becomes indigenized as part of the political culture is an important—and often neglected—part of this debate. I argue that a secular consensus often emerges as a result of an engagement with and a transformation of religious ideas toward politics. Normatively, secularism should not be imposed by the state on society but should emerge bottom-up, from within civil society, based on democratic negotiation and bargaining over the proper role of religion in politics. In other words, in developing societies where religion is a key marker of identity, in order for religious groups to reconcile themselves with secularism, a religious-based theory of secularism is required.

Equally significant are the different models of secularism that liberal democracy might accommodate. The literature on democratic theory is particularly weak in clarifying the precise relationship and parameters of coexistence between religion and liberal democracy. How we define secularism is an important part of this conversation. I argue that there is greater room for flexibility on this topic than is generally acknowledged, and consequently, a rethinking of the relationship between secularism and liberal democracy is needed. This is especially important in the context of advancing a liberal-democratic theory for Muslim societies, given that religion is a key marker of identity for a significant percentage of the population and secularism has a troubled legacy.[2]

(2) In societies where religion is a marker of identity, the road to liberal democracy, whatever other twists and turns it makes, cannot avoid passing through the gates of religious politics. While mainstream social science theory has long maintained that religious politics and democratization/liberalization are antithetical, a critical reading of the historical record suggests otherwise. Historically, the development of liberal democracy in the West (especially in the Anglo-American tradition) emerged not in strict opposition to religious politics but often in concert with it. In many long-standing liberal democracies, debates over the place of religion in the polis were some of the most hotly contested and divisive issues. Democratic negotiation and bargaining over the normative role of religion in government were an inherent part of this development process. The prominence of religious politics—particularly in the public sphere—is an important part of the history and struggle for liberal democracy that has been underappreciated by democratic theorists (particularly when commenting on the politics of the Muslim world after 11 September 2001). The primary theoretical implication that flows from this argument that is relevant for the study of liberal democracy in Muslim societies is that the process of democratization and liberalization cannot be disconnected from debates about the normative role of religion in government.

(3) An intimate and often-ignored relationship exists between religious reformation and political development. The first typically precedes the second, although the processes are deeply interwoven and connected. This is particularly true in societies under the sway of an illiberal or undemocratic religiopolitical doctrine. Democratization and liberalization do not necessarily require a rejection or privatization of religion, but what they do require is a reinterpretation of religious ideas with respect to the moral basis of legitimate political authority and individual rights. By engaging in this reinterpretation, religious groups can play an important role in the development and consolidation of liberal democracy. This observation applies both to the historical development of liberal democracy in the West (especially in the case of Catholicism) and to Muslim societies today.

Overall, this book argues for a rethinking of democratic theory so that it incorporates the variable of religion in the development and social construction of liberal democracy. By approaching this topic historically and comparatively, a more nuanced and balanced treatment of this subject can be obtained.

From the Fall of the Berlin Wall to the Fall of the Twin Towers: The Intellectual Context

In the immediate aftermath of the Cold War, religious fundamentalism—in particular its Muslim variant—emerged as one of the greatest perceived threats to liberal democracy. The al Qaeda attacks on 11 September 2001 resolved a debate that had surfaced after the fall of the Berlin Wall about new and emerging threats to international peace and security. From the outset, Islamic fundamentalism was a leading candidate for the position.[3] Influential journals such as the *Economist*, the *Atlantic Monthly*, *Time*, and *Foreign Affairs* were busy debating this subject, most certainly influenced by prominent Western politicians such as Jacques Chirac, Helmut Kohl, Daniel Quayle, and Yitzhak Rabin, who were warning that the "green peril" of Islam had replaced the "red menace" of communism as the chief threat to Western civilization.[4]

Public opinion in the United States was not far behind elite opinion on this issue. In 1993—almost a decade before the September 11 attacks—a comprehensive nationwide poll found that 42 percent of Americans agreed with the statement that there "should be restrictions on the number of Muslims allowed to immigrate to the U.S.," and 43 percent concurred with the view that Muslims "tend to be religious fanatics."[5] Dramatic events from the Arab and

Islamic world in the last two decades of the twentieth century are arguably responsible for these attitudes.[6]

A partial list of the emotionally charged and defining images that have shaped public opinion, American foreign policy, and academic scholarship toward Muslim societies in recent decades includes the 1979 Iranian revolution and the concomitant seizure of the U.S. embassy in Tehran, the 1981 assassination of Anwar Sadat, the 1983 bombing of the U.S. embassy and Marines barracks in Lebanon, the 1989 fatwa against Salman Rushdie and *l'affaire du foulard* in France, the annexation of Kuwait by Saddam Hussein and subsequent Gulf War in 1991, the misogynist rule of the Taliban in Afghanistan throughout the 1990s, two Palestinian intifadas and a wave of suicide attacks against Israeli civilians in 2000, and finally and most dramatically, the coordinated attacks in 2001 against the Twin Towers in New York and the Pentagon in Washington, D.C. The chaos, mayhem, and bloodshed in Iraq, post-Saddam Hussein, have further solidified these views.

Intellectual debates prior to 11 September 2001 gave a stamp of respectability to this pejorative image of Muslim societies. From Francis Fukuyama's thesis on "the end of history" and Benjamin Barber's argument about "jihad vs. McWorld" to Robert Kaplan's suggestion about "the coming anarchy" and, most influentially, Samuel P. Huntington's essay and subsequent book on "the clash of civilizations," all have collectively reinforced, in different ways, the idea that the Muslim faith and Islamic civilization are incongruent with liberty, democracy, human rights, gender equality, and other emancipatory principles.[7] Francis Fukuyama articulated a widely held belief when he said:

> There does seem to be something about Islam or at least the
> fundamentalist versions of Islam that have been dominant in recent
> years, that makes Muslim societies particularly resistant to modernity.
> Of all contemporary cultural systems, the Islamic world has the fewest
> democracies (Turkey alone qualifies), and contains no countries that
> have made the transition from Third to First World status in the
> manner of South Korea or Singapore.[8]

The events of 11 September 2001 and their aftermath have erased any lingering doubt about the relevance and urgency of this topic, which now far transcends a concern about military security and terrorism.[9] The question of Islam's compatibility with liberal democracy is at the heart of current debates about immigration, multiculturalism, citizenship, political community, the universality of human rights, the future of Algeria, Turkey's relationship with the European Union, the Israel-Palestine peace process, U.S. foreign policy, and the wars and reconstruction efforts in Afghanistan and Iraq—just to name a few. This debate is subsumed by larger theoretical questions that have immense significance at the dawn of the twenty-first century: What are the core values and ideals of liberal democracy? Can they be found or promoted in non-Western societies? In what ways are the values and ideals of liberal democracy conflictual and problematic? For example, can the ideas of democracy and human rights take hold in cultures where ideas of personhood are based on values other than those of liberal individualism? Are some religious systems more compatible with liberal democracy than others? These are the broad questions that shape this inquiry.[10]

"The Great Political Problem of Our Times": Religion and Democracy

In *Democracy in America*, Alexis de Tocqueville, writing in 1831 about life in the early American republic, discusses what he calls the "great political problem of our times." Tocqueville's primary audience, it should be remembered, were not Americans but rather the educated classes in his native Europe, whose political problems shaped his consciousness, especially in his native France.

According to Tocqueville, "the organization and the establishment of democracy in Christendom is the great political problem of our times."[11] This observation, although 178 years old, reminds us that the problem of religion's relationship with democracy is not an exclusively Muslim phenomenon but one that other religion traditions—Christianity in particular—have had to struggle with. To the extent that Tocqueville's observation is correct, it could be extrapolated that in the same sense that the "great political problem" facing Europe in the nineteenth century was the question of democracy in Christian lands in the twenty-first century, arguably the great problem of our time is the establishment and organization of democracy in the Muslim world.

In the voluminous scholarly literature that is produced annually on democratic theory, there has been scant mention of religion's relationship to democracy until recently. In three recently published "democracy readers," edited by prominent scholars in the field, for example, one searches in vain for any mention of this topic in the table of contents.[12] Yet, on reflection, this omission is understandable. The question of religion's relationship to democracy and its proper role in political society has been largely resolved in the West (the United States being an arguable exception). A broad secular consensus exists within and among Western liberal democracies on this question, and any remaining tension is negotiated via existing democratic processes and institutions that enjoy broad legitimacy. The same cannot be said for most Muslim societies today. This difference is important. One of the key analytical errors often made when discussing Muslim politics is to fall into the seductive trap of a "false universalism." What I mean by this is the mistaken belief that the Western experience with religion-state relations has been the universal norm for the rest of humanity. In other words, it is wrong to assume that because the West has achieved a broad democratic consensus on the normative relationship between religion and state then the rest of humanity must have done so as well. A concomitant of this misguided belief is that any manifestation of religion in politics that challenges comfortable Western assumptions about secularism must surely be a sign of religious fascism.

For most Muslim societies, the question of religion's normative relationship with government has not been democratically resolved. The reasons for this are complex and critically important if one is to understand the crisis of liberal-democratic politics in the Muslim world today. It is accurate to say that democracy, in particular its liberal variant as understood in the West, is a contested concept in Muslim societies. Recent American intervention in the Middle East—in the name of spreading liberal democracy—has complicated the internal debate on this issue even further.[13] Far from a comprehensive treatment of this topic, this book seeks to untangle these complex and emotionally charged questions and make them more intelligible.

A discussion of the general relationship between Islam and democracy is theoretically subsumed under the broader conceptual relationship between religion and democracy. Their compatibility is dependent, in part, on the definitions of religion and democracy that are employed. In this book, religion is broadly conceived of as a specific system of belief about the divine, including a code of ethics, rituals, and a philosophy of life.[14] Of particular importance are the normative ideals of a believer with respect to themes of political community, citizenship, human rights, the rule of law, and—critically—the moral basis of legitimate political authority. With respect to Muslim societies, the key question that is often asked is whether liberal democracy can coexist with Islam—or, as a leading scholar on the topic has eloquently put it,

> There is an agonizing question at the heart of the present debate about democracy in the Islamic world: Is liberal democracy basically compatible with Islam, or is some measure of respect for law, some tolerance of criticism, the most that can be expected from autocratic governments? The democratic world contains many different forms of government—republics and monarchies, presidential and parliamentary regimes, secular states and established churches, and a wide range of electoral systems—but all of them share certain basic

assumptions and practices that mark the distinction between democratic and undemocratic governments. Is it possible for the Islamic peoples to evolve a form of government that will be compatible with their own historical, cultural, and religious traditions and yet will bring individual freedom and human rights to the governed as these terms are understood in the free societies of the West?[15]

This book seeks to engage with these questions.

The working definition of liberal democracy employed in this book is one that has its origins in the political theory of John Locke (consent), Jean Jacques Rousseau (popular sovereignty), and John Stuart Mill (individual liberty).[16] Though more robust than a Schumpeterian view, where democracy is no more than the ability to vote for or against potential state leaders, the conception employed here is more modest than that of, for example, the participatory or deliberative democrats.[17] In other words, it is a moderately robust definition of liberal democracy according to which political authority is rooted in the consent of the governed, the people rule via their elected representatives, and basic human rights, as enshrined in the United Nations Universal Declaration of Human Rights, are upheld.[18] Robert Dahl's famous definition of "polyarchy," with one significant caveat, approximates the working definition of liberal democracy employed in this study.[19]

"Polyarchy," according to Dahl, "is a political order distinguished at the most general level by two broad characteristics. Citizenship is extended to a relatively high proportion of adults, and the rights of citizenship include the opportunity to oppose and vote out the highest officials in the government."[20] For these characteristics of a liberal democracy to exist, eight institutional guarantees are required: (1) freedom to form and join organizations; (2) freedom of expression; (3) inclusive suffrage; (4) the right to run for office; (5) the right of political leaders to compete for support and votes; (6) availability of alternative information; (7) free and fair elections; and (8) the existence of institutions for making government policies depend on votes and other expressions of preference.[21] While these institutional guarantees are necessary for a liberal democracy, they are by themselves insufficient. Constitutional guarantees are also needed to ensure protection of basic rights and liberties and to ensure that democratically elected governments rule within the framework of the constitution. These broad provisions map out the rough working conception of liberal democracy that informs this book.

In adopting Dahl's list, I am agreeing with an important component of what has come to be called modernization theory, namely, that there are a number of goals appropriate to any society that aspires to democracy or to the deepening of democracy. At the same time, I disagree with claims that sometimes accompany this view that a society that lacks these characteristics is simply void of any democracy whatsoever or that once Dahl's character- istics are present, democracy is forever secure and consolidated without the possibility of rollback.

The second caveat about modernization theory pertains to what Alfred Stepan has called the fallacy of "unique founding conditions."[22] The fallacy pertains to a historical argument that a particular set of social conditions and constellation of forces are needed to produce a new political phenomenon (such as democracy or civil society) and then to assume that if the exact same conditions are not reproduced, the social invention in question cannot emerge. "The fallacy of course is to confuse the conditions associated with the invention of a phenomenon with the possibilities of *replication*, or probably more accu- rately *reformulation*, under different conditions, of the same general phenome- non."[23] The critical methodological caveat that flows from this argument and that informs this book is to be wary of committing the fallacy of unique founding conditions when discussing political development in non-Western societies. This fallacy is implicit in early modernization theory and is premised on an ahistorical and culturally superior reading of the European political history, particularly with respect to the relationship between religion, secular- ism, and liberal democracy. A consequence of this fallacy is the belief that in non-Western societies that have been strongly influenced by local traditions, liberal democracy cannot be achieved by drawing on local cultural resources.[24] Samuel P. Huntington's religious-civilizational approach to the study of de- mocracy in the post–Cold War world is a reflection of this perspective.

In his widely discussed book *The Clash of Civilizations and the Remaking of the Modern World*, Huntington reserves special attention for Christianity and secularism in arguing why Western civilization is distinct from other civiliza- tions. "Western Christianity . . . is historically the single most important charac- teristic of Western civilization," he argues.[25] For Huntington, Western culture is unique precisely because it has incorporated secularism and liberal values as part of its civilizational ethos from the beginning. "God and Caesar, church and state, spiritual and temporal authority, have been a prevailing dualism in Western culture."[26] Similarly, he suggests that "a sense of individualism and a tradition of rights and liberties" is unique to Western civilization, and thus "The West was West long before it was modern."[27] He then immediately seeks to contrast the West with other societies precisely on this point. "In Islam, God is Caesar, in China and Japan, Caesar is God; in Orthodoxy, God is Caesar's junior partner."[28]

Huntington then proceeds to advance an argument about how "kin cultures" increasingly support each other along "civilizational fault lines," warning of an Islamic-Confucian alliance that will challenge the West in the twenty-first century. While Huntington does discuss other rival civilizations, he clearly views Islam as the greatest challenge. Near the end of his book he boldly asserts that "the underlying problem for the West is not Islamic fundamentalism. It is Islam."[29] On the relationship between Confucianism and democracy, he implies a certain culture essentialism when he asserts that China's "Confucian heritage, with its emphasis on authority, order, hierarchy, and supremacy of collectivity over the individual creates obstacles to democratization."[30] This book seeks to challenge these assumptions.[31]

Theoretical Tensions between Religion and Democracy

The tension between religion and democracy is as old as political philosophy itself. Recall that democratic Athens brought Socrates to trial on two charges: corrupting the minds of the young and religious impiety. It remains a matter of dispute among historians whether Socrates' accusers were more concerned with his alleged religious crimes or his political ones.[32]

In the modern period, at first glance the relationship between religion and democracy seems inherently contradictory and conflictual. Both concepts speak to different aspects of the human condition. Religion is a system of beliefs and rituals that is related to the divine and the sacred. In this sense, it is decidedly metaphysical and otherworldly in its orientation and telos. While religions may differ in their various manifestations, most religions share these features.

Democracy on the other hand is decidedly this-worldly, secular, and egalitarian. Regardless of religious belief, race, or creed, democracy (especially its liberal variant) implies an equality of rights and treatment before the law for all citizens without discrimination. Its telos is geared toward the nonviolent management of human affairs in order to create the good life on this earth, not in the hereafter. Critically, unlike religious commandments, the rules of democracy can be changed, adjusted, and amended. It is precisely the inclusive nature of democracy that separates it from religion and theologically based political systems.

One way to conceptualize the theoretical tension between religion and democracy is to imagine a horizontal and vertical axis.

As the diagram below demonstrates, religion is primarily a vertical relationship between an individual and his or her God. In its most basic form, it need not affect or concern other members of society. Democracy on the other

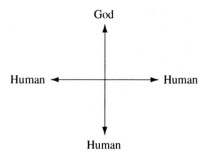

FIGURE 1.

hand is a system of political organization that fundamentally implies a horizontal relationship among individuals in society. Its basic definition is devoid
of any reference to the divine or the transcendent. A point of tension arises
where these lines become crossed.[33]

An obvious point of friction is when members of society seek to interject
their vertical relationship with God into the horizontal public sphere as a way
of regulating social relationships. In other words, when the moral foundation
of legitimate political authority is no longer based exclusively on the horizontal
axis (popular sovereignty) but shifts in the direction of the vertical axis (divine
sovereignty), democracy is compromised. This is a main reason why religious
politics is deemed antithetical to democratic politics and why democratic
theorists insist that a liberal-democratic polity necessitates a retreat or separation of religion from politics.[34] The objection to religious politics from the
perspective of liberal-democratic theory is often justified on the following
grounds. Religion claims to be in possession of universal truths. The ideological rigidity often associated with this religious belief undermines tolerance,
pluralism, and compromise—all crucial aspects of liberal-democratic politics.[35]

Second, religion is exclusionary because it sets up insurmountable boundaries between believers and nonbelievers. Democracy on the other hand is
inclusive, egalitarian, and nondiscriminatory; citizenship is not based on adherence to God but rather on membership in political society.

Third, religion undermines the secular order of society that is needed to
sustain liberalism and maintain a democratic peace.[36] In other words, it seeks
to collapse the distinction between the horizontal and vertical axes by dragging
God from the heavenly heights and injecting God into the center of public debate.
The danger to minorities from religious majorities is particularly salient here.

These observations are implicit today in much of the literature on liberal-
democratic theory. They fit with an understanding of religion's role in liberal
society based on the received wisdom from the European Enlightenment. This

book seeks to expand our understanding of these widely held assumptions. Specifically, *this book challenges the thesis on the structural incompatibility between religious politics and liberal-democratic development.*[37] In the course of doing so, I will advance three key arguments.

The first argument pertains to the relationship between liberal democracy and secularism. While acknowledging that liberal democracy requires a form of secularism (properly understood) to sustain itself two caveats are offered. First, religious traditions do not emerge in human society with an inherent prodemocratic and secular predisposition.[38] These ideas must be socially constructed by members of the host community before they take root. *How* secularism becomes indigenized in an emerging democracy is an important part of this debate that has yet to receive sufficient scholarly attention. This book argues that a secular consensus often emerges and is intimately tied to an engagement with, and a transformation of, religious ideas toward politics. As noted, normatively, in a religious society, the long-term prospects for political secularism are better when it is not imposed top-down but rather when it emerges bottom-up, based on a democratic consensus over the proper role of religion in government. In other words, in order for religious groups to reconcile themselves to a conception of politics that separates religion from state, a religious-based theory of political secularism is required.

A concomitant of the foregoing observation pertains to the different models of secularism that liberal democracy might accommodate. Democratic theorists have generally avoided clarifying the parameters of coexistence between religion and liberal democracy. How secularism is defined is a critical part of this conversation. I argue in this book that there is more room for flexibility on this topic than is generally appreciated, and consequently a rethinking of the concept of political secularism is needed. This is especially important in the context of advancing a liberal-democratic theory for Muslim societies, given the salience of religion in public affairs in the Muslim world today and the negative perceptions many Muslims have of the concept of secularism.[39]

The second core argument I will advance is that in societies where religion is an overriding marker of identity, the road to liberal democracy, whatever other twists and turns it makes, cannot avoid passing through the gates of religious politics. This claim is a historically contingent one. It is based on the precise historical moment and part of the world under consideration in this book (late twentieth- and early twenty-first-century Muslim societies). It is not claimed that at all times and in all places the transition to secular democracy in the Muslim world (or elsewhere) must pass through the gates of religious politics.

To date, there has been a broad consensus in the social sciences that religious mobilization and liberal-democratic development are antithetical. I argue that this is an inaccurate reading of the history of liberal democracy. The development of liberal democracy in the West (especially the Anglo-American tradition) is intimately tied to changing religious ideas. Similarly, religious discourse was a precondition of the rise of the early modern public sphere.[40] In many long-standing liberal democracies, the place of religion in the polis were some of the most hotly contested and divisive issues.

Democratic negotiation and bargaining over the normative role of religion in government were an inherent part of the transition to, and consolidation of, liberal democracy. The prominence of religious politics—particularly in the public sphere—forms an important part of the history and struggle for liberal democracy that has been underappreciated by democratic theorists (especially when discussing the politics of the Muslim world after 11 September 2001).[41] The primary theoretical implication that emerges from this argument that is relevant for the study of liberal democracy and its problems in Muslim societies is that the process of democratization and liberalization cannot be artificially separated from discussion about the normative relationship between religion and government.

The third argument of critical significance is that there is an intimate relationship—theoretical as well as historical—between religious reformation and political development. The first typically precedes the second, although they are deeply interconnected and mutually reinforcing. This argument has special relevance in religious societies where a significant part of the population is under the sway of an illiberal or undemocratic set of political ideas. Liberal-democratic development does not require a rejection or privatization of religion, but what it does require is a reinterpretation of religious ideas, especially with respect to the moral basis of legitimate political authority and the centrality of individual rights. By engaging in this theological reformulation, religious groups can play a constructive and important role in the development and consolidation of liberal democracy.

Clarification of Theoretical Approaches and Assumptions

The book seeks to ruminate on the theoretical and practical relationship between religion and democracy. The main problematic of this book is that liberal democracy requires a form of political secularism, yet in the Muslim world today the primary intellectual, political, and cultural resources at the disposal of Muslim democrats are theological. Imbedded in this problematic is the relationship between political culture and democracy. In pursuing this kind of study, there is a danger of assuming that the variable of political culture is being elevated as *the* most salient factor in explaining the absence of democracy in the Muslim world. There is also the related danger of assuming a simple causation between changes in political culture and democratization. This book aims to avoid both assumptions. For the most part, it also refrains from positing causal relations among cultural, political, economic, and other factors, except as tentative hypotheses where this helps to explicate a broad argument that a path to secular democracy can emerge through the framework of religious politics. An assumption this book does make is that there are numerous historical, structural, and cultural variables that explain the obstacles to democracy in the developing world. A comprehensive analysis would require exploring the economic, sociopolitical, military, and international contexts that influence the process of democratization. Some of the key prerequisites for democracy that social scientists generally agree on include social and economic modernization (i.e. industrialization and high GNP, literacy, mass communications), class structure (a sizeable middle class and an independent bourgeoisie), and finally a democratic political culture (the cultural norms, values, and beliefs that shape political behavior).[42]

An influential McGill University study on political liberalization and democratization in the Arab world noted that political culture "should not be seen as the prime or overriding variable in any process of regional democratization. Cultural attitudes . . . not only influence political realities but are also themselves influenced by political context."[43] According to this view, political culture is thus not a fixed variable but is subject to multiple influences. No nation's political psyche, on this assumption, is rigidly fixed in either a pro- or antidemocratic direction. To assert this would be ahistorical. In this context, Larry Diamond has written that "there is considerable historical evidence to suggest that democratic culture is as much the product as the cause of effectively functioning democracy."[44] This study is in broad agreement with these observations.

Rather than addressing claims about the general causal relationship between political culture and democracy, this book focuses on the coherence of a picture of the relationship between religion and democracy in which the former contributes positively to the latter. The discussion of Muslim politics in Turkey and Indonesia with respect to emerging secular norms is speculative and is meant simply to identify an emerging political trend. I argue that these observations are valid to the extent that this emerging secular shift among Muslim political parties and actors affects the process of democratization.

Methodological Approach: Toward a Comparative Political Theory

The primary methodological approach of this book is historical and comparative. Drawing on insights and lessons from Western political theory and
history, I will examine the relationship between liberal-democratic development and religion both theoretically and in the context of the Muslim world.[45]
I will briefly discuss three Muslim majority countries—Iran, Turkey and
Indonesia—as a means of reinforcing the theoretical claims of this book.

In specific terms, this approach is meant to compensate for the weakness in
academic scholarship on the subject of Islam and democracy.[46] A historical and
comparative approach demonstrates this weakness. Mainstream modernization
theory and Orientalist interpretations of the relationship between Islam and
liberal democracy have enjoyed a resurgence in some influential circles after 11
September 2001.[47] With rare exceptions, this body of literature has clouded rather
than illuminated debate on this subject. I will argue that many of these scholars
have not only misdiagnosed the relevant politics and history of the Muslim
societies with respect to the relationship between religion, secularism, and democracy but also have selectively interpreted the history of political development in the
West by downplaying the role of religious politics and its connection to democratization. In other words, a double misdiagnosis has taken place.[48] This point is
important and is connected to one of the preliminary subthemes of this book. In
order to comprehend the challenges facing liberal democracy in Muslim societies
today, we must reacquaint ourselves with what Sheri Berman has called "the very
turbulent backstory" of the development of liberal democracy in the West.[49]
Progress in grasping the problems of democratization in one region is dependent
on an understanding of its historical development in the other.

Finally, this book's orientation has been inspired by the emerging field of
comparative political theory. Lying as it does at the intersection of two subfields
of political science, political theory and comparative politics, as Fred Dallmayr
has noted, in "contemporary academia, comparative political theory or philosophy is either completely nonexistent or at best an embryonic and marginalized
type of endeavour."[50] Universalist in its scope while simultaneously sensitive to
local context, as defined by Dallmayr, the task of the practitioner of comparative
political theory is to go beyond the traditional analytical frameworks and
theoretical approaches that define these two subdisciplines of political science.
"Properly pursued, comparative political theorizing would need to be genuinely
global in character" and should be pursued "not through unilateral fiat but only
through mutual interrogation, contestation and lateral engagement."[51]

Sudipta Kaviraj, in a more recent contribution to this emerging field, has noted that "to understand political modernity in the non-Western world is impossible without Western social theory; it is equally impossible entirely within the terms of that tradition."[52] In keeping with Dallmayr's interciviliza-tional approach to comparative political theory, which seeks to strike a balance between the universal and the particular, Kaviraj observes that "the process of modernity are universal, but these processes are realized through a trajectory of historical events which are specific to each society." His advice to Western social scientists interested in theorizing about non-Western societies is to "learn from Western social theory, but not expect it to tell us about our precise future. Therefore we must climb this essential and edifying ladder, but learn to dispense with it when the time comes; that time comes precisely when histori-cal sociology begins."[53] This book is informed by these observations and seeks to make a contribution to this emerging field of comparative political theory by rethinking the theoretical and practical relationships between religion, secu-larism, and liberal democracy.

Overview of the Chapters

If is often assumed—erroneously—that the development of democracy, human rights, pluralism, and secularism in the West was a smooth process. This idea is implicit in much of the mainstream scholarship and media commentary on this subject, which makes political development in Muslim societies appear arrested and retarded by comparison. Why the strong appeal of religion in the Muslim world and calls for "an Islamic state" at the dawn of the twenty-first century, two hundred years after the French Revolution? Where are the secular-democratic opposition groups? Why do Islamist parties triumph in elections? Why such hatred and bitterness toward the West? Why so many manifestations of conser-vatism and violence? Why so much anger and political conflict in the Islamic world? Are all these things inherent in Muslim societies, in their culture and religion? In the words of one prominent scholar, "what went wrong?"[54]

These are legitimate questions. A comprehensive answer, however, re-quires a sense of history, not only of the Islamic world but of the West as well. It is often implicitly assumed in discussion about non-Western societies that the West has always been secular, liberal, and democratic or that a straight line can be drawn, without any detours or setbacks, from ancient Athenian democracy and the age of Pericles to modern American democracy and the writings of John Rawls. This assumption distorts perceptions of the struggle for democracy in non-Western societies.[55]

Francis Fukuyama's widely debated post–Cold War thesis on the "end of history" and the triumph of liberal democracy illustrates this point. He includes a chart in his famous book that classifies countries, such as the United States, as "liberal democracies" from as early as 1790. No qualification is offered. Recall that in 1790, however, the majority of Americans, women and African Americans in particular, were legally disenfranchised.[56] Acknowledging the novelty of the liberal-democratic project, as it historically evolved in Europe and North America and its recent consolidation during the twentieth century, is a precondition for understanding the challenges and obstacles to the emergence of this form of government in Muslim societies today. Chapter 1 of this book discusses this point.

This preliminary chapter explores the historical background needed to comprehend a liberal-democratic theory for Muslim societies. After briefly surveying the literature on political liberalism and modernization theory with respect to religion, a critical reading of this literature is offered. I argue that this literature has been unhelpful in understanding the theoretical relationship between religion and democratic development. Alternatively, by taking a longer view of history, a more balanced understanding of the topic is possible. Drawing on the work of the historian Fernand Braudel and the political philosopher Michael Walzer, I propose a more nuanced approach.

The main subtheme of chapter 1 is the relationship between Islam, modernization, and political development. By end of the twentieth century, most Muslim societies were marked by two key political characteristics: the general absence of democracy (or conversely the persistence of authoritarian politics) and the poor state of human rights. Two major reports, one by the United Nations Development Program (UNDP) and the other by Freedom House, have confirmed this observation and have painted a grim picture of the Muslim world's political future.[57] The strength of Islamist opposition groups in most Middle East societies further casts doubt on the prospects for liberal-democratic development.

Chapter 1 explores the question of Islamic fundamentalism's relationship to political development. Focusing on the sociological impact of Islamic fundamentalism, rather than its ideological content, and comparing it with the rise of English Puritanism, I offer a dissenting interpretation of the origins and political impact of Islamism. I argue that radical religious protest movements often emerge in the context of a rapidly modernizing societies and the social upheaval that accompanies the breakdown of the traditional order. This is a common occurrence throughout history and is linked to the longer term process of political modernization. Islamic fundamentalism, I argue, is a much more complicated social phenomenon than is generally realized, which may carry latent development benefits, especially when observed from the perspective of history and sociology. A comparative historical treatment of politics in the early modern period of Europe and the contemporary Middle East helps to illustrate this point, while also serving to challenge the popular view of the structural incompatibility between religious politics and democratization.

Chapter 2 examines the relationship between religious reformation and liberal democracy via the political theology of John Locke. Not only is Locke a founding father of modern liberal democracy but the relationship between church and state preoccupied his thinking throughout his life. While the enduring insights contained in his writings remain a staple of the Western philosophical canon, to date no one has attempted to systematically apply his political theory to the question of social change in the Muslim world.[58] Chapter 2 will attempt to do so.

Locke is an exemplary political philosopher to call on in the context of a book on religion, secularism, and liberal democracy in Muslim societies. An analysis of his work demonstrates how it is possible to find theoretical space within religion to advance an argument for popular sovereignty and human rights.

Furthermore, Locke is useful not only because he is widely credited with writing the first outline of modern liberal democracy but also because the sociopolitical context in which he wrote has critical parallels with Muslim societies today. First, religion was a marker of identity for large numbers of people in both societies. Second, the process of modernization had produced similar social and economic dislocations with comparable effects on popular religious consciousness. In this sense, the discussion in chapter 1 of the rise of English Puritanism and its parallels with Islamism is relevant to the themes of this chapter and will be explored further. Third, a theological conception of politics was shared by large numbers of people, in terms of the moral basis of legitimate political authority. Recall that Locke was writing in an era when political authority was often justified by invoking the "divine right of kings."[59] It was in this context that he wrote two of his most famous political tracts, *A Letter Concerning Toleration* (1689) and the *Two Treatises of Government* (1689). These seminal texts will be combed for insights on the relationship between emerging liberal-democratic ideas and religious values.

In the second part of chapter 2, I attempt to apply Locke's political theology to the case of the contemporary Muslim world. While political and religious debates in the Islamic Republic of Iran will form the immediate basis of comparison, I argue that the underlying political lessons are transferable beyond Iran's borders to other Muslim societies. Central to this discussion is the unique methodology of Locke's argument in constructing new liberal and democratic ideas from within a social milieu of a deeply religious society.

Locke's political writings on the question of religious toleration and political authority can be understood as emerging out of a dissenting religious exegesis. It is this context—within John Locke's political theology—that is relevant to the construction of a theory of liberal democracy for Muslim societies.

Chapter 2 concludes by arguing that in societies that are under the sway of an illiberal and undemocratic religiopolitical doctrine, liberal democracy can be advanced by a reinterpretation of religious ideas with respect to government. This is a more successful and more cohesive alternative to the complete privatization or rejection of religion from the public sphere. This development can be observed both in seventeenth-century England and in the Middle East today. To the extent that this is accurate, an important connection has been established between religious reinterpretation and liberal-democratic development. It also suggests a possible universalism to this aspect of democratic theory (i.e. how religious societies can develop liberal-democratic arguments) that may be valid across time and between cultural traditions.

Chapter 3 tackles the question of secularism. It seeks to clarify the theoretical relationship between religion, secularism, and liberal democracy. In much of the scholarly literature on liberal-democratic theory, this relationship is assumed rather than argued and rarely discussed in any detail. Today, the term "secularism" is bandied about with an imprecision that comes at the expense of understanding. What are the historical roots of secularism? What problems does it seek to overcome and what values does it promote? When it is affirmed that liberal democracy requires secularism, what does this actually mean, institutionally, constitutionally, and in terms of state-society relations? These theoretical questions are answered in this chapter.

Specifically, I will examine the point at which religion and liberal democracy come into conflict, and then give a clear statement as to why a form of secularism is an essential condition for liberal democracy. As a result of this investigation, several important questions arise: is there more than one model of secularism that liberal democracy might accommodate? If so, what are possible other models? Second, what minimum boundaries must the state and groups within civil society respect in order to uphold a liberal democracy? How fluid (or rigid) are the boundaries of secularism? These questions are investigated in the first part of the chapter. They are answered, in part, by first looking at the writings of two influential political philosophers, Alexis de Tocqueville and Richard Rorty. While they arrived at different conclusions about the desirability and compatibility between religion and democracy I seek to bridge the chasm by turning to the recent theoretical contributions of Alfred Stepan on the relationship between liberal democracy and the world's religious systems. Specifically, I will examine his thesis on the "World

Religious Systems and Democracy: Crafting the 'Twin Tolerations',," with a focus on its relevance to contemporary Muslim societies.[60]

Chapter 4 examines the question of secularism and its discontents in Muslim societies. The propagation of secularism in Muslim societies today faces several obstacles, of which some are theoretical but most are practical. The theoretical obstacle pertains to the often-heard argument that both doctrinally and historically Islam, unlike Christianity, is utterly incompatible with secularism. The most articulate proponent of this position has been Bernard Lewis, who has long maintained that there is no moral basis or historical precedent for the separation of politics and religion in Islam. His argument is a popular one and is rooted in a comparison of the inner doctrines of Islam and Christianity as well as their early religious histories.[61] In short, Lewis's argument boils down to a claim that history is destiny. This claim runs contrary, however, to the fact that for over a millennium, Christendom, notwithstanding Jesus' famous instruction to "render unto Caesar the things which are Caesar's, and unto God the things that are God's," is marked by a very long history of the mutual interdependence and sometimes union of church and state, not only in the form of Caesaropapism in Eastern Orthodox Christianity but in Latin Christendom as well.[62] Lewis's argument obscures this fact, both in terms of the assumptions he makes of an enduring dualism between church and state in the West and in terms of his applied analysis of Muslim societies. In this book I will offer an alternative explanation on the theoretical obstacles and prospects for political secularism in Muslim societies.

Abdou Filali-Ansary has insightfully noted that in "the Muslim world, secularization is preceding religious reformation—a reversal of the European experience in which secularization was more or less a consequence of such reformation."[63] The relationship between religious reformation and secularism is critical to understanding the weak intellectual roots of secularism in the Muslim world. I will investigate this relationship by drawing on the work of Marshall Hodgson, whose comparative treatment of the modernization of Europe and the Middle East can be read as a counternarrative to that of Bernard Lewis. Specifically, Hodgson, while not speaking to the topic of Islam and secularism directly, suggests that a radical rupture with the Islamic past has prevented the matching and harmonization of technological modernization from above with "steady social and intellectual transformation" from below.[64] As this chapter demonstrates, this radical rupture between tradition and modernity has had profound negative consequences for political development in Muslim societies during the twentieth century.

In addition, secularism faces important ideological challenges at the practical level. First, in the popular imagination of many Muslims, the concept of secularism has a credibility problem because of its perceived linkage with colonialism and imperialism. Second, secularism is seen as contributing to the failure of the postcolonial state in the Muslim world, which often ruled in the name of a secular political ideology (for example, Ba'athism, various forms of socialism, Arab and Iranian nationalism). Mounting socioeconomic disparities, the suppression of internal dissent, and the political subservience of many regimes to the (secular) West together have made the concept of secularism a deeply suspect one in many Muslim societies.[65]

Recent events outside of the Muslim world have further damaged secularism's reputation. The decision of the French government in 2004, for example, to ban the wearing of the hejab in French public schools—in the name of secularism—entrenches the idea, in the eyes of Muslim communities globally, that secularism is an inherently anti-Muslim political doctrine that persists at the expense of the civil rights of Muslims.

A consequence of secularism's poor reputation in the Muslim world is that for many politically active segments of society, a rejection of the normative idea that religion and state should be separated has now morphed into a core component of "Muslim identity." This is easily discerned when Muslim political activists are asked to comment on the topic.[66] Given this situation, the key tension in the debate with respect to religion, secularism, and liberal democracy in Muslim societies today is the following. Liberal democracy requires a form of political secularism, yet simultaneously secularism is anathema to many Muslims. How can this chasm be bridged? Put differently, how can a version of secularism be socially constructed to assist the process of democratization and liberalization in the Muslim world?

By way of conclusion, I argue that real gains for liberal democracy in Muslim societies require the development of an "indigenous theory of Islamic secularism." Akeel Bilgrami has perceptively observed that in the East, secularism "has to be earned, not assumed at the outset."[67] Though he was writing about the interesting case of Indian secularism, his advice has special relevance to Muslim-majority societies where in the past the most vocal defenders of secularism have been elite members of society who have projected their own secularity onto the wider society, which remains deeply religious. Secularism, in other words, lacks organic roots in Muslim societies. Based on recent historical experience, it is widely viewed as an ideology of repression (especially in the Arab world) rather than as a prerequisite for a just political order. Altering this perception demands that religious groups and religious intellectuals in Muslim societies morally engage with the topic of secularism, in an attempt to reconcile their own religious values with a form of government that is both secular and religion-friendly. Recent empirical evidence from Indonesia and

Turkey suggests that when this does occur, the project of liberal democracy can be advanced as a result.

Conclusion

The late Canadian scholar of comparative history and religion Wilfred Cantwell Smith was concerned throughout his life with the future development of Muslim societies. He concluded his *Islam in Modern History*, published over fifty years ago, by anticipating the destabilizing effects of Muslim politics on global affairs. He wrote: "the various intellectual and moral issues are today themselves internationalized. We would contend that a healthy, flourishing Islam is as important not only for the Muslims but for all the world today."[68] This observation has a unique poignancy after 11 September 2001.

If there is one general lesson to be taken from this transformative event, it is that the world is indeed a global village whose actors ignore long-standing problems of democratic governance and sustainable development at their collective peril. The topic of religion and democracy, after September 11, is now one of the most important and pressing questions of our age. This is especially true in light of the general absence of democracy and respect for human rights throughout most of the Muslim world. The destabilizing effects that emanate from the Middle East now affect us all.

Looking back over the last decade since the end of the Cold War, it is apparent that global politics has been marked by two key events: (1) the cross-cultural diffusion of democratic ideas, and (2) the reappearance of ethnic/religious identities in public affairs. While democracy as a normative ideal is ubiquitous in international affairs, in political theory, it raises as many questions as it lays to rest. David Held has suggested that the "uncritical affirmation of liberal democracy essentially leaves unanalyzed the whole meaning of democracy and its possible variants."[69] Therefore, any discussion of liberal democracy's global future must address as a central problem the question of difference.[70] This book does so, by rethinking the theoretical and practical relationship between religion, secularism, and liberal democracy in Muslim societies. Furthermore, by examining the broad relationship between religion and democracy, both historically and comparatively, and by relying on insights from Western political theory, this book aims to contribute to the development of a liberal-democratic theory for Muslim societies.

This study challenges the widely held assumption that religious politics and liberal-democratic development are structurally incompatible. It does so first by critically reexamining the role of religion in the development of liberal democracy in the West, highlighting the place of religious politics in this developmental trajectory. Next, I apply the lessons of this investigation to several key countries in the Muslim world. I conclude that the struggle for liberal democracy, both in the West historically and in the Muslim world today, cannot be disconnected from debates about the normative status of religion in government. In other words, the road to liberal democracy, whatever other twists and turns it makes, cannot avoid passing through the gate of religious politics.

Furthermore, I argue that there is an inherent link between the reformation of religious thought and political development. While this is often assumed as part of the grand narrative of Western history, liberal-democratic theorists rarely acknowledge this point, especially when commenting on Muslim politics.[71] This relationship between religion and liberal democracy is especially important in societies where religion is a key marker of identity and where religious values shape the political culture. Recognizing this point can help democratic theorists untangle the complicated relationship between religion, secularism, and democracy in the Muslim world today.

Finally, there is the question of secularism. No liberal-democratic theory can ignore this topic, especially in the context of emerging democracies in the Muslim world. Empirical evidence from several countries, where advances have been made in the area of democracy and human rights, suggest that an indigenous theory or understanding of Muslim secularism can contribute to the development of liberal democracy. When Muslim groups develop a "political theology of secularism" whereby signing onto the liberal-democratic project is not deemed a rejection of Islamic values but rather an affirmation of them, liberal democracy in the Muslim world gains the support of a critical political constituency. Given the salience of religious values in shaping political norms in the Muslim world today, reconciling Islamic political thought with secularism is a critical precondition for the construction of a liberal-democratic theory for Muslim societies. I conclude this book by arguing this point.

I

Toward a Democratic Theory
for Muslim Societies

The Historical Background

Islamic fundamentalism is a temporary, transitory movement, but it
could last another 30 or 50 years—I don't know how long. Where
fundamentalism isn't in power it will continue to be an ideal, as
long as the basic frustration and discontent persist that lead people
to take extreme positions. You need long experience with clericalism
to finally get fed up with it—look how much time it took in Europe!

—Maxime Rodinson

In his insightful theoretical discussion of the relationship between
religious systems and democracy, Alfred Stepan engages in a critique
of liberal-democratic theory with respect to the role of religion in
public affairs.[1] Stepan's argument is that liberal political philosophers
such as John Rawls and Bruce Ackerman, when discussing a just
political order, attach great weight in their writings to *liberal arguing*
but almost no weight to *democratic bargaining.*[2] This is a problem
for democratic theory, Stepan maintains, particularly as it relates
to religious societies in the non-Western world where democratic
transitions and consolidations have yet to occur. Stepan argues that
liberal political theory has clouded rather than illuminated our
understanding of the struggle for democracy, especially in societies
where the normative role of religion in politics remains a heated
topic of debate. The assumption that religion's proper role in political
life has been democratically negotiated—in favor of secularism and
liberal democracy—is a common analytical error social scientists

make when commenting on the politics of the Muslim world. This chapter is devoted to explicating this idea.³

In broad terms, this chapter reexamines the relationship between religion and political development. Specifically, I will map out a historical context that will form the foundation for the development of a liberal-democratic theory for Muslim societies. After a review of the place of religion in liberal-democratic and political modernization theory, the bulk of this chapter will provide an alternative reading of the rise of Islamic fundamentalism. The accent will be on situating the rise of religious fundamentalism as an integral yet temporary phase in the long-term process of political development, which has little to do with religious essences but rather is deeply connected to the onset of modernity and the social upheaval that often accompanies the rapid transformation of traditional societies.

I argue three specific but interrelated points in this chapter.

(1) Mainstream scholarship in the field of liberal-democratic theory and modernization theory has been largely unhelpful in understanding the theoretical questions related to the struggle for liberal democracy in Muslim societies.

(2) Islamic fundamentalism is a much more complicated social phenomenon than is generally recognized. Its emergence and persistence in the Muslim world, in the latter half of the twentieth century, was predictable and is understandable.

(3) Radical religious protest movements, such as Islamism, have a proto-modern character to them. Their impact and relationship to the development of liberal democracy can be better appreciated by focusing on their sociological effects over the long term rather than on their doctrinal content.

The central theoretical claim of this chapter is that historical depth is required to understand the complicated relationship between religion, modernization, and democracy. It is often assumed—mistakenly—that the development of democracy, human rights, and pluralism in the West was a smooth process. A critical reading of history indicates that this was not the case; thus a complication-free path to political development should not be assumed in other regional or cultural contexts.

As to methodology, this chapter adopts a comparative historical approach. Because many of the preeminent political questions within the Muslim world today directly relate to the relationship between religion and democracy in a way that echoes the debates on religion and the emergence of democracy in Europe during the sixteenth and seventeenth centuries, I emphasize the parallels between the two periods and regions. By approaching this topic from such a vantage point I seek to counter a key axiom of the clash of civilizations thesis which after 11 September 2001, has resurfaced and has understandably won new followers.[4] This axiom emphasizes a fundamental ontological incompatibility between civilizations, Islam and Latin Christendom in particular. A comparative historical methodological approach that focuses on civilizational commonalities and political development serves as a counternarrative to this widely debated and popular thesis.

Similarly, this comparative approach to the study of Muslim politics is meant to provide an alternative reading to the widely held perspective that interprets Islamic fundamentalism as a unique peculiarity located in the cultural essence of Muslim civilization. I argue that Western observers of the Muslim world today should recall their own history of political development and recognize distinct parallels with Muslim societies, where violence and religious radicalism marked the transition between tradition and modernity and where the origins of liberal democracy can be located.

John Rawls and Religion: Normative and Empirical Caveats for Liberal Theory

In John Rawls's influential book *Political Liberalism*, he is concerned with how a plural society in which citizens have a variety of socially embedded, reasonable, but deeply opposed comprehensive doctrines can arrive at an overlapping consensus.[5] His normative recommendation is that on major questions of quasi-constitutional importance, individuals should only advance political causes and arguments based on freestanding conceptions of justice that are not rooted in one of the comprehensive, but opposing, doctrines found in a polity.[6] Rawls thus argues that certain types of disputes—such as disputes about religion—should be taken off the political agenda. He writes: "when certain matters are taken off the political agenda, they are no longer regarded as appropriate subjects for political decision by a majority or other plurality votings."[7] *Political Liberalism* leaves democratic theorists with the normative injunction—buttressed by the preeminent philosophical standing of Rawls himself—that important public arguments about the place of religion in society are only appropriate if they employ freestanding conceptions of political justice.[8]

While Rawls's theory is both persuasive and internally consistent, Alfred Stepan points out that there is a serious flaw in his approach. Stepan contends that Rawls devotes no attention to the subject of *how* actual polities have consensually and democratically arrived at quasi-constituent agreements to "take religion off the political agenda." Indeed, if we are interested in political struggles over the role of religion in the polis that are arrived at via consensual democratic agreements, "it is important to stress that almost none of them empirically, discursively, or even normatively, were confined to the Rawlsian liberal normative map."[9]

In an important note, Stepan cites a private communication with Bruce Ackerman on this point. Ackerman confirms that his and Rawls's endeavors are aimed at providing fully developed philosophical arguments for an ideal end state for a liberal-democratic society. Scholars such as Alfred Stepan and his colleague, Juan Linz, are concerned with the historically different and prior question of *how* concrete polities have created the minimal conditions for democracy.[10] It is this question that is germane for our discussion here and our larger concern about the development of liberal democracy in Muslim societies.

Politics involves conflict. The development of liberal democracy provided a path to regulate and institutionalize the management of conflict.[11] Often forgotten, however, in democratic theory is that in many long-standing liberal democracies the major source of conflict for a long period of time was the place of religion in society. In many of these countries, the political containment or marginalization of religious conflict was only constructed after long, emotional, and often bitter public arguments. Extensive political negotiation had to take place prior to the reaching of a consensus on the proper relationship between religion and government.[12]

To arrive at a consensus on the role of religion in political society, Stepan reminds us that an emerging democracy normally entertains public theological arguments. During the process of political debate and contestation some proponents of the democratic bargain are able to gain ascendance, or at least acquiescence within their religious community for the democratic bargain, by employing religious doctrinal arguments that are *not* conceptually freestanding, but rather are deeply and sometimes uniquely embedded in their own religious communities' experience and comprehensive doctrine.[13] The thrust of Stepan's argument is summarized as follows:

> One can expect, therefore, that in polities where a significant component
> of one of the world's major religions may be under the sway of a
> nondemocratic doctrinally based religious discourse, one of the major
> tasks of political and spiritual leaders who would like, for whatever
> reason, to revalue democratic norms in their own religious community
> will be continually to mount theologically convincing public arguments
> about the legitimate multivocality of their religion. Such arguments
> may violate Rawls's requirement for freestanding public reasoning—but
> they may be vital to the success of the democratization process in a
> country in the midst of a contestation over the meaning and the

appropriateness of democracy. *Liberal arguing* has a place in a
democracy, but it would empty meaning and history out of political
philosophy if we did not leave a place for *democratic bargaining*, and for
some forms of nonliberal public argument within religious
communities, in such democratic bargaining.[14]

As Ackerman concedes, the paradigm of political liberalism assumes not only
that a democratic transition has taken place but that liberal democracy has long
been consolidated and its core values entrenched within the political culture.
In the case of non-Western societies that have yet to make a transition to
democracy, the dominant paradigm in the scholarly literature for the past
fifty years has been modernization theory. Both the theory of political liberalism and modernization theory are paradigms that share common epistemo-
logical and teleological assumptions about social change, the idea of progress,
the proper course of political development, and the role of religion within this
developmental trajectory. As Irene Gendzier has noted, "theories of Political
Development and, more generally, interpretations of Third World political
change were based on contemporary theories of liberal democracy." She
adds, "set in historical perspective, Political Development theories, as exten-
sions of contemporary liberal-democratic theories, share a common historical
origin."[15] The next section is devoted to explicating these common origins.

Political Modernization Theory and Religion

The predominant claim of modernization theory is that economic development is
linked to coherent and predictable changes in cultural and sociopolitical life.[16] As
a society moves forward and makes a transition from an agrarian-based economy
to an industrial one, this leads to occupational specialization, higher literacy rates,
and growing income levels. The cultural changes that result from this process
lead to changes in gender roles, attitudes toward authority, and sexual mores;
declining birthrates; and eventually greater political participation.

   In a broad sense, the process of modernization simply means replacing old
patterns of thought, action, association, and belief with new ones. When
students in the social sciences read the influential works in the Western
canon, from Hobbes, Locke, and Rousseau to Hegel, Mill, and Marx, they are
doing so against the backdrop and evolution of modernity in Europe. This
process of social change and evolution was organic to Europe. In the context of
many developing societies, however, the social transformations that modernization brought was largely not a result of an indigenous process—as it was in

Europe, where it was connected to changes in civil society—but rather was driven by the exogenous forces of European colonialism and imperialism in alliance with local elites. This partly explains modernization's destabilizing effects and will be explored in greater depth in the final chapter.

As far as the academic literature about Third World development is concerned, its origins date back about a half century to when two important processes coincided: the emergence of the United States as a superpower and the decolonization of large parts of Africa and Asia after World War II. The political macrophenomena of social change and economic development of these regions received new attention from the U.S. government whose new-found superpower status expanded its national interests globally. The upswing of this development in international relations was increased funding for the study of the Third World in the United States, which manifested itself most significantly in the work of the American Social Science Research Council Committee on Comparative Politics. The body of literature that emerged from this committee gave strong impetus to theory construction and set the parameters for mainstream scholarly discussion of the problems of political development in the Third World. Collectively, this body of scholarship is known as "modernization theory," and it is intellectually indebted to the theories of Max Weber and Talcott Parsons.[17] The academics who were most intimately connected with this school of thought and who wrote extensively and influentially in this area include Gabriel Almond, Lucien Pye, David Apter, Samuel Huntington, James Coleman, Cyril Black, Sidney Verba, Dankwart Rustow, Daniel Lerner, and David McClelland.[18]

In a 1968 article on the social aspects of modernization in the developing world, Daniel Lerner, a widely cited modernization theorist, defined his topic as "the social change whereby less developed societies acquire characteristics common to more developed societies."[19] The diffusion of values from the West to the non-West, increasing urbanization, literacy, political participation, material consumption, and the ability to control nature via modern technology were all deemed essential aspects of the modernization process. Similarly, Gabriel Almond and G. Bingham Powell defined political development as "the increased differentiation and specialization of political structures and *the increased secularization of political cultures.*"[20]

The focus on secularization is important to this discussion. While there was no single monolithic "modernization theory" but rather "theories," most political modernization theorists implicitly subscribed to the view that a core problem afflicting development in Asia, Africa, and the Middle East was that these societies were excessively "traditional" and could only move forward via a process of modernization. In other words, the replacing of traditional patterns of thought, belief, habit, and custom with secular-rational thinking was required.

Traditional societies were thought to be static and unchanging; the rhythm of life in them was seen as circular, not linear and progressive; creativity and innovation were thought to be nonexistent; and, critically, religion was viewed as a significant barrier to progress because it promoted notions of fatalism, superstition, and otherworldliness. The secularization thesis is thus the sine qua non of modernization theory, as religion—drawing on a key axiom of Enlightenment liberal thought—was considered to be the very embodiment of tradition. As Donald E. Smith noted over twenty-five years ago—representing the dominant view at the time, which remains largely unchallenged—"Political development includes, as one of its basic processes, the secularization of polities, the progressive exclusion of religion from the political system."[21] Summarizing the academic field of political development with regard to modernization theory, Fred R. von der Mehden has observed:

> The high point of the modernization and development field in the
> United States lasted about two decades from the early 1950s to
> the early 1970s. It began with the social sciences accepting most of
> R. Nisbet's premises regarding social evolution: that change is natural,
> directional, immanent, continuous, necessary, and proceeds from
> uniform causes, and that "one could categorize non-Western peoples
> as not simply exotic or difficult but as reflecting lower stages of an
> evolutionary advancement that was thought to be universal." This
> picture changes over the years as the process of development was
> found to be more complex, but the portrayal of religion as at the very
> least not conducive to modernization continued to be far less
> challenged in the general conceptual literature than it was in
> particularistic empirical studies.[22]

Islamic Fundamentalism and Democracy: A Dissenting Perspective

In an article on the dismal prospects for democracy in the Arab world, Lisa Anderson begins by recalling the scholarly contribution of two prominent political scientists on the theoretical preconditions for democracy.[23] The first scholar, Harvard professor Samuel P. Huntington, in a widely read essay in 1984, "Will More Countries Become Democratic," disputed an earlier thesis by

Dankwart Rustow, that the only essential precondition for democracy was a shared national identity.[24] Huntington responded that other factors were important as well, most significantly economic growth. He discussed an economic "zone of transition" that corresponded to the upper third of the World Bank's middle-income countries that could lead to a transition from authoritarianism to either communism or democracy. He further theorized that a market economy and a bourgeoisie were necessary but not sufficient for the emergence of democracy.[25] Turning to the Muslim world, Huntington bluntly stated that its prospects for democracy were not good, as it lacked the essential preconditions needed for a democratic transition.

> Among Islamic countries, particularly those in the Middle East, the prospects for democratic development seem low. The Islamic revival and particularly the rise of Shiite fundamentalism, would seem to reduce even further the likelihood of democratic development, particularly since democracy is often identified with the very Western influences the revival strongly opposes.[26]

Huntington's observation that the rise of Islamic fundamentalism in the public sphere of Muslim societies is antithetical to democratization seems axiomatic and difficult to dispute—at first glance. This is particularly true when one discusses the prospects for liberal democracy in light of mainstream Islamist positions that often qualify the concept of popular sovereignty with religious safeguards and take issue with universal standards of human rights as embodied in international law.[27] In this chapter, however, I offer a dissenting view on the relationship between Islamic fundamentalism and democratic development.

The main difference between my dissenting view and the conventional perspective, as represented by Samuel Huntington, for example, is that Huntington's view is only valid from a short-term perspective. The emphasis he places on the doctrinal incompatibility of Islamic fundamentalism with liberal democracy is beyond dispute. However, if one takes the longer view of history, the emergence of Islamic fundamentalism and its contributions to democratization—in certain national contexts—can be interpreted differently.[28]

I argue in this chapter that the actual content of Islamic fundamentalist thought is less important than the social conditions that give rise to it. The process of the rapid modernization of traditional societies sometimes produces a radical interpretation of religion as a response to social dislocation and political uncertainty. Islamic fundamentalism is a much more complicated social phenomenon than is generally appreciated, and its long-term effect may include latent benefits for the development of liberal democracy in the Muslim world.[29] In order to appreciate this argument I will emphasize the sociological impact of Islamism, while viewing its doctrinal orientation—albeit highly significant in its immediate influence on society—as a less important element in the long-term political development of Muslim societies.[30]

Comparing Histories: Islam and Christianity

More than a decade ago, Gregg Easterbrook suggested that in terms of the ebbing and flowing of religious passions, Islam was in the same historical space once occupied by Christianity during the High Middle Ages and early modern period. He wrote:

> Ought Islam to be considered barbarian because the religion
> sometimes sparks rioting and has followers who endorse that
> internally contradictory concept, the "holy war"? Neither speaks well
> of Islamic values, but consider an intriguing historical parallel.
> Today's Moslem extremism is occurring about 1,300 years after the
> death of Mohammed, in 632 A.D. The low ebb of Christianity—the
> Inquisition, followed by decades of mutual slaughter among Catholics
> and Protestants—began approximately the same number of years
> after the death of Christ. A low point of Judaism—the final loss of the
> Holy Land to the Romans—came in 70 A.D. , a few centuries more
> than a thousand years after Moses led the flight from Egypt. This
> could be nothing but coincidence. But perhaps major religions,
> involving as they do deep-seated webs of philosophy, emotion and
> politics, require a millennium to shake themselves out.[31]

To compare religious traditions is not to equate them. The study of history, however, would be rendered meaningless unless one could draw on relevant historical analogies to illuminate contemporary phenomena. A major assumption of this book is that the similarities between Islam and Christianity—and the radical protest movements they have spawned at approximately the same time (in their respective histories) and for many of the same reasons—are significant enough to merit a comparison.[32] Before proceeding with this comparison, I shall pause to consider some potential objections.

Problems of Civilizational Comparison

Any comparison is fraught with danger. This is particularly true when comparing cases that at first glance seem unconnected: political change in seventeenth-century Europe and the twenty-first-century Middle East. Initial objections are likely to be raised on methodological grounds because the comparison is not adhering to formats for comparison that are generally used in the comparative politics literature: the longitudinal (diachronic) and the crossnational (synchronic).[33] Thus, contemporary Iran and nineteenth-century Iran can be compared; or contemporary Iran and contemporary Turkey can be compared; but comparing contemporary Iran and seventeenth-century England is problematic. According to Arend Lijphart, comparisons should be made between similar cases so that differences can be analyzed with systematic precision. Comparing social phenomena with too many different variables poses a problem for a rigorous comparative inquiry, especially when dealing with only two case studies.[34]

Objections are also likely to be raised that a comparison between political development in (sixteenth- and seventeenth-century) Europe and the (twentieth- and twenty-first-century) Middle East suffers from a modernization theory bias. In particular, the linear teleological assumptions of modernization theory with respect to the dichotomy between "tradition" and "modernity" and the inevitable triumph of secular liberal democracy might be raised as an objection. Dependency theorists might argue that the economic contexts in the two cases are significantly different both globally and within each of the regions under consideration, making a comparison difficult. Finally, cultural essentialists are likely to be offended by the very notion of a comparison between Christianity/Europe and the Middle East/Islam either in the past or present. Their objections would likely increase in the context of a discussion of the similarities between Islamic fundamentalism and radical Protestantism as precursors to the development of a liberal-democratic polity.[35]

These objections are misplaced. This chapter demonstrates that traditional societies on the brink of modernity undergo and experience similar processes of dislocation, anxiety, breakdown, and reconstruction for many of the same reasons and with outcomes that are comparable. This is especially true in societies where religion is a key marker of identity. Particularly salient for this discussion is the rise of religious radicalism during the time of transition. Social scientists familiar with the political history of both early modern Europe and the contemporary Middle East, will be immediately struck by the similarities. As one author has astutely noted, "as the years pass, the choices being made in the Muslim countries seem increasingly familiar to the student of tumultuous early-modern Britain, when the fabled British sobriety gave way to religious radicalism, armed struggle and a bloody civil war."[36]

Fred Dallmayr has also raised a number of important caveats with respect to historical analogies. They are "always hazardous," he observes. "There may indeed be superficial historical parallels; but their occurrence is often peculiarly twisted and their significance counterintuitive." The reason for emphasizing this interpretive point is due to a "lack of linearity." The study of history, Dallmayr reminds us, "is a dense fabric of multiple strands whose status and interrelation are open to multiple interpretations and reinterpretations. Even if one strand at a given time and place could be comparable with a similar strand elsewhere, the immense complexity of historical contexts would thwart any simple analogy."

The problem is "compounded or accentuated," he notes, in crosscultural or crosscivilizational comparisons "where the terms 'culture' or 'civilization' stand for inherited frames of meaning and ways of life shared among larger groups of people." Prudence is warranted because

> although perhaps not impossible, any attempt to move laterally
> beyond or across such frames is likely to be suspect on epistemic as
> well as experiential grounds. The suspicion is bound to be particularly
> strong among historians whose professional training tends to alert
> them more to concrete particularities than to bland uniformities,
> more to fine nuances than to glib abstractions. Even non-historians,
> however, can see the problem: there is no prima facie evidence for
> assuming that the histories of cultures—and the stories of their
> people—are synchronized or readily convertible.

In the end, however, after considering the potential drawbacks in making broad historical analogies—especially across time and between cultures—Dallmayr cautiously endorses this methodological approach. His observations, while theoretical, are made in the concluding essay of a volume—entitled *An Islamic Reformation?*—that presents numerous parallels between the earlier religious reformations that took place in Christendom and the contemporary Muslim Middle East.[37] I am in broad agreement both with Fred Dallmayr's caveats against and arguments for a comparison between religious and political developments in Christian Europe and the Muslim Middle East.[38]

One further point bears directly on the development of a liberal-democratic theory for Muslim societies. When religious societies are under the sway of an illiberal and undemocratic political doctrine, transitions to liberal democracy cannot avoid dealing with the topic of political authority, in particular the moral basis of legitimate political authority. Some doctrinal reformulation or reconsideration is required in this area. I will explore this topic in greater detail in chapter 2; suffice it to say here that the historical analogy I will draw between Islam and Christianity is strongly congruent with a construction of liberal-democratic theory that has as one of its central components the clash between authoritarian and democratic conceptions of government.

Both Christianity in the early modern period and Islam today had to grapple with the idea of the moral basis of legitimate political authority. More important, they had to do so in the context of rival notions of political legitimacy rooted in holy scripture. The emergence and social construction of an indigenous version of political secularism was an integral part of this development trajectory. Overcoming religious opposition to emerging liberal-democratic ideas was also part of this long-term political process that scholarship on the development of liberal democracy has generally ignored. To better appreciate this critically important relationship between religion and democratic development, a discussion of an obscure event that took place in a small town in the heart of Europe almost five hundred years ago is most illustrative.

The Case of Münster

On 25 February 1534, the German town of Münster was taken over by Anabaptist zealots who established a radical theological dictatorship.[39] Those who refused to undergo rebaptism were expelled without food or belongings in the middle of a snowstorm. The new regime restructured the local government by canceling all debts, burning financial records, and confiscating food, money, and other valuables. A new moral tyranny was imposed on the citizenry, the most dramatic example being the burning of all books except the Bible. Blasphemy, seditious language, scolding one's parents, backbiting, adultery, even complaining were now considered sins and punishable by death. Polygamy was instituted, and unmarried women were ordered to marry the first man who asked them. Forty-nine women were executed and their bodies dismembered as a result of their failure to comply with this new law. A harsh dress code was also implemented; houses were routinely searched and surplus goods confiscated.

It was not long before news of the plight of Münster reached the outside world. Franz van Waldeck, a Catholic bishop from Münster who managed to escape, recruited a mercenary army that surrounded and laid siege to the town. Confusion and chaos soon took over Münster as the siege tightened. From within the Anabaptist rebel ranks, a new leader emerged by the name of John Beukels of Leiden, popularly known as John of Leiden. One of his first acts was to call a town meeting in which he proclaimed: "Now God has chosen me to be king over the whole world. . . . But what I am doing I must do, for God has elected me therefor. Dear brothers and sisters, Let us for this thank God."[40]

As the siege continued and starvation set in, John retained power through periodic prophetic outbursts, often invoking religious scripture. When this was insufficient, outright terror and brute force were his modus operandi; all dissent was ruthlessly suppressed. After a failed coup attempt, John oversaw the torture and beheading of the plotters. Their bodies were buried in two mass graves in the marketplace. Executions and dismemberment were frequent, and the bodies of the dead were nailed to trees and gateways as a reminder to others.

On 25 June 1535—sixteen months after the rebel takeover—Münster was finally liberated. The bishop's troops managed to capture John of Leiden alive, and over the next several months he was led in chains from village to village across northern Germany as a prisoner of war. On 22 January 1536, he was brought back to Münster, and in a public ceremony he was tortured to death with red-hot irons. His body was then put in a cage and suspended from St. Lambert's Church. Reportedly, this cage still hangs in Münster today.

Recalling the Anabaptist uprising in Münster is instructive in shedding light on contemporary problems of political development in the Islamic world.[41] The Muslim world today is at the beginning of the fifteenth century of the *hijra* (hegira),[42] corresponding to approximately a century before Martin Luther nailed his ninety-five theses to the door of the Castle Church in Wittenberg. Christendom in the early sixteenth century, like Islam at a similar age in its historical development, was marked by intellectual, political, and religious upheavals.

In 1516, Sir Thomas More published his *Utopia*, a book that reflected new Renaissance thinking by posing fundamental and heretofore unexamined questions about the relationship between church, state and society. A year later Martin Luther launched his protest against the sale of indulgences by the Catholic Church, an event that unofficially marked the beginning of Protestantism. Early sixteenth-century Europe also witnessed the emergence of a wide range of scientific discoveries and overseas exploration as the era of modern capitalism and colonialism began in earnest. The printing press created a media revolution that brought new ideas, partisan rhetoric, and a spirit of inquiry to the people. Most significantly, it made the Bible accessible to the masses in the local vernacular. Thomas Hobbes was to complain that this was one of the principal causes of the English Revolution (1640–1660). He wrote in *Behemoth*:

> For after the Bible was translated into English, every man, nay, every
> boy and wench, that could read English, thought they spoke with
> God Almighty, and understood what he said. . . . the reverence and
> obedience due to the Reformed Church here, and to the bishops
> and pastors therein, was cast off; and every man became a judge
> of religion, and an interpreter of the Scriptures to himself.[43]

Soon the Reformation and Counter-Reformation engulfed Europe, dividing the continent both religiously and politically.[44]

Similarly, the latter half of the twentieth century has ushered in profound social and political changes for Muslim societies. The ending of the era of colonialism saw the emergence of many nominally independent Muslim majority states, marked by an abundance of military coups detat, inter-state wars, revolutions, an oil boom, foreign interventions, high rates of population growth and urbanization, and growing socioeconomic inequality.[45] The forces of economic and cultural globalization have significantly transformed the traditional way of life in Muslim societies, and coupled with a general absence of democracy, this has produced numerous social pathologies, the most significant being the rise of Islamic fundamentalism.

Social scientists who have studied the period note that there was "nothing very unusual about the rebellion that occurred in Münster, or that it took the form of a religious movement. Similar events were common in medieval Europe."[46] In other words, it was a sign of, and a reaction to, the changing times. The turbulent world of English politics in the sixteenth and seventeenth centuries was not far removed from events in Münster. It was similarly going through the early stages of modernization, with its accompanying destabilizing effects, a subject I will explore in greater depth later in terms of its parallels with Islamic fundamentalism.

According to the historian John Trumpbour, many of the radical Protestant sects in England "were haunted by the spectre of Münster and they talked about it often."[47] In *Puritanism and Revolution: Studies in Interpretation of the English Revolution of the Seventeenth Century*, Christopher Hill reports on this connection.

> Henceforth its memory and that of John of Leyden remained as a horror story to make the flesh of heretics creep, or to justify suppression of the lower orders if they chanced to get out of hand. The thirty-eighth article of faith of the Church of England is directed against Anabaptist communism: "The riches and goods of Christians are not common as touching the right, title, and possession of the same, as certain Anabaptists do falsely boast." The forty-first article of 1552, omitted in the Elizabethan prayer-book, was aimed specifically against the millenarian doctrine. In 1594 Thomas Nashe, in *The Unfortunate Traveller*, expressed a typical ruling-class attitude when he spoke of John of Leyden and his fellows as "such as thought they knew as much of Gods minde as richer men." It was not for the poor to give themselves such airs. In the sixteen-forties Oliver Cromwell, Sir

Arthur Hesilrige, and John Lilburne were all referred to as "John of Leyden" by political enemies wanting to discredit them. But for the more radical groups Münster was not a horror story at all. The Leveller William Walwyn spoke of "that lying story of that injured people . . . the Anabaptists of Münster." Another Leveller, Richard Overton, asked, "Who writ the Histories of the Anabaptists but their Enemies?" John Bunyan is said to have reflected the ideal of Münster in his picture of the town of Mansoul in *The Holy War*.[48]

Returning to the case of the Muslim world, the emergence of radical Islamist movements at the end of the twentieth century can be understood in the same social and historical context which characterized Europe during the early modern period. The parallels between the two time periods are worth emphasizing as a counterpoint to the generally accepted view that interprets Islamism as a sui generis ideology rooted in the cultural essence of Muslim societies. In reading about the religious zealotry and ferocity of John of Leiden and his followers, one is reminded of Osama bin Laden, Ayman al-Zawahiri, and the Taliban.[49] The parallels are striking, and in significant ways the similarities between both groups outweigh their differences, not only in their political motivations, social origins, and idiom of expression but also in their religiohistorical context.

In attempting to explain the motivations that lay behind the attack on New York on 11 September 2001, Fouad Ajami observed that Islam did not produce Mohammed Atta, the lead hijacker, but rather he was born of his country's struggle to reconcile tradition with modernity.[50] Similarly, Thomas Friedman perceptively wrote that almost "all of the fifteen Saudi hijackers on Sept. 11 came from one of the country's poorer regions, 'Asir, which has recently undergone *a rapid but socially disruptive modernization*."[51]

While there are many similarities between radical Protestant movements of the sixteenth century and radical Sunni groups in the late twentieth century, one should also be aware of the differences. Lewis Spitz draws attention to some wild sexual excesses among the most radical Christian groups. He observes that there "were even cases of radicals indulging in sexual intercourse while lying on an altar, no doubt to demonstrate the triumph of pure spirit over the flesh."[52] Their Muslim counterparts today would undoubtedly be horrified by such religiously sanctioned public behavior.

When comparing religiously inspired protest movements in Europe in the sixteenth century with those in the Middle East in the late twentieth century, two observations are worth noting. Democracy and human rights in the West did not emerge from documents but rather from social struggle, in particular from contentious and disputatious politics of which religion was a central point of conflict. Europe has indeed traveled a long way in terms of its own political development in the last five hundred years. Any objective attempt to explore the problems of democracy and political development in non-Western societies, particularly Muslim societies, requires a rethinking of the development of democracy in the West—especially with respect to the role of religion in politics—and an appreciation that the road has been extremely rough and bumpy with many potholes and detours along the way.

Second, we should be wary of the tendency to read history backward instead of forward. There is an implicit assumption in much of the commentary about the Muslim world today, both scholarly and journalistic, that in comparison, the West has always been liberal and democratic and that one can draw a straight line from Socrates, Plato, and Aristotle in ancient Greece to Isaiah Berlin, John Rawls, and Ronald Dworkin in late twentieth-century England and North America. As a counterpoint, Mark Mazower has suggested that it is fundamentally wrong to see Europe as the natural home of democracy and freedom. Rather, in the last one hundred years it was "frequently a nightmarish laboratory for social and political engineering, inventing and reinventing itself through war, revolution and ideological competition."[53]

Communism and fascism, Mazower argues, "should be regarded not as exceptions to the general rule of democracy, but as alternative forms of government that attracted millions of Europeans by offering different solutions to challenges of the modern world. By 1940 the prospects for democratic government looked bleak, and Europe's future seemed to lie in Hitler's hands."[54] These are sobering reminders for a Western audience struggling to understand the politics of Muslim societies in the aftermath of 11 September 2001.

Islam, Modernization, and Development

The rise of Islamic fundamentalism at the end of the twentieth century was a baffling development for many observers of the Middle East. It seemed to confirm the worst prejudices and stereotypes about Islam and Muslims. How could large numbers of people, in the age of secular reason, at the end of the twentieth century identify in such a profound way with a militant version of religion as the primary source of their identity? This not only challenged the received wisdom of both the Enlightenment and social science theory but also gave credence to an "essentialist" and reductive interpretation of Muslim politics that was allegedly dominated by an antidemocratic core set of values. Bernard Lewis, Ernest Gellner, and Martin Kramer are three prominent representatives of this school of thought.

The emergence of fundamentalism in the Muslim world instead of liberal democracy is often explained as a function of the unique peculiarities of Islamic civilization. Despotism—according to this theory—is at the very core of the Muslim faith, as it demands submission both to God and to those who rule in his name.[55] In an often-cited Orientalist cliché, Islam does not recognize a separation between religion and politics but is a total way of life, the implication being that a totalitarian system is the natural state of affairs.[56]

Bernard Lewis explains that one reason for the absence of liberal democracy in the Muslim world is that Islam discouraged the formation of independent groups that might have challenged despotic rule. In what is today a standard Orientalist trope, the problems of contemporary Muslim societies can be located in medieval Muslim history. "Islamic law," Lewis writes, "knows no corporate legal persons; *Islamic history* shows no councils or communes, no synods or parliaments, nor any other kind of elective or representative assembly. It is interesting that the jurists never accepted the principle of majority decision—there was no point, since the need for a procedure of corporate decision never arose."[57] Delving deeper into the history of medieval Islam to explain the contemporary absence of democracy, Lewis adds: "the political experience of the Middle East under the caliphs and sultans was one of almost unrelieved autocracy, in which obedience to the sovereign was a religious as well as a political obligation, and disobedience a sin as well as a crime."[58]

Ernest Gellner, a towering figure in the social sciences, similarly locates the modern problems of political development in the Muslim world in a cultural essence located deep in the annals of Muslim society and history (which he assumed was uniform).[59] According to Gellner, the "High Culture" of the urban *ulama* (clergy) and bourgeoisie in Muslim society was characterized as scriptural and puritanical and is normative for the urban life of the entire Islamic world. This is to be contrasted with the "low culture" of folk Islam, which was more tolerant and flexible. Under modern conditions this scriptural puritanism is appropriated at the mass level as part of the process of political centralization, urbanization, and mass education. Islamic fundamentalism is thus "the demand for the realization of this norm, and the popular support it enjoys stems from the aspiration to the High Culture by the newly urbanized masses." This explanation of Muslim politics, Gellner argues, is "entirely congruent with the requirements of industrialisation and of political modernity, contrary to the previously dominant assumptions of social theory that modernity requires secularization."[60] In short, the rise of Islamic fundamentalism in the late twentieth century is an authentic representation of the totality of Muslim society.

Martin Kramer is the most recent author of repute who works within the foregoing doctrinal framework when writing about Muslim societies. In a discussion about modern Middle Eastern history, he has written: "of the many fundamentalisms that have emerged within Islam during recent years, perhaps none has had so profound an impact on the human imagination as Hizbullah—'the Party of God.'"[61] In attempting to explain their political behavior, he has noted that "more than any other fundamentalist movement in recent history, Hizbullah evoked the memory of the medieval Assassins, who had been feared in the West and Islam for their marriage of fierce militancy with destructive deeds."[62] The linking of the activities of Hizbullah, a late twentieth-century Islamist group, with the twelfth-century Assassins is typical of how some Orientalist scholars interpret contemporary events in the Muslim world in a way that seems to suggest that the more complex modern forces of demographic shifts, economic disparity, cultural transformation, and foreign interventions should not be taken into account.

Juan Eduardo Campo, in an incisive and acerbic response to Kramer, has noted: "One can only imagine the objections that would be raised if a respected American Studies scholar were to interpret Chicano or African American gang activity in American cities in terms of ancient Aztec or African warrior religions, while neglecting to discuss the immediate social, cultural, and economic causes."[63] Campo's comment on the modern socioeconomic crisis of state and society in the Middle East and its relationship to the emergence of religious fundamentalism merits some investigation as an alternative reading of the problems of Muslim political development.[64]

The Malaise of Modernity and Political Islam

While fundamentalism is often considered an exclusively Muslim phenomenon, it is important to acknowledge that all the major religions have experienced this form of militant religious piety.[65] The fact that it first emerged in the West (recall the Anabaptists uprising in Münster) is not accidental, given that the process of modernization had its initial and most consequential impact in Europe and later the United States.

The momentous transformation of society and culture over the last two centuries has profoundly altered the way human beings relate to one another and view the world around them. In the twentieth century in particular, there has been a discernible shift away from large extended families and a group-based identity and toward a more individual-centered existence. This passing of traditional society has also included a weakening of parental authority, the questioning and rejection of religious authority, changing sexual mores, the rise of individualism, and the reliance on instrumentalism reason. While these trends are not visible in equal magnitude in every country, they do exist to varying degrees across most societies and are intimately connected to what Charles Taylor has termed the "malaise of modernity."[66]

Modernity has also been identified with an increase in social problems such as higher divorce and crime rates, alcohol and drug addiction, neurological disorders, and family breakdown. These social problems has given rise in troubled times to questions of authenticity and a search for "identity" that can help the individual and his or her community navigate through the troubled waters of the modern age.

Throughout human history, during times of great social transformation and political turmoil, a natural concomitant has been the revival of religion. During the Mongol occupation of Russia (1237–1480), for example, the Orthodox Church experienced one of its greatest periods of growth.[67] A similar phenomenon occurred in the United States in the mid-nineteenth century with the onset of the rapid industrialization of America. Put simply, social upheaval induces a reaction where people seek stability and security by returning to the basic and the familiar. Muslim societies are no different in this regard.[68] Writing specifically about the Muslim reaction to modernity, James Piscatori observes:

> Muslims are in a sense looking for what Daniel Bell called "new rites of incorporation" which link today's deracinated individual to a community and a history. And yet, in another sense, they are looking, rather, for *old* rites of incorporation that appear to be new even as they are familiar. Religion, precisely because in the past it answered questions about life and death and provided its followers with moral links to each other, becomes the means by which individuals hope to answer the new question of what it is to be modern, and, in so doing, to gain perhaps a reassuring, common world-view. In this respect, born-again Christians and veiled-again Muslims are responding to the same broad phenomenon.[69]

A common target for all fundamentalist groups is secularism, particularly the consumer-oriented culture and materialism that is identified with our secular age. These movements are all literalist when it comes to interpreting sacred scripture and generally view critical readings of the religious texts as heretical. To quote from a popular saying among Islamist activists: *kulu bid'aten dallalah* (all innovation is forbidden/on the path of loss).

What fundamentalist groups seek to do is bring God down from heaven and place religion at the center of social and political debate. "Every fundamentalist movement I have studied," Karen Armstrong notes, "in Judaism, Christianity and Islam, is rooted in a profound fear of annihilation—a conviction that the liberal, secularist establishment wants to wipe out religion. This is as true of the militant Christian groups in the United States as it is of Muslim extremists in Egypt and Iran." The need to "defend Islam," a common refrain of Muslim fundamentalists, indicates a sincere belief that their faith is under assault. "Fundamentalists believe they are fighting for survival, and when people feel that their backs are to the wall, they can lash out violently like a wounded animal."[70]

Secondly, the primary audience for fundamentalists is members of their own faith who are deemed to have gone astray and lack sufficient piety to attain personal salvation. Fundamentalists are against the idea of pluralism in matters of faith while firmly believing that there is only one correct school of interpretation of scripture, religion, and law.

Significantly, it is important to point out that these movements are not traditional in the sense of trying to roll back the clock to a pristine age and disengage completely with modern society in the way of Amish Christians or Hasidic Jews. Rather, these movements are modern, in terms of both the values they are reacting against and their use of modern technology, support for postsecondary training, and urban lifestyle. This is most apparent in the educational backgrounds of many of their adherents, who tend to come disproportionately from the professions of applied science, engineering, and medicine, where the answers are precise and the formulas exact. Ambiguous meanings, multiple correct responses, shades of grey, and an appreciation for nuance are not part of their intellectual or professional training. Their response to contemporary social and political questions is informed by this cognitive rigidity. Reflecting on the new millenarian movements, John Sigler writes: "there are those . . . who have a need for clear rules and directions, for right and wrong, and . . . modern culture, with its relativism, and uncertainties, clearly fails to provide this needed direction. These new militant movements provide not only inerrant scriptural authority, but new families and support in an age of loneliness and exaggerated individualism." Sigler adds: "these movements offer alternatives to the major cultural trends of modernity. They emphasize stability, security, solidarity and community. Many people find it hard to face the harsh realities of modern life without some sense of order."[71] The stable and supportive communities that these groups offer have been attractive to many people in the modern and postmodern eras.

In commenting on the parallel processes of religious resurgence in disparate societies, two scholars have made the important point that the "resurgence of 'fundamentalistic' promotion of particularistic ideologies and doctrines" should be seen as the "recent globe-wide assertion of particularist ideas," and should be comprehended in the context of "increasing *globality*."[72] Globalization, in other words, based on profound changes in technology and communications, has greatly heightened awareness of the plurality of cultures and lifestyles in our world among previously segmented and isolated populations. The concept of "identity" at its core is relational, in that individuals and groups define themselves in relation to other individuals and groups in society. The more we are aware of others, the more this forces the question: what is distinct about me and my community in a globalized world? In a widely read book, *Jihad vs. McWorld* (1995), Benjamin Barber argued this point, specifically that the rise of ethnoreligious nationalism in the late twentieth century is a reaction to the increasing political, economic, and cultural interdependence of our planet.[73] In short, the rise of particularist identities is a concomitant of globalization.

The foregoing political, cultural, and sociological insights suggest a need for a longer term perspective on the rise of religious fundamentalism, particularly as it relates to problems of democracy in the Muslim world. In the pursuit of this end, Fernand Braudel's concept of the longue durée is highly relevant.[74]

Fernand Braudel and the Longue Durée: The Modernization of Muslim Societies

Fernand Braudel is one of the most widely cited and influential historians of the twentieth century. He belongs to the *Annales* school of historians, which has made significant contributions to historical research and theory. Departing from traditional historical approaches, these historians assume that history needs to be comprehended in the context of forces that underlie human behavior and not as a simple recalling of discrete human actions. Braudel was one of the most prominent historians to suggest that history should synthesize data from the social sciences, in particular economics, and thus provide a broader historical overview of human societies.

His concept of the "longue durée" (the study of history as a long duration), should be understood in contrast with "l'histoire événementielle," event history (the study of history as battles, revolutions and the actions of great people).[75] Braudel's concept of the longue durée extends the perspective of historical space as well as time. Until the *Annales* school, most historians had taken the juridical political unit of the nation-state, duchy, or principality as their starting point. Yet when large time spans are considered, geographical features, economic systems, or political processes may have more significance for human populations than national borders. In his doctoral thesis, a seminal work on the Mediterranean region during the reign of Philip II of Spain, Braudel treated the geohistory of the entire area as a "structure" that exerted a myriad of influences on human life beginning with the first settlements on the shores of the Mediterranean Sea. "By *structure*," Braudel wrote, "observers of social questions mean an organization, a coherent and fairly fixed series of relationships between realities and social masses" that affects the flow and outcome of history.[76] For example, the structure of mercantile capitalism in Europe between the fourteenth and eighteenth century would be a phase of history that lasted over the longue durée and could be studied on its own. "Despite all the obvious changes which run through [this period]," Braudel notes, "these four or five centuries of economic life had a certain coherence, right up to the upheavals of the eighteenth century and the industrial revolution.... These shared characteristics persisted despite the fact that all around them, amid other continuities, a thousand reversals and ruptures totally altered the face of the world."[77]

Returning to the study of Muslim societies, Braudel's concept of the longue durée is helpful in assessing the political process of modernization in the Middle East and its connection to Islamic fundamentalism. Braudel criticizes l'histoire événementielle because of its limited explanatory value; in the same way, focusing exclusively on the doctrinal-ideological component of religious fundamentalism in Muslim societies—at the expense of a sociological and historical perspective—also carries an analytical cost that inhibits a deeper understanding of the obstacles to political development in the Muslim world. In this context, several points should be noted.

Modernization and Its Discontents in Muslim Societies

Modernization is a traumatic process. The West took several hundred years to develop its secular and democratic institutions through a process of trial and error. The Protestant Reformation and Counter-Reformation, the wars of religion, political and religious persecution, genocide, the Industrial Revolution, the exploitation of workers, the rise of nationalism, and World Wars I and II resulted in a profound change in all spheres of life—political, economic, intellectual, and religious. Today we are witnessing a similar process of transformation in developing countries, with the concomitant destabilizing affects.

In L. Carl Brown's comparative treatment of modernization in Europe and the Middle East he observes that a "case can be made that the Muslim world today is seized with the equivalent of all such [destabilizing] factors plus more." He lists common modernizing developments such as rising literacy rates, the increase in publication of printed material (books, newspapers, journals), rural to urban migrations, and growing economic interdependence but notes a critical difference with respect to the changes affecting Muslim societies: "the time involved [is] squeezed down for today's Muslims to a few decades as opposed to at least a century and a half, if not more, for Reformation Europe."[78] This time compression has added to the instability afflicting Muslim societies today.

Furthermore, other significant differences can be highlighted in the process of modernization and its destabilizing consequences in Europe as opposed to the Muslim world. Unlike in Europe, where it was largely an indigenous and organic process, in Muslim societies, modernization began as a direct result of the colonial encounter with Europe. Instead of innovation, their modern experience was one of imitation in an attempt to catch up with the West. Muslim countries in the postcolonial era have been largely split unhealthily into two camps: the elites who have received a Western-style education and have internalized secular values and a large majority who have not. Many regimes are in effect gerontocracies of aging men while the majority of their populations are under the age of thirty. Most political change since the era of formal independence has been forced top-down on society in an accelerated manner, not bottom-up via an indigenous process of social evolution, civil society engagement, and democratic negotiation.

In 1935, for example, Reza Pahlavi (the father of the monarch deposed in 1979) ordered his troops to go into the streets of Tehran to forcibly remove—at bayonet point—the veil from women's heads. These policies were matched in neighboring Turkey by Mustafa Kemal Atatürk's harsh secularization and Westernization of Turkish society. Two generations later, in the same authoritarian way that the Pahlavi monarchy forcibly removed the veil, Ayatollah Khomeini and his Islamic revolutionaries imposed it on Iranian women with equal determination and rigor. Similarly, the rise of political Islam in Turkey can partially be explained as a counterreaction to Kemalist secularist policies that were imposed on a religious society—99.8 percent of whose people are Muslims—in a top-down manner, to the exclusion of Turkey's Islamic identity.[79] In short, before there was religious fundamentalism in the Muslim world a modernist form of fundamentalism prevailed. It is against this backdrop that we should situate and explore the emergence of religious fundamentalism as a broad historical phenomenon.

This is not the first time societies undergoing intense periods of social change have given rise to militant religious movements seeking stability and order. Western observers of the Muslim world need to overcome their amnesia about their own history and recognize distinct parallels between what is happening today in the Middle East and the early phases of modernization of the West. In the current post-September 11th euphoria about the superiority of Western values, it needs to be repeatedly stated that Western history did not begin with human rights, democracy, and free markets but rather that their origins lay elsewhere. In this context Michael Walzer's thesis of the "Revolution of the Saints" is worthy of discussion.

The Walzer Thesis

Michael Walzer, the prominent American political philosopher, wrote his doctoral dissertation at Harvard on the Puritan Revolution in England in the seventeenth century, a period of civil war and intense turmoil. He provided a comprehensive framework for understanding what he called "the revolution of the saints," which was fundamentally "a study in the origins of radical politics."[80] Walzer's arguments merit extended summary, since he offers a thoughtful and analytically useful discussion of this topic that sheds considerable light on contemporary Muslim politics.

The early modern period in England was a time of intense social transformation marked by population growth, rural to urban migration, and a receding of feudalism.[81] According to Walzer, the following social problems provided a fertile soil for the emergence of Puritanism in England in the sixteenth and seventeenth centuries.

First, the "problem of rural 'depopulation,' vagabondage, and extensive... poverty" due to "rapid population growth [and]... the dislocation of men from the old rural society set thousands of beggars wandering the roads."[82] For over a century, "these beggars quite literally formed a distinct social group, completely alienated from the work-a-day world on whose fringes they dwelt.... Other men, driven from the land, poured into the cities... where they were newly subject to the calamities of depression and urban unemployment."[83]

Second, the "problem of rapid urbanization [and]... with it intensification of the dangers of plague and fire... brought new men into London who could not be absorbed by the existing civic institutions." In the midst of this turmoil, "Puritanism flourished also in the city and especially in the suburbs: in the records of the bishop's court recent immigrants turn up often as members of sectarian religious groups. Deprived of village solidarity, disoriented in the great crowds, many men must have found solace in Puritan faith and even Puritan discipline."[84]

On a related point, Walzer discusses "the problem of the religious vacuum left by the slow decay and then abrupt collapse of the old church. At a fairly early point, both in London and the country, this vacuum began to be filled by

Puritanism," as "once again, for many men, Puritanism provided an alternative set of social and spiritual activities."[85] "Finally . . . there was the basic problem of social organization raised by the . . . end of rural 'housekeeping,' the disappearance of urban confraternities and the weakening of guild ties, the increased rate of social and geographic mobility, the creation of the urban crowd and the urban underworld. How were men to be reorganized, bound together in social groups, united for co-operative activity and emotional sustenance? It was in response to such questions," Walzer observes, "that there emerged, in the course of the sixteenth and seventeenth centuries, so many new forms of organization and relationship, so many theories of contract and covenant. Debate over the precise nature of the new organizations—and especially the Puritan organization—makes up considerable part of the tractarian literature of the period."[86]

The political order during this period was rife with corruption, nepotism, and anarchy. The Puritans, driven by a militant religious fervor and informed by a Calvinist ideology, sought to bring order and stability to their society by overthrowing the corrupt establishment and beheading the king. These "saints," as Walzer calls them, were motivated by two things: "a fierce antagonism to the traditional world and the prevailing pattern of human relationships and a keen and perhaps not unrealistic anxiety about human wickedness and the dangers of social disorder. The saints attempted to fasten upon the necks of all mankind the yoke of a new political discipline."[87] In assessing their behavior in the context of a changing Europe, Walzer describes the Puritans as "an agent of modernization, an ideology of the transition period."[88]

Near the end of his study, Walzer attempts to link his findings about English Puritanism to other cultural contexts and societies undergoing intense social change. He writes that the "Puritan concern with discipline and order . . . is not unique in history. Over and over again, since the days of the saints, bands of political radicals have sought anxiously, energetically, systematically to transform themselves and their world." The key development that gives rise to militant religious piety is the breakdown of the old order. The choice of sainthood in such circumstances, Walzer observes, "seems reasonable and appropriate" and in light of the above discussion, "given similar historical circumstances, Frenchmen and Russians would predictably make similar choices. Englishmen became Puritans and then godly magistrates, elders and fathers in much the same way and for many of the same reasons as eighteenth-century Frenchmen became Jacobins and active citizens, and twentieth-century Russians [became] Bolsheviks."[89] Echoing sentiments discussed earlier about the rise of political Islam in the Middle East, Walzer writes:

In different cultural contexts, at different moments in time, sainthood will take on different forms and the saints will act out different revolutions. But the radical's way of seeing and responding to the world will almost certainly be widely shared whenever the experiences which first generated that perception and response are widely shared, whenever groups of men are suddenly set loose from old certainties.[90]

Puritanism, therefore, "provided what may best be called an *ideology of transition*. It is functional to the process of modernization not because it serves the purposes of some universal progress, but because it meets the human needs that arise whenever traditional controls give way and hierarchical status and corporate privilege are called into question."[91]

During more tranquil times when a semblance of peace is restored, the radical ideology of the saints no longer has a popular appeal, and they gradually disappear from society. In the context of seventeenth-century England, Walzer writes, "after the Restoration [of the Stuart Monarchy], its energy was drawn inward, its political aspirations forgotten; the saint gave way to the nonconformist. Or, Lockeian liberalism provided an alternative political outlook." This suggests "only that these problems were limited in time to the period of breakdown and psychic and political reconstruction. When men stopped being afraid . . . then Puritanism was suddenly irrelevant."[92]

Summarizing his theory of radical politics based on the history of early modern England, Walzer concludes that his "model may serve to reveal the crucial features of radicalism as a general historical phenomena and to make possible a more systematic comparison of Puritans, Jacobins, and Bolsheviks (and perhaps other groups as well)."[93]

Walzer lists the main points of his model as follows:

(1) At a certain point in the transition from one or another form of traditional society (feudal, hierarchical, patriarchal, corporate) to one or another form of modern society, there appears a band of "strangers" who view themselves as chosen men, saints, and who seek a new order and an impersonal, ideological discipline.

(2) These men are marked off from their fellows by an extraordinary self-assurance and daring. The saints not only repudiate the routine procedures and customary beliefs of the old order, but they cut themselves off from the various kinds of "freedom" . . . experienced amidst the decay of tradition. The band of the chosen seeks and wins certainty and self-confidence by rigidly disciplining its members and teaching them to discipline themselves. The saints interpret their ability to endure this discipline as a sign of their virtue and their virtue as a sign of God's grace.

(3) The band of the chosen confronts the existing world as if in war. Its members interpret the strains and tensions of social change in terms of conflict and contention. The saints sense enmity all about them and they train and prepare themselves accordingly.

(4) Men join the band by subscribing to a covenant which testifies to their faith. Their new commitment is formal, impersonal, and ideological; it requires that they abandon older loyalties not founded upon opinion and will—loyalties to family, guild, locality, and also to lord and king.

(5) The acting out of sainthood produces a new kind of politics.

(6) Within the band of the chosen, all men are equal. . . . The activity of the chosen band is purposive, programmatic, and progressive in the sense that it continually approaches or seeks to approach its goals.

(7) The violent attack upon customary procedures set the saints free to experiment politically. Such experimentation is controlled by its overriding purposes and the right to engage in it is limited to the chosen few who have previously accepted the discipline of the band. It is not a grant of political free-play, but it does open the way to new kinds of activity, both public and secret. The saints are entrepreneurs in politics.

(8) The historical role of the chosen band is twofold. Externally, as it were, the band of the saints is a political movement aiming at social reconstruction. It is the saints who lead the final attack upon the old order and their destructiveness is all the more total because they have a total view of the new world. Internally, godliness and predestination are creative responses to the pains of social change. Discipline is the cure for freedom and "unsettledness."

(9) [This is a transitional movement.] One day . . . security becomes a habit and zeal is no longer a worldly necessity. Then the time of God's people is over. . . . Once that order is established, ordinary men are eager enough to desert the warfare of the Lord for some more moderate pursuit of virtue. Once they feel sufficiently secure as gentlemen and merchants, as country justices and members of Parliament, they happily forego the further privilege of being "instruments." Hardly a moment after their triumph, the saints find themselves alone; they can no longer exploit the common forms of ambition, egotism and nervousness; they can no longer convince their fellow men that ascetic work and intense repression are necessary.

(10) [The saints] helped carry men through a time of change; they had no place in a time of stability. They had been elements of strength in an age of moral confusion and of cruel vigor in an age of vacillation. Now it was suggested that saintly vigor had its own pathology and conventionalism its own health.[94]

Gateways to Modernity: Puritanism and Islamism?

The crux of Walzer's argument is that English Puritanism had a proto-modern character.[95] Historians Lawrence Stone, Michael Mullet, Christopher Hill, and Perez Zagorin have suggested similar ideas in their writings.[96] Specifically, the new "Puritan state of mind, outlook of assertiveness and individual responsibility [had] transformed societies from medieval subservience and Catholic resignation to modern individualism and mass participation."[97] There are echoes here of Max Weber's famous thesis on the Protestant ethic and rise of capitalism. Weber suggested that shifts in religious doctrine had sociological implications. While Weber emphasized economics and the rise of capitalism, Walzer focused on politics, in particular the rise in radical religious politics.[98]

According to Walzer, "the idea that specially designated and organized bands of men might play a creative part in the political world, destroying the established order and reconstructing society according to the Word of God . . . did not enter at all into the thought of Machiavelli, Luther or Bodin."[99] Instead, these writers of the early modern period focused their attention on the activities of "the prince," stressing the important role of the individual in politics and his relationship to political power.

With the benefit of hindsight, however, Walzer suggests that "this is an incomplete vision, for in fact the revolutionary activity of saints and citizens played as important a part in the formation of the modern state as did the sovereign power of princes." In other words, politics from below not only mattered but mattered profoundly in the political development of the West. "In Switzerland, the Dutch Netherlands, Scotland, and most importantly in England and later in France, the old order was finally overthrown not by absolutist kings or in the name of reason of state," Walzer observes—and one might add *or* in the name of secularism/liberal democracy—"but by groups of political radicals, themselves moved by new and revolutionary ideologies."[100] Such ideologies, judged by the standards of today, would be viewed by social scientists as decidedly illiberal and fundamentalist, yet they played a vital role in the long-term modernization and democratization of the West.

In identifying the modern character of English Puritanism, Walzer lists seven ways that seventeenth-century revolutionary religious politics was significantly different from medieval religious politics. The contrast between the traditional political passivity of the masses and their now more active involvement in public affairs is the key interpretive point that suggests a historical break with the past and the beginnings of a transition to modernity.

Walzer's seven themes of proto-modern politics, derived from his study of religious politics in seventeenth-century England, are as follows:

(1) *Political authority:* the trial and beheading of King Charles I in 1649 "was a bold exploration in the very nature of monarchy rather than a personal attack upon Charles himself."

(2) *Military innovations:* the establishment of a "well-disciplined citizen's army in which representative councils arose and 'agitators' lectured or preached to the troops, teaching even privates (cobblers and tinkers in the satiric literature) to reflect upon political issues."

(3) *Constitutionalism:* "the effort to write and then to rewrite the constitution of a nation, thus quite literally constructing a new political order."

(4) *Reorganization of state institutions:* "the public presentation of whole sets of clamorous demands, many of them from previously passive and nonpolitical men, for the reorganization of the church, the state, the government of London, the educational system, and the administration of the poor laws."

(5) *Civil society:* "the formation of groups specifically and deliberately designed to implement these demands, groups based on the principle of voluntary association and requiring proof of ideological commitment but not of blood ties, aristocratic patronage, or local residence."

(6) *Political journalism:* "the appearance of political journalism in response to the sudden expansion of the active and interested public."

(7) *Complete social reform:* "Finally and above all, the sharp, insistent awareness of the need for and the possibility of *reform.*" Walzer identifies this call as "one of the decisive characteristics of the new politics, this passion to remake society." In support of this argument, he cites a sermon delivered before the House of Commons in 1641:

> Reformation must be universal [exhorted the Puritan minister
> Thomas Case] ... reform all places, all persons and callings; reform
> the benches of judgement, the inferior magistrates .... Reform the
> universities, reform the cities, reform the countries, reform inferior
> schools of learning, reform the Sabbath, reform the ordinances,
> the worship of God ... you have more work to do than I can
> speak. ... Every plant which my heavenly father hath not planted
> shall be rooted up.[101]

In summary, the transformation of Englishmen, from a state of political passivity and isolation into a state of political engagement and active citizenship was embodied in the figure of the Puritan saint. Walzer credits the ideology of Puritanism with transforming the lives of private men by pushing them into new collective associations that were determined to change the political status quo, in particular the dominance of traditional elites. In this broad sociological sense, one can recognize distinct parallels with Islamic fundamentalism in the Muslim world today, in not only the revolutionary content of its ideology, its transformative impact on traditional society, and the social origins of its adherents but also, arguably, its developmental potential with respect to the gradual emergence of liberal democracy.[102]

Political Islam's Rupture with Tradition

A significant body of literature in Middle Eastern studies describes political Islam as a sharp rupture with Muslim tradition and a fundamentally modern social phenomenon.[103] Sami Zubaida, arguably the most insightful scholar in this vein, notes that "modern [Islamic] fundamentalists represent a departure rather than continuity with Islamic political traditions or precepts. This break is accentuated by the fact that modern Islamic groups are operating ideologically and politically within the context of modern nation-state and the political concepts related to it."[104]

In a study of Ayatollah Khomeini's political theory, Zubaida demonstrates that notwithstanding the vocabulary of Shia Islamic discourses that permeate Khomeini's writings and the absence of any explicit borrowing from Western social science categories, "Khomeini's doctrine of government . . . is nevertheless based on the assumptions of the modern state and nation, and in particular on the idea of modern forms of popular political action and mobilization." There is one exception, however, when the borrowing is explicit: when Khomeini borrows from the European concept of a "republic." Zubaida observes: "Perhaps Khomeini's modernist innovation, otherwise implicit, is manifested in the term 'Islamic Republic,' a form of government never before conceived of in an Islamic history dominated by dynasties whose rule was for the most part accepted by Sunni and Shi'i jurists."[105]

Similarly, there is a near consensus among scholars that Ayatollah Khomeini's doctrine of the *wilayat al-faqih* (Farsi, *velayat-e faqih*) that called for the "rule of the Islamic jurist" marked a significant break with Shia tradition in terms of the relationship between religion and politics. Senior ayatollahs within the Shia world (including in Iran at the time) strongly objected to Khomeini's political doctrine primarily because it was considered an innovation and a radical break with the historically quietist role played by the clergy in political society.[106]

Zubaida's discussion of the Muslim Brotherhood in Egypt bears a striking resemblance to Walzer's discussion of the Puritan movement. The Muslim Brotherhood, according to Zubaida, is a "populist Islamic movement or party...[that in] terms of ideology and organization...represent a radical departure from historical forms of Islamic political agitation and actions. It is primarily urban and orthodox, distinct from the rural heterodox movements...[and] it is also distinct from urban movements in previous centuries."[107] By contrast, the urban protest movements of the past in Egypt were

> sporadic, led by ulama or lesser shaykhs in response to aggravations of oppression, mostly fiscal—prices of bread or other commodities—in support of one or other princely faction in situations of open conflict and civil war. Basically they were movements to redress perceived injustice in the name of religious norms. There were not usually calls for the institution of an Islamic state and society, these being assumed to be extant under the prevailing sultan or caliph. Historically, calls for the institution of a legitimate state as against an allegedly ungodly one were always made in the name of an alternative prince, usually designated in terms of lineage.... The [Muslim] Brotherhood is distinguished from these past patterns in being a modern political party, with a systematic organization and recruitment, and a political programme imbued with the assumptions of the modern national political field.... The objectives of this organization were the displacement of the existing order with one based on Islamic law and principles of social justice. This was to be done through popular organization and mobilization; the "people" mobilized in relation to abstract political principles, not in the cause of a more legitimate prince or charismatic. The desirable future order is postulated in terms of an organic unity between community and government, mediated by institutions of representation (through elections), legislation (but within the limits of shari'a), economic and social policies and plans. That is to say, an Islamic form of the nation state, assuming modern political forms and processes.[108]

John Sigler concurs with this interpretation, noting that what is "new" in the Islamist phenomenon is "not the continuing hold of Islamic beliefs and practice, but the strong political orientation to achieve political power and the control of the territorial state. Hence the phrase political Islam, for the goal is the achievement of state power."[109] In this context, both of the leading theorists of Islamism in the Sunni Muslim world, Sayyid Qutb (1906–1966) and Mawlana Mawdudi (1903–1979), developed a decidedly modern concept of a "vanguard" party of Muslim followers that would lead Muslim society to its utopia. Gilles Kepel has described this vision of a vanguard party as based on a "Leninist model" of Islamic revolution.[110]

The socioeconomic origins and educational backgrounds of many of the participants in the Islamist movement also reveal distinct parallels with Puritanism. Adherents tend to disproportionately come from middle and lower middle classes and have benefited from rising literacy rates and exposure to higher education. In the case of political Islam, one of the most influential early studies was conducted by Saad Eddin Ibrahim in the late 1970s. The majority of the Islamic activists he interviewed were between twenty and thirty years old, had a college or postgraduate education, and came from a rural or small-town background.[111] Carrie Wickham's more recent study on religion and political mobilization in Egypt confirms these trends.[112]

The recruiting of Egyptian men into the ranks of the Islamists is taking place against the backdrop of two explosions: a population explosion and a university explosion. The Egyptian population has increased from 21.8 million (in 1950) to 70.3 million (in 2002)—an increase of 222 percent—while the university explosion has been even greater: from about 37,000 students in 1951–52 to almost 1.5 million in 2001–2, an increase of 3,954 percent.[113] High rates of increase in population and in numbers of university students coupled with a lack of employment opportunities in the context of a repressive political atmosphere is a volatile mix.

In the case of England, Lawrence Stone describes a similar relationship between rising levels of education, socioeconomic instability, and religious militancy. "Another disturbing factor" Stone observes in early seventeenth-century England "was the growing realization that the numbers of the leisured class equipped with higher education were increasing faster than the suitable job opportunities."[114] Put simply, universities like Oxford and Cambridge were putting out graduates faster than the existing economy and institutions could absorb them. Between 1530 and 1630, for example, enrolment in these universities grew by 163 percent or twice as fast as the existing population.[115] "Neither the central bureaucracy, nor the army, nor colonial expansion in Ireland, nor even the law could absorb them all," Stone adds. "The result was frustration and resentment among large numbers of nobles, squires and gentry."[116] The destabilization this development wrought for English society was significant enough for Lawrence Stone to list it as one of the major causes of the English revolution in his widely acclaimed study of the topic. He concludes:

> One result of this educational over-expansion, coupled with the
> development and the spread of a series of ideologies antagonistic to the

status quo, was the appearance of that sinister precursor of a time of political troubles, the alienation of the intellectuals. The Puritan ministers and lecturers in the cities and the villages, some dons behind the greying walls of their colleges . . . all increasingly felt themselves cut off in spirit and in reality from the central institutions of government. In so highly literate a society as that of early seventeen-century England, this alienation of many members of the most articulate segments boded no good for the regime. Moreover, this was merely one aspect of the wider phenomenon of a deepening split between two cultures, one represented by the bulk of the political nation, and the other by a minority at Court and among the higher clergy and judges. It was a split which was symbolized by the emergence of clearly antithetical myths and ideologies: Obedience versus Conscience; the Divine Right of Kings versus Balanced Constitution; the Beauty of Holiness versus Puritan austerity; Court versus Country.[117]

In this passage, one can substitute the word *Islamist* for *Puritan*, *Egypt* for *England*, and *presidents/generals* for *kings*, and the result describes the politics of not only contemporary Egypt but many Muslim societies today. Particularly salient is the sense of alienation and estrangement large segments of the rising educated classes feel toward the political status quo. In this context, Hazem Ghobarah astutely observes: "It is thus the frustration and the anxiety over the prospect of sinking that is the primary obsession of most individuals in both cases. The different global environments and historical contexts of the two cases are secondary to the core of the problem, which is human anxiety in times of change."[118]

By way of conclusion, Ellis Goldberg's four points of convergence between radical Protestantism and Islamic fundamentalism are worth considering. Goldberg's essay is the most thorough scholarly investigation and crosscomparison of the topic and succinctly summarizes the foregoing argument. He lists historical, ideological, social, and institutional factors that give both Puritanism and Islamism a protomodern character:

Calvinism and the contemporary Islamist Sunni movements in Egypt are discourses on the nature of authority in society. Historically both movements arose as central state authorities made absolutist claims to political power and, in the process, sought to dominate transformed agrarian societies in new ways. Ideologically, both movements asserted that the claims of sweeping power by nominally religious secular central authorities were blasphemous egotism when contrasted with the claims of God on the consciences of believers.

Socially, both movements transferred religious authority away from the officially sanctioned individuals who interpret texts to ordinary citizens. Institutionally, both movements create communities of voluntary, highly motivated and self-policing believers that yield greater degrees of internal cohesion and compliance than the absolutist authority can achieve, and they therefore can become the basis of postabsolutist political authority in an authoritarian and antidemocratic fashion.[119]

The Modernizing Force of Political Islam

The latest scholar to discuss the modernizing character (of certain strands) of Islamic fundamentalism is Bjorn Olav Utvik, a Middle East historian at the University of Oslo. He agrees with the basic assumptions and arguments outlined here and similarly affirms that "contemporary Islamism in the Middle East and North Africa should be . . . seen as part of the breakthrough of the 'modern age' in Muslim societies" and "as an important modernizing agent within current Middle Eastern society."[120] He expands the comparison between religious protest movements in Christianity and Islam by exploring the case of Hans Neilsen Hauge (1771–1824) and Lars Oftedal (1838–1900), two nineteenth-century Norwegian Christian revivalist leaders whose sociological impact and contributions to political development he compares positively with the Puritans in England and the Muslim Brotherhood of Egypt. He concludes his Norwegian-Egyptian comparison by stating that the "importance [of the Norwegian religious radicals] to the gradual democratisation of Norwegian society can hardly be overestimated" and argues that a similar development is occurring in the Islamic world today.[121]

In reflecting on the influence of radical religious protest movements in Islam and Christianity, Utvik poses the critical question: "why did religion and not some secular ideology deliver the vocabulary for the social and political assertion of the upstart groups mobilized by Puritans and Islamists respectively?"[122] The question is important particularly for those social scientists who lack a historical perspective on the relationship between religion and political development. The suggestion that religious fundamentalism (of any sort) can contribute to political development—least of all liberal-democratic development—may be difficult to accept at first glance. But this is only a problem when fundamentalism is viewed exclusively as a doctrinal phenomenon and not a sociological one that cannot mutate, evolve, or transform. When observed from the perspective of sociology and the longue durée, a different social scientific interpretation can be extracted.

The answer Utvik provides as to why religious ideology trumped secular ideology in the case of both English Puritanism and Egyptian Islamism is that "there were no ideological options outside of religion." This is more easily understood in the case of seventeenth-century England, which was at the dawn of modernity and firmly situated in the pre-Enlightenment era; but what explains the turn to religion in the Muslim world today—almost three hundred years after the French Revolution? The short and partial answer is that the perceived failure of secular ideologies in the Middle East during the late twentieth century (primarily nationalist and socialist) has created an ideational vacuum in Muslim politics that has been filled by political Islam. This is a huge topic that I will explain in greater detail in the chapters that follow. The essence of the argument, however, is that among the ideological options available to Englishmen (in the seventeenth century) and Egyptians and Muslims (today), the radical religious option was often the most realistic, probable, and rational one available. Cultural essences and clashing civilizations had little to do with these developments.

A concomitant to the foregoing observation—and the larger historical point that deserves emphasis—is that "common to the context of both Puritans and Islamists is that the traditional societies, in which religion had provided moral legitimation to the existing order, were rapidly dissolving. A deep-felt dismay at the ensuing perceived chaos led to the reassertion of religious values, but in a reformed shape, more fit to secure moral order in the new environment created by social change."[123] One need only think about the prominence and plethora of religious actors in Iraq today (post–Saddam Hussein) who have emerged out of chaos and the breakdown of the older order to appreciate this point.[124]

In this context, it is also important to recall that for many people religion is not a private affair than can be easily restricted for home use only. If one's moral universe is deeply connected to a religious understanding of human affairs and if religion provides meaning to one's life, a rigid separation between the public and the private cannot easily be established (notwithstanding its institutional and constitutional necessity in a functioning liberal democracy). This was certainly true for many people in the West until relatively recently and is indeed true for large segments of the Muslim world today. Appreciating this point is key to understanding the persistence of religious themes in Muslim politics.

Returning to the sociological impact of radical religious protest movements and their modernizing influence on traditional societies, Utvik's study of Norway confirms and complements the analysis of Michael Walzer, Lawrence Stone, and Sami Zubaida on the relationship between religion and political development.[125] But note that these contributions are primarily sociological in nature. The context is that of a traditional society on the verge of modernity and the transformation in patterns of thought, association, and values brought about as a result of radical religious protest movements.

Individualization and Islamism

Islamism, like its Puritan counterpart, has been responsible for breaking up primordial ties to family, clan, tribe, and village. These traditional ties, often structured on a hierarchical and vertical basis, have been replaced with horizontal ties that are organic and revolve around themes of loyalty and solidarity among equals. Traditional patron-client ties and networks have also been broken up, and new bonds among members of society have been created on a more egalitarian basis. According to Andrea Rugh, there is an emphasis among Islamists on individual accountability and personal responsibility in realizing the values of an Islamic polity. This contrasts with the traditional notion of locating the responsibility of the individual as an integral part of the primary group to which he or she belongs. For Islamists, "the higher authority for which the individual is accountable is . . . [God], even when the compliance with that authority requires that individuals take actions which contradict the guidance of mundane authorities."[126]

This process of individualization is linked to an emerging hostility toward traditional sources of authority in society, particularly religious authority. Both Puritans and Islamists have demonstrated this attitude and believe that the religious establishment has been corrupted and has deviated from the true path of God's calling; hence the need for individual responsibility and action to set things right. In Saad Eddin Ibrahim's widely cited survey of Islamist opinion in Egypt, for example, he noted that "attitudes [toward religious authority] ranged from indifference to hostility. None had anything positive to say about the 'ulama' as a group," and those who were most hostile viewed the clergy "as hypocrites and opportunists and described them as people who would reverse religious edicts . . . to suit the whims of rulers. So much were the 'ulama' considered a disgrace to Islam that members [of one Islamist faction] . . . were strongly advised not to pray behind them or in mosques where official 'ulama' [clergy] presided."[127]

Given this perceived failure of moral leadership among traditional religious leaders, radical Islamists are of the view that each individual believer is responsible for his or her own personal salvation, and interlopers are not needed to interpret religious scripture. In the words of one Islamist leader, "the Koran was delivered in Arabic; it is therefore clear, and the only tool that may be needed for explaining the meaning of some of its terms is a good dictionary."[128]

Utvik weighs in at this point with the following clarification directed to the skeptical reader. He writes: "it might seem contradictory to regard a duty to devote one's life to the struggle for a cause, in the interest of God and mankind, as linked to a process of individualization." Emphasizing a sociological perspective, he adds: "the crucial point here is that what is demanded is not a step backwards into some kind of primordial form of group identification, where the individual is subordinate to the perceived collective will of the group, but rather a step forward into a situation where the individual must constantly choose of his or her own free, conscious, and informed will to act for the cause."[129] This freedom of individual choice, particularly in developing societies that have recently experienced mass education and have been exposed to mass communication, enhances the process of individualization, Utvik suggests.

James Piscatori and Dale Eickelman discuss a related concept they call the "objectification of Muslim consciousness," which they suggest is a salient feature of Muslim politics today. While they do not link it explicitly to the rise of political Islam, their discussion of the topic suggests that the objectification of Muslim consciousness is operating in a mutually reinforcing way with potential positive outcomes for the long-term development of liberal democracy. By "objectification" they mean "the process by which basic questions come to the fore in the consciousness of large numbers of believers: 'what is my religion?' 'Why is it important in my life?' and 'How do my beliefs guide my conduct?'" Disillusionment about religious authority, as discussed earlier in the case of Islamism, enhances this process. Piscatori and Eickelman write:

> Objectification does not presuppose the notion that religion is a uniform or monolithic entity (although it is precisely that for some thinkers). These explicit, widely shared, and "objective" questions are modern queries that increasingly shape the discourse and practice of Muslims in all social classes, even as some legitimize their actions and beliefs by asserting that they advocate a return to purportedly authentic traditions. Objectification is thus transclass, and religion has become a self-contained system that its believers can describe, characterize, and distinguish from other belief systems.[130]

Critical to this objectification process is the rise of publishing and mass education. Piscatori and Eickelman suggest that in the same way the Christian Reformation was called "'the daughter of printing' because printing made possible a broader dissemination of ideas," higher levels of education and exposure to dissenting interpretations of religion "contribute to objectification by inculcating pervasive 'habits of thought.' . . . They do so by transforming religious beliefs into a conscious system, broadening the scope of religious authority, and redrawing the boundaries of political community."[131] In other words, a democratization of religious interpretation is taking place in Muslim societies today. "A . . . facet of objectification," according to Piscatori and Eickelman, "is that authoritative religious discourse, once the monopoly of religious scholars who have mastered recognized religious texts, is replaced by direct and broader access to the printed word: More and more Muslims take it upon themselves to interpret the textual sources, classical or modern, of Islam."[132] In this sense, Osama Bin Laden has the same right to issue a fatwa as a Pakistani cab driver in New York. It is up to the individual believer to decide which religous leader to follow, if any.

Who really speaks for Islam? Can there be multiple correct and morally legitimate interpretations of the Islamic faith? And how does a believing Muslim choose among the plethora of new and often conflicting interpretations of his or her religion? These questions are now central to Muslim politics and are linked to the emergence of new social movements that are challenging traditional authority structures in Muslim societies. In this context, one Tunisian Islamist, albeit from the liberal end of the Islamist spectrum, has observed that "it is difficult to say that because my father was a Muslim, I should be one." He then proceeded to quote the Prophet Muhammad to the effect that people should have the freedom to choose their own religious affiliation on the basis of their personal convictions.[133]

According to Jose Casanova "if there is anything on which most observers and analysts of contemporary Islam agree it is on the fact that the Islamic tradition in the very recent past has undergone an unprecedented process of pluralization and fragmentation of religious authority, comparable to that initiated by the Protestant Reformation."[134] This change marks a clear contrast with the past in how Muslims approach their religion and suggests the emergence of new patterns of individual autonomy that bode well for the long-term development of liberal democracy. In synthesizing these trends, Bjorn Olav Utvik sees in political Islam, when observed from the perspective of history, a "double democratizing potential."

> By placing responsibility for the affairs of this world and the hereafter squarely on the individual conscience it simultaneously sets the individual free to become an active participant in the shaping of society and politics, and provides her or him with the self-discipline and restraint necessary for a truly civil society characterised by mutual respect among citizens, vital to any genuinely democratic polity.[135]

Utvik suggests two other ways political Islamist movements are contributing to the modernization of Muslim societies: by depersonalizing public life and by promoting a culture of meritocracy.

The reigning corruption of traditional ruling elites and power holders in many Muslim societies is a major source of grievance among Islamist activists. Islamists distinguish themselves from these elite groups—and increase their popularity by doing so—by living very frugal and humble lives among the masses. The contrast between Ayatollah Khomeini's humble lifestyle and diet of raisins and yogurt versus the opulence and extravagance of the Shah of Iran's peacock throne comes to mind. Similarly and more recently, the contrast between the image of Osama Bin Laden, living in a cave in the mountains of Afghanistan, with the image of the Saudi royal family, ensconced in their luxurious palaces and protected by an alliance with the United States, could also be cited in this context. These contrasting images mark a clear dividing line in the eyes of many people between political friends and foes within Muslim societies.

The larger point here is that political Islamists routinely condemn the opulence and extravagance of the power elite. They are generally very critical of the misuse of public funds in pursuit of personal gain, the prevalence of vote rigging and kickbacks, and the general culture of nepotism that pervades political life. This is not to suggest that they are immune from such practices when they achieve political power but rather that when in opposition they routinely decry these practices. A significant part of their appeal, therefore, is their stated moral commitment to roll back and end these abuses.

Utvik suggests that this aspect of the political Islamist movement "has a modernizing aspect, for in many of its aspects current corruption is a continuation of time-honoured practices that, until recent times, were seen as quite legitimate: the duty of individuals who gain influence and control over material resources to use their position for the benefit of their relatives, neighbours, friends, clients, or patrons." Islamists often condemn such practices on political as well as moral grounds, describing such behavior as a "sin" and its practitioners as *al mufsidun fi al-ard* (the corrupters of the earth) who are explicitly condemned in the Quran. What Islamists are doing, inadvertently, is challenging the existing patron-clientist ties and "age-old social structures based on the reciprocal solidaric obligations of kinship and client networks, and the institutions of the modern market and modern state." The net outcome of this sociological trend, suggests Utvik, is that it carries potential positive consequences for political development when viewed from the perspective of history.[136]

Similarly, political Islamists support the principle of meritocracy in public life, not in an ideal sense but with a greater commitment than the traditional ruling elites. Individual merit and religious piety should be the main criteria for promotion to positions of responsibility, not class, family, or political ties. Utvik notes that when the Muslim Brothers appeared on the political scene in

Egypt in the 1930s, their policy of meritocracy immediately distinguished them from the traditional nobility and land-owning classes, who were guided by a different set of criteria regarding social promotion and career advancement. In the Brotherhood's "real leadership structures promotion was always based on merit," Utvik observes. Furthermore, Islamism in Egypt worked "to open the road for the idea of individual career, individual life projects. This has been shown to be a characteristic [in] setting young Islamist students in the 1980s off from their parent[s'] generation."[137]

Mass Politics, Modernity, and Political Islam

Collective action by ordinary people to change their political destiny is the epitome of modernity. In Europe this idea first emerges with Puritanism; I am arguing that a similar development has taken place in the Middle East with respect to the rise of Political Islam.[138] To appreciate the positive developmental change that Islamism has engendered, both historically and sociologically, one should keep in mind the contrast with political life in Muslim societies prior to the advent of this social phenomenon. To the extent that these observations are true, Islamism has structurally altered the pattern and form of political life in Muslim societies and shifted it in a modernizing direction.

In specific terms, Islamism has been responsible for bringing new social groups into the political process, particularly from the previously marginalized sectors of society. In this sense, its contribution has been both novel and modernizing. As noted, the socioeconomic origins of a typical Islamist activist are from the middle and lower middle classes, and he or she is the recent recipient of postsecondary education, is upwardly mobile, and is now demanding a voice in shaping the political destiny of his or her society. This represents a significant sociological change in Muslim politics.

Utvik suggests that another aspect of this novelty is the form and method of political organizing adopted by the Islamists. The advent of mass assembly, mass petition, group pressure, appeal to public opinion—and, critically, "the political association of men and women not connected by kinship or other primordial ties of loyalty for the purposive furtherance of political change"— is both new and transformative. Such new forms of social solidarity, on a mass level, mark a break with the past, and in both "theory and practice [the Islamists] challenge the power monopoly of the established ruling classes."[139] These new populist forms of politics that the Islamist phenomenon has engendered are a few of the reasons why some social scientists consider them to be modern and modernizing agents in the political development of Muslim societies.

Objections might be raised at this point that the forces of secular Arab and Iranian nationalisms as well as the Community Party were also powerful political currents during the mid–twentieth century that drew large numbers of people into the street in similar ways to Islamism. This is undoubtedly true; however, Islamism is significantly different. It has sustained itself for a longer periods of time (primarily in the case the Muslim Brotherhood, which dates back to the 1920s), has sunk deeper roots in society (partially due to the social welfare services it provides), and arguably has a greater organic connection with its adherents (due to its religious orientation in still very religious societies).

Furthermore, a large part of the political agenda of the secular nationalists and socialists has been adopted by the Islamists and is now an integral part of their political platform. In this sense, the term "religious nationalists" is a more apt description of these social movements. "The Islamist movements were the natural continuations of independence movements that stalled before attaining their final goal," Lisa Anderson observes. "Apparent political independence did not produce freedom, either for the country in the international system or for the individual at home, nor did it lead to economic prosperity or cultural renewal."[140] The core grievances and complaints that secular political groups in the Muslim world and Islamists share are: resisting Western intervention, supporting a just global political order, redistribution of domestic wealth, challenging the political dominance of elite groups, and finally, support and solidarity for the national and human rights of the Palestinian people.[141]

In summary, the populist, nationalist, and grassroots orientation of the mainstream Islamist phenomenon, for this historical moment, has made it an enduring feature of Muslim politics. While Islamists' political ideology is far from liberal-democratic, they can be viewed as protomodernizing agents because of their ability to mobilize large numbers of people from heretofore marginalized sectors of society and initiate a pattern of political mobilization and behavior that is in stark contrast with the past.

Conclusion

The main goal of this chapter is to rethink the relationship between religion and political development. Three separate but related arguments were advanced.

First, liberal philosophers and social scientists interested in developing societies have been slow to recognize the connection between religion and political development. An ahistorical approach to these difficult social science questions is partly to blame, but more particularly it is the secular and Orientalist biases that inform their political assumptions and hence limits their scholarly contribution. This is especially true when they are discussing the rise of religious radical movements and their relationship to the development of liberal democracy against the backdrop of what Fernand Braudel called the longue durée.

Second, the rise of Islamic fundamentalism is a much more complicated social phenomenon than has generally been realized or appreciated. This chapter is not suggesting that political Islamists are liberal democrats in Muslim garb; far from it. What I do suggest is that the rise of religious protest movements such as Islamism should be viewed as a consequence of the social upheaval that follows the break down of the old political and religious order. The anxiety and uncertainty that is unleashed in traditional societies undergoing rapid social transformation often manifests itself in the form of mass-based religious groups whose popularity is temporary and coincides with the onset of modernity and the period of breakdown and reconstruction. The parallels between Puritanism and Islamism were highlighted and are particularly enlightening in terms of the cross cultural and regional similarities of societies undergoing the same social transformations.

Third, radical religious protest movements have a protomodern character. This fact can be appreciated by focusing on the sociological changes they engender, not the political ideology they espouse. Discerning how very different the method, form, and pattern of political life were prior to their emergence in society, especially with respect to the rise of individualism and mass mobilization, assists in understanding their novelty and their contribution to political modernization.

In this context, I should mention an important caveat about the relationship between political modernization and liberal democracy: the two are not synonymous. It is critical to note that modernization does not necessarily lead to democracy, pluralism, and respect for human rights. In Barrington Moore's classic study *Social Origins of Dictatorship and Democracy*, he reminds us of the different paths political modernization can take. Besides the "bourgeois revolutions culminating in the Western form of democracy" that many people take for granted, Moore also explored modernization's "alternative routes and choices." Two of these choices were decidedly undemocratic and illiberal: "conservative revolutions from above ending in fascism, and peasant revolutions leading to communism."[142] What political trajectories Muslim societies will follow in the coming decades is open to speculation. They are likely to be numerous and diverse. There are no guarantees that liberal democracy will emerge triumphant. What is less disputatious, however, is the transformative and modernizing influence of political Islam in the Muslim world today, for the reasons I have discussed here.

A historical and comparative approach is particularly beneficial in comprehending these difficult and emotionally charged questions. Bjorn Olav Utvik
suggests that historical amnesia has prevented many people from understanding the relationship between religion, modernization, and democracy. He
correctly notes that "too often we tend to think of the development of democracy,
tolerance and secularism in Western societies as a smooth process, which it was
definitely not, and it cannot be expected to be so elsewhere."[143] The case of the
Islamic Republic of Iran over the last decade is a perfect illustration of this point.
During the two-term presidency of Muhammad Khatami (1997–2005) a profound and important debate and seesawing struggle took place in Iran between
former revolutionary radicals—many of whom were and are now championing
pluralism, tolerance, and democracy—and a conservative clerical oligarchy, buttressed by support from lower middle classes, who are trying to maintain the
revolutionary status quo. To date, the conservatives have won most of the political
battles and prevented the institutionalization of democratic reform, but the
struggle is far from over, and the internal preconditions for democratization
seem good in Iran over the long term.[144]

I will briefly examine Iran at the end of the next chapter, but I would like to
make some preliminary remarks here. During the 1960s and 1970s, Iran
experienced a state-led modernization process that dramatically affected existing social relationships, cultural patterns, and economic life. The land reform
program disrupted the ebb and flow of rural life, leading to massive migration
into the major cities with its concomitant destabilizing effects on urban life.
The state-led "modernization programs did not, however, encompass change
in the political power structure, nor did they introduce cultural and political
modernity. On the contrary, through the modernization process, a more
structured and powerful autocratic state power was built."[145]

It was during this time that religion in Iran became politicized, in large
part due to the destabilizing effects of rapid modernization on a traditional
society and also as a reaction to the authoritarian policies of the state. Said
Amir Arjomand, in his comparative treatment of the Iranian revolution, has
observed that the "reaction of privileged groups and of autonomous centers of
power against the expansion and centralization of the state is a major source of
most if not all the early modern European revolutions." Throughout this
period, a common thread that consistently reappeared in Spain, Portugal, the
Netherlands, France, and Britain was that "estates and corporations reacted
when their autonomy and inherited privileges were threatened by the state;
and they usually found allies in Calvinist preachers and iconoclasts." The Shia
ulama in Iran, Arjomand suggests—demonstrating the relevance of the Walzer paradigm to modern Middle Eastern politics—were the equivalent of the

Calvinist preachers who played a similar role in the early phases of European modernization.[146]

To the extent that Walzer's model and its concomitant, the Puritan-Islamist analogy, are valid for understanding the process of modernization in Muslim societies, this analytical approach suggests that the actual content of the ideology is less important than the enveloping socioeconomic context that produces a transitional force of saints during a time of turmoil. One of the added benefits of recalling Walzer's thesis is that it provides an alternative framework to the Bernard Lewis–Samuel Huntington paradigm that emphasizes the "sacred rage of Islam" and the inherent "clash of civilizations" rooted in an alleged inherent Islamic hatred for the West. The above analytical framework also carries the latent benefit of forcing Western social scientists and public intellectuals to recall their own history of political development, in which violent periods have marked the transition from tradition to modernity.

Furthermore, Walzer's thesis and the Puritan-Islamist comparison, when applied to Muslim societies, reveal how the ideational bias of modernization theory and liberal-democratic theory has inhibited an understanding of sociopolitical change in the Muslim world. The lesson here is that historical depth is needed for an objective understanding of political development in the Middle East—particularly with respect to the role of religion in politics—and that the Orientalist argument about Islam's intrinsic problem with modernity does not stand up to critical scrutiny when viewed from this perspective. This will become abundantly clear in the next chapter, where I explore the political theology of John Locke and the lessons it offers about democratization in Muslim societies today.

2

Dueling Scriptures

The Political Theology of John Locke and the Democratization of Muslim Societies

For Obedience is due in the first place to God, and afterwards to the Laws.

—John Locke

Many democratic theorists trace the origins of modern democracy to the writings of Jean-Jacques Rousseau. The choice is an obvious one, given Rousseau's heavy emphasis in *Du Contrat Social* (1762) that sovereignty is rooted in "the general will" and that the public good and popular deliberation are the foundations of a just political order. In a recent essay on democratic theory, however, Ian Shapiro challenges conventional wisdom on this topic. "Many commentators [are mistaken in] treating Rousseau as the father of modern democratic theory," Shapiro argues. It is his belief "that John Locke merits the distinction. [Locke] developed the elements of an account of democracy that is more realistic, far-reaching, and appealing than is Rousseau's, and it has greater continuing relevance than does Rousseau's to contemporary democratic thinking."[1]

At first glance Shapiro's assertion is difficult to accept, given that Locke is generally regarded by political philosophers as the father of modern liberalism and individual rights rather than modern democracy and public participation ("democracy" and "liberalism" are often mistakenly equated in popular discussion). Locke is famous for his argument that legitimate political authority is based on the "consent" of the governed; however, one scholar has noted that

"Locke's notion of government by consent is not democracy. The people can consent to whatever form of civilian or constitutional rule they like.... It is to a system or structure of government that consent is required not to particular governments, let alone to particular decisions or policies."[2] Shapiro responds by conceding that while "Locke was no theorist of *democratic participation*," what is significant is that "he was an innovative theorist of *democratic legitimacy*" and thus merits the unique distinction of being the true founding father of modern democracy.[3]

Regardless of what position one takes on this debate, there is no denying that Locke is a seminal figure in the development of liberal-democratic political thought.[4] His writings are required reading in any introductory Western political philosophy course, and his name is intimately linked with the Enlightenment tradition and the development of a human rights discourse. What is often forgotten, however, when reading Locke today, is that his seminal contributions to political theory were philosophically rooted in a dissenting religious exegesis. All of his arguments—whether about freedom of conscience and belief, the moral basis of legitimate political authority, family, consent, property, and equality—can be understood as emerging from a political theology that was rooted not in a rejection of Christianity but rather in a reinterpretation of it. An inherent part of his political methodology, therefore, was a recasting of religious norms as an antecedent to advancing a new theory of government. The relationship between religion and political development might seem bizarre to undergraduate students studying political philosophy today; however, historians of Western political thought can certainly appreciate its significance.[5]

The rise of Christianity shifted debate away from the ideal of an active citizen in the Greek polis to that of the true believer in the Christian commonwealth. A new conception of political community had emerged. "Christianity succeeded where the Hellenistic and late classical philosophies had failed, because it put forward a new and powerful ideal of community which recalled men to a life of meaningful participation," Sheldon Wolin has observed. "Although the nature of this community contrasted sharply with classical ideals ... [and] its ultimate purpose lay beyond historical time and space, it contained, nevertheless, ideals of solidarity and membership that were to leave a lasting imprint, and not always for good, on the Western tradition of political thought."[6]

Augustine's *City of God* (410–423) and Aquinas's *Summa Theologica* (1267–1273), regarded as authoritative texts for over a millennium, established a normative framework for the discussion of Western political theory.[7] As David Held reminds us, the "Christian world-view transformed the rationale of political action from that of the *polis* to a theological framework," such that the notion of "good lay in submission to God's will. How the will of God was to be interpreted and articulated with systems of secular power preoccupied Christian Europe for centuries, until the very notion of single religious truth was shattered by the Reformation."[8] In light of this forgotten truism about the religious foundations of Western political thought, one might ask: what lessons from the development of Western political philosophy are applicable to other religious traditions and societies—Islam and Muslim societies in particular? More precisely—what can Muslim democrats learn from reading Locke today in terms of their own struggle for democracy and human rights? In what ways are Locke's writings on religion and politics relevant to debates confronting Muslim societies, especially with respect to the relationship between religion, secularism, and liberal democracy? These are the broad theoretical questions this chapter will explore.

The discussion begins with an overview of Locke's political thought and evolving views on political authority. I will then examine Locke's two seminal political texts, *A Letter Concerning Toleration* (1689) and the *Two Treatises of Government* (1689). I will devote special attention to the religious arguments Locke invokes within these texts with respect to changing political norms. In this context, Locke's dispute with Sir Robert Filmer on the origins of government and the moral basis of legitimate political authority will also be given special attention.

The second half of the chapter will attempt to apply the lessons learned from Locke's political theology to the case of the Muslim world. While the focus will be on the Islamic Republic of Iran, these lessons have wider transferability to other societies in the Islamic world. The core thesis I will advance is that a reinterpretation of religious norms—not a rejection or marginalization of religion—is a precondition for liberal-democratic development. I make this argument in two broad but interrelated ways: first, I warn of the dangers of introducing fundamental political and theological innovations in communities with weak liberal and democratic traditions. Second, I claim this thesis to be relevant in emerging democracies where large segments of the population are under the sway of an authoritarian and illiberal religious doctrine—as in Locke's England in the seventeenth century and much of the Muslim world today. In such cases, a reevaluation of religious norms with respect to government is a prerequisite to liberal-democratic development.[9]

This chapter is meant to serve as a long preamble to some ruminations on the theoretical relationship between religion, secularism, and democracy in Muslim societies. The fact that a religious reformation in Europe preceded and then led to secularization (and by extension liberal democracy) seems to suggest something important about both the sequence and process of liberal-democratic development in general—when viewed from the perspective of history—and especially with respect to the relationship between religion, secularism, and democracy in particular. In noting this fact, I draw on an observation by Abdou Filali-Ansary, who perceptively wrote: "in the Muslim world, secularization is preceding religious reformation—a reversal of the European experience in which secularization was more or less a consequence of such reformation."[10] He was referring to a state-imposed, top-down imposition of secularism instead of an organic, bottom-up, democratically negotiated version. There is much more to say on the topic of secularism and Muslim societies. I will explore this subject in greater depth in chapter 4.

Relevant Background Notes on the Political Philosophy of John Locke

The historical context that is relevant to understanding John Locke's political theory is the social breakdown and chaos unleashed by the early phase of modernization in Europe. Post-Reformation Europe saw the emergence of new debates about religious toleration, not only between Catholics and Protestants, but among the various Protestant sects in particular. In an age of gross intolerance, most Christian denominations were interested in enforcing religious uniformity on their societies, each of them claiming exclusive knowledge of God's will on earth and warning of the dangers of social disorder if religious toleration were allowed to flourish.[11] This widely held belief led to the infamous wars of religion that engulfed Christendom during the sixteenth and seventeenth centuries and was as an important background development that informed and shaped Locke's political philosophy.

The second seminal and more localized event during the seventeenth century was the English Civil War (1642–60). This event and its aftermath (specifically the "Exclusion Crisis") formed the immediate political context that influenced Locke's political thought.[12] Locke was not only an observer of these events but also an indirect participant. The main forces in the battle for political power were those loyal to Parliament (the side Locke supported) and the royalist supporters of the Stuart monarchy. As a result of this conflict, new questions emerged in English society about the moral basis of authority, the nature of political obligation, and the best way to preserve political order.

In addition, Locke stood at the brink of the scientific revolution that was just emerging in Europe. In a very genuine sense, he straddled the divide between tradition and modernity, or as one scholar has aptly described it, Locke stood "between the age of faith that was passing and the age of the Enlighten-ment that was dawning."[13]

As a man of science living in a very religious society (and coming from a Puritan background), Locke tried to reconcile reason epistemologically and ontologically with revelation, both of which served as complementary sources of moral authority for him. For example, at the beginning of book 1 of the *Two Treatises of Government*, Locke commences his attack on Robert Filmer (the leading intellectual champion of the "divine right of kings") by affirming that "*Scripture or Reason* I am sure doe not anywhere say so notwithstanding the noise of divine right, as if Divine Authority hath subjected us to the unlimited Will of another."[14] Similarly, in *A Letter Concerning Toleration*, Locke affirms that "we must not content ourselves with the narrow measures of bare justice; charity, bounty, and liberality must be added to it. *This the Gospel enjoins, this reason directs*, and this that natural fellowship we are born into requires of us."[15] In short, moral and ethical debates about religious toleration and political power and the emergence of rationalist and skeptical thought establish a framework in which one can situate and attempt to understand the evolution of Locke's political philosophy.[16]

Locke: From Intoleration to Toleration

By the standards of his time, Locke was as intellectually gifted as he was politically progressive. The reputation that he now enjoys, however, as a pioneer of modern liberal-democratic thought was the result of a gradual evolution of his thinking. It is largely forgotten that in his early years Locke opposed religious toleration and was a firm proponent of an authoritarian state.[17] "As for myself, there is no one [who] can have a greater respect for and veneration for authority than I," he wrote. Elaborating on his early authoritarian concep-tion of politics following the restoration of the Charles II. He added:

> I find that a general freedom is but a general bondage, that the popular
> asserters of public liberty are the greatest engrossers of it too. . . . All
> the freedom I can wish my country or myself is to enjoy the protection
> of those laws which the prudence and providence of our ancestors
> established and the happy return of his Majesty hath restored.[18]

In the early 1660s, Locke wrote his first major political treatise, the *Two Tracts on Government*. He was at Oxford University at the time, where he set out to answer the following questions on religious toleration: (1) "Whether the civil magistrate [could] lawfully impose and determine the use of indifferent things in reference to religious worship" and (2) whether "the civil magistrate [could] specify indifferent things to be included within the order of divine worship, and impose them upon the people." After considerable reflection, his answer to both questions was an unequivocal yes. The dispute consuming England at this time revolved around the question of religious toleration and the extent to which a diversity of worship should be allowed in society without provoking a civil war. A related and equally important question was who was to be the final arbiter in making these decisions, the will of the civil magistrate or the conscience of the individual.

The immediate political relationship the *Two Tracts on Government* sought to address was the normative one between religious toleration and political order. This issue was one of the most hotly contested and emotionally charged controversies in post-Reformation Europe, dominating political life. Due to its overall importance, it preoccupied Locke's thinking throughout his adult life. While it is largely forgotten today, it is instructive to recall—in the context of recent debates about Islam's relationship with violence—that until fairly recently Christianity was arguably the most intolerant of the world's religious traditions. In Voltaire's famous phrase, "Of all religions, the Christian is without doubt the one which should inspire tolerance most, although up to now the Christians have been the most intolerant of all men."[19] Accusations of heresy and the persecution of heretics was a long-running theme for over a millennium in Christian Europe, replete with inquisitions, expulsions, and forced conversions. "It was not until the religious conflicts generated in the sixteenth century by the Protestant Reformation and in the actual struggle against persecution," Perez Zagorin reminds us, "that genuine theories of religious toleration first made their appearance in Europe."[20]

The term "indifferent things" that Locke chose to write about in his first political tract referred to those aspects of religion that were not explicitly commanded or forbidden by scripture. They were neither inherently good nor evil and included items such as church ornaments, rites, ceremonies, fasts, and other forms of external church worship and observance. While most Christian denominations allowed for a degree of liberty of conscience in matters of faith, disagreement soon emerged in deciding whether something was indifferent or not. Much of the religious dispute in England during the seventeenth century between the Anglican Church and dissenting Protestant sects revolved around this question. Given the general climate of intolerance of this era and the passionate views that informed people's approach to matters of faith, a holy war over "indifferent things" was never far away.[21]

Locke's position in the *Two Tracts* was to favor political order over liberty of conscience. His views were a product of his time, oriented to the English Civil

War and the ensuing chaos that had enveloped England. He lamented: "all those tragical revolutions which have exercised Christendom these many years turned upon this hinge, that there hath been no design so wicked which hath not worn the vizor of religion, nor rebellion which hath not been so kind to itself as to assume the specious name of reformation . . . none ever went about to ruin the state but with pretence to build the temple."[22] Locke feared that people would use religious freedom not to be good citizens but to sink their country "in perpetual dissension and disorder."[23] Locke's remedy for this state of affairs was to defend the cause of political order, embodied in the divine right of kings, against claims for the liberty of religious conscience.

What is interesting about Locke's worldview at this early stage of his adult life is his belief in the "firm subordination of religious sentiment to the demands of politics. Whatever its origins, political authority, to be adequate to its tasks, must be total."[24] In this sense, Locke was adhering to the reigning Hobbesian consensus that the sovereign authority had the right to proclaim a state religion and to regulate the public manifestations of religion in society.[25] The alternative to a confessional state, it was widely believed, was chaos and social anarchy. Thomas Hobbes speaks to this issue directly in chapter 26 of his *Leviathan*:

> if men were at liberty, to take for Gods Commandments, their own dreams, and fancies, or the dreams and fancies of private men; scare two men would agree upon what are Gods commandments; and yet in respect of them, every man would despise the Commandments of the Common-wealth. I conclude therefore, that in all things not contrary to the Morall Law . . . all Subjects are bound to obey that for divine Law, which is declared to be so, by the Lawes of the Commonwealth.[26]

Seven years later, while serving as confidante and assistant to Lord Anthony Ashley Cooper (the first earl of Shaftesbury, a prominent figure in English politics), Locke revisited the questions he had debated during his Oxford years, albeit from a different angle. The conclusions he reached this time were poles apart. In his posthumously published *Essay Concerning Toleration* (1667), in a reversal of his earlier authoritarian views, he affirmed that civil peace and social harmony could be advanced by "making the terms of Church communion as large as may be."[27] This shift of opinion on the merits of religious toleration was more fully articulated in his longer and more influential essay *A Letter Concerning Toleration* (1689). As James Tully has noted, the 1667 *Essay* "marks the transition to Locke's radically subjective view of religious worship" in the 1689 *Letter*.[28] The latter document has great importance in the overall development of Western liberal-democratic thought. I will discuss first Locke's articulation in it of the relationship between theological innovation and political norms, and then discuss potential lessons to be learned that can be transferred and applied to current debates within Muslim societies.

Locke's Argument for "True Religion"

In 1683, as the battles over religious toleration intensified in England (and indeed throughout Europe) and became inextricably linked with struggles for political power, Locke was forced to flee Britain for the relative safety of Holland. He wrote his famous *Letter Concerning Toleration* there during the winter months of 1685, "with an intensity of moral conviction and of moral outrage unparalleled in western political theory."[29]

In the *Letter*, Locke summarizes and codifies a debate that had been raging in England (and Europe) over the previous half century. Specifically, he advances a series of prudential and moral arguments in defense of religious toleration that are rooted in a reconceptualization of the normative relationship between political authority and religious conscience. By linking the question of toleration to the language of individual rights, Locke's *Letter* marks a significant shift in the historical development of liberal democracy. As James Tully has noted,

> the collection of assumptions, arguments, terms, distinctions and
> justifications of toleration of dissent, of civil and religious liberty, many
> of which are Locke's, has come to be a fairly stable and traditional
> part of one of the two main western political and juridical discourses;
> that of the sovereign individual and his or her subjective rights.[30]

What concerns us here is less the explicit content of Locke's argument in defense of toleration (and by extension political secularism and liberty of conscience) and more the religious foundations of his thesis. A close reading of the *Letter* reveals that Locke is advancing two novel ideas about Christianity and what it means to be a good Christian, ideas that heretofore had little public support. This new theory of Christianity and Locke's passionate defense of it mark a radical break in the way religion had been understood by seventeenth-century English society.[31]

At the outset of his *Letter Concerning Toleration*, Locke attempts to redefine Christianity and to draw a sharp distinction between what he calls "true Religion" and, by implication, false religion. At six separate points in the *Letter*, one encounters the catchword "true Religion." In two other places, Locke invokes the terms "true Christian" or "true Christianity" and on five other occasions the term "true Church."[32] The early parts of the *Letter* are filled with such references. These terms reflect Locke's attempt to shift the normative definition and redirect the moral compass of Christianity by contrasting his new tolerant interpretation of Christianity (the true version) with the intolerant interpretations he sees around him (the false versions). The entire *Letter* arguably is premised on this distinction between the "true tolerant Christianity" and the "false intolerant Christianity." In other words, Locke suggests that if only his fellow citizens had a proper understanding of "true" Christianity, England and the rest of Christendom would not be engulfed in turmoil.[33]

Locke delves into this debate on the first page of his *Letter*. The first sentence asserts that toleration is an inseparable part of the Christian faith: "since you are pleased to inquire what are my Thoughts about the mutual Toleration of Christians in their different Professions of Religion, I must needs answer you freely . . . that I esteem that Toleration to be *the chief* Characteristical Mark of the True Church."[34] What is interesting to note here is how, prior to any overt discussion of politics, Locke advances an argument in the first paragraph of his *Letter* (and on three separate occasions in this same paragraph) in favor of what he calls—"the True Church," "a true Christian," and "the Business of True Religion."[35] Criticizing the so-called Christians who "boast of the Antiquity of Places and Names, or of the Pomp of their Outward Worship, he says: "these things . . . are much rather Marks of Men striving for Power and Empire over one another, *than of the Church of Christ*."[36] If a man pursues these narrow and self-serving ends in the name of religion yet simultaneously is "destitute of Charity, Meekness, and Good-will in general towards all Mankind, even to those that are not Christians, he is certainly yet short of being a true Christian himself."[37]

Pushing this argument further, Locke suggests that "the Business of True Religion is quite another thing. It is not instituted in order to the erecting of external Pomp, nor to the obtaining of Ecclesiastical Dominion, nor to the exercising of compulsive Force; but to the regulating of Mens lives according to the Rules of Vertue and Piety." Locke continues in this vein with the statement "no Man can be a Christian without *Charity*, and without *that Faith with works*, not by Force but by *Love*."[38]

Addressing more directly the problem of religious toleration, Locke affirms that most people have lost their focus when it comes to religion. They have misdirected their anger away from identifying real social problems afflicting English society. Working within a narrow religious framework, Locke argues that religious pluralism is not a source of corruption and moral decay— unlike the persistence of basic immoralities that are explicitly condemned in the Bible and do lead to social breakdown. Authentically pious people who are genuinely interested in doing God's work, Locke suggests, should get their moral bearings straight and focus their attention on these "real" dangers plaguing society, not the false danger of religious pluralism and toleration.

> Now, tho' the Divisions that are amongst Sects should be allowed to be
> never so obstructive of the Salvation of Souls; yet, nevertheless,
> *Adultery, Fornication, Uncleanliness, Lasciviousness, Idolatry, and such-*
> *like things, cannot be denied to be Works of the Flesh;* concerning which
> the apostle has expressly declared that *they who do them shall not*
> *inherit the kingdom of God.* Whosoever, therefore, is sincerely solicitous
> about the Kingdom of God and thinks it his Duty to endeavour the
> Enlargement of it amongst Men, ought to apply himself with no less
> care and industry to the rooting out of these Immoralities than to the
> Extirpation of Sects. But if anyone do otherwise, and whilst he is cruel
> and implacable towards those that differ from him in Opinion, he be
> indulgent to such Iniquities and Immoralities as are unbecoming the
> Name of a Christian, let such a one talk never so much of the Church,
> he plainly demonstrates by his Actions that 'tis another Kingdom he
> aims at and not the Advancement of the Kingdom of God.[39]

Recalling the example of Jesus Christ, Locke proceeds to argue that many people have jettisoned Christ's authentic example of spreading the message of God. "If, like the Captain of our Salvation, they sincerely desired the Good of Souls, they would tread in the Steps, and follow the perfect example of that Prince of Peace" who tried to spread the gospel "not armed with the Sword, or other Instruments of Force, but prepared with the Gospel of Peace, and with the Exemplary Holiness of the Conversation. This was his method." The conclusion Locke reaches, therefore, is that "toleration of those that differ from others in Matters of Religion, is so agreeable to the Gospel of Jesus Christ and to the genuine Reason of Mankind, that it seems monstrous for Men to be so blind, as not to perceive the Necessity and Advantage of it, in so clear a Light."[40]

Two items are worth noting here. By invoking "reason," Locke is suggesting that his new interpretation of Christianity should be self-evident to anyone who contemplates his suggestion. Second, toleration is good because it is in keeping with the will of God. A good Christian, in other words, is not someone who is interested in the "extirpation of sects" or spreading the word of Jesus "with the sword, or other instruments of force" but one who believes in toleration, peace and the nonviolent spread of the message of Christ. According to Locke, both reason and revelation support this new interpretation of religion.

To modern ears this interpretation of Christianity sounds quite familiar, but the larger political point to remember is that in seventeenth-century

Europe it was a radical position. To better appreciate the novelty of Locke's project, it bears repeating that for most of its history prior to the eighteenth century, Christianity was not about "turning the other cheek" and "loving one's neighbor" but rather was driven by a burning zeal to create a godly society by punishing heretics, crushing dissent, and opposing religious toleration—often by brute force. As Perez Zagorin writes in his comprehensive study on the topic, *How the Idea of Religious Toleration Came to the West,*

> it was only in Western society . . . and only since the sixteenth century because of the conflicts and debates between contending Christian churches, sects and confessions, that there has appeared a massive body of writings . . . exploring the problem of religious toleration from many angles and presenting an array of arguments in behalf of the principles of liberty and conscience, mutual tolerance and religious coexistence and diversity. This literature was produced at a time when, as in the previous five centuries of Christian history, an accusation of heresy could mean death for the person charged.[41]

When viewed in its proper historical context, Locke's moderate and tolerant interpretation of Christianity was a novel idea that carried considerable personal danger for him and marked a significant departure from the reigning Christian and English consensus.[42]

The second innovation in Christianity that Locke's *Letter* advances is the notion that religious belief should be voluntary and truth claims in matters of faith are normatively subjective. All churches in essence possess the same moral message, and all believers in God are fundamentally equal and subject to human fallibility in matters of religion. In making this claim, Locke was not suggesting moral parity of all religious expressions and all interpretations of scripture. His reference was mainly to the Protestant churches, not the Catholic Church, which, along with most English Protestants, he truly despised. More significantly, Locke believed that anarchy would not emerge if religious toleration was accepted because most people could reasonably agree on a common-sense interpretation of Christianity—in particular the tolerant and peaceful "true Religion" he was advocating—if they rationally reflected on his new proposition.[43]

Building on his support for the freedom of religious conscience and his belief that each individual is responsible for the care of his own soul and personal salvation, Locke puts forward a new definition of a church. "A Church then I take to be a voluntary Society of Men, joining themselves together of their own accord, in order to the publick worshipping of God, such a manner as they judge acceptable to him, and effectual to the Salvation of their Souls."[44]

The key words in this sentence are "of their *own* accord" and in "a manner as *they judge* acceptable." Locke is undermining the notion of the moral superiority of a state church and the need for religious uniformity. His support of the moral sovereignty of individual conscience includes the right to change churches if a believer deems it necessary. "For if afterwards he discovers any thing either erroneous in the Doctrine, or incongruous in the Worship of that Society to which he has join'd himself, Why should it not be as free for him to go out as it was to enter?"[45]

Elaborating on the point of the fundamental moral equality of churches, Locke raises two questions: if two churches come into conflict with each other, on what moral basis can we settle their dispute? And which one of them is right? Locke's initial answer was that "it is the Orthodox Church which has the Right of Authority over the Erroneous or Heretical." But he immediately qualifies this answer—and by doing so moves Christianity in a new normative direction—by stating that this initial response sheds no light on the question itself, because "every Church is Orthodox to it self; to others, Erroneous or Heretical. For whatsoever any Church believes, it believes to be true; and the contrary unto those things, it pronounces to be Error. So that the Controversie between these Churches about the Truth of their Doctrines, and the Purity of their Worship, is on both sides equal."[46] Concluding his argument, Locke affirms that there is no objective judge who can settle a dispute between churches, as the "Decision of that Question belongs only to the Supreme Judge of all men, to whom also alone belongs the Punishment of the Erroneous" (i.e. God).[47]

The fundamental moral equality of churches was premised on Locke's belief in the fundamental moral equality of all Christian believers. This new position is staked out in Locke's *Letter* on several occasions and is intimately linked to his defense of the freedom of religious conscience. The targets of his criticisms are the traditional figures of authority in English society: the monarchy and the clergy. "Princes indeed are born Superior unto other men in Power," Locke observes, "but in Nature equal. Neither the Right, nor the Art of Ruling, does necessarily carry along with it the certain Knowledge of other things; and least of all the true Religion."[48]

With respect to the moral authority and indispensability of the clergy in matters of faith, Locke writes: "some perhaps may object, that no such Society can be said to be a true Church, unless it have it in a Bishop, or Presbyter, with Ruling Authority derived from the very Apostles, and continued down unto the present times by an uninterrupted Succession." Locke, however, disagrees with this opinion. Anticipating criticism, he disarms his Christian critics by both quoting scripture and arguing that the will of God is on his side. "Let them shew me the Edict by which Christ has imposed that Law upon his Church. And let not any man think me impertinent if, in a thing of this consequence, I require that the Terms of that Edict be very express and positive. For the Promise he has made us, that *wheresoever two or three are gathered together in his Name, he will be in the midst of them* [Matt. 18:20], seems to imply the contrary."[49] What is noteworthy here is Locke's appeal to the moral authority of scripture. "Show me evidence," he is saying to his fellow Christian critics. The fact that there is no explicit command in the Bible on this topic suggests that alternative conceptions of the role of clerics in worship and in the life of a Christian can be envisioned and given legitimacy.

In summary, Locke's *Letter Concerning Toleration* realigns the broad moral and social relationship between religious toleration and political order. Staking out a clear position that it is imperative to distinguish "the Business of Civil Government from that of Religion, and to settle the just Bounds that lie between the one and the other," Locke argues for a separation between church and state and freedom of religious conscience. "True and saving Religion consists in the inward perswasion of the Mind," he writes, "it cannot be compell'd to the belief of any thing by outward force."[50]

Locke arrives at these new religiopolitical positions by reflecting on the relationship between religion and government. According to one Locke scholar, "the main argument of the *Letter* does have to rest on its distinctively Christian foundations."[51] While this is indeed true, the unique point I have been trying to demonstrate is that Locke's argument is not only based on Christianity but more significantly *is based on a decidedly distinctive and novel reading of Christianity.* Locke has shifted the moral compass of Christianity in the direction of toleration, religious liberty, peaceful persuasion of the mind, and the fundamental moral equality of Protestant churches and believers.[52] This reinterpretation of religion serves as a critical precondition to advancing a new political theory of state-society relations. A revised interpretation of Christianity also serves as a critical preface to Locke's more popular and influential work the *Two Treatises of Government.*

Locke's Political Theology

The *Two Treatises of Government* (1689) was Locke's attempt to address the relationship between individual freedom and political authority. Recall the tumultuous times. In England, the traditional symbols of authority—the Church of England, the monarchy, and the House of Lords—had been abolished and then resurrected. In 1649, King Charles I had been publicly beheaded, and England had become a republic under the short-lived Puritan rule of Oliver

Cromwell. In 1660, Charles II made a triumphant return to England, the Stuart monarchy was restored, and the Church of England reestablished. The old symbols of authority suddenly reappeared, and new allegiances were required. Add to this mix the devastation wrought by the bubonic plague (1665), the Great Fire of London (1666), growing controversies about religious toleration, and rising tension between an assertive Parliament and a conservative monarchy. In the midst of this confusion, fundamental questions about the moral basis of political authority, citizen obligation, consent, and the liberty of individual conscience were being asked, written about, and debated.

In responding to these controversies, Locke relied on his two most trusted sources: reason and revelation. The *Two Treatises* can be understood through these complementary lenses. The often-neglected *First Treatise* encapsulates the revelatory and scriptural part of Locke's argument, while the *Second Treatise* contains the more rational and secular aspects of his political vision. What concerns us in this discussion are the theological arguments of the *First Treatise*, particularly their relationship with Locke's attempt to reorient existing religious and political norms as a prelude to advancing his quasi-liberal-democratic thesis on government.

The Locke-Filmer Debate

To better understand of the origins of Locke's argument requires some reference to the political ideas of Sir Robert Filmer, a royalist ideologue, polemicist, and highly influential English author. Locke wrote the *Two Treatises*, in large part, with the motivation of refuting Filmer's views. As the title of his most famous tract—*Patriarcha or The Natural Power of Kings* (1680)—indicates, Filmer was a traditionalist who believed in the divine right of kings.[53] He was the leading intellectual defender and theoretician of the principle of absolute hereditary monarchy in England during the seventeenth century, and his writings were republished after his death in 1653 and circulated in the context of an emerging dispute between the Whig-dominated Parliament and the Stuart monarchy. Filmer's main argument was that the power of a monarch was analogous to the natural power a father exercises over his offspring. Such power was not only absolute but was a form of personal property that the monarch owns and is entitled to pass on to his heirs.

Filmer's views were based on scripture and history. He traced his argument back to the biblical Adam; according to his interpretation of scripture, God granted the right of ownership over the earth to Adam and his progeny. It "*is a truth undeniable,*" Filmer asserted, "*that there cannot be any Multitude of*

Men whatsoever ... gathered together from the several corners and remotest Regions of the World, but that in the same Multitude ... there is one Man amongst them, that in Nature hath a Right to be King of all the rest, as being the next Heir to Adam, and all the other Subject to him."[54] According to Filmer, the monarchy of Adam is "*the Original Grant of Government*" of which "*the Supream Power is settled in the Fatherhood, and limited to one kind of Government, that is to say Monarchy.*"[55]

There can be little doubt that Locke's main intellectual target in the *Two Treatises* was Robert Filmer.[56] One need look no further than the front cover of Locke's book, where the full title is displayed: *Two Treatises of Government: In the Former, the False Principles and Foundation of Sir Robert Filmer, and His Followers, are Detected and Overthrown. The Latter is an Essay concerning the True Original, Extent, and End of Civil-Government.*[57] More significantly, aside from Locke's general description of Filmer's ideas as "*glib Nonsense*" replete with "*Inconsistencies*" and "*Obscurities,*" Locke clearly states at the outset why Filmer's writings must be taken seriously. "*I should not speak so plainly of a Gentleman, long since past answering, had not the Pulpit, of late Years, publickly owned his Doctrine, and made it the Current Divinity of the Times.*"[58]

It was thus the widespread acceptability of Filmer's views—aided and abetted by a wide cross-section of the religious establishment in England—that made Filmer's ideas relevant to English politics. As Locke elaborates in his preface: "*For I should not have Writ against Sir Robert Filmer, or taken the pains to shew his mistakes, [and] Inconsistencies ... were there not Men amongst us, who, by crying up his Books, and espousing his Doctrine, save me from the Reproach of Writing against a dead Adversary.*"[59] It is clear from these comments that the general popularity of Filmer's divine-right-of-kings thesis necessitated an undermining of the reigning religiopolitical orthodoxy before a new one could be submitted in its place. This was the task Locke set out to accomplish.

The *First Treatise of Government* is fundamentally about divine providence, political authority, and the relationship between man and God. Locke launches a major assault on the philosophical and theological foundations of Filmer's discussion of these themes.[60] The theological underpinnings of the Locke-Filmer dispute have been noted by Locke scholars before. Dunn has written that "Jesus Christ (and Saint Paul) may not appear in person in the text of the *Two Treatises* but their presence can hardly be missed," and Jeremy Waldron has more recently noted that "it is intriguing that Locke chose to devote 120 pages of biblical refutation to Filmer's six pages of biblical argument," adding: "the only sustained passage of the *First Treatise* that is not scriptural in focus is the core passage on inheritance in Chapter IX, about ten pages at most."[61] The reasons for this heavy dosage of theological disputation, as an integral part of and antecedent to a larger political argument, have been largely missed by Locke scholars.

This intimate relationship between theology, politics, and the historical development of liberal democracy is extremely significant both for this chapter and this book as a whole, and will be discussed in greater detail in the pages that follow. But first the basic outlines of the Locke-Filmer dispute require attention.

In his preface, Locke tells us that the foundation of Filmer's argument (of the divine right of kings) is "*Scripture-proofs.*" In fact, Filmer claims—like many political Islamists in the Muslim world today—that the sole standard for assessing the moral legitimacy of government is the revealed word of God.[62] "It is a shame and scandal for us Christians," Filmer observes, "to seek the original of government from the inventions or fictions of poets, orators, philosophers and heathen historians, who all lived thousands of years after the creation . . . and to neglect the scriptures, which have with more authority most particularly given us the true grounds and principles of government."[63] Revealingly, Locke concurs with Filmer that the scriptures are the most authoritative standard for measuring political legitimacy. However, he confidently affirms—and this is where he undermines Filmer's thesis—that Filmer's argument does not stand up to critical scrutiny according to his own standard of proof.

Locke writes that if "*the Assignment of Civil Power is by Divine Institution*" and confirmed by scripture, then "no Consideration, no Act or Art of Man can divert it from that Person, to whom by this Divine Right, it is assigned."[64] Locke thus acknowledges the ultimate authority of scripture in matters political especially in determining the head of state. The problem, however, according to Locke, is that Filmer has misread and misunderstood the Bible. The scriptural evidence of the *jure divino* of Adam's monarchy is simply absent from the text. Locke argues:

> If he [Filmer] has . . . given any other Proofs of *Adam's Royal Authority*,
> other than by often repeating it, which among some Men, goes for
> Argument, *I desire any body for him to shew me the Place and Page, that
> I may be convinced of my mistake*, and acknowledge my oversight. If no
> such Arguments are to be found, I beseech those Men, who have so
> much cryed up this Book, to consider whether they do not give the
> World cause to suspect that it's not the Force of Reason and Argument,
> that makes them for Absolute Monarchy, but some other by Interest,
> and therefore are resolved to applaud any Author, that writes in favour
> of this Doctrine.[65]

As noted earlier, according to Robert Filmer, all humans owed their obedience to their rulers because God had given the earth to Adam and his posterity, which, Filmer suggests, extends to the English monarchy. "Divine appointment had ordained it to be *Monarchical*," Locke wrote, paraphrasing Filmer.[66]

The relationship between ruler and commoner was essentially a master-slave relationship, one for which Locke in his earlier writings, as noted earlier, had demonstrated some sympathy.

In specific terms, Locke charged that Filmer was guilty of misinterpreting the scriptures. While this thread of reasoning runs throughout Locke's critique of Filmer, with respect to the nature of political power, Filmer's mistake, according to Locke, was twofold. Filmer mistakenly claimed that (1) God gave Adam exclusive authority to rule the earth as his private domain as a monarch (and by extension the current claim to political authority in seventeenth-century England can be traced back through the Bible to Adam). In other words, a linear line of moral authority, Filmer claimed, can be traced from Adam to the Stuart monarchy; and (2) monarchical rule is absolute, and the king is above the law. In the same way a father has absolute control over the welfare of his children, a monarch has absolute control over his subjects. Put differently, paternal power, Filmer argued, is synonymous with political power.

On both accounts, Locke argues that Filmer's thesis is fundamentally misleading and his conclusions erroneous. More precisely, Locke accuses Filmer of shoddy biblical scholarship, poor argumentation, and weak reasoning. Locke says the general pattern of the entire corpus of Filmer's writing is that "Incoherencies in Matter, and Suppositions without Proofs put handsomely together in good Words and a plausible Style, are apt to pass for strong Reason and good Sense, till they come to be look'd into with Attention."[67]

Having thoroughly investigated Filmer's thesis, Locke concludes that Filmer has in general "warp[ed] the Sacred Rule of the Word of God,"[68] by severely misreading the scriptures with respect to the idea of the divine origins of government and in particular with respect to the exclusivist claims to land and power by Adam (and down throughout history to the Stuart monarchy). In short, Filmer's claim that the original grant of government is located in the story of Genesis is bereft of any evidentiary support. Furthermore, Locke accuses Filmer of engaging in a "false inference"[69] when he assumes that paternal power is analogous to political power. The two are decidedly separate, and neither scripture nor reason supports Filmer's position. To better appreciate the style and manner of Locke's critique—in particular the relationship between competing exegeses and political thought—consider the following example.

A Case Study of Dueling Scriptures: The Book of Genesis

Chapter 5 of the *First Treatise*, "Of Adam's Title to Sovereignty by the Subjection of Eve," is a representative sample of Locke's biblical hermeneutics. In brief, it is an alternative commentary on several passages from the Book of Genesis that Filmer partially relies on to support his thesis about the divine origins of kings. The central verse in dispute is "Unto the woman he said, I will greatly multiply thy sorrow and thy conception; in sorrow thou shalt bring forth children; and thy desire shall be to thy husband, and he shall rule over thee" (3:16).

According to Filmer's interpretation, in this verse God has announced that *"the Original Grant of Government"* begins with Adam, in that *"the Supream Power is settled in the Fatherhood, and limited to one kind of Government, that is to Monarchy."*[70] Locke argues that Filmer has misread the scriptures and that his conclusion cannot be sustained by any rational and "sober" examination of the text.[71] In other words, God has not prescribed a model of government for the human race either in this verse or any other part of the Bible. The scriptures are silent on this question of the proper form of government, or as Locke says more explicitly in *A Letter Concerning Toleration*, "there is absolutely no such thing, under the Gospel, as a Christian Commonwealth."[72]

Locke begins his analysis by noting the general context and moral direction of the Book of Genesis, in particular the early verses. The broad theme is God's condemnation of Adam and Eve for disobeying an explicit order to not eat from the forbidden tree—an act that results in their expulsion from heaven. According to Locke, "God says here to our first Parents, that he was Denouncing Judgement, and declaring his Wrath against them both, for their Disobedience."[73]

Locke fires his first salvo at Filmer by pointing out a serious contradiction between God's demotion of Adam (in the Bible) and Filmer's elevation of Adam's status (in his own book, *Patriarcha*). "We cannot suppose that this was the time," Locke observes, "wherein God was granting *Adam* Prerogatives and Priviledges, investing him with Dignity and Authority, Elevating him to Dominion and Monarchy," when by virtue of his defiant conduct he was a "helper in the Temptation, as well as a Partner in the Transgression . . . yet he too had his share in the fall, as well as the sin." In other words, Locke poses the question, as Adam has just engaged in a serious moral transgression (by defying God's will), how could God simultaneously be rewarding him?

Locke brings forward further evidence, in verses that immediately follow in Genesis, to suggest that Filmer has misunderstood God's intent: "In the sweat of thy [i.e. Adam's] face shalt thou eat bread, till thou return unto the ground; for out of it wast thou taken: for dust thou *art*, and unto dust shalt thou return" (3:19); and "Therefore the Lord God sent him forth from the garden of Eden, to till the ground from whence he was taken" (3:23). Locke points out that in comparing these three passages and reading them in context, "twould be hard to imagine, that God, in the same Breath, should make him Universal

Monarch over all Mankind, and a day labourer for his Life; turn him out of *Paradise, to till the Ground, ver.* 23. and at the same time, advance him to Throne, and all the Priviledges and the Ease of Absolute Power."[74] Locke's conclusion is that Filmer must have misread the Book of Genesis and extracted an interpretation that cannot be justified by any honest reading of the Bible. Summarizing his dissenting exegesis, Locke writes:

> This was not a time, when *Adam* could expect any Favours, any grant
> of Priviledges, from his offended Maker. If this be *the Original Grant of*
> *Government,* as . . . [Filmer] tells us, and *Adam* was now made
> Monarch, whatever Sir *Robert* would have him, 'tis plain, God made
> him but a very poor Monarch, such an one, as our . . . [Filmer] himself
> would have counted it no great Priviledge to be. God sets him to work
> for his living, and seems rather to give him a Spade into his hand, to
> subdue the Earth, than a Scepter to Rule over its Inhabitants. *In the*
> *Sweat of thy Face thou shalt eat thy Bread,* says God to him, *ver.* 19.[75]

The next exegetical disagreement Locke has with Filmer pertains to the relationship between husbands and wives. Locke first quotes the relevant passage in full: "*Unto the woman he said, I will greatly multiply thy sorrow and thy conception; in sorrow thou shalt bring forth children; and thy desire shall be to thy husband, and he shall rule over thee*" (Gen. 3:16). He then offers his own interpretation of the passage. Locke sees nothing overtly political in these words, only a very general description of a natural reality. He observes: "God, in this Text, gives not, that I see, any Authority to Adam over Eve, or to Men over their Wives, but only foretels what should be the Womans Lot, how by his Providence he would order it so, that she should be subject to her husband, as we see that generally the Laws of Mankind and customs of Nations have ordered it so; and there is, I grant, a Foundation in Nature for it."[76] In other words, this is a purely descriptive verse and not a prescriptive one with any connection to political norms that have divine sanction.

Locke then proceeds to puncture holes in Filmer's argument by raising a series of illuminating questions. He asks: "neither will anyone, I suppose, by these Words, think the weaker Sex, as by a Law [of nature] so subjected to the Curse contained in them, that 'tis their duty not to endeavour to avoid it. And will anyone say, that *Eve*, or any other Woman, sinn'd, if she were brought to Bed without those multiplied Pains of God threatens her here with?" Locke's hermeneutical point is that biblical passages cannot be translated literally into absolute factual events for all peoples and at all times; exceptions to this alleged moral imperative often exist. Deepening his critique, Locke draws on recent English political history. Addressing specifically the question of a wife's absolute subjection to her husband (Filmer's position), Locke asks rhetorically whether "Queens *Mary* or *Elizabeth*, had they Married any of their Subjects, had been by this Text put into a Political Subjection to him? or that he thereby should have had *Monarchical Rule* over her?"[77]

Concluding his dissenting exegesis, Locke posits an alternative interpretation of these verses.

> But if these words here spoke to *Eve* must needs be understood as a Law to bind her and all other Women to Subjection, it can be no other Subjection, than what every Wife owes her Husband, and then if this be the *Original Grant of Government* and the *Foundation of Monarchical Power*, there will be as many Monarchs as there are Husbands. If therefore these words give any Power to *Adam*, it can be only a Conjugal Power, not Political, the Power that every Husband hath to order the things of private Concernment in his Family, as Proprietor of the Goods and Land there, and to have his Will take place before that of his wife in all things of their common Concernment; but not a Political Power of Life and Death over her, much less over any body else.[78]

Like a good trial lawyer summarizing his closing argument, Locke concludes that Filmer has not proven his case beyond a reasonable doubt. His arguments are too weak, unconvincing, and superficial to be believed. Rather than proving his case, Locke suggests that Filmer has merely stated it. "He ought to have proved it by some better Arguments than by barely saying, That *thy desire shall be unto thy Husband*, was a Law whereby Eve and all that should come of her, were subjected to the absolute Monarchical Power of Adam and his Heirs."[79]

Furthermore, the verses in question from the Book of Genesis are too abstract and vague for one to be able to derive any conclusive or definitive meaning from them, least of all a divine-sanctioned theory of government. In Locke's own words, these verses are "too doubtful an expression, of whose signification Interpreters are not agreed, to build so confidently on."[80]

Summarizing his refutation of Filmer, Locke observes:

> according to his way of Writing, having once named the Text, [Filmer] concludes . . . that the meaning is, as he would have it. Let the words *Rule* and *Subject* be but found in the Text or Margent, and it immediately signifies the Duty of a Subject to his Prince, the Relation is changed, and though God says *Husband*, Sir *Robert* will have it *King*; *Adam* has presently *Absolute Monarchical Power* over *Eve*, and not only over *Eve*, but *all that should come of her*, though the Scripture says not a word of it, nor [has] our . . . [Filmer] a word to prove it.[81]

Having undermined Robert Filmer's authoritarian conception of legitimate political authority, Locke then proceeds in the *Second Treatise* to lay out his quasi-liberal-democratic political vision. He returns to a consideration of the "state of nature," affirming that human beings are divinely created in this state as naturally equal and free and thus "no Absolute or Arbitrary power" can be exercised over them. In the state of nature, the "fundamental, sacred, and unalterable law of *self-preservation*" exists, and the earth is not the private domain of kings and their progeny but rather it has been "given . . . to Mankind in common."[82]

Still deeply committed to a view of politics that is rooted in divine providence, Locke argues—in contrast to Filmer—that because people are naturally born free and equal, the only moral basis for exercising political authority lies in the voluntary "consent" of the governed. "Men being . . . by Nature, all free, equal and independent, no one can be put out of this Estate, and subjected to the Political Power of another, without his own *Consent*," Locke observes. "When any number of Men have so *consented to make one Community* or Government, they are thereby presently incorporated, and make *one Body Politick*, wherein the *Majority* have a Right to act and conclude the rest."[83]

Assessing Locke's Political Theology

What are the larger political lessons to be learned from the foregoing discussion, and how does it shed light on the struggle for liberal democracy in Muslim societies today? I have tried to show that Locke's argument for religious toleration and his quasi-democratic defense of government by consent have a unique pattern and sequence. In both *A Letter Concerning Toleration* and the *Two Treatises*, he prefaces his new political theory with a theological discussion—or, more precisely, a dissenting religious exegesis that challenges the conventional norm. This is not an insignificant fact but rather it significantly illuminates our understanding of how new ideas can be advanced in religious-based societies.

As noted, Waldron has written that "it is *intriguing* that Locke chose to devote 120 pages of biblical refutation to Filmer's six pages of biblical argument."[84] But there is much more to this point than mere questions of curiosity and intrigue or the related fact that Filmer (unlike Locke) attempted to explicitly integrate into his political philosophy the writings of non-Christian thinkers such as Aristotle and Cicero, while Locke's authoritative references are decidedly and exclusively Christian—the Anglican theologian Richard Hooker and Jesus Christ.[85] The strong religious orientation of Locke's political theory is worth noting. Are these merely accidental developments or do they provide a deeper insight into the historical development of liberal democracy that has crosscultural potential? Similarly, why did Locke choose this approach to advance his political argument? In other words, why did he believe it was necessary to refute Filmer with a biblical exegesis as a prelude to advancing a new political theory on government?

Recall that the new political positions Locke was defending, both on toleration and on government by consent, were minority views that did not enjoy broad support in seventeenth-century England. The idea that political order could somehow be enhanced by embracing religious toleration and that human beings were fundamentally created equal in the state of nature were highly controversial propositions in Europe at the time. Waldron notes that these ideas were "like communism in America in the 1950s. . . . [It was thought that if it was] let loose in politics and in moral belief generally . . . there was no telling the harm it could do." Proponents of these ideas "were widely regarded as unsound and dangerous to the point of incendiary, the last people respectable opinion would rely on for an account of the grounding or the reform of stable and effective political institutions."[86]

In large part, Locke's proto-liberal-democratic theories were deemed offensive because they seemed to violate basic moral presuppositions rooted in divine providence and the natural order of human civilization. Seventeenth-century England was a deeply conservative and religious society. Judging by today's standards, many would consider Locke and his compatriots Christian fundamentalists. Due to his indirect participation in English politics (as an advisor to the first Earl of Shaftsbury), Locke had an interest in changing hearts and minds and thus had to situate his arguments within the existing moral framework of English political culture if they were to be taken seriously. Whether he did this instrumentally, as Leo Strauss and his disciples claim, or because of his own deeply held Christian convictions is beyond the scope of this chapter.[87] The more important point for this discussion relates to the transformation of a political culture—particularly one with weak or nonexistent democratic and liberal ideas. It is the legitimacy and authenticity of new ideas on government and the introduction of new moral values that concerns us here. For Locke's political theory to receive a fair hearing, he had to work within the existing (religious) values of his host community. In short, to construct an argument that political change was in keeping with Christianity was to render it legitimate and acceptable.[88]

In the *First Treatise*, as I have shown, Locke accepts the Bible as the ultimate standard for assessing the moral basis of legitimate political authority. His argument against Filmer is based on rejecting Filmer's reading of the Book of Genesis and offering his own dissenting religious exegesis. His idea of legitimate government is rooted in the idea of the state of nature, in which human beings, all created by the same divine source, are fundamentally free and basically equal, and he argues that the only form of political authority that can be morally (i.e. religiously) justified is by the expressed consent of the governed. He goes to considerable length to prove that his idea is perfectly consistent with God's providence, implying that any pious Christian could comfortably support his theory on both theological and rational grounds. In short, having first undermined Filmer's very dubious reading of the Bible and its concomitant political argument, while firmly remaining within the existing moral/Christian consensus of his time, Locke then proceeds to construct his alternative theory of government which we recognize today as being the outline of modern liberal democracy.

In *A Letter Concerning Toleration*, Locke follows the same trajectory of argument. Accepting the assumptions of a religious worldview, he first sets out to shift the moral compass and normative direction of Christianity, *before* beginning a discussion about church-state relations, political secularism, and the social benefits of religious toleration. He argues that toleration is to be embraced not only for prudential reasons but fundamentally because it is the Christian (i.e. moral) thing to do. "True Christianity" and "true religion" require it, and both scripture and reason support it. His new liberal political vision, in other words, is predicated on this prior moral claim.

The key point here is that in Locke's contribution to the historical development of liberal democracy, religious reformation (or reformulation) *precedes* new moral claims about the legitimate basis of political authority. Religious reformation is an antecedent to political secularization and movement toward liberal democracy. An integral part of Locke's argument was an effort to change the values and norms that informed the political culture of his age. This is understood more easily if we remember that the political culture of seventeenth-century England was deeply infused by conservative Christian values and thus any discussion of the moral basis of government had to factor this reality into political discussion. If anyone sought to change the political culture with respect to ideas of government, they logically had to alter the normative interpretation and understanding of Christianity. A religious reformation, therefore, was a precondition to political secularization and the evolution of arguments that contributed to the development of liberal democracy. This is the first broad conclusion this chapter derives from rereading the political theology of Locke. The question that remains for this chapter is what does the foregoing discussion have to do with understanding political development in Muslim societies today? In short, everything.

The Relevance of John Locke to Liberal-Democratic Theory in Muslim Societies

To compare religious traditions is not to equate them. The study of history, however, is rendered meaningless if one cannot draw on relevant historical analogies to illuminate contemporary political phenomena. The historian Marc Bloch has in fact suggested that one of the principal purposes of historical comparison is the identification of differences.[89] It is a major assumption of this book that the similarities between Islam and Christianity as religious faiths—and the political consequences flowing from their reformulation—is significant enough to merit a comparison.[90] Both religions, albeit at different times, have been used in similar ways as the key legitimating principle of government—both in justifying political authority and citizen obligation and in opposing the emergence of more democratic and liberal principles. The ongoing political battle in Iran between reformists and conservatives is an illustration of this point.

A comparison between Locke's England and Iran today is justified on the following grounds. Both societies, albeit at different times, were under the sway of an illiberal and undemocratic political doctrine, and in both societies religion has been a key marker of political identity. Furthermore, in both Iran and England liberal or democratic traditions were nonexistent or at best very weak, and popular ideas on what constituted legitimate government were decidedly nondemocratic.[91] More pertinent, in both societies, the emergence of new arguments about the moral basis of legitimate political authority emerged as a result of a clash between notions of the divine right of kings/clerics and popular sovereignty. It was the "lived experience" of monarchical-clerical despotism that produced a series of lessons, in both societies, that were central to the struggle against political authoritarianism. Finally, progress in advancing liberalization and democratization was intimately linked to the reinterpretation of religious norms and the indigenization of a soft form of political secularism.[92]

In 1997, a grassroots democratization *process* had gained new momentum in Iran following a series of electoral victories for reformist candidates in consecutive presidential, parliamentary, and municipal elections. Iranian society during the two-term presidency of Muhammad Khatami (1997–2005) was engaged in full-scale internal debate about the relationships between tradition and modernity, democracy and theocracy, civil law and religious law, human rights and religious duties. The key axis of controversy around which this debate unfolded was the normative relationship between religion and government in Iranian society.

Following the 1979 overthrow of the Pahlavi monarchy, the postrevolutionary power struggle had been convincingly won by the Islamist supporters of Ayatollah Khomeini, vanquishing nationalist and leftist forces in the process. In simple terms, the crisis of Iranian democracy during the Khatami period can be understood as an internecine ideological war among past and present political Islamists vis-à-vis the future of Iran's Islamic revolution. The dominant group is a narrow, cleric-conservative coalition that controls all of the major levers of power and who can draw on a solid and loyal following among the deeply religious segments of the lower middle class and the bazaar. A Weltanschauung that grants ultimate political authority to the Islamic jurists and limits the exercise of popular sovereignty has informed this dominant group's political theology.[93] To date, they have won most of the major political battles for control of state institutions—but critically not the ideological ones at the level of civil society—yet they remain firmly in control of the Iranian state.

What is significant here is that despite this group's hold on power, the postrevolutionary Islamist consensus on the question of legitimate political authority has been shattered in Iran, especially within critical segments of Iranian civil society (intellectuals, women, youth). Since the early 1990s, following the death of Ayatollah Khomeini, an emerging democratic critique of cleric authoritarianism has been produced by influential members of the religious intelligentsia, both lay and clerical, that has sunk deep roots within Iran's political culture with an attempt to reorient it in a liberal and democratic direction.[94]

Known internally in Iran as the *no-andish-an-e dini* (New Religious Thinkers), this group of writers, political activists, and public intellectuals has developed a powerful, coherent, and penetrating theoretical critique—from within an indigenous Iranian Islamic framework—of the ruling religious orthodoxy. Their ideas in large part formed the philosophical foundation of the reform movement that won Muhammad Khatami the presidency in 1997 and 2001. The titles of some of the more popular books that have been produced—and widely consumed by the public—speak volumes about the revisionist political and religious reformation that engulfed Iran during this period: *Reason in the House of Religion* (Hassan Yousefi Eshkevari); *The Fascist Interpretation of Religion and Government: Pathology of Transition to the Democratic and Development-oriented State* (Akbar Ganji); *A Critique of the Official Reading of Religion* (Mohammed Mujtahid Shabistari); *Crises of Religious Government* (Mohsen Kadivar); *The Tragedy of Democracy in Iran* (Emadeddin Baghi); and *From the Sacred Witness to the Profane Witness: The Secularization of Religion in the Sphere of Politics* (Saeed Hajjarian).[95]

Central to the reformist-conservative dispute has been disagreement about the proper location of sovereignty. A statement by Ayatollah Ahmad Jannati, a leading clerical hawk and head of Iran's powerful Guardian Council, concisely captures the perspective of the ruling conservative establishment: "The people of Iran are considered in [view of Islamic] law, as orphans and minors, and Islamic scholars and clerics are their guardians and parents, who have to see to all of their needs."[96]

On the other side of the political spectrum, a diverse coalition of religious thinkers and laypersons responded with a prodemocratic interpretation of religion. In a rejoinder to Ayatollah Jannati, Iranian reformers wrote an editorial of their own the following day:

> How can a society which has more than one million university
> students and 17 million high schoolers, and overall the people have
> adequate access to international media, be considered as orphans and
> in need of a guardian, especially from one class [of society]? If their
> understanding of Islam is really this, why are they being polite—put
> aside the constitution of the Islamic Republic once and for all! Why do
> you spend so much money then on colourful elections? In this
> geometry of command, all of these are unnecessary extras.[97]

The important phrase to pay attention to in this riposte is: "If their understanding of Islam is really this." Much of the political debate in Iran during this period took place within a religious framework and idiom. In the words of Eric Rouleau, a longtime French observer of Muslim politics, "en Iran, islam contre islam."[98] The references and debates, therefore, were fundamentally about what type of Islam should be followed, who the interpreters of Islam should be, and—critically—where does sovereignty lie, with the people or the clerics? For a sampling of this debate, consider the case of Yusuf Saanei.

One of Iran's ten grand Ayatollahs, Yusuf Saanei comes from a distinguished family of theologians and possesses impeccable religious and revolutionary credentials. A close confidante and protégé of Ayatollah Khomeini—who once said "I raised Ayatollah Saanei like a son"—Saanei was appointed to several high-ranking positions in government soon after the revolution, including membership in the influential Guardian Council and the Assembly of Experts, and ultimately to the position of prosecutor-general. In these capacities, he played a significant role in Islamicizing the Iranian political system, especially in transforming Iran's secular legal code to a Shariah-based system. In 1984, however, he withdrew from politics and moved to the city of Qum, a center of Shia Islamic learning, to teach, study, and gradually develop a new modern interpretation of Islam. In a recent interview, he affirmed that the

Quran equates between men and women and gives everyone equal
rights. Color, ethnicity, nationality and religion are not standards that
can be used to discriminate between people when it comes to their
rights. For example, regarding the rights of non-Muslims, when the
Quran refers to disbelievers, it does not mean those who follow a
different religion than Islam. . . . Non-Muslims around the world are
not infidels. Christians, Marxists, Jews, and Zoroastrians are all non-
Muslims but they are not disbelievers. Unfortunately, the majority of
Muslim clerics and scholars do not differentiate between disbelievers
and non-Muslims, which is the root of many problems. This is a very
important matter that must be discussed in a conference between Shia
and Sunni [theologians]. All people are equal in their rights.
Personally and from my perspective of Islam, I respect all mankind
and the Quran respects all mankind not only Muslims.[99]

To promote his ideas, in the late 1990s, Saanei issued a series of bold
fatwas forbidding discrimination based on race, gender, or ethnicity. His new
reformist exegesis even allowed abortion in the first trimester. He observed that
while abortion is generally forbidden, "Islam is also a religion of compassion
and if there are serious problems, God sometimes doesn't require his creatures
to practice his law. So under some conditions—such as parents' poverty or
overpopulation—then abortion is allowed." He went out of his way to clarify,
however, that "this doesn't mean that we're changing God's laws . . . it just
means we're reinterpreting laws according to the development of science—
and the realities of the times."[100]

Notwithstanding his modernist orientation, lest anyone believe that he could
be a poster boy for the American Civil Liberties Union, Saanei wrote in one of his
books that the wearing of the hejab is mandatory for Muslim women and that
"even a working woman must receive her husband's consent to work."[101] Despite
these illiberal positions, his religious views have significantly evolved since the
1979 Iranian revolution. In explaining his changing religious convictions, he has
observed that when he was in political office he "could not feel the pain of the
people as much [in] those days. . . . But now, I am among people and I feel the
pressures." He added: "How can we say Islam is a religion of justice if its laws
consider women and non-Muslims unequal to Muslim men? Indeed, a man and
woman are both humans, and Islam considers all humans of an equal value."[102]

On the sensitive question of the normative relationship between religion
and state, while not stating this explicitly, Saanei, echoing Locke, suggests that
he favors a soft form of political secularism primarily because it preserves the
integrity of religion. "The spiritual leadership has lost its holiness because it's

become part of the power elite," he noted. "I've realised how power corrupts. The unity between power and religion does great damage. Power is always linked with lies, theft, oppression and betrayal. Religious leadership, however, is holy. And for that reason religious leaders can't say: I will lead the people to prayer, I will show them the good... and at the same time be part of the government. Government requires boxing people's ears, deceiving them. The world of government is a world of oppression."[103]

All things considered, Saanei's religious views, while still representative of a minority bloc within the Shia seminaries, does suggest an evolution of theological thought—at the highest level in Iran—with direct consequences for the struggle for democracy. Feminist groups and reformist politicians, for example, have relied on Saanei's rulings in support of their democratization and liberalization efforts. "His willingness and courage to say things against the traditional mainstream is what makes him different from other clerics," one Iranian secular feminist observed.[104] Furthermore, citing Saanei as a religious authority helps shield Iranian democracy and human rights activists from conservative charges that they are at war with God's revealed word and thus are enemies of Islam.

Real versus False Islam: Lockean Parallels in Iran

Scrutinizing the speeches by reformers and their conservative critics, one can discern that both groups invoke religion in defense of their political ideals. The reformists criticize conservative Iranians who (as former president Khatami put it) "suppose that the more retarded a society is, the better protected its religion will be" and ask (as did former minister of culture Atoallah Mohajerani) "why does the Koran carry the harshest criticisms of the prophet? [Because] it was not in the nature of the prophet to stifle discussion of opposing points of view."[105] The conservative clerics fire back (as did former speaker of the Majlis, Ali Akbar Nateq Nouri) that the "threat coming from nationalists and liberals is serious. We must be aware. They are weakening the beliefs and convictions of our people"[106] and argue (as did supreme leader Ayatollah Khamenehi) that "it will be a great danger to the national security and people's faith if the enemies of the Islamic revolution control or infiltrate the press."[107] Thus conservatives warn that the reformist agenda threatens both political order and Islam. "You cannot save Islam with liberalism and tolerance," Ayatollah Jannati asserted, after a major press crackdown in August 2000. "I am announcing clearly and openly that the closure of the newspapers was the best thing the judiciary has done since the revolution."[108]

Consider the following speech by Ayatollah Abolghassem Khaz'ali, a hard-line cleric and former member of the influential Guardian Council. During the height of the reformist-conservative battles in 1999, Khaz'ali delivered a fierce-ly worded attack on the reform movement in Iran and in particular the policies of President Khatami. "That gentleman [Khatami] says that there exist different interpretations of the fundamentals of Islam and religious belief," Khaz'ali told his audience. Addressing Khatami specifically, Khaz'ali asked: "Are you above the sources of emulation [in the Shia seminaries]? When a jurisprudent and philosopher like Ayatollah Mesbah Yazdi [a leading clerical hawk] says some-thing, you should say 'I shall listen and I shall obey.'" Khaz'ali continued:

> If there is a danger, it is coming from the slogan of "civil society,"
> alongside which we are getting various readings of the fundamentals
> of religiousness, and now the situation has reached the point when the
> existence of God is being debated at the universities.... A handful of
> writers who are being supported by the US are writing against
> religion's fundamental and our sacred values. It is people like the
> former press deputy of the Minister of Islamic Guidance,
> Mr. Borghani, who had spent 13 years in the US, and Saeed Hajjarian
> who was kicked out of the Information Ministry, who are the ones who
> are now playing with us. If Mr. President does not prevent insults
> against the sanctities of Islam, then we shall see a day that he will
> escape from the country with makeup on his face [a reference to Iran's
> first president, Abdul Hassan Banisadr, who disguised himself as a
> woman to flee Iran]. Mr. President! Why aren't you thinking about
> your turban? Do you think that people are stupid?[109]

The reformist coalition responded with their own appropriation of reli-gious texts and symbols to bolster their campaign for political liberalization and democratization. Speaking at an academic seminar in Tehran in 2002 entitled "Democracy and Religion," Mohsen Armin, a leading reformist par-liamentarian from Tehran, drew on the legacy of the Ali ibn Abu Talib (the first Shia imam, the fourth Sunni caliph, and a revered companion and relative of the Prophet Muhammad) in support of freedom of expression and in defense of civil rights. Referring to Ali's rule of the fourth Muslim caliphate (656–660), which Armin characterized as a model of democracy and tolerance, he stated that no one was ever imprisoned for expressing an opinion under Ali's leader-ship—unlike in Iran today, where "several [reformist] religious clerics and individuals have been sent behind bars on the very same charges."

Armin continued by observing that "Ali ... told his most dangerous ene-mies, the Kharijites, who had called [Ali] an atheist, that they were free to use

[the] Muslim's public treasury and could pray at mosques with others as long as they did not take up arms against him and the government." This is the proper moral standard for tolerating different points of view in society, Armin insisted. Applying Ali's moral standard for freedom of political expression to contemporary Iranian politics, Armin noted that charges against reformist activists who have been jailed on allegations of attempting to overthrow the Iranian government are unjust and divorced from Ali's Islamic standard for toleration because "they have not taken up arms against the [current Iranian] government." Furthermore, Armin noted, Ali never called his opponents "apostates" but merely said that they were "misled from the path of truth." Returning to the case of Iran, Armin noted that "here in Iran, a university lecturer [Hashem Aghajari] has been accused of blasphemy for the remarks he has made while in Imam Ali's . . . government no Kharijite was accused of such charges."[110] The implicit message Armin was conveying was that the conservative clerics in Iran were violating basic tenets of Islamic government as established by the revered moral figure Ali himself. Thus, the clerical claim to moral legitimacy based on Islamic values—which is the bedrock of their justification for political authority—was seriously open to dispute. A "true" Shia Muslim (such as the reformists claimed to be) normatively should tolerate dissenting points of views, and by extension democracy and human rights. Those who stood in opposition to this principle (i.e. the conservative clerics) were not upholding Islamic standards of government and were thus guilty of practicing a false version of Islam.

In a set of remarks broadcast on Iranian state television, President Khatami made the same point about Ali, one of the most revered figures in Shia Islam. In fact, he came very close to suggesting that Ali, despite his seventh-century origins, was really a proto-liberal democrat.

> He was a human being who at the height of religious piety and devotion was brave in action and sympathetic to the people. A great human being who was angered when a bangle was forcibly taken away from a non-Muslim living under his rule. A human being who openly called on the people to criticize him, to understand their rights and to demand their rights. He believed that government was to serve people. He wanted justice for society. His earthly rule lasted less than five years, during which he had to deal with many wars, clashes, rebellions, tensions but at the end he was not satisfied if there was a human being living in the domain of his rule without wheat or shelter. [He was] a human being whose charter of government and compassion for humanity is still alive and a model for us.[111]

Similarly, at a meeting in Isfahan entitled "With the Intellectuals of the Nation," the head of the reformist Mosharekat (Participation) Party, Mohammad Reza Khatami (the president's younger brother) drew on similar Islamic themes to bolster the democratic claims of his party. He said that Iranians would never accept an interpretation of religion that was devoid of freedom and justice for its followers. "Mankind has a bitter memory of certain religious governments, where violence was practiced in the name of religion," he affirmed. Directing his ire at his conservative rivals, he noted: "in religious governments, except for Prophet Mohammad's ... and Imam Ali's ... there have always been certain social strata in power who declared themselves as sacred and misused people's beliefs for their own gain."

He then switched to the Lockean theme of differentiating between "real" and "true" religion. Khatami claimed that liberalism and democracy were the "true" form of Islam supported by his reformist coalition in contrast to the inauthentic and false version of Islam practiced by his conservative rivals. "The religious leaders must introduce real Islam to the people as it was the people who followed the leaders to make the revolution." This responsibility of leadership was critical, so that people could get to know real Islam, in contrast to what "others are trying to make us believe as real Islam." Speaking directly to his right-wing adversaries, he asked: "How can you compare an Islam which propagated justice and freedom for all, with the one that advocates disgracing intellectuals?" Affirming his revolutionary credentials, Khatami cited the late Ayatollah Khomeini, who once said that the public vote was to be the final determining factor in all of the affairs of the country. "How can you compare that [democratic version of] Islam with the fact that there are now ten to twelve people [in the Guardian Council who] can nullify all the demands of the people?"[112] The implication was that conservatives were in violation of not only core Islamic tenants but also the explicit preferences of the leader and founder of the Islamic revolution himself. Two weeks later, as the internal struggle in Iran intensified, President Khatami echoed the foregoing themes when he said that the conservative Guardian Council "must end its policy of systematic obstruction" of parliamentary legislation, adding: "the battle [inside Iran today] is between a democratic Islam and a despotic Islam."[113]

The more one investigates the political and religious parallels between Locke's England in the seventeenth century and Khatami's Iran in the twenty-first century, the more one is struck by certain similarities. In both cases, authoritarianism is justified by invoking the concept of the divine right of kings and clerics. "The right of fatherly government was ordained by God, for the preservation of mankind," Filmer asserted[114] while his Iranian counterpart, Ayatollah Ali Akbar Meshkini, similarly has asserted that the "powers and rights of the [Supreme Leader] are the same as those of the prophet [Muhammad]. He can dispose of all the nation's wealth, but also those belonging to the individuals."[115]

A key component of Filmer's absolutist political theory in the seventeenth century was that paternal power was synonymous with political power. Clerical hard-liners in Iran draw on a similar analogy to bolster their authoritarian conception of government. Ayatollah Ahmad Azari-Qumi has in fact suggested that the Islamic Republic of Iran is the de facto personal domain of the supreme clerical leader.

> The powers delegated to the [supreme] leader in the constitution
> are the [extension of the] monopoly of the leader in his duties and
> responsibilities and do not impose restrictions on his powers. . . . [The
> leader] is like the head of the family who, although in the division
> of labour takes the responsibility of outside shopping, he leaves for
> himself the right to interfere in the house where he has delegated
> the housework to his son.[116]

Moreover, Ayatollah Khomeini himself, in his famous lectures on "Islamic Government," where he first outlined his vision for a Shia Islamic state, invoked the Filmerian theme of equating paternal power with political power. "The governance of the *faqih* [Islamic jurist] is a rational and extrinsic matter," Khomeini asserted, "it exists only as a type of appointment, like the appointment of a guardian for a minor. With respect to duty and position, there is indeed no difference between the guardian of a nation and the guardian of a minor."[117]

In terms of democratic theory, the most salient parallel in this comparison is the clash between divine and popular sovereignty. One of Locke's most vocal opponents was the Anglican priest Charles Leslie (1650–1722). In his book *The Finishing Stroke, Being a Vindication of the Patriarchal Scheme of Government . . .* (1711), Leslie observed:

> The Sum of the Matter betwixt Mr. *Hoadly* [an English bishop and
> outspoken opponent of ecclesiastical political authority] and me is
> this, I think it most Natural that *Authority* shou'd *Descend*, that is, be
> *Derived* from a *Superior* to an *Inferior*, from *God* to *Fathers* and *Kings*,
> and from *Kings* and *Fathers* to *Sons* and *Servants*: But Mr. *Hoadly* wou'd
> have it *Ascend*, from *Sons* to *Fathers*, and from *Subjects* to *Sovereigns*;
> nay to *God* Himself, whose *Kingship* the Men of the *Rights* say, is
> *Derived* to *Him* from the *People!* And the Argument does Naturally
> Carry it all that Way. For if Authority does Ascend, it must Ascend to
> the Height.[118]

The conservative clerical establishment in Iran invokes nearly identical arguments. Compare Charles Leslie's comments with those of Ayatollah Ali Akbar Meshkini in a Friday prayer sermon in Qum on March 20, 1998:

> If the experts [Assembly of Religious Experts] reached consensus on the leadership of a person and someone said that he did not accept this then he should be made to change his mind by reasoning with him. And if he still did not accept, then he should be sorted out with a sword.... I should say something about this. We see a group of people [the reformists], who have been given pens to write, call into question the meaning of the absolute leadership. Once upon a time, I explained the meaning of absolute, but they did not seem to have understood it. Once again they have said: "why should leadership be forever? Leadership should be for a limited period of time. Three or four years as a leader is enough for one person." Leadership is one of the most dignified aspects of the issue of *imamate* [vice-regency of the Prophet Muhammad]. If what they say is right, then we shall also say that Imam Sadiq [the sixth Shia imam, 702–765] was an imam for a few years and that was enough. Similarly, the prophet [Muhammad] was also a messenger for a few years in Mecca, that was enough for him. Similarly, we shall even say that God has been God since time immemorial and that was enough for Him. Such people come up with a different plan every day. Then they distort things, saying that the Guardian Council's supervisory role should be abolished. They want the Guardian Council to just sit idly by, watching people go to the Majlis [parliament] and say nothing about it. They want the road to the Majlis to be left open so that everyone who wants to enter the Majlis can do so freely. This is the Majlis, the Majlis which has been formed thanks to the immaculate blood of 100,000, 150,000 martyrs being spilt. These people's blood has been spilt for God. *Leadership is a divine issue.*[119]

Despite the separation of 287 years, both Charles Leslie and Ayatollah Meshkini justify political leadership on divine grounds and reject the notion of popular sovereignty for near identical reasons. Leslie is aghast at the notion that political authority "is derived ... from the people," while Meshkini similarly expresses open opposition to the idea that "the road to the Majlis ... be left open so that everyone who wants to enter the Majlis can do so freely."

One could continue in this vein by comparing the similarities in political argumentation between proponents of *jure divino* and government by consent. The larger theoretical point in terms of democratic theory is the following. In the case of both England and Iran, emerging democratic voices pursued similar strategies and invoked comparable arguments to justify a transition from religious authoritarianism to an emerging liberal-democratic order. These individuals relied on a theological reinterpretation of religious norms as a central part of their strategy in rearticulating the moral basis of legitimate government. Proponents of this new position accepted many long-standing assumptions about the religious foundations of political society—in particular the centrality of scripture and religious tradition and history as a moral reference point—while simultaneously reorienting the normative principles of religion in the direction of liberal democracy.

Conclusion

Of primary interest in this chapter was how deeply religious societies under the sway of an illiberal and undemocratic religio-political doctrine can invoke arguments to theoretically rationalize and support a transition to democracy. An analysis of Locke's political theology indicates that a reinterpretation of religious ideas with respect to government, as well as a competition between "dueling scriptures," was an integral part of the development of Western liberal-democratic theory. Even though the Lockean example was drawn from a geographically and religiously distinct part of the globe (in Western Protestant Europe over three hundred years ago), a similar development can be observed in Muslim societies today. This suggests a *possible* universalism, that may be valid across time and between cultures, to the way religious societies can develop liberal-democratic arguments.

The parallels between the principle of the divine right of kings and the divine rights of clerics, the Bible and the Koran, Christianity and Islam, and the eras of John Locke and Muhammad Khatami are striking. In both cases, the debate about the future direction of English/Iranian society has occurred and is occurring by a reinterpretation—not outright rejection—of religious thought and a subtle movement in the realm of ideas, in the direction of political pluralism, toleration of dissent, and representative government. Atheists, agnostics, and French-inspired secularists are not driving this process. It is not a coincidence, for example, that the magnum opus of one of Iran's leading philosophers, Abdol Karim Soroush, is devoted to the theme of a reinterpretation of religious knowledge, *Qabz va Bast-i Tiorik-i Shari'at* (The Theoretical Contraction and Expansion of the Shariah).[120]

Furthermore, the incarceration and banning of the writings of, for example, the senior cleric Grand Ayatollah Ali Hossein Montazeri and the junior clerics Mohsen Kadivar and Hassan Yousefi Eshkevari speaks to the Iranian regime's legitimacy problem. Such religious personalities pose a special threat to conservative clerical rule, primarily because their quasi-liberal and democratic interpretation of Islam is popular and undermines the monopoly on religious interpretation that Iran's conservative elite seek to enforce. Secular political figures can be more easily dismissed by the regime as no threat to the moral basis of political authority because of their perceived lack of authenticity; theologians and Muslim democratic activists pose a more serious challenge precisely because they accept the basic religious framework of politics the conservative clerics uphold yet offer a dissenting interpretation of the relationship between Islam and politics.

Even the 2003 Nobel Peace laureate Shirin Ebadi is mindful of working within the parameters of Iran's Islamic political culture in her defense of universal human rights. She treads a very careful line that avoids articulating a defense of human rights based exclusively on secular principles that cannot be reconciled by an innovative reading of Islamic jurisprudence. "The piecemeal reform of Islamic laws that she proposes would mean using 'rationality,' which she describes as 'the scales for the weighing and apprehension of the holy word,' to determine which anachronistic laws should be discarded."[121] In speech after speech, she has gone out of her way to emphasize that there is no inherent contradiction between Islam and democracy or human rights. "The lack of democratization in the Islamic world," she has stated, "does not emanate from the essence of Islam. Rather, it is due to the unwillingness for numerous reasons of Islamic states *to embrace an interpretation of Islam* that is compatible with human rights, preserves individual and social freedoms, and advocates democratic statecraft."[122]

Personalities such as Shireen Ebadi, Yusuf Saanei, Mohsen Kadivar, and Abdolkarim Soroush remind us of the critical role played by what we might call "religious intellectuals" in promoting political development in conservative religious political environments. By situating their moral arguments with one foot in tradition and the other in modernity, they act as a critical bridge in the transition from authoritarianism to liberal democracy. This is particularly true when it comes to introducing new philosophical and theological innovations in societies with nonexistent or weak liberal-democratic traditions.

Locke can also be viewed as a religious intellectual. While this suggestion might seem shocking to a secular Western audience used to thinking of Locke as a founding father of the (secular) Enlightenment, historians of political thought should be comfortable with this characterization. Due to his grounding in the traditional religious norms of his society, Locke was able to break with the reigning consensus in his society and advocate a new political philosophy without alienating his entire political constituency. Ian Shapiro has perceptively noted that: "Locke is something of a hybrid figure. He makes arguments that endure as defining features of political argument in the modern West, yet he does so in ways that reflect and embody premodern concerns. Reading Locke reveals that we have more complex links to our past than we might otherwise perceive."[123]

When studying political philosophy in the early 21st century, the religious roots of modern liberal democracy often escape our attention. A critical re-reading of the political theology of John Locke, however, reminds us of the theological origins of modern politics. It also helps us shed light on struggles for liberal democracy in non-Western polities where religion is a key marker of identity and where religious groups, religious intellectuals, and religious-based political parties are active in society.

Locke is credited with writing the outline of modern liberal democracy. His ideas were taken up and expanded further by other philosophers such as Rousseau, Paine, and Mill. The methodology Locke used in articulating his political philosophy, however, should not be forgotten. With hindsight, we can see that it was central to the history of liberal democracy. In his critique of royal absolutism and intolerance, the core thrust of Locke's argument was that his opponents had fundamentally misunderstood and misapplied the moral teachings of the Bible. "The Scripture says not a word of it," was Locke's common refrain as he proceeded to break new ground in Western political philosophy.[124]

In the Muslim world today, a similar rethinking of religious ideas has emerged with parallels to seventeenth-century England. The day after his election to a second term in office, President Khatami commented that the "people showed their commitment to *the real meaning of religion* and demands for freedom and justice.... The need of the moment and the future is to stabilize and deepen democracy and realize the rights of the people alongside religion."[125]

We are all observers of this Muslim political drama as it plays itself out. As the late Eqbal Ahmad once observed, a primary lesson to be learned from the European experience of political modernization that is relevant to a Muslim context is that "no significant political change occurs unless the new form is congruent with the old. It is only when a transplant is congenial to a soil that it works."[126] This truth about social change applies as much to Locke's England in the seventeenth century as it does to Khatami's Iran in the twenty-first century, where a reinterpretation of religious thought is a critical variable, influencing the process and trajectory of democratization and liberalization.

3

A Concise Anatomy
of Secularism

Examining Its Linkages to Liberal Democracy

One of the major failures of most Arab and Western intellectuals
today is that they have accepted without debate or rigorous scrutiny
terms like secularism and democracy, as if everyone knew what
these words mean.

—Edward W. Said

This chapter explores the history of secularism and its relationship
with politics. The aim is to deepen our grasp of the concept of political
secularism and to understand its connection with liberal democracy.
Far from attempting a comprehensive treatment of the topic, I will
examine various definitions of secularism, the historical background
that gave rise to it, and the political problems it seeks to resolve.
I will also examine the writings of key political philosophers who
have contributed insights into this subject, along with the various
political models of secularism that have been bequeathed to us
from the political history of the West.

The first theme I will explore is the historical roots of secularism.
This is necessary because the term "secularism" is often bandied about
with an imprecision that comes at the expense of analytical clarity. Any
serious discussion of secularism, therefore, must first begin with an
attempt to define the concept politically. I will argue that while the
concept of secularism is ambiguous, a minimum common denomi-
nator does exist whereby political secularism suggests a form of

separation (that can vary) between the domain of religion and the domain of government.

An illustration of the ambiguous nature of secularism can be found in the different historical experiences of church-state relations in Europe. This has allowed for more than one form of political secularism to emerge. In the Western tradition, the two distinct but related forms of secularism are what could be called the Anglo-American "religion-friendly" (weak) version and the French Republican "religion-hostile" (strong) version. These examples suggests that secularism is not a monolithic entity but varies markedly in accordance with the historical experiences of church-state relations and nation building in various emerging democracies.

The second theme this chapter explores is the precise relationship between secularism and liberal democracy. While writers from Alexis de Tocqueville in the early nineteenth century to Richard Rorty in the late twentieth century have written about this relationship, rarely have authors theorized about the constitutional and institutional boundaries between religion and state that are needed to sustain a liberal democracy. A key problem in grappling with this topic is that secularism is often assumed, but its necessity for liberal democracy is rarely argued. In tackling this critical issue I will draw on the recent theoretical work of Alfred Stepan.

Stepan's theory on religion and democracy is useful for many reasons but primarily because it concentrates attention on the precise points of friction between religious groups and the liberal-democratic state. While Stepan insists that a form of religious-state separation is necessary to sustain liberal democracy, he also develops a theory that is versatile, allowing for multiple possible scenarios in which religion and liberal democracy might coexist. Stepan's thesis has special relevance to the contemporary debate on Islam and democracy precisely because of the nuanced way he approaches the theoretical relationship between religion, secularism, and liberal democracy.

Toward a Conceptual Definition of Secularism

What does the word "secularism" actually mean? What values does it promote and what problems does it seek to resolve? Does secularism imply anticlericalism, atheism, disestablishment, state neutrality and equidistance toward all religions, the rejection of religious symbols in the public sphere, the separation of the public and private spheres, the complete separation of religion from politics, or more narrowly the separation of the institutions of the state from the influence of religion? All of the above, some of the above, or none of the above? If there is one thing that can be affirmed with certainty, it is that the concept itself is deeply contested, or as Charles Taylor has observed, "it is not entirely clear what is meant by secularism."[1]

In tracing the etymology of the term "secular," Nikki Keddie notes that the word is "derived in Middle English from the Old French word *seculer* (itself from the Latin *saecularis*). The word originally referred to clergy who were not bound by the religious rules of the monastic order." Keddie adds: "In Middle English, it could also refer to the realm of the 'this-worldly' as opposed to the divine—the sacred and 'other-worldly' realms historically monopolized in Western Europe by the Roman Catholic Church."[2]

John Keane suggests that the "intellectual roots [of secularism] run deep," and he expresses surprise that to date "a comprehensive scholarly genealogy of these roots remains unwritten."[3] In his own brief survey of the concept, Keane observes that during the sixteenth century the term "secular . . . underwent modernisation" and came to be understood as "converting from ecclesiastical to civil use. . . . 'Secularisation' connoted a process of reducing the influence of religion, as when the term was used in legal and ecclesiastical circles to describe the transfer of religious institutions or property to lay ownership or temporal use."[4] Quoting from the first English-language dictionary, organized by Samuel Johnson (published in 1755), Keane observes that secularism at this moment in English history was described as "worldliness; attention to the things of the present life . . . to convert from spiritual appropriations to common use . . . to make worldly."[5]

Talal Asad, in an anthropological study, traces the term to mid-nineteenth-century northwestern Europe. He notes that "secularism" and "secularists" were first introduced by liberal freethinkers to avoid the charge of atheism, which suggested immorality in what was still a largely religious society. He credits George Jacob Holyoake (1817–1906), a social reformer and working-class activist, with coining the term "secularism" in 1851.[6] In Holyoake's book *The Principles of Secularism*, the concept is defined as follows:

> Secularism is the study of promoting human welfare by material
> means; measuring human welfare by the utilitarian rule, and making
> the service of others a duty of life. Secularism relates to the present
> existence of man, and to action, the issues of which can be tested by
> the experience of this life—having for its objects the development of
> the physical, moral, and intellectual nature of man to the highest
> perceivable point, as the immediate duty of society: inculcating the
> practical sufficiency of natural morality apart from Atheism, Theism,
> or Christianity: engaging its adherents in the promotion of human

improvement by material means, and making these agreements the ground of common unity for all who would regulate life by reason and ennoble it by service.[7]

By the twentieth century, secularism had emerged as a scholarly category that was used in the social sciences and connected with the work of Auguste Comte, Emile Durkheim, Max Weber, Karl Marx, Ferdinand Toennies, and Ernst Troeltsch. Nikki Keddie lists three ways "secularization" is commonly understood today: as (1) "an increase in the number of people with secular beliefs and practices"; (2) "a lessening of religious control or influence over major spheres of life"; and (3) "a growth in state separation from religion and in secular regulation of formerly religious institutions and customs."[8]

One simple way of thinking about secularism is in relation to three core disciplines in the social sciences: philosophy, sociology, and political science. Philosophically, secularism refers to a rejection of the transcendental and the metaphysical with a focus on the existential and the empirical. This is what Harvey Cox was referring to when he referred to secularism as "the liberation of man from religious and metaphysical tutelage, the turning of his attention away from other worlds and toward this one."[9] Sociologically, secularism correlates with modernization: a gradual process that leads to the declining influence of religion in social institutions, communal life, and human relationships. This is an understanding of secularism which is most common in popular discussion of the topic and it is what Peter Berger has called a "process by which sectors of society and culture are removed from the domination of religious institutions and symbols."[10] Politically, secularism is about a separation of the public and private spheres and in particular the separation of religion and state.[11] This threefold breakdown is very similar to Charles Taylor's recent tripartite categorization of secularism. According to Taylor:

- Secularity 1 is the retreat of religion from the public sphere, the diminution of religion in people's lives or the separation of church and state in public spaces.
- Secularity 2 is the decline of religious beliefs and practices that can be seen in Western liberal democracies in the form of church attendance. It is related to Secularity 1 but it is different in scope.
- Secularity 3 is the place of our self-understanding toward religion and the recognition that something has eclipsed it with the rise of alternative belief systems. It is the problematization in Latin Christendom on this topic between 1500–2000 that looks at background conditions and the development of secularism from the *longue duree*.[12]

The European Roots of Secularism

Charles Taylor's third definition of secularism (secularity 3) draws our attention to the changing perception of the concept over the course of history. He reminds us that in 1500, atheism was not an ideological option, as "it was virtually impossible not to believe in God," whereas today it "is one human possibility among others."[13] As a result, social questions related to religion are today deeply contested and embattled issues. In affirmation of Taylor's position, one need only think about contemporary debates in the West about abortion, stem-cell research, and same-sex marriage, all of which are connected to issues of religion and state.

In his attempt to locate the political roots of secularism, John Keane refers to the writings of John Wycliffe (*Tractatus de civili dominio*, 1374), William of Ockham (*A Short Discourse on the Tyrannical Government*, 1334–1347?), and Marsilius of Padua (*Defender of the Peace*, 1324).[14] The conflict between these men with their dissident writings and the Pope during the fourteenth century led to an early tension and fissure between religious and secular authority in Latin Christendom.[15]

The Protestant Reformation and the Wars of Religion in Europe during the sixteenth and seventeenth centuries were seminal events in the historical development of political secularism.[16] According to Charles Taylor, "the origin point of modern Western secularism was the Wars of Religion; or rather, the search in battle-fatigue and horror for a way out of them. The need was felt for a ground of coexistence for Christians of different confessional persuasions."[17] As a consequence of these events, the question of religious toleration came to be a hotly contested political question in Latin Christendom for hundreds of years.[18] Religion, it should not be forgotten, was a key organizing theme in Europe for over a millennium. In an era marked by intolerance toward religious dissent and the persecution of heretics, the idea that political order and religious pluralism could somehow coexist was widely viewed as anathema during this period. The dominant view at this time was that in order to maintain social order an established church and religious uniformity was required in the public sphere. This is why Hobbes firmly insisted in his *Leviathan* (1651) that a solution to the English civil war necessitated not a separation of church and state but rather a union of these two domains. As the subtitle of his *Leviathan* clearly spells out, this is a book about "The Matter, Forme, and Power of A Commonwealth *Ecclesiasticall* and Civill."[19] In chapter 12, "Of Religion," Hobbes spoke directly to this point:

> But where God himself, by supernaturall Revelation, planted Religion;
> there he also made to himselfe a peculiar Kingdome; and gave
> Lawes, not only of behaviour towards himselfe; but also towards
> one another; and thereby in the Kingdome of God, the Policy, and
> lawes Civill, are a part of Religion; *and the distinction of Temporall,
> and Sprituall Domination, hath there no place.*[20]

Notwithstanding Hobbes's overt antisecularism in the realm of politics, embodied in his insistence that all public manifestations of religion were to be decided by the sovereign, Charles Taylor points out that there were secular consequences to Hobbes's political theory. He refers to the discussion of the relationship between state and religion that appears in the latter part of the *Leviathan* (part 3, "Of a Christian Commonwealth"). The issue Hobbes was attempting to resolve was the tension between obeying the will of God and the will of the sovereign. What happens when an individual perceives that the two are in conflict? Who should he follow? His conscience or his monarch? According to Hobbes, this problem was "the most frequent praetext of Sedition, and Civill Warre, in Christian Common-wealths. . . . of obeying at once, both God, and Man, then when their Commandements are one contrary to the other."[21]

Hobbes's strategy in chapter 43 is to recast this politico-theological problem by noting that "it is manifest enough that when a man receiveth two contrary commands, and *knows* that one of them is God's, he ought to obey that, and not the other, though it be the command of his lawful sovereign."[22] In this passage, Hobbes introduces an important restriction in the debate. He suggests that in order to disobey the sovereign's authority it is not enough to merely *believe* that the sovereign has violated the word of God; one must in fact *know* this to be true. One of the key purposes, however, of Hobbes's entire discussion in part 3 of *Leviathan* is to demonstrate that a subject is dependent on his sovereign to know God's will, so that in theory, the possibility of conflict is absolutely precluded.[23]

Hobbes demonstrates his support for absolute political sovereignty by noting that even in the hypothetical case where the sovereign is an infidel, to "resisteth him, sinneth against the Laws of God . . . that admonisheth all Christians to obey their Princes . . . in all things. And for their *Faith*, it is internall, and invisible. . . . they ought to expect their reward in Heavan, and not complain of their Lawfull Soveraign; much lesse make warre upon him."[24] According to Taylor, what Hobbes is suggesting is that "the demands of the Christian faith, as confessionally defined, [are] irrelevant to the public sphere" and in "the private realm, the believer can and must do what conscience demands, but he commits no sin in respecting publicly established forms and ceremonies." The thrust of Hobbes's entire argument, Taylor suggests, has a secularizing potential, in that "when pushed further this logic can lead to the extrusion of religion altogether from the public domain."[25]

While Martin Luther spoke about "two governments, the spiritual which fashions true Christians and . . . the secular government which holds the Unchristian and wicked in check and forces them to keep the peace outwardly," it was left to John Locke to issue one of the first theoretical treatises justifying the institutional separation of church and state.[26] As explicated in the previous chapter, the backdrop to his argument was implacable debates in Europe on the relationship between religious toleration and political order, in particular the "Exclusion Crisis" (1679–1681) in England that sought to deny Charles II's Catholic brother James II (Duke of York) the succession to the English throne.[27] In a famous passage in his *A Letter Concerning Toleration* (1689)— reversing a previously held position that supported the firm union of church and state—Locke argued:

> I esteem it above all things necessary to distinguish exactly the
> Business of Civil Government from that of Religion, and to settle the
> just Bounds that lie between the one and the other. If this be not done,
> there can be no end put to the Controversies that will be always
> arising, between those that have, or at least pretend to have, on the
> one side, a Concernment for the Interest of Mens Souls, and on
> the other side, a Care of the Commonwealth.[28]

Locke's position at the time, when judged by twenty-first-century standards of tolerance and political pluralism, was deeply exclusionary and very narrow in scope. His argument for toleration was primarily directed to resolving intra-Protestant feuding and did not apply to Catholics, for example. Nonetheless, Locke's *Letter* was an attempt to morally justify a new conception of church-state relations. His argument had a significant influence on English politics at the time and marked a historical break with past thinking on the relationship between religion and politics, church and state, the public and the private realm. This is not to suggest that Locke was the primogenitor of these ideas, but he did play a unique role in codifying and constructing a set of rational moral arguments that eventually sank deep roots in Western political culture.

From Locke's seventeenth-century argument in support of freedom *of* religion to Mill's nineteenth-century argument that political development necessitated freedom *from* religion, one can discern a gradual yet clear trajectory toward the secularization of politics and society in Europe.[29] "The old opinions in religion, morals, and politics," Mill observed in his autobiography, "are so much discredited in the more intellectual minds as to have lost the greater part of their efficacy for good."[30] Earlier, in his now classic work *On Liberty*, he wrote:

It is accordingly on this [religious] battlefield, almost solely, that the
rights of the individual *against* society have been asserted on broad
grounds of principle, and the claim of society to exercise authority over
dissentients openly controverted. The great writers to whom the world
owes what religious liberty it possesses have mostly asserted freedom
of conscience as an indefeasible right, and denied absolutely that a
human being is accountable to others for his religious belief.[31]

The French Revolution

The French Revolution and the rise of modern nationalism were also central
developments in the story of secularism. Religious identity was gradually being
replaced by new forms of social attachment connected to the emergence of the
nation-state and the idea of citizenship. The Catholic Church's close identification with the *ancien régime* led to the confiscation of Church assets, and priests
were required to swear allegiance to the new French republic rather than the
Pope. Those who did not were persecuted, especially during Robespierre's
infamous reign of terror (1793–1794). William Doyle points out that the
Church was the "mainspring of opposition to the new order," and it was not
until 1801 that Napoleon Bonaparte was able to reach a concordat with the
Pope that "reconciled Catholics to the new regime by re-establishing their
Church," albeit firmly under state control.[32] During this period, the tension
between Paris and Rome was so great that it led French troops to march on
Rome, not once but twice (in 1798 and 1809), including in the process the
abduction of recalcitrant popes. All of this gave the new secular order a
decidedly anticlerical and antireligious flavor that has remained a staple of
French secularism. The concordat lasted approximately a century until 1905,
when the Third Republic, amid a new anticlerical militancy, codified a law on
the separation of church and state. This law was recently updated in 2004
amid concerns that French secularism was threatened by Muslim immigrants.
      In retrospect and on closer scrutiny, one can discern two related but
distinct models of political secularism that have emerged over time in the
West. According to Bhikhu Parekh,

> the secularist thesis can take several forms of which two are the most
> common. In its weaker version it separates *state* and *religion* and
> maintains that the state should not enforce, institutionalize or
> formally endorse a religion . . . and should in general retain an attitude
> of strict indifference to religion. In its stronger version it also

separates *politics* and *religion* and maintains that political debate and deliberation should be conducted in terms of secular reasons alone.[33]

In light of these different models of secularism, perhaps it is more accurate to speak of *secularisms* in the plural rather than a singular monochromatic form. This recognition that political secularism is nonmonistic allows us to think about secularism's prospects in non-Western societies. The implication is that these societies might be able to develop a home-grown version of secularism that, as I will argue later, is essential for the consolidation and development of liberal democracy. Charles Taylor has noted that "there is truth in the claim that secularism has Christian roots, but it is wrong to think that this limits the application of its formulae to post-Christian societies."[34] What is required here is an investigation of comparative secularisms in the non-Western world. How did emerging democracies in these parts of the globe deal with the question of religion-state relations and negotiate an accommodation based on a broad consensus? What obstacles had to be overcome? Which models of European secularism, if any, did they seek to emulate? How were local traditions accommodated? More broadly, what social conditions produced a form of political secularism that has allowed democracy to flourish? This is a huge topic that is beyond the scope of this chapter; instead I will focus more narrowly on the Western tradition and the comparative lessons to be learned for Muslim societies.[35]

The two dominant traditions of political secularism in the West, the Anglo-American and the French, both have their origins in the lived experience, over a long period of time, of the interaction and tension between religion and politics.[36] A gradual process of democratic bargaining and negotiation over the normative relationship between religion and politics has taken place— often after heated, acrimonious, and contentious debate—and today a broad consensus exists on religion's role in the polis and the limits of its reach.[37] This consensus, over time, has sunk deep roots in the political cultures of France, England, and the United States and has given shape to the current models of political secularism we are familiar with. One noticeable difference between the Anglo-American and the French versions of secularism, when looked at in the context of church-state relations, is in their attempts to locate the source of the political problem that secularism is trying to remedy. Is the very nature of religion the problem or is the problem state imposition of religion? T. Jeremy Gunn's comparison between French and Anglo-American secularism captures this predicament:

> Unlike France, where "laïcité" might have the connotation of the state protecting itself from the excesses of religion, the term "religious freedom" in the United States would be more likely to have the

connotation of religion being protected from the excesses of the state. Thus Americans are more likely to be predisposed to have suspicions about state laws regulating religion while the French are more likely to be suspicious of an absence of regulation of religious activity. At least this is the theory.[38]

John Bowen locates the difference between English and French secularism in the different ways each society thinks about the normative relationship between the individual, the state, and society. In the case of France, an active and intervening state is central to the French conception of the good life. The French attach a critical role to the state by giving it the responsibility to create good citizens, promote liberty, and maintain public order. Seeking out the roots of laïcité, Bowen interviewed the political philosopher Blandine Kriegel, a key participant in the contentious debates in France on secularism and integration and an influential policy advisor to President Jacques Chirac. In her reflections on the topic she located the difference between these two variants of secularism in the writings of Locke and Rousseau and the influence of these philosophers on their societies political traditions.[39]

Kriegel attempted to differentiate laïcité from Anglo-American secularism by noting that idea of freedom of religion was understood in special way in France. "In Anglo-Saxon thinking, in Locke and Spinoza, it is the concrete individual who has rights; freedom of conscience is the foundation," she told Bowen. "In our tradition these liberties are guaranteed through political power [of the state], which guarantees a public space that is neutral with respect to religion." The idea of "public space" in France is intimately tied to the active intervention of the state. "The public school is part of the public because it is where civic education takes place. And so is public administration. There will never be Sikh civil servants in France!," Kriegel affirmed.[40] The reference here is to practicing Sikhs in England and Canada who won the right to wear their turbans and keep their ceremonial daggers while still working in the public service. This would never be tolerated in France, as l'affaire du foulard and the recent debate on laïcité has amply demonstrated. In short, the normative relationship between state and society and the place of the individual and his or her relationship to community are interpreted and understood differently by French society. Summarizing Kriegel's explanation of laïcité, Bowen noted:

Here Rousseau stands against Locke, freedom through the state against freedom from the state, society as a "coming together" and "living together" against society as isolated rights-bearing individuals or (worse) as isolated communities defined by religion, race or ethnicity. In the Anglo-Saxon mirror image of France, agents of the state display their separateness in their turbans or their headscarves, and the people follow suit.[41]

Investigating the roots of these different forms of secularism any further is beyond the scope of this chapter.[42] Fundamentally, the disparity can be traced back to different historical experiences with church-state relations and nation building in England, the United States, and France. The historian Patrice Higonnet has summarized this point quite succinctly by noting that "the American Revolution was carried out *through* religion; by contrast, the French revolution was made *against* religion. Everything before flowed into that; and many things since then have followed from that."[43]

Arguably, one of the salient factors that has influenced the substance and character of French versus Anglo-American secularism has been the relative heterogeneity of Protestant denominations in England and the United States versus the homogeneity and hegemony of Catholicism in France. The contrast between the authoritarianism of the Catholic Church and the imposition of its religious teachings on society and the relatively greater tolerance for noncon-formists in England, particularly in the period following the English Toleration Act of 1689, could partly explain different European attitudes with respect to church-state relations. Core doctrinal differences between Catholicism and Protestantism could be listed as well; for example, the contrast between the Catholic requirement that all believers must follow the teachings of the Vatican versus the centrality of the liberty of individual conscience in Protestantism has arguably shaped attitudes toward the role of religion in political society.[44]

To summarize the discussion up to this point, the following broad general-izations about secularism have been made. (1) Secularism is an amorphous concept that is difficult to precisely define. (2) Politically, secularism suggests some form of separation between state and religion. (3) Secularism has a long history, with roots in Latin Christendom that emerged against the backdrop of the "problem of religion" in government. (4) Secularism has various models; the two most prominent ones in the Western tradition are the Anglo-American model (relatively religion-friendly) and the French model (relatively religion-hostile). Both of these models are by-products of these countries' unique historical experiences in grappling with the relationship between religion and democracy. John Ruedy's summary of secularism is difficult to improve upon.

> Secular is a term used to distinguish the temporal or worldly from the spiritual, while secularism has come to denote a philosophy that privileges the domain of the temporal and diminishes that of the spiritual. The former grows to cover civil affairs and education, while the latter is increasingly restricted to the areas of private belief,

worship, and conduct. While secularism as a philosophy is central to the Western experience, it should be borne in mind that the concept has evolved historically and that it is still doing so. What was considered the proper province of human rational decision was different in the fifteenth century than in the nineteenth century and is even more different in the late twentieth. Secondly, it should be stressed that the struggle over the frontier between the secular and the religious is one characterized by continuous tension and that, up to now, the exact line of the frontier between the two has never been agreed upon. One must also recognize that in the West there has seldom been agreement among secularists as a group, nor among the religious as a group, as to where exactly that frontier should be.[45]

The questions that are now germane for this chapter are as follows: what is the precise relationship between secularism and liberal democracy? Does liberal democracy require secularism and if so, in what form? How secular does a political system need to be in order to sustain a liberal democracy? In other words, what are the minimum conditions in terms of state-church relations needed to sustain a liberal democracy? An examination of these questions is the focus of the following subsections.

Mapping the Minimum Conditions of Secularism and Liberal Democracy

The relationship between secularism and liberal democracy is subsumed by and intimately connected to the broader relationship between religion and democracy. At first glance, the theoretical tension between religion and democracy seems inherently contradictory and conflictual. Both concepts speak to different aspects of the human condition. Religion is a system of beliefs and rituals related to the "divine" and the "sacred." In this sense, it is decidedly metaphysical and otherworldly in its orientation and telos. While religion may differ in its various manifestations, most religions share these features in common. It is precisely the dogmatic claim—for which many religions and sects are infamous—that they alone are in the possession of *the* absolute truth and the concomitant shunning of skepticism in matters of belief that makes religions a source of conflict. Furthermore, many religions and sects tend to set insurmountable boundaries between believers and nonbelievers. Entry into the community of a religion often demands an internalizing of its sacred and absolute truths.[46]

Democracy on the other hand is decidedly this-worldly, secular, and egalitarian, at least in theory. Regardless of religious belief, race, or creed, democracy (especially its liberal variant) implies an equality of rights and treatment before the law for all citizens without discrimination. Its telos is geared toward the nonviolent management of human affairs in order to create the good life on this earth, not in the hereafter. Critically, unlike religious commandments, the rules of democracy can be changed, adjusted, and amended. It is precisely the inclusive and relativistic nature of democracy that separates it from religion and theologically based political systems.

The core tension between religion and democracy is rooted in the moral basis of legitimate political authority. Where does this authority fundamentally lie and who is ultimately sovereign? Political constitutions that contain dual notions of sovereignty violate the definition of democracy at a core level when the democratic consent of the governed is filtered through the consent of an unelected minority group. Hobbes recognized the problems of dual sovereignty over 350 years ago. Unless sovereignty was absolute, he argued, there would be no peace, for "what is it to divide the Power of a Common-wealth, but to dissolve it? for powers divided mutually destroy each other."[47]

Tocqueville on Religion, Secularism, and Democracy

One of the first people to systematically reflect on the relationship between democracy and religion was the nineteenth-century French aristocrat Alexis de Tocqueville. In the context of democratic theory, Tocqueville is usually remembered for his warnings about the problem of the "tyranny of the majority" and his observation about the "equality of conditions" in early America.[48] It is generally forgotten, however, that he also was deeply interested in the relationship between religion and democracy.

"On my arrival in the United States," Tocqueville observes in *Democracy in America*, "the religious aspect of the country was the first thing that struck my attention."[49] Tocqueville describes religion in the United States "as the first of their political institutions; for if it does not impart a taste for freedom, it facilitates the use of it."[50] He saw religion as a moderating force in the United States that existed in natural harmony with its democratic character. "The Americans combine the notions of Christianity and of liberty so intimately in their minds," he noted, "that it is impossible to make them conceive the one without the other."[51] His ruminations on this theme are not only explored in several chapters of *Democracy in America* but are peppered throughout this work. In his introduction he makes several perspicacious observations.

Tocqueville is tremendously prescient in observing, as early as 1831, that the tide of democracy is emerging as an unstoppable force in human history. "To

attempt to check democracy," he tells us, "would be . . . to resist the will of God."
For this reason, it must be studied "to discover lessons from which we may
profit." He adds: "the various occurrences of national existence have everywhere
turned to the advantage of democracy: all men have aided it by their exertions,
both those who have intentionally labored in its cause and those who have
served it unwittingly." *Democracy in America*, he says, "has been written under
the influence of a kind of religious awe produced in the author's mind by the
view of that irresistible [democratic] revolution which has advanced for centuries in spite of every obstacle and which is still advancing in the midst of the
ruins it has caused."[52]

The reference to the negative potential and consequences of democracy
speaks to the nuanced and dispassionate approach Tocqueville brings to his
investigation of this topic. He is not an ideologue of democracy but rather
realizes that untamed "democracy . . . has wild instincts, and it has grown up
like those children who have no parental guidance, who receive their education
in the public streets," and it can be "enfeebled by its own excesses."[53] The
balance, objectivity, and insight Tocqueville brings to the study of democracy
are on display in this passage:

> There will be less splendor than in an aristocracy, misery would also be
> less prevalent; comfort would be more general; the sciences might be
> less perfectly cultivated, but ignorance would be less common; the
> ardor of the feelings would be constrained, and the habits of the nation
> softened; there would be more vices and fewer crimes.[54]

With respect to the institutions of religion, Tocqueville sees them as
promoting both equality and upward social mobility. The "clergy opened their
ranks to all classes, to the poor and the rich, the commoner and the noble," he
tells us. "Through the church, equality penetrated into the government, and he
who as a serf must have vegetated in perpetual bondage took his place as a priest
in the midst of nobles, and not infrequently above the heads of kings."[55] Also in
his introduction, Tocqueville insightfully observes two paradoxes, which I call
the "paradox of religion and democracy" and the "paradox of advancing democratic change in religious societies."

The paradox of religion and democracy for Tocqueville revolves around the
following tension. Religion, in his view, supports a general equality of believers,
yet its adherents had been on the wrong side of the political barricades, supporting the conservative status quo, in recent democratic upheavals. Tocqueville
suggests that this can be corrected if religion is properly understood and interpreted. In his ruminations on the topic he comes very close to saying that there is
no fundamental antagonism between religion and democracy and the two can

and should be natural allies in the development of human civilization. "Christianity, which has declared all men equal in the sight of God," Tocqueville observes, "by a *strange coincidence of events*... has been for a time entangled with those institutions which democracy destroys; and it is not infrequently brought to reject the equality that it loves and curses freedom as an opponent would, whereas it *could* support freedom's struggle by taking it by the hand."[56]

The second paradox, relating to the dilemma of promoting democratic change in religious societies, is manifested, Tocqueville observes, in the tension between two groups of people: the virtuous nondemocrats and the morally dubious democrats. The first group is made up of "virtuous and peaceful individuals whose pure morality, quiet habits... and talents fit them to be leaders of their fellow men"; but it is problematic that while "their love of country is sincere.... civilization often finds them among its opponents; they confound its abuses with its benefits, and the idea of evil is inseparable in their minds from that of novelty." The second group (of morally dubious democrats) are people "whose object is to materialize mankind, to hit upon what is expedient without heeding what is just, to acquire knowledge without faith, and prosperity apart from virtue; claiming to be the champions of modern civilization." The core paradox with respect to democratization, therefore, is the following:

> The religionists are the enemies of liberty, and the friends of liberty
> attack religion; the high-minded and the noble advocate bondage, and
> the meanest and most servile preach independence; honest and
> enlightened citizens are opposed to all progress, while men without
> patriotism and without principle put themselves forward as the
> apostles of civilization and intelligence.[57]

Tocqueville, it should be recalled, was not writing for an American audience but rather for the educated classes in Europe, particularly in his native France, where the normative relationship between religion and politics was still unresolved; as he put it, "the organization and the establishment of democracy in Christendom is the great political problem of our times."[58] The core problem as he saw it was that in Europe the "spirit of religion and spirit of freedom [were almost always] marching in opposite directions. But in America ... they were intimately united and ... they reigned in common over the same country."[59] Tocqueville concludes his reflections on religion and democracy by stating that while the Americans have not completely "resolved this problem... they furnish useful data to those who undertake to resolve it."[60]

One of the confident claims that Tocqueville made about the peaceful coexistence of religion and democracy in the United States was the decidedly secular character of the American political system. Everyone he spoke with on this matter—in particular the clergy of the various Christian denominations—were in unanimous agreement in that "they all attributed the peaceful dominion of religion in their country mainly to the separation of church and state."[61] The anticlericalism of American politics and society was particularly intriguing to Tocqueville. He observed that he "learned with surprise that they [clerics] filled no public appointments; I did not see one of them in the administration, and they are not even represented in the legislative assemblies." When he investigated the topic further, he learned that most clergy "seemed to retire of their own accord from the exercise of power, and they made it the pride of their profession to abstain from politics." One consequence of the separation between church and state in America, Tocqueville insightfully observes, is "that the real authority of religion was increased by a state of things which diminished its apparent force."[62]

Revealingly, Tocqueville invokes the alleged absence of the separation of religion and politics in the case of Islam, in contrast to Christianity, to explain its democratic deficit.

> Mohammed professed to derive from Heaven, and has inserted in the Koran, not only religious doctrines, but political maxims, civil and criminal laws, and theories of science. The Gospel, on the contrary, speaks only of the general relations of men to God and to each other, beyond which it inculcates and imposes no point of faith. This alone, besides a thousand other reasons, would suffice to prove that the former of these religions will never long predominate in a cultivated and democratic age, while the latter is destined to retain its sway at these as at all other periods.[63]

In making these observations, Tocqueville was simply repeating the standard view of what is now a sacred and unexamined equation: no secularism equals no democracy. He reaches this conclusion despite his sympathetic treatment of the role religion can play in encouraging and sustaining democracy. Richard Rorty arrives at a similar conclusion about democracy's relationship with secularism, despite his far greater skepticism about the extent to which religion might contribute to democratic development.

Richard Rorty and the Jeffersonian Compromise

Richard Rorty (1931–2007) is one of the most influential and widely cited philosophers of the late twentieth and early twenty-first century. Born into an

American family of socialists, he relates in an autobiographical essay that "the most salient books on my parents' shelves were two red-bound volumes, *The Case of Leon Trotsky* and *Not Guilty* [the Dewey Commission report on Stalin's purges of the Communist Party]." Rorty thought of these books "in the way in which other children thought of their family's Bible: they were books that radiated redemptive truth and moral splendor."[64] As a result of these early influences, Rorty recalls that he "grew up knowing that all decent people were, if not Troskyites, at least socialists."[65] It might come as a surprise, therefore, that notwithstanding his Marxist upbringing, he came to view the United States as a prototypical democratic society. In this same essay he says:

> I see America pretty much as [Walt] Whitman and [John] Dewey did, as opening a prospect on illimitable democratic vistas. I think that our country—despite its past and present atrocities and vices, and despite its continuing eagerness to elect fools and knaves to high office—is a good example of the best kind of society so far invented.[66]

On the topic of religion, Rorty, in contrast with Tocqueville, is deeply skeptical about any religious contribution to democratic politics. In 2000, he told an overflow crowd at the University of Virginia that he was a "militant secularist" and that "the Enlightenment was right to suggest that religion is something that the human species would be better if it could outgrow."[67] It was Diderot, Rorty approvingly reminded his audience, who said that "the last king should be strangled with the entrails of the last priest."[68] In his numerous interviews, when Rorty is reminded of the religious underpinnings of American democracy and how our contemporary notions of justice, fairness, and equality are intimately tied to what Rousseau called "civil religion," he refuses to concede any ground to religion. References to the important contributions to democracy by distinguished religious figures such as Martin Luther King, Malcolm X and Mahatma Gandhi also fail to sway him. "Whether the possibility of rearing new Martin Luther Kings," he observed "is worth the risk of rearing new Jerry Falwells is a matter of risk management. To my mind, the advantage of getting rid of the Falwells is worth the risk of getting rid of the Kings.... I just suspect that the continued existence of churches is, by and large, more of a danger than a help to the rise of global democratic society."[69]

While Rorty did not write a full-length monograph on religion, he addressed the topic in several scattered essays and in various interviews.[70] In a short but widely referenced essay on the relationship between religion and democracy, written over a decade ago, Rorty referred to religion as a "conversation stopper." The occasion was a review of Stephen L. Carter's *Culture of Disbelief: How American Law and Politics Trivialize Religious Devotion*.[71] As the subtitle suggests,

Carter is critical of how the secular segments of American society have pushed religion to the sidelines. While accepting the need for a separation of church and state, he argues that religious faith should not be privatized but rather brought into the public sphere and accepted as a legitimate reference point on debates about public policy questions. Disagreeing with this proposition, Rorty responded:

> Carter puts in question what, to atheists like me, seems the happy, Jeffersonian compromise that the Enlightenment reached with the religious. This compromise consists in privatizing religion—keeping it out of what Carter calls "the public square," making it seem bad taste to bring religion into discussions of public policy. . . . We atheists, doing our best to enforce Jefferson's compromise, think it bad enough that we cannot run for public office without being disingenuous about our disbelief in God; despite the compromise, no uncloseted atheist is likely to get elected anywhere in the country. We also resent the suggestion that you have to be religious to have a conscience—a suggestion implicit in the fact that only *religious* conscientious objectors to military service go unpunished. Such facts suggest to us that the claims of religion need, if anything, to be pushed back still further, and that religious believers have no business asking for more public respect than they now receive.[72]

According to Rorty, the "Jeffersonian Compromise" is vital for the continued health, flourishing, and survival of a democratic society. Liberal democracy can only be sustained, he argues, if "religious believers remain willing to trade privatization for a guarantee of religious liberty."[73]

Rorty's point is a simple and often-heard one in contemporary debates among liberal philosophers. Not everyone in society shares the same religious convictions, and some, such as atheists, have no religious convictions at all. In short, religion tends to be "a conversation-stopper" when it is invoked as a moral reference point in public debate. Moreover, religion, like bowling, bird watching or badminton, is irrelevant to public affairs and should be relegated to the private sphere. According to Rorty, Thomas Jefferson "thought it enough to privatize religion, to view it as irrelevant to social order but relevant to, and possibly essential for, individual perfection."[74] To introduce private matters such as God or religion into the public conversation is to threaten the communication and deliberation that is vital to sustain a liberal democracy. Normatively, Rorty suggests that the "'restructuring . . . [of] arguments in secular terms' just means 'dropping reference to the source of the premises of the arguments,' and that this omission seems like a reasonable price to pay for religious liberty."[75]

In 2002, Rorty had the opportunity to revisit and update his views on the relationship between religion and democracy. The occasion was a symposium at the University of Richmond entitled "Religion and Democratic Culture: The Role of Faith in Public Discourse," and his interlocutor was Yale University Professor of Theological Philosophy Nicholas Wolsterstorff. Rorty began his remarks by recalling his review of Stephen Carter's *Culture of Disbelief.* He noted that on reflection he now realizes that his "response to Carter was hasty and insufficiently thoughtful." He then proceeded to offer a restatement of what he called "my anti-clerical views."[76]

Rorty began by drawing a distinction within the broad category of religion. From the perspective of democratic theory, there is a difference between "congregations of religious believers ministered by pastors" and "ecclesiastical organizations" that "offer authoritative guidance to believers." It is the latter groups that "are the target of secularists like myself," he affirmed. "Our anti-clericalism is aimed at Catholic bishops, the Mormon General Authorities, the televangelists, and all other religious professionals who devote themselves not to pastoral care but promulgating orthodoxy and acquiring economic and political clout. We think that it is mostly religion above the parish level that does the damage ... by deliberately creating ill-will toward people ... whose behavior they presume to call immoral."[77]

Proceeding with his strong indictment of ecclesiastical organizations, Rorty hoped that they would eventually disappear from society, noting that religion "will, in this secularist utopia, be pruned back to the parish level." Referencing the ideas of his most revered twentieth-century philosopher, he further qualified his views on religion. "We share Dewey's feeling that militant atheism is as unattractive as militant religious proselytizing, but we want to distinguish between atheism and anti-clericalism." Acknowledging that there is some social utility for religion, Rorty conceded that a rapid removal of religious institutions "would leave a gap in the lives of religious believers, for they will no longer have a sense of being part of a great and powerful worldly institution." He hoped this gap would gradually be filled "by an increased sense of participation in the advance of humanity—theists and atheists together ... toward the fulfillment of social ideals."[78] Elaborating on these ideas, Rorty wrote elsewhere:

> But there is a second sort of philosopher who describes himself or herself as an atheist. These are the ones who use "atheism" as a rough synonym for "anticlericalism." I now wish that I had used the latter term on the occasions when I have used the former to characterize my own view. For anticlericalism is a political view, not an epistemological

or metaphysical one. It is the view that ecclesiastical institutions, despite all the good they do—despite all the comfort they provide to those in need or in despair—are dangerous to the health of democratic societies.[79]

Rorty does not believe that there is something intrinsically wrong with religious language. He has little problem with it as long as it is privatized. "Religious belief," he noted, "according to the 'ethics of belief' that I share with William James, is not irrational, or intrinsically wrong-headed. But . . . putting political convictions in religious terms gives aid and comfort to ecclesiastical organizations, and thus to religious exclusivism." It was precisely because of his strong criticism of religious institutions that Rorty said: "I see liberal Protestant-ism as the form of Christian religious life most congenial to liberal democracy."

> Protestantism has often, and rightly, been thought to be more congenial to liberal democracy than Catholicism. This is because the idea of "the priesthood of all believers" encourages the believer to interpret Scripture, theology and devotional literature on his own, rather than simply waiting to be informed by church officials about what is required to be a member in good standing of a given denomination. The latter attitude does seem to be the sort of thing democratic societies have a right to discourage.[80]

Rorty has also updated his claim that religion is a "conversation stopper." Crediting Jeffrey Stout with forcing him to reconsider his views, he noted that it is only "one variety of expression of religious belief [that] does indeed stop the conversation, as when somebody says, 'Don't ask me for reasons. I don't have any. It is a matter of faith.'" Rorty notes that secularists can fall into the same conversation-stopping trap as well. "I would not consider myself to be seriously discussing politics with my fellow citizens if I simply quoted passages from Mill at them, as opposed to using those passages to help me articulate my views." Recasting his views on the role of religion in the public sphere, Rorty now maintains that "instead of saying that religion was a conversation-stopper, I should have simply said that citizens of a democracy should try to put off invoking conversations-stoppers as long as possible. We should do our best to keep the conversation going without citing unarguable first principles, either philosophical or religious."[81]

Taken together, both Tocqueville and Rorty, while representing contrast-ing views on the role of religion in democratic life, converge on the need for secularism—albeit secularisms of different qualities—as a prerequisite for democ-racy.[82] This suggests room for variance between Tocqueville's religious-friendly perspective and Rorty's religious skepticism. But how far can the boundaries between religion and democracy be stretched before democracy is broken and fundamentally compromised? Neither Tocqueville nor Rorty address this critical question in their writings. One scholar who does speak directly to this topic is Alfred Stepan. An examination of this recent theoretical contributions on religion, secularism, and democracy—which will considerably illuminate this conversation—is the focus of the next subsection.

Stepan's Model: Crafting the "Twin Tolerations"

In *Arguing Comparative Politics*, Stepan writes a short but profoundly insightful chapter on the relationship between religion and democracy.[83] His methodological approach is rooted in comparative politics and political theory, with an emphasis on the role of political institutions and democratization.

Stepan begins his theorizing by introducing the term "twin tolerations," which he defines as "the minimal boundaries of freedom of action that must somehow be crafted for political institutions *vis-à-vis* religious authorities, and for religious individuals and groups *vis-à-vis* political institutions."[84] He then proceeds to ask three important questions:

1. What are the minimal core institutional and political requirements for democracy? Building on this analysis, what can be inferred about the "twin tolerations"?

2. How have a set of long-standing democracies (the fifteen European Union countries) actually met these minimal boundary requirements and what "maps of misreading" can be extracted from this experience?

3. On the basis of the answers to the foregoing questions, what lessons can be learned and applied to other religious systems, in particular the ones Huntington has identified as having a civilizational problem with democracy (i.e. Islam, Confucianism, and Eastern Orthodox Christianity)?[85]

Democracy and Its Core Institutions

There is a general consensus among democratic theorists that Robert Dahl's eight conditions of polyarchy are core requirements for democracy. These institutional requirements, which support the basic freedoms needed to have an electoral democracy, are (1) freedom to form and join organizations; (2) freedom of expression; (3) the right to vote; (4) the eligibility of all citizens for public office; (5) the right of political leaders to compete for support and votes; (6) availability of alternative sources of information; (7) free and fair elections; and (8) the existence of institutions for making government policies depend on votes and other expressions of preference.[86]

While these institutional guarantees are necessary, they are insufficient for the consolidation of liberal democracy. What Dahl fails to consider, observes Stepan, is what happens *after* the election. Basic liberties and minority rights must be protected in a democratic constitution. Furthermore, democratically elected governments must rule within the framework of the law and the constitution and be bound by a set of vertical and horizontal institutions that help ensure accountability.[87]

It is important to remember that democracy is a system of conflict regulation that allows peaceful competition over values, goals, and policies. As long as individuals and groups agree to work within the framework of the law and respect the rights of other citizens, *all* groups should be granted the opportunity to advance their interests. According to Stepan, all citizens have the right to have a say in public policy-making that will affect their lives: "this is the minimal institutional statement of what democratic politics entails and does not entail. No more, no less."[88] But what does this statement imply about religion and democracy and what are the necessary boundaries that preserve elected governments' freedom from the domination of religious groups and religious groups' freedom from the domination of government?

Stepan answers that religious institutions should not have a constitutionally guaranteed privilege to dictate, limit, or veto decisions made by democratically elected governments. Likewise, religious groups should have complete autonomy to worship privately *and* advance their private interests in the public sphere and to sponsor organizations and movements, as long they do so nonviolently and without violating the liberties of others. No religious group can a priori be excluded from participation in politics. It is only *after* a violation has occurred, Stepan affirms, that constraints can be placed on religious groups and organizations, and this is to be decided solely by the courts. Casting his theoretical net quite broadly, Stepan asserts: "In light of this broad framework of minimal freedom for the democratic state and the minimal freedom of citizens, it would appear, from a purely theoretical perspective, that there can be an extraordinarily broad range of concrete patterns of religion-state relations in political systems that would meet our minimal definition of [liberal] democracy."[89]

Western Europe and the Twin Tolerations: Maps of Misreading?

Turning to the case of Europe, Alfred Stepan poses the important question—
what has been the pattern of religion-state relations in Europe and how have
the "twin tolerations" been socially constructed?

According to Stepan. many prominent social scientists, particularly when
discussing the prospects for democracy in non-Western societies, *ahistorically*
assume that a rigid form of church-state separation is not only a core aspect of
Western civilization but of democracy as well. For such analysts, a religious
system like Eastern Orthodox Christianity—where there is an established
church—poses serious problems for democratic transition and consolidation.
Likewise, when Islamic parties emerge victorious in democratic elections,
there is widespread sympathy when the military intervenes to thwart democratization in the name of protecting secular, Western-style democracy, as
happened in Algeria in 1992 and Turkey in 1996. Stepan poses the question
"Are these correct readings, or dangerous misreadings, of the lessons of the
relationship of church and state in Western democracy?"[90]

To answer this question, Stepan conducts the following experiment. He
sets out to test empirically the extent to which an actual separation of church
and state exists in the fifteen European Union (EU) member countries, against
the backdrop of Robert Dahl's eight institutional guarantees of polyarchy, plus
his stipulations about human rights protection, civil liberties, and constitutionalism. What Stepan discovers is that as of 1990, five of the fifteen members of
the European Union—Denmark, Finland, Greece, Sweden, the United Kingdom (as well as Norway, not a member of the EU)—had established churches.

Furthermore, *every* long-standing western European democracy with a
strong Lutheran majority—Sweden, Denmark, Iceland, Finland, and Norway—had an established church. Stepan draws our attention to the following
articles from the Norwegian constitution:

[Article 2] The Evangelical Lutheran religion shall remain the official
religion of the state. The inhabitants professing it are bound to
bring up their children in the same.

[Article 4] The King shall at all times profess the Evangelical Lutheran
religion and uphold and protect the same.

[Article 12] Half the members of the King's Council shall profess the
official religion.

[Article 21] The King after consultation with his Council appoints senior ecclesiastical officials.[91]

Similarly, succession to the British throne continues to carry very strict religious guidelines. According to the official website of the British Monarchy,

> The succession to the throne is regulated, not only through descent, but also by statute; the Act of Settlement confirmed that it was for Parliament to determine the title to the throne. The Act laid down that only Protestant descendants of Princess Sophia—the Electress of Hanover and granddaughter of James I—are eligible to succeed. Subsequent Acts have confirmed this. Parliament, under the Bill of Rights and the Act of Settlement, also laid down various conditions which the Sovereign must meet. *A Roman Catholic is specifically excluded from succession to the throne; nor may the Sovereign marry a Roman Catholic.* The Sovereign must, in addition, be in communion with the Church of England and must swear to preserve the established Church of England and the established Church of Scotland. The Sovereign must also promise to uphold the Protestant succession.[92]

In a similar vein, article 3 of the Greek Constitution (1975) declares the "prevailing religion in Greece is that of the Eastern Orthodox Church of Christ," and article 14 (paragraph 3a) states that "insult to the Christian and all other known religions" can be a cause for the seizure of published material. Similarly, article 16 of the Constitution of Spain reads: "the public powers shall take into account the religious beliefs of Spanish society and maintain the appropriate relations of cooperation with the Catholic Church and other denominations."[93]

This is a mere sampling of a general European pattern. In the Netherlands, Austria, and Germany extensive state support exists for private religious education. Similarly, Christian-Democratic parties have frequently ruled in Germany, Austria, Italy, Belgium, and the Netherlands. The only EU member whose constitution explicitly prohibits political parties from using religious symbols is, surprisingly, Portugal.[94]

Recent empirical research by Jonathan Fox supports Stepan's nuanced reading of religion-state relations. Drawing on the Religion and State Database, Fox has exhaustively investigated, empirically, the extent of religion and state separation in all 152 countries with a population of one million or more. His focus is on the behavior of national governments, not regional or local governments and not general societal practices. He compared data for the years 1990 and 2002 to assess whether separation of religion and state (SRAS) and government involvement in religion (GIR) had changed during this time period and if so in what direction. His analysis of the data challenges common assumptions on the topic and complements what Stepan calls the common "maps of misreading" that inform popular and scholarly discussion of church-state relations.

Fox's primary conclusion is that "more than a century since the founders of social sciences began to predict the demise of religion in modern times, SRAS is the exception and GIR is the norm for most of the world. Using the strictest interpretation of SRAS—no support for religion and no restrictions on religious practices—only one country, the United States, has no GIR. Furthermore, even using a looser interpretation of scoring . . . less than 22% of states have even marginal SRAS."[95]

In a follow-up study, Fox investigates a simple yet important question: do democracies have separation of religion and state (SRAS)? Again, drawing on the Religion and State Database, which includes sixty-two variables in six broad categories measuring different aspects of the separation of religion and state for all 152 countries with a population of one million or more and data from the Polity and Freedom House datasets, Fox's conclusions compliment and reinforce Stepan's argument. Specifically, Fox demonstrates that "most democracies do not have SRAS. This is true whether democracy is measured through its procedures via the Polity dataset or whether it is measured with the civil and political rights measures of the Freedom House dataset. It is also true for Western democracies. These empirical results strongly indicate that SRAS, no matter which operationalization of the concept one uses, is not necessary for a functioning democracy or liberal democracy."[96]

A critical distinction Fox makes in his analysis that is vital for the debate on religion and democracy is the existence of an upper threshold for government involvement in religion that democracies respect. "The major difference between democracies and non-democracies is not the presence of SRAS but rather an upper limit on GIR."[97] This upper limit coincides with one side of what Stepan has defined as the twin tolerations.

Fox's analysis of the empirical data lends strong support to the theoretical claims advanced by Stepan, who consolidates his argument by noting that

> virtually no Western European democracy now has a rigid or hostile separation of church and state. Indeed, most have arrived at a democratically negotiated freedom of religion from state interference and all of them allow religious groups freedom, not only of private worship, but to organize groups in civil society. . . . The "lesson" from

Western Europe, therefore, lies *not* in church-state separation but in the constant political construction and reconstruction of the "twin tolerations." Indeed, it is only in the context of the "twin tolerations" that the concept of "separation of church and state" has a place in the modern vocabulary of West European democracy.[98]

A similar caveat applies to the concept of secularism. "Discursive traditions," Stepan observes, "as dissimilar as the Enlightenment, liberalism, French republicanism, and modernization theory argued, or assumed, that modernity and democracy required secularism. But from the viewpoint of empirical democratic practice, the concept of secularism must be radically rethought."[99]

Stepan's two key analytical points that are relevant to clarifying the precise relationship between secularism and liberal democracy are the following.

(1) "If we are looking at the defining characteristics of democracy *vis-à-vis* religion, 'secularism' and the 'separation of church and state' are not an intrinsic part of the core definition, but what we have said about the 'twin tolerations' is."[100]

(2) "The 'lesson' from Western Europe, therefore, lies *not* in church-state separation but in the constant political construction and reconstruction of the 'twin tolerations.' Indeed, it is only in the context of the 'twin tolerations' that the concept of 'separation of church and state' has a place in the modern vocabulary of West European democracy."[101]

A Comment on the Stepan Thesis: Secularism by Stealth?

Stepan's claim is a bold one. His argument that the "separation of church and state" is not "intrinsic" to the normative relationship between religion and democracy but what he has said about the "'twin tolerations' is," strikes the reader, at first glance, as extremely controversial. It might look like a violation of conventional wisdom, arrived at after centuries of conflict and evolution and embodied in the sacred formula "No secularism equals no democracy." But does democracy in fact demand secularism?

In examining Stepan's unconventional approach to this question, it helps to recall his definition of the "twin tolerations." The "twin tolerations" are "the minimal boundaries of freedom of action that must somehow be crafted for political institutions *vis-à-vis* religious authorities, and for religious individuals and groups *vis-à-vis* political institutions." Are these "boundaries" that Stepan insists "*must* somehow be crafted (emphasis added)" between the "political institutions [of the state]" and "religious . . . groups [in society]" not simply another way of calling for a separation of church and state, albeit by another name?

After all, what is a "boundary" if not a form of separation? What Stepan has ingeniously done is recast the debate on the relationship between religion and liberal democracy by effectively saying that yes, liberal democracy does demand secularism, but I will simply give it a different name, the "twin tolerations" instead of calling it secularism. However, before dismissing Stepan's thesis as merely a game of semantics, closer examination will show that he does succeed in deepening our grasp of the emotionally charged relationship between religion and democracy.

Stepan's definition of the "twin tolerations" refers to "the *minimum* boundaries of freedom of action" that both religious organizations and the state must mutually recognize and respect in order to sustain a liberal democracy. The emphasis should be on the word "minimum." What Stepan is revealing is that he is subscribing to a weak version of the secularization thesis (as defined earlier by Bhikhu Parekh) that merely separates *state from religion* rather than demanding a more robust separation of *politics from religion*, which is embodied in the stronger version of secularism. In other words, Stepan is effectively siding with Tocqueville over Rorty—endorsing the Anglo-American variant of secularism over the French one.

There are several benefits in drawing upon Stepan's approach in order to clarify the theoretical relationship between religion, secularism, and liberal democracy. First, his thesis is theoretically very precise, in part because his definitions are plain and unambiguous. He begins with a clear description of liberal democracy that draws on Dahl's idea of polyarchy, with added stipulations about civil rights protection and constitutionalism. He calls his definition a "core institutional 'threshold' approach to democracy" that affirms the obvious: that no societal group should be denied the right to participate in public affairs as long as it does so within the framework of the law and without violating the rights of others. This, he asserts, is the "minimal institutional statement of what democratic politics entails and does not entail. No more, no less."[102]

Building on this preamble, Stepan then focuses his analytical lens on the crux of the tension between religion and democracy. The root of the problem is trying to ascertain the "necessary boundaries of freedom for elected governments from religious groups, and for religious individuals and groups from government."[103] Stepan locates these boundaries between church and state in the following area:

> The key area of autonomy that must be established for democratic institutions is that the institutions that emanate from democratic procedures should be able, within the bounds of the constitution and human rights, to generate policies. Religious institutions should not

have constitutionally privileged prerogatives which allow them authoritatively to mandate public policy to democratically elected governments.[104]

Stepan's "twin toleration" approach, outlining the necessary boundaries of freedom for religious groups from government and for elected governments from religious groups, allows for "an extraordinarily broad range of concrete patterns of religion-state relations."[105] This is the second advantage of Stepan's thesis: its versatility, especially with respect to the role of religious groups in a liberal democracy. It allows them full participation in public affairs while clearly spelling out the theoretical limits of their political reach. This approach is particularly useful for democratic theorists when discussing emerging democracies in the non-Western world, where religious groups are often politically active and part of the mainstream of public debate.

Finally, Stepan's thesis is helpful because of the terminology he employs, or more precisely, does not employ. By using the term "twin tolerations" instead of "secularism," he provides prodemocrats with a useful rhetorical device they can use to advance democracy while simultaneously shielding themselves from the charge of promoting alien ideas. This has special value in societies that are sensitive to the perceived threat of cultural imperialism, where terms such as "secular," "secularity" and "secularization" have weak cultural roots and are often used pejoratively to criticize political opponents whose ideas allegedly lack cultural authenticity.

In short, Stepan's thesis on religion and democracy is perfectly suited for understanding the obstacles to and the path toward liberal democracy in Muslim societies. Having surveyed some of the relevant historical and theoretical background on secularism and its relationship to liberal democracy, the next chapter explores the unique history, background and political challenges facing secularism in the Muslim world today.

Conclusion

This chapter began with an attempt to define the concept of secularism. To reach this end the etymological and historical roots of secularism were investigated. It was discovered that at a bare minimum, political secularism implies a firm yet undetermined form of separation between the realm of religion and the realm of government. While secularism does have European roots, this does not imply monism. There is more than one history of political secularism, and different models of it have emerged over time, principally a weak version, which merely demands a separation of religion from the state, and a stronger version that insists on a more robust separation of religion from politics. These two distinct but related versions of political secularism were called "Anglo-American Secularism" and "French Republican Secularism." It was also argued that both models of secularism are a by-product of the unique history of the church-state relations and nation building experiences of these countries which emerged after a long period of experimentation, often accompanied with violence, conflict and acrimonious debate.

Subsequently, the relationship between secularism and liberal democracy was explored. Contrasting perspectives from two prominent political philosophers, Alexis de Tocqueville and Richard Rorty, were examined. While both men have written insightfully and influentially on the topic—and agree that liberal democracy requires secularism—a deeper analysis of the precise relationship and tension between secularism, religion and liberal democracy was sought in the writings of Alfred Stepan. His novel and groundbreaking theoretical contribution argued that while liberal democracy necessitates a form of secularism, the boundaries between religion and state are much more flexible and fluid than is generally appreciated. He suggested that clarity could be gained by shifting attention away from the ambiguous and emotionally charged concept of secularism and replacing it with the term "twin tolerations." The benefit of Stepan's thesis is that it argues that there is more than one model of secularism that liberal democracy can accommodate. His theory has special relevance for emerging liberal democracies where religious groups are part of the mainstream of public debate and the question of religion's role in the polis is a matter of ongoing debate and controversy.

Equally important is Stepan's point on the lessons to be learned from European history. He reminds us that European societies were not born with a secular proclivity embedded in their political cultures but rather a church-state separation needed to be democratically negotiated and socially constructed around an emerging consensus over a long period of time. The "'lesson' [for the development of liberal democracy] from Western Europe," Stepan observed, "lies *not* in church-state separation but in the constant political construction and reconstruction" of the boundaries between religion and state. The versatility, nuance and theoretical depth of Stepan's theory on religion and democracy, it was argued, have particular applicability to contemporary debates on Islam, secularism and democracy in Muslim societies where these issues are currently being debated and contested.

4

Secularism and Its Discontents in Muslim Societies

Indigenizing the Separation between Religion and State

Those who thought that religion could be separate from politics understand neither religion, nor politics.

—Mahatma Gandhi

The main claim of this chapter is that the development of an indigenous theory of Islamic secularism will significantly increase the prospects for liberal democracy in Muslim societies. Building on the arguments of the previous chapter where the theoretical relationship between religion, secularism, and liberal democracy were examined, in this chapter the crisis of secularism in Muslim societies will be the focus.

A broad set of arguments will be mapped out explaining why Muslims have compelling reasons to be skeptical toward secularism. Rejecting an Orientalist interpretation that locates the problem of secularism in the inner doctrines of Islam and the early religious history of the Muslims in Arabia, I argue that the modern period of Muslim history is a more appropriate place to investigate this topic. Specifically, the crisis of secularism in the Muslim world today is deeply connected to the failure of modernization programs and policies. In contrast with the West, where modernization is broadly associated with democracy, human rights, and pluralism—in short, social justice—in Muslim societies, with a few exceptions, modernization has been synonymous with dictatorship, repression, and corruption—in short, social injustice. All of this is intimately connected to the colonial and post-colonial encounter between Muslim societies and the West, especially the role of the state in being the primary vehicle where secular ideas, policies, and practices were promulgated. In light of this negative legacy associated with secularism, a seemingly irreconcilable paradox confronts Muslim democrats: on the one hand, liberal democracy necessitates a form of secularism to sustain itself, yet simultaneously secularism suffers from ill repute. Where can one turn for answers and solutions to this dilemma? How can this paradox be reconciled? Answering these questions will be the focus of the latter half this chapter. I argue that a solution to the crisis of secularism in Muslim societies can be located in two separate areas: (1) understanding the different historical experiences between Europe and the Islamic world in terms of the relationship between a religious reformulation and political secularization, and (2) learning the lessons from recent political gains for democracy in Turkey and Indonesia.

Approximately ten years ago, Abdou Filali-Ansary made the prescient observation that in contrast to Europe, where a religious reformation preceded and then led to secularization, in Muslim societies this sequence has been reversed. I will argue that this fact contributes significantly to explaining the weak intellectual roots of secularism in Muslim societies. State-led modernization from above has not been matched by a concomitant transformation of Muslim political culture from below, especially in crafting a normative relationship between religion and government that is capable of supporting liberal democracy (i.e. at a minimum a soft form of political secularism). In exploring this point I will draw on the work of the eminent world historian and scholar of Islam Marshall Hodgson. He has suggested that the modernization of Muslim societies, in contrast to that of Europe, has been marked by a radical social and intellectual rupture with its past that has had profound consequences for the political development of the Muslim world during the twentieth century.

Next, I will briefly explore recent gains for democracy in two Muslim countries, Indonesia and Turkey. I argue that these gains are directly attributable to the emergence of an indigenous theory of Muslim secularism. Muslim intellectuals and political parties from Indonesia and Turkey, with strong connections to civil society, have managed to reconcile their political theologies with the concept of a separation of religion and state. An important reformation of Islamic political thought has occurred that is profoundly significant for the democratization of Muslim societies. This development has arguably sunk deep roots in the political culture of these countries, allowing Muslim political parties to play a leading role, not unlike Christian democratic parties in Europe, in the development and promotion of liberal democracy. I will suggest that the construction of an indigenous understanding or theory of Muslim secularism carries the added benefit of bringing new recruits into the democracy camp from previously marginalized segments of society. This development bodes well for the long-term prospects of democratic consolidation in Turkey and Indonesia.

This chapter builds on my earlier argument that because religion is a key marker of identity in Muslim societies, reconciliation between Islamic political thought and secularism is a necessary precondition for the consolidation of liberal democracy in these societies. Such reconciliation holds the prospect for a transformation of Muslim political culture, allowing religious groups to play a constructive role in the development of democracy and the protection of human rights.

Secularism and Its Discontents in the Muslim World

Translating the term "secularism" is the first problem. There is no word in classical Arabic, Farsi, or Turkish that is exactly synonymous with "secular," "secularity," or "secularism." Seyyed Hossein Nasr has written that "there is the word *'urfi* which refers essentially to law, *dunyawi*, which means this-worldly in contrast to other-worldly, and *zamani* which means temporal as opposed to eternal, but none of these has exactly the same meaning as secular."[1]

An early illusion to the term was drawn from the Koranic word, *dahr*, whose semantic evolution came to refer to atheists.[2] This term was associated with Jamal Eddin Al-Afghani, a prominent late-nineteenth-century Muslim political activist who engaged in a debate on religion and science with the French philosopher Ernest Renan. Afghani wrote a famous treatise, originally in Persian in 1881, that became known in Arabic as *Ar-rad 'ala ad-Dahriyin* (Refutation of the materialists).[3] The immediate context was Afghani's stay in India and his criticism of the modernization efforts of pro-British Muslims affiliated with Sir Seyyed Ahmad Khan (1817–1898).[4] The first Arabic translation of this book came from the pen of his famous disciple Muhammad Abduh in 1885, under the title *Risala fi ibtal madhhab al-dahriyyin wa-bayan mafasidihim wa-ithbat anna 'l-din asas al-madaniyya wa 'l-kufr fasad al-'umran* (An Epistle on the Refutation of Materialist Thought and Demonstrating Its Falsehoods and on Proving that Religion Is the Anchor of Civility and Its Absence Is the Reason for the Corruption of Civilization). A later French translation appeared in 1942 simply entitled *Réfutation des matérialistes*.[5]

Afghani has been described as "a man whose life touched and deeply affected the whole Islamic world in the latter quarter of the nineteenth century."[6] While he did not invoke the term "secularism" in his writings, nor was his immediate concern the relationship between religion and state, Abdou Filali-Ansary has suggested that given the stature of Afghani as one of the founding fathers of modern Islamic political thought, his attack on materialism was later equated with an attack on secularism, so that the concept slowly became a bête noir of Muslim political activists during the late twentieth century. Arguably, this was because some of the arguments of the materialists in the nineteenth century (whom Afghani was critiquing), and proponents of secularism in the twentieth century, especially their critique of religion, were similar. Khaled Abou El Fadl suggests that a more accurate Arabic translation of the title Afghani's famous treatise, observed through the lens of twentieth-century Muslim politics, would be *A Treatise on the Refutation of Secular Materialism: Demonstrating the Critical Importance of Religion to Civil Societies, and Proving That Its Absence [Kufr] Leads to the Corruption of Civilized Societies.*[7]

In short, choices in terminology bequeathed a legacy. When influential early modernist Muslim thinkers equated "nineteenth-century positivists with seventh-century opponents of the Prophet [Muhammad]," this effectively meant that from the beginning "secularism was seen as being intimately related to, if not the same thing as, atheism." The result, according to Filali-Ansary, was a "large and enduring misunderstanding" of the topic of secularism in general in Muslim politics that lasts until today.[8]

The misunderstanding increased in subsequent decades when other Muslims, looking for a proper translation of the word "secularism," chose *ladini*, which translates as "nonreligious" or "irreligious."[9] A subsequent neologism was *ilmaniyyah* (from *ilm*, science) or *almaniyyah* (this-worldly) and came in response to the French word *laïcisme*, which first appeared in the Muslim world at the end of the nineteenth century in the dictionary of a Christian Lebanese scholar.[10] Thus, a binary opposition between Islam and secularism was created from the outset in the Muslim world that eventually left an imprint in the collective consciousness of Muslims. Filali-Ansary captures this legacy with the following summary:

> The feeling that has prevailed since then among Muslims is that there is a strict and irreducible opposition between two systems—Islam and non-Islam. To be a secularist has meant to abandon Islam, to reject altogether not only the religious faith but also its attendant morality and the traditions and rules that operate within Muslim societies. It therefore has been understood as a total alienation from the constituent elements of the Islamic personality and as a complete surrender to unbelief, immorality, and self-hatred, leading to a disavowal of the historic identity and civilization inherited from illustrious ancestors. It is worth noting that the vast majority of Muslims in the nineteenth century, even those who were part of the educated elite, lived in total ignorance both of the debates going on in

Europe about religion and its role in the social order and of the historical changes reshaping European societies. They were not aware of the distinction between atheism and secularism. The consequences of this misunderstanding still profoundly shape the attitudes of Muslims today.[11]

The problems with secularism in Muslim societies, however, are far greater than a matter of etymology and translation. They are rooted in the actual lived experiences of Muslim communities over the past two hundred years. The most politically salient part of this lived experience—what William Shepard has called "*the* dominating fact of life for the Islamic world"—has been "Western imperialism in its various dimensions, military, political, economic and cultural."[12] The 2003 American-Anglo invasion and occupation of Iraq is the just the latest chapter in a long series of interventions that has drastically shaped the political and moral context in which debates on modernization and secularism have taken place.[13] As Muhammad Khalid Masud has noted in a recent scholarly contribution to this topic, "Muslim thinkers found it very difficult to understand new ideas like secularism in isolation from Christian (Western colonial) supremacy."[14]

As we begin our investigation into the topic of secularism and its discontents in Muslim societies it should be recalled that in the West, the now harmonious accommodation between religion, secularism and liberal democracy was arrived at via an indigenous process of social transformation that took several centuries to work itself out.[15] Sometimes this process was bloody, often times it was violent. The important point to stress is that this process of negotiation and bargaining over the normative relationship between religion and state was organic to Europe and North America. It was not imported from the outside or imposed by force from above but rather it emerged organically from the bottom up. Any remaining tension between religion and government has now been institutionalized and a broad consensus exists on the basic framework of the debate and how conflict should be resolved. In Muslim societies, by contrast, the political manifestation of secularism was imposed from the outside via Western hegemony in the form of colonialism and imperialism and kept alive by local elites who lived their lives alienated from the religious sentiment of the masses. According to Vali Nasr, the role of the state was central to this development:

> In the Muslim Middle East and Asia, secularism was not a product of
> socio-economic, technological, or cultural change—it was not
> associated with any internal social dynamic. In fact, it was not even an
> indigenous force. Secularism was first and foremost a project of the

state—first the colonial state, and later the postcolonial state. It was a Western import, meant to support the state's aim of long-run development. As a result, from the outset a religious-secular divide came to reflect the increasingly contentious relations between the society and the colonial state.[16]

While a comprehensive history of secularism and its discontents in the Muslim world remains to be written, the case of Iran during the twentieth century perfectly illustrates Nasr's point. Similar developments have taken place across the Muslim world, with some variation, but the collective result and the lessons learned have been the same: the concept of secularism, as perceived by most Muslims, has been discredited and its image severely tarnished.

The Postcolonial State and the Demise of Secularism:
Lessons from Iran

While Iran was never formally colonized, it has been referred to in the scholarly literature as a "semicolony."[17] The description is a fitting one considering the long history of foreign intervention and periodic military occupations of Iran, particularly during the first half of the twentieth century. According to Nikki Keddie and Mehrdad Amanat, "to discuss Iranian politics as distinct from Iran's foreign relations is to imply an artificial separation between them. It must be borne in mind that the internal politics [of Iran]...were to a considerable degree controlled not only from behind the scenes...but even from beyond Iran's borders."[18]

The emergence of the modern state of Iran begins with the founding of the Pahlavi monarchy in 1925. Reza Khan (1878–1944), a commander of the imperial guard and Minister of War, consolidated power amid the chaos of tribal insurrections, Soviet and British penetration, economic decay and the corrupt rule of the decrepit Qajar dynasty.[19] Proclaiming himself the new king of Iran, he ruled autocratically while launching a massive modernization and secularization program that was comparable, though not identical to, that of Mustafa Kemal Atatürk in neighboring Turkey. The infrastructure of a centralized and modern state, with new roads, railways, a modern education system, a bureaucracy, a banking system, and a conscripted army began to take shape.[20] The transformative effect of these policies was felt throughout Iranian society, but especially by the clergy, whose powers and privileges were significantly curtailed in the area of law and education. Commenting on the diminution of the role of religion in public affairs, Karen Armstrong writes that "Shah

Reza Pahlavi would...not only equal but even surpass Atatürk's ruthless secularization."[21] Gavin Hambly disagrees and notes that in "his dealings with the ulama, Riza Shah, contrary to what is often asserted, was quite circumspect, and there is no evidence that he ever considered launching an assault upon Islam such as Atatürk mounted in Turkey. He preferred to ignore rather than confront the ulama [clergy]."[22] The truth lies somewhere in between. Pahlavi was forced to abdicate in 1941 by the Allied Powers because of his pro-German sympathies. He was replaced by his twenty-one-year-old son, Mohammad Reza Pahlavi (1919–1980), who continued his father's modernizing and secularizing policies, gradually at first but with more intensity and determination as he consolidated power. The key developments, however, that significantly affected the perception of secularism in Iran were to unfold after the 1953 coup d'état that restored Mohammad Reza to the throne after he fled the country following a period of democratization led by the charismatic liberal-democratic prime minister Mohammad Mossadeq. At the time, the nationalization of the British-controlled Iranian oil industry, coupled with fears of a communist takeover, led to a joint CIA-MI6 coup that restored the young Pahlavi king to power and returned Iran to the orbit of pro-Western allies in the Middle East.[23]

The ruling ideology of the new Pahlavi order was not as dogmatically secular and overtly hostile toward religion as the Kemalist project in Turkey. Rather, the ideological orientation of the regime was based on a unique form of monarchical nationalism that viewed the nation as inseparable from the Pahlavi monarchy and the kingdoms that had preceded it. In the official pronouncements of the state, Iran's Islamic identity was downplayed and its pre-Islamic identity elevated, specifically in terms of a glorification of ancient Persian empires, kings, and dynasties.[24]

The new regime that emerged in the aftermath of the 1953 coup resembled other postcolonial regimes in the Muslim world in its political authoritarianism, commitment to modernization, and secular developmental goals. According to one Iran scholar, "as a generalization, it can be said that the phrase, 'L'état, c'est moi', accurately describes how the country [of Iran] was managed during this period."[25] All independent political forces, from the communist left to the religious right, were crushed, and a powerful centralized state quickly established its hegemony over society.

The pattern of state-society relations that unfolded in Iran in the ensuing decades was reproduced in other Muslim societies in the post-World War II era: an autocratic modernizing state, often with critical external support, suffocated secular civil society, thus forcing oppositional activity into the mosque, inadvertently contributing to the rise of political Islam.[26] A set of top-down, forced modernization, secularization and Westernization policies by the state—within a short span of time—generated widespread social and psychological alienation and dislocation. Rapid urbanization and changing cultural and socioeconomic relationships coupled with increasing corruption, economic mismanagement, rising poverty, and income inequality undermined the legitimacy of the state. These developments reflected badly on secularism, since the ruling ideology of many postcolonial regimes in the Muslim world, Iran included, was openly secular-nationalist.[27]

Despotism, dictatorship, and human rights abuses, for a generation of Muslims growing up in the postcolonial era, thus came to be associated with secularism. Muslim political activists who experienced oppression at the hands of secular national governments logically concluded that secularism was an ideology of repression.[28] This observation applies not only to Iran but also to Tunisia, Algeria, Egypt, Syria, Iraq, Yemen, Turkey, and many other Muslim majority countries in the latter half of the twentieth century. This point seems to be underappreciated by some scholars who write on the topic of Middle East and Islamic politics. John Waterbury, for example, has demonstrated sympathy for the polices of the Mubarak regime in dealing with its domestic opposition. In a widely cited essay on the prospects for political liberalization in the Middle East, he asserted: "it is not at all self-evident that repression will fail. Here too Mubarak has been exemplary."[29] His overall discussion of democracy in the Middle East suffers from a secular and modernization theory bias such that he mistakenly assumes that the question of religion's normative relationship with government has been democratically negotiated in Egypt and thus any public manifestation of religious identity in the public sphere is an abnormality and a threat to political development. In short, the Islamists are the problem, and the secularists are their potential victims, who face "immense risks." The point that seems lost on Waterbury is that the secularists within Muslim societies are often allied with the repressive apparatus of the authoritarian state, thus delegitimizing them (and the perception of secularism) in the eyes of the rest of the population.

Nilüfer Göle develops this point further in the context of Turkey. She observes that contrary to the Western experience with secularism, in the Middle East, secularism "is not neutral and power-free."[30] The authoritarianism of the colonial and postcolonial state, along with its secularizing policies, has made it an active and biased participant in the modern political history of Muslim societies. It has accumulated a track record, a list of failed policies and also a list of victims. Far from being neutral and democratic, the secular postcolonial state in Muslim societies and the elites that support it have generally bolstered authoritarianism rather than political liberty. "This fact explains why, contrary to common belief, the westernized elites in the Middle

East are very often not the most democratic," Göle observes.[31] In contrast to the West, therefore, where secularism has historically been a force for political and religious pluralism, in Muslim societies, secularism's legacy has been almost the exact opposite. Armstrong succinctly captures this key interpretive point when she writes that in "the West, secularization has been experienced as liberating; it had even, in its early stages, been regarded as a new and better way of being religious." But in Muslims societies, "secularization was experienced as a violent and coercive assault. When later fundamentalists claimed that secularization meant the destruction of Islam, they would often point to the example of Atatürk."[32]

The concept of secularism, therefore, has become highly politicized in Muslim societies due to the modern encounter between Europe and the Middle East in the form of colonialism and imperialism and subsequently to the behavior and failure of post-colonial regimes whose reigning ethos has been decidedly secular. According to Vali Nasr:

> Secularism in the Muslim world never overcame its colonial origins and never lost its association with the postcolonial state's continuous struggle to dominate society. Its fortunes became tied to those of the state: the more the state's ideology came into question, and the more its actions alienated social forces, the more secularism was rejected in favor of indigenous worldviews and social institutions—which were for the most part tied to Islam. As such, the decline of secularism was a reflection of the decline of the postcolonial state in the Muslim world.[33]

Contributing Factors

One can add to this picture specific domestic and foreign policy positions adopted by prominent Western liberal democracies that have had a negative impact on Muslim sensibilities. Collectively, these policy positions have served to delegitimize the concept of secularism in Muslim societies. Consider the following examples.

The fact that the West both loudly and proudly proclaims itself to be secular and is often viewed as propping up repressive regimes in the Muslim world has undercut any positive image of secularism. Arguably, the most dramatic example of this was the United States' support for the Shah of Iran from 1953 to 1979. Strong French support for the Algerian military junta, especially in the aftermath of the aborted democratic process in 1992, along with uniform Western support in 2007 for Mahmoud Abbas and his secular

Fatah party in Palestine against the democratically elected Hamas government could be listed in this context as well.[34]

Similarly, the 2003 American-Anglo invasion and occupation of Iraq have further alienated Muslim societies from the West.[35] For example, two members of an American nongovernmental organization working on pro-democracy projects in the Middle East published a revealing opinion piece in the *Christian Science Monitor* after the ouster of Saddam Hussein, entitled "Even the Word 'Democracy' Now Repels Mideast Reformers." Their argument was that in the aftermath of the U.S. occupation of Iraq, even in previously friendly parts of the Middle East, a U.S. affiliation is now viewed as "radioactive," and any ties to the United States "would damage the credibility of legitimate activists." They observed: "on a recent trip to Syria, Bahrain, and Jordan, reformers told us, with great distress, they can no longer even use the words 'democracy' and 'human rights' in their communities, let alone work publicly on U.S.-funded democracy promotion projects."[36]

These views are corroborated by recent public opinion surveys among Jordanian students, whose government is the most pro-American in the Muslim world. When asked to form word associations with terms such a "democracy" and "terrorism," almost half of the students surveyed connected the term "democracy" with "colonization" or "killing," while the most common responses to the term "terrorism" were "Israel," "USA," and "George W. Bush."[37]

On a related point, the public debate in France on *l'afffaire du foulard* has further eroded the reputation of secularism among large swathes of the global Muslim community. This was amply demonstrated in the lead-up to and immediate aftermath of the March 2004 law passed by the French National Assembly calling for a ban on clothing and insignia in public schools that "conspicuously manifest a religious affiliation." Despite the official claims of neutrality, the legislation was aimed at Muslims. This was clearly evident from the fact that the public debate on secularism centered primarily on the hejab and Muslims, not the turban and Sikhs, yarmulkes and Jews, or crosses and Christians.[38]

Significantly, the moral justification for this law was based on the widespread belief that *laïcité* was under threat and a new law was needed to bolster and protect French secularism. Public opinion in France strongly backed the new legislation, as was reflected in the final vote: 494 to 36 in the National Assembly and 276 to 20 in the Senate. This development and the news surrounding it were transmitted around the globe. In some Muslims countries, it even resulted in street demonstrations.[39] The message Muslims received from this series of events was unambiguous—"secularism" is a punitive ideology that works to the collective detriment of the human and civil rights of Muslims.[40]

Finally, there is the topic of Muslim identity and secularism. A noticeable aspect of Muslim identity in the latter part of the twentieth century is that it is being constructed in relationship to, and in rejection of, the "West." According to Khaled Abou El Fadl, "Islamic thinking . . . has remained reactive . . . [in] that it defines its position vis-à-vis democracy . . . or human rights, always with an eye toward how the other defines himself."[41] Developing this thought further, he observes:

> In the age of post-colonialism, Muslims have become preoccupied with the attempt to remedy a collective feeling of powerlessness and a frustrating sense of political defeat, often by engaging in sensational acts of power symbolism. The normative imperatives and intellectual subtleties of the Islamic moral tradition are not treated with the analytic and critical rigor they rightly deserve, but are rendered subservient to political expedience and symbolic displays of power.[42]

He describes this condition and the identity that is constructed around it as resulting from the predominance of a "theology of power."[43] He also notes that this new identity marks a radical rupture with the Islamic past and is "thoroughly a by-product of colonialism and modernity." The group of politically active Muslims that he is describing

> define Islam as an ideology of nationalistic defiance of the other, a rather vulgar form of obstructionism vis-à-vis the hegemony of the Western world. Therefore, instead of Islam being a moral vision given to humanity, it becomes constructed into the antithesis of the West. In the world constructed by these groups, there is no Islam; there is only opposition to the West.[44]

Tariq Ramadan makes a similar point in the context of the Muslim embrace of corporal and capital punishment that is mandated by Islamic law. In calling for a moratorium on these punishments, Ramadan noted: "The unilateral condemnations that we hear in the West will not help things evolve. For the moment, we're living through exactly the opposite phenomenon: Muslim populations convince themselves of the Islamic character of these practices *by virtue of Western rejection*. The less Western it is, the more Islamic it is [perceived to be]."[45]

These observations apply with special reference to the topic of secularism. For many Muslims, a rejection of the idea that religion and state should be separate has morphed into a core aspect of Islamic identity and is synonymous with one's status as an authentically "good Muslim."[46] When asked about the topic, Muslim activists will repeat this mantra as if it were a sacred equation that is beyond dispute and inextricably linked to Muslim authenticity in the early twenty-first century. The evidence of this is easy to discern; one need only pay attention to how political Islamists, both Sunni and Shia, discuss—and subsequently dismiss—the topic of secularism.

Political Islam's Rejection of Secularism

In his famous lectures on "Islamic Government," delivered while in exile in Najaf, Iraq, in the winter of 1970, Ayatollah Khomeini observed:

> This slogan of the separation of religion and politics and the demand that Islamic scholars not intervene in social and political affairs has been formulated and propagated by the imperialists; it is only the irreligious who repeat them. Were religion and politics separate in the time of the Prophet. . . . Did there exist, on one side, a group of clerics, and opposite it, a group of politicians and leaders? . . . These slogans and claims have been advanced by the imperialists and their political agents in order to prevent religion from ordering the affairs of this world and shaping Muslim society, and at the same time to create a rift between the scholars of Islam, on the one hand, and the masses and those struggling for freedom and independence, on the other. They have thus been able to gain dominance over our people and plunder our resources, for such has always been their ultimate goal.[47]

Khomeini's successor, Seyyed Ali Khamenehi, has repeatedly echoed these sentiments during his tenure as the supreme leader of the Islamic revolution. In an address to the members of the Assembly of Experts, for example, he asserted that "colonialist powers have always advocated a separation of religion from politics," adding that under the regime of the shah, "Iran experienced the secular form of government which brought wide-scale ethical corruption." He concluded by noting that the "Iranian nation has established a religious-oriented government which, thanks [be to] God, has brought enormous social, political and administrative blessings so that the Iranian nation will never substitute the religious administration with a secular one."[48]

Khamenehi's counterparts in the Sunni Muslim world, even those of a relatively liberal Islamist persuasion, have similarly interpreted secularism very negatively. This is clearly demonstrated in their writings; they blame nearly all problems within Muslim societies on the forces of secularism. For example, Munir Shafiq, a Palestinian Islamist, writes in his essay "Secularism and the Arab-Muslim Condition" that "the trend in Islamic history, which disrupted the relationship between religion and the state (and thus brought an end to the model of the [seventh-century] Rightly Guided Caliphate), bore the seeds of secularism in government." In modern times it has been these "seeds of secularism [that have] germinated to produce despotism, injustice, immorality, misuse of public wealth, persecution of minorities and instigation of tribal and ethnic conflicts."[49]

In a similar vein, the Egyptian Islamist Abdelwahab Elmessiri writes about how secular humanism in Europe and North America "has been dealt an almost deadly blow by two world wars, environmental disasters, the increase of some negative social phenomena (crime, suicide, pornography, teenage pregnancy, etc.)." On the other side of the Cold War divide, he observes, the "socialist illusion lies dead in the ashes of the Soviet Union and [with] its obituary writ large by the syndicates or organized crime that control many Russian cities." All of these "ravages of secularism are now evident and its total reality is clearer than ever."[50]

The roots of Sunni Islamist views on secularism can be traced back to Sayyid Qutb and Maulana Mawdudi, the two key theoreticians of modern Sunni political Islam.[51] More recently, representing a popular perspective, the influential Al Azhar University–educated cleric Yusuf Qaradawi, in a book revealingly titled 'Al-Hulul al Mustawradah wa Kayfa Jaat 'alaa Ummatina' (How the Imported Solutions Disastrously Affected the Muslim Community), has written that "secularism may be accepted in a Christian society but it can never enjoy a general acceptance in a Muslim society.... Secularism among Muslims is atheism and a rejection of Islam."[52]

The Egyptian jurist and moderate Islamist intellectual Muhammad Imara reaches a similar conclusion, although his views are more nuanced. "Secularism is not our preference for an option to progress," he told a Beirut conference on Islam and Arab nationalism. "Those among us who are committed to secularism ... are consciously or unconsciously imitators."[53] In his book al-Almaniyya wa Nahdatuna al-Haditha (Secularism and Our Modern Renaissance) he contrasts a utopian vision of Islam with a dystopian view of secularism, which he describes as an appealing yet flawed ideological system. He concludes that Islam is a superior alternative to secularism in large part because it is concerned with social justice and the public interest, while secularism is utilitarian and focuses on the narrow self-interest of individuals.[54]

Muslims in Southeast Asia discuss secularism in very similar terms. On 28 July 2005, for example, the Indonesian Council of Ulama issued a series of fatwas, the most controversial and widely cited one being fatwa number 7, which condemned liberalism, pluralism, and in particular secularism.[55] Twenty years earlier, the respected Malaysian scholar Syed Naquib al-Attas published Islam, Secularism and the Philosophy of the Future, where he wrote: "Islam totally rejects any application to itself of the concepts secular, or secularization or secularism as they do not belong and are alien to it in every respect."[56] Invoking arguments similar to Yusuf Qaradawi, al-Attas argued that the very nature of Islam and Christianity are different, so that secularism could develop in one and not the other. He cited the absence of a revealed law in Christianity to explain why it was prone to secularization, unlike Islam, which is grounded in the Shariah and thus represents a more complete and self-sufficient system of belief.[57]

Similarly, in the summer of 2007, the deputy prime minister of Malaysia, Najib Razak, emphatically declared that Malaysia was not a secular state but an Islamic one. "Islam is the official religion and we are an Islamic state. But as an Islamic state, it does not mean that we don't respect non-Muslims," he told reporters after officiating at the International Conference on the Role of Islamic States in a Globalized World in Kuala Lumpur. When asked by one reporter whether Malaysia was not seemingly moving toward being a secular state, Razak fired back: "I have to correct you. We have never, never been secular because being secular by the Western definition means separation of the Islamic principles in the way we govern a country. We have never been affiliated with that position. We have always been driven by our adherence to the fundamentals of Islam. So, your premise is wrong."[58]

These dismissive comments on secularism were similarly on display in post-Saddam Hussein Iraq. In the lead-up to the January 2005 elections and the ensuing debate on the founding principles of Iraq's new constitution, the relationship between religion, state, and politics was extensively commented on by leading Iraqi political parties and religious figures. If there was one thing they could agree on, it was the complete rejection of secularism. Adnan Soliman, spokesperson for the Sunni Congress, affirmed that separating state and religion is "against [the] Islamic culture we have been bred on."[59] Sheikh Ibrahim Ibrahimi, representative of Grand Ayatollah Mohammad Ishaq Fayad, one of the four senior sources of religious authority (*marja al-taqlid*) who determine policy for Iraq's majority Shia community, has made a similar claim: "all of the *ulema* . . . and the majority of the Iraqi people, want the national assembly to make Islam the source of legislation in the permanent constitution, and to reject any law that is contrary to Islam." He added: "we warn officials against a separation of state and religion, because this is completely rejected by the *ulema* . . . and we will accept no compromise on this question."[60]

Iraq's new president, Jalal Talabani, confirmed the pejorative status of the term "secularism" in Muslim political discourse. After publicly asserting "we the Kurds will never accept the establishment of an Islamic regime in Iraq," he was asked if as an alternative he would support a secular political regime instead. He revealingly and sagaciously replied: "Yes, I will, but we do not use the term 'secularism.' What we say is: a democratic, federal, parliamentarian, united and independent Iraq, which respects the Islamic identity of the Iraqi people."[61]

Mahmoud Abbas, President of the Palestinian National Authority, made similar comments on an October 2007 trip to Malaysia. Speaking at a press conference in Kuala Lumpur, Abbas said: "I'm not a secularist. I'm a good Muslim and I don't have to be with Hamas to be a good Muslim." He added: "Even if you're in Hamas, you're not necessarily a good Muslim. I'm a good Muslim and if some people want to portray me as a secularist, it is up to them. But I'm not a secularist."[62]

Finally, arguably the clearest indication on the grim prospects for secularism in the Arab world was revealed in Iraq in the aftermath of the removal of Saddam Hussein. Against the backdrop of what was perceived by many Iraqis as the demise of secular Ba'athist tyranny, it was reported that the Iraqi Communist Party—now allowed to resume activity after years of suppression—had adopted the politics of religion to spread its message.[63] So woeful were the prospects for secularism that they had no choice. We can conclude from the foregoing analysis that secularism is a deeply suspect concept in Muslim societies for the following reasons:

- The early translation of the word constructed a dichotomy between Islam and secularism such that secularism was interpreted as synonymous with atheism.
- Secularism as a political concept is intimately connected to authoritarianism because it was introduced into the region by colonial and imperial powers and subsequently tied to the developmental failures and repressions of the postcolonial state.
- Particular domestic and foreign policies of leading Western powers have been perceived as negatively affecting the human and civil rights of Muslims (secularism in France, U.S. support for repressive regimes and intervention in the Middle East).
- Muslim identity and debates on authenticity in the late twentieth century have been constructed in relationship to, and in rejection of, the secular West.[64]

Toward Secular Liberal Democracy in the Muslim World: Historical and Empirical Lessons

What does the foregoing analysis suggest about the advancement of a democratic theory for Muslim societies? At the beginning of this chapter I argued that liberal democracy demands a form of secularism; yet secularism has been discredited in the Muslim world. Given this paradox, what are the prospects for advancing a secular liberal democracy in Muslim societies? Where can democratic theorists turn for insight in reconciling this tension?

One of the most insightful scholars writing today on the relationship between Islam and democracy is Abdou Filali-Ansary. In his article "The Challenge of Secularization," written over a decade ago, he noted: "In the Muslim world, secularization is preceding religious reformation—a reversal of the European experience in which secularization was more or less a consequence of such reformation."[65] Unfortunately, he did not expand on this insight. Doing so would have shed considerable light on two important subjects: (1) the symbiotic relationship between religion, secularism, and political culture, and (2) the way liberal democracy in Muslim societies can be advanced.[66]

In the historical development of the West, a religious reformation preceded and then led to the onset of secularization. It is philosophically inconceivable to think of the emergence and spread of secularism without reference to the Protestant Reformation and the ensuing Wars of Religion that tore Europe asunder.[67] In the historical development of secularism in Europe, Martin Luther's ninety-five theses (1517) preceded and indirectly led to Locke's *Letter Concerning Toleration* (1689), one of the first theoretical and moral justifications for the separation of religion and state in Western political thought.[68] The reverse sequence would be difficult to fathom, primarily because the political culture in Europe at the time was unwilling to support the idea of a separation of church and state.

Indeed, any religious innovation whatever, prior to the Enlightenment, was viewed with deep skepticism, in large part because religion was *the* source of moral authority. This is why Hobbes "was frequently attacked, in print and from the pulpit, for his supposed atheism, denial of objective moral values, and promotion of debauchery."[69] At the start of his *Leviathan*, he anticipates that this will happen and that his fiercest critics will be upset primarily with his novel religious arguments, not his overt political ones. In his dedicatory epistle, he writes: "that which perhaps may most offend are certain Texts of Holy Scripture, alleged by me to other purpose than ordinarily they use to be by others."[70] His new religious ideas were simply viewed as too unorthodox to be authentic, despite his clear commitment to Christianity.[71]

Recall also the discussion in Chapter 2 on the theme of a religious reinterpretation in the political theology of John Locke. In both of his major political tracts, *Two Treatises of Government* and *A Letter Concerning Toleration*, Locke's political arguments—which had significant consequences for the development of secularism in the West—were *preceded* by a re-interpretation of

Christian doctrine. In the *Two Treatises*, the moral basis of legitimate political authority are relocated, away from the "Divine Right of Kings" (the focus of the *First Treatise of Government*), and newly situated in the "consent" of the governed (the focus of the *Second Treatise of Government*). As we have seen in Chapter 2, in *A Letter Concerning Toleration*, Locke's religious reinterpretation of Christian doctrine acts as a preface to his new conception of church-state relations where he diverges from the reigning Hobbesian consensus and argues that religious toleration is indeed compatible with political order on the condition that one can "distinguish exactly the Business of Civil Government from that of Religion, and to settle the just Bounds that lie between the one and the other."[72] In other words, the normative relationship between religion and politics is first reshaped by Locke via a dissenting religious exegesis upon which a new conception of church-state relations is subsequently built. The clear lesson from European history is that a religious reformation of ideas about government *preceded* the movement toward secularization and democratization.[73]

By contrast in the Muslim world, as Filali-Ansary has correctly noted, the reverse process has taken place—"secularization [has] preced[ed] a religious reformation." This has had profound negative consequences for political development in Muslim societies. The introduction of secularism into the region, first due to the colonial encounter with Europe and secondly due to the modernizing and repressive policies of the post-colonial state, effectively meant that secularism in Muslim societies was a top-down process of state imposition, rather than a bottom-up process that emerged via an organic connection with civil society.

According to Vali Nasr, the strong centralizing and authoritarian policies of the Turkish state under Mustafa Kemal Atatürk became "a model of state formation in much of the Muslim world; Iran during the Pahlavi period, Arab nationalist regimes, Indonesia, Pakistan—all to varying degrees emulated the Turkish model."[74] An integral part of this development scheme meant that "social engineering went hand in hand with the conscious secularization of the judiciary and the educational system, and with the nationalization of religious endowments, thus truncating the social political role of religion."[75] Marshall Hodgson discusses this theme in his comparative treatment of the modernization of Europe and the Middle East. A critical difference he uncovers—which had serious consequences for political development—was that the Muslim encounter with modernity, unlike in Europe, has been marked by an "acceleration of history" that resulted in a radical rupture with the past. The tragic consequence of this development has been that modernization has *not* been accompanied by a parallel transformation of religious, intellectual, and political values on a mass level.

In his essay "Modernity and the Islamic Heritage," Hodgson tells the story of nineteenth-century Egypt. In the aftermath of Napoleon's occupation of Egypt (1798–1799), an Albanian officer of the Ottoman army, Muhammad Ali (1769–1849), seized power in 1805, destroying the old Mamluke military class and launching an extensive modernization program that transformed Egyptian society.[76] Due to his sweeping reforms, Muhammad Ali is credited with being the founding father of modern Egypt. According to Hodgson, however, while Ali was successful in destroying the old traditional order and modernizing Egypt, "he found that the background of *two centuries of steady social and intellectual transformation*, which Western Europe had known, was totally lacking, and this lack restricted his ability to build certain narrow limits—limits then unfamiliar, but which were to become commonplace."[77]

Muhammad Ali's attempt to construct a new intellectual life for Egypt was embodied in the modern school system he established, modeled on the Western system, with an emphasis on schools of engineering and science. The results, according to Hodgson, despite noble intentions, had a "destructive aspect." Over time, society became bifurcated between a small elite who were the recipient of a Western and secular education and the majority who were not. The first group "had no serious knowledge of the Islamic past of Egypt, and found little sympathy for—or from—the masses of their families."[78] The second group, the recipients of a traditional education, "were left to support the cultural continuity of the land." The final result, which has significantly influenced the contemporary debate on religion, secularism, and democracy, was "one group possessed of much modern book learning which alienated them from their own people and who knew almost nothing of the very religion they professed; [and] another group, increasingly incompetent custodians of that religion, who knew nothing of the intellectual springs of modern life."[79]

Pressing his comparison further, Hodgson compares the social impact of Napoleon's invasion of Germany (1813) with that of Egypt. The historical change that resulted "was no less rapid in Egypt than in Germany," but the critical difference was that "while in Germany it made for a more vigorous economic, social, and intellectual life, the same world-historical events had largely contrary results in Egypt." Hodgson explains that

> in Germany the innovations in administrative technique, in machine production, and the rest, if not quite so far advanced as in France or in England, nevertheless had been prepared by the *gradual* training of generations of former medieval clerks and craftsmen in more and

more technically-advanced ways—as had been the case in England and France themselves; for fundamentally Germany was part of the same general society as were England and France. In Egypt, on the contrary, the same events tended to destroy what craftsmen's skill and what intellectual soundness had in fact existed there in the eighteenth century.[80]

Hodgson goes on to note that the "story of Egypt was repeated—usually rather less neatly, and in a wide variety of circumstances—among most of the lands of urban and literate civilization of the Eastern hemisphere. . . . a large proportion . . . [of which were] more or less Islamic."[81] His radical rupture thesis—or, as he called it, the "drastic discontinuity" of Muslim modernity—has been discussed and argued by other scholars who have reached similar conclusions.[82] The key point here is that Hodgson's analysis complements and confirms the views of Filali-Ansary that "in the Muslim world, secularization is preceding religious reformation—a reversal of the European experience in which secularization was more or less a consequence of such reformation."[83]

While Hodgson does not explicitly refer to the relationship between religious reformation, secularization, and democratization (he was a historian, not a political scientist), his statement that the Muslim world did not experience a "steady social and intellectual transformation" from below to match state-induced modernization from above is a reference to the underdevelopment of Muslim political culture. In other words, due to the absence of a religious reformation of the normative relationship between religion and government, political secularism has had weak intellectual roots in the Muslim world. Summarizing this thought, Nikki Keddie writes:

> the needs, first, of governmental self-strengthening and then of nationalist movements and states were the primary factors in secularist policies, changes and achievements. Although some secularist intellectuals and secularizing social trends existed in most of these countries before secularism was adopted by a twentieth-century movement or state, these were not the main forces in the decisions to adopt secularizing policies. In all the above countries, secularism was tied to nationalism, to modernization, and to the centralization of control [by the state] over politics, economic life, ideology, and society.[84]

This chasm between state secularism from above and the nonsecular political culture from below also explains, in part, why support for religious parties and calls for the establishment of an "Islamic state" have an appeal today. Except for a minority of the population who have been the recipients of a Western education and have internalized a secular outlook, a significant portion of Muslim society today is responsive to political appeals that call for the integration of religion and state and a rejection of secular political principles. This is because the religious underpinnings that shape and inform Muslim political culture allow for it.[85]

While this is the pessimistic side of the story, the foregoing analysis simultaneously provides grounds for optimism, as well as suggesting the way forward. If a religious reformation can contribute to secularization—and by extension democratization—an appropriate question to ask is whether these developments are occurring anywhere in the Muslim world today. If so, where are they taking place and what lessons do they offer about ways to promote liberal democracy that might have an appeal across Muslim societies? Recent events in Indonesia and Turkey suggest an answer.

Indigenizing Muslim Secularism and Advancing Liberal Democracy

Two countries in the Muslim world where the prospects for liberal democracy seem brightest are Indonesia and Turkey. In recent years, both have registered significant gains for political development, despite their different historical experiences. This is reflected in the annual rankings by Freedom House, in which Indonesia and Turkey have registered some of the highest scores for political rights and civil liberties in comparison to the other members of the Organization of Islamic Conference.[86] What is relevant for this book is the correlation between the formation of Muslim political parties and the emergence of democratization and political secularism in these countries. This relationship has received little attention to date in the scholarly literature, yet by focusing on this connection it greatly illuminates our understanding of the theoretical relationship between religion, secularism, and liberal democracy in general and the obstacles to political development in Muslim societies in particular. While a comprehensive examination of the politics of Turkey and Indonesia is beyond the scope of this book the following brief comments are offered.

One of the intriguing aspects of Turkish and Indonesian politics in recent years has been the central role played by Muslim intellectuals and political parties in advancing liberal democracy. This development on its own shatters one of the key assumptions of modernization and dependency theory—and the writings of many liberal philosophers in the West who have long maintained that religious politics and political development are structurally incompatible. Critically, the same religious parties and groups have gradually reconciled their political theologies with secularism, thereby allowing themselves to make important contributions to the democratization and liberalization of their societies. In both Turkey and Indonesia, at the national level, calls for the creation of an Islamic state and the implementation of Shariah law do not have popular appeal, in contrast with other parts of the Muslim world.[87] An acceptance of pluralism, universal standards of human rights, and political secularism has flourished in recent years in these countries, significantly transforming their respective political cultures and orienting them in a liberal-democratic direction.

Muslim Secularism in Turkey

One of the important aspects of recent gains for liberal democracy in Turkey is that this movement is being led by a political party whose roots lie firmly within the Turkish Islamist movement.[88] Recep Tayip Erdoğan, the current prime minister and leader of the Adalet ve Kalkinma Partisi (AKP; Justice and Development Party), was himself banned from political office in 1998 and sentenced to a ten-month jail term for his Islamist leanings, yet today he is leading Turkey toward the very secular European Union. How did this happen?[89]

The story of Turkey's struggle for liberal democracy is most instructive. Officially, the country is a secular democratic republic. The version of secularism that was adopted by the founder of modern Turkey, and subsequently defended by the military and the Kemalist establishment, was a militantly antireligious version of secularism whose intellectual roots can be traced to August Comte (1798–1857), and the French concept of laïcité.[90] The emergence of a series of Muslim-based parties, as political space has opened up, has dominated Turkish politics for the past twenty years. Despite repeated electoral victories, these parties have been banned, only to reappear again with new names and increased political support. They represent an important and heretofore marginalized political constituency in Turkey, and when judged in terms of their commitment to the principles of liberal democracy, revealingly, they have a better track record than their adversaries in the Turkish secular establishment.

These contrasting orientations to liberal democracy were on display during the spring and summer of 2007. The ruling AK Party nominated its foreign minister, Abdullah Gül, as a candidate for president. Ahmet Necdet Sezer, the outgoing president and a staunch defender of Kemalist traditions, issued a series of dire warnings that the future of the country was at stake if the government did not withdraw Gül's nomination.[91] These fears were echoed across the Kemalist establishment, particularly by the media. On 27 April 2007, the general staff of the Turkish military released a statement that the *New York Times* described as a "thinly veiled threat" against the democratically elected civilian government—a perception shared almost universally by outside observers, given the long history of military coups d'état in Turkey. The statement read in part:

> Recently the main issue emerging in connection with the presidential election has focused on a debate over secularism. This is viewed with concern by the Turkish armed forces. It should not be forgotten that the Turkish armed forces are partial in this debate and are a staunch defender of secularism. The Turkish armed forces are against those debates (questioning secularism) . . . and will display its position and attitudes when it becomes necessary. No one should doubt that.[92]

A series of public demonstrations followed. They were organized by mainstream secular parties, retired military officers, and various civil society associations that self-identified with a Kemalist interpretation of secularism. Slogans were chanted against the AK Party, the United States, and the European Union and in defense of secularism. Some of the lead organizers came perilously close to welcoming the intervention of the Turkish military in politics. For example, on 30 April 2007, Türkan Saylan, president of the Association for the Promotion of Contemporary Living and one of the organizers of the demonstrations in the city of Samsun, released an open letter to Europe saying that the "Turkish public regards the army as those who come to their rescue at the time of earthquakes, floods and disasters. . . . it is not possible for either the EU or [the] USA . . . to comprehend the bond of love and respect between the public and the army. However, the frequent intimidating messages of [the] EU about the army . . . is also a major factor in [the] Turkish republic distancing themselves from EU." She added that the "European Union must understand that the army, whose main task is to protect the secular republican order, has just as much right to voice its opinion as any NGO in the event of initiatives being taken that exploit children and are based on religious law and tolerated by people in positions of authority."[93] The Association of Kemalist Ideology was another organization behind these mass rallies. Necla Arat, director of the Faculty for Systematic Philosophy at Istanbul University and a senior member of this organization, saw nothing unusual in the recent memorandum issued by the military. She noted that engineers, entrepreneurs, politicians, and intellectuals all express their opinions in public. "Why do we get jittery when soldiers express theirs?" she asked.[94]

By the end of the summer, the forces of moderation, democracy, and political pluralism had prevailed. Bolstered by a strong economy, the AK Party won a landslide victory, securing 46.5 percent of the popular vote, the first time in fifty years that a ruling party was returned to power with a bigger share of the vote. This resounding triumph allowed Gül, a former Islamist and practicing Muslim, to become the eleventh president of the Republic of Turkey, ushering in a new era in Turkish politics.[95]

One of the important background developments that have significantly contributed to the process of consolidation of democracy in Turkey has been a gradual internal ideological transformation within religious-based parties and among Muslim intellectuals. These groups have effectively reconciled their political theologies with secularism, albeit a secularism of a different sort. While considerable tension still exists between the Anglo-American model of secularism (preferred by these groups) and the French model of secularism (which the Turkish military insists on), all mainstream expressions of political Islam in Turkey today have not only philosophically accepted the principle of the separation of religion and state but also reject the idea of the state enforcement of Shariah law and support Turkey's bid for entry into the European Union. According to M. Hakan Yavuz, these developments have taken place because there has been an "internal secularization of religion" in Turkey.[96]

A healthy democracy, however, cannot rely on constitutions, legal safeguards, and politicians alone. Ultimately, the consolidation of liberal democracy in Turkey will depend on the maturity of civil society. Turkish civil society in quantitative terms compares favorably with other postindustrial democracies. Ersin Kalaycio-glu's survey of the existing data revealed that Turkey has approximately 56,000 active voluntary organizations and 59,000 cooperatives. This translates into one voluntary association for every 543 citizens, a ratio similar to figures of those in the United Kingdom and Canada, where there are 436 and 429 citizens per voluntary organization, respectively.[97]

One influential civil society association is the Islamic-oriented Fethullah Gülen movement. The interpretation of Islam that guides this group is based on a reformulation of the teachings of Jalaluddin Rumi (1207–1273), Yunus Emre (1238–1320), and the writings of Said Nursi (1878–1960). It strives to promote an understanding of faith that is modern, democratic, and secular.[98] According to Yavuz, the Gülen movement is the "most dynamic, transnational, wealthy and faith-based Islamic movement in Turkey." It is completely auton-omous from state control, and "one of the main doctrines of this group is the idea that religious consciousness is formed and perpetuated through engaging in social practices and institutions." Yavuz writes that "an examination of this movement reveals how new political and economic opportunities [have] affected the internal secularization of Turkish Islam in terms of modernity, nationalism, and the global discourses on human rights."[99]

The reach and popularity of the Gülen movement in civil society—mainly in the areas of education, the media, and the business community—is extensive, and the political theology of democratic secularism that has emerged from it has had an indirect and salutary effect on Turkish politics. Elizabeth Özdalga suggests that notwithstanding the strong religious revivalist appeal of the Gülen movement, its sociological effect on Turkish society "actually leads to secularization (disenchantment)." Her argument is that in the same way leading strands of Western Protestantism in the nineteenth century contributed to secularization by virtue of their support for universal values and humanism, the Gülen movement is having a similar effect on Turkish Islam when viewed over the long term. This phenomenon is tied to the subtle way universal and humanistic values can undermine particular and parochial identities. "The followers of Fethullah Gülen may well be fervent believers. Nevertheless, the way in which they formulate their mission—as a humanistic project—undermines their own theological foundation as Muslims—a development that has meant that the role of religion, Islam, has become destabilized."[100]

Despite the Gülen movement's preference for remaining aloof from politics, it has not succeeded. The polarized nature of Turkey's political landscape, with most of the conflict revolving around the role of religion in society, has forced an engagement, albeit a quiet one. To its credit, however, the Gülen movement has sought to act as a moderating and stabilizing force in Turkey, even when its own leadership has been targeted.[101] Yavuz notes that "Gülen's neo-Nur movement has distinguished itself from other faith movements through its soft and conciliatory voice on the most hotly debated subjects, such as secularism, the Kurdish question, and the headscarf issue."[102] Domestically, it has sought to play the role of a bridge-builder between rival political currents, and internationally it has been a strong supporter of ecumenism, crosscultural understanding, and peace.

The charismatic leader of this movement, Fethullah Gülen (b. 1938), known affectionately as Hocaefendi by his supporters, has written extensively about his political and religious thought. "Islam does not propose a certain unchangeable form of government," Gülen says; "instead, Islam establishes fundamental principles that orient a government's general character, leaving it to the people to choose the type of government according to time and circumstances."[103] His interpretation of Islam is decidedly tolerant, pluralistic, modern, and compassionate. According to Gülen, "Islam . . . upholds the following fundamental principles:

1. Power lies in truth, a repudiation of the common idea that truth relies upon power.
2. Justice and the rule of law are essential.
3. Freedom of belief and rights to life, personal property, reproduction, and health (both mental and physical) cannot be violated.
4. The privacy and immunity of individual life must be maintained.
5. No one can be convicted of a crime without evidence, or accused and punished for someone else's crime.
6. An advisory system of administration is essential."[104]

Gülen's views on secularism are worth noting as well. He was a signatory of the Abant Declarations, signed by leading Turkish secular and Islamic intellectuals in response to the crisis of religion and politics that gripped Turkey during the 1990s. The first statement issued by these intellectuals (in July 1998) was, understandably, entitled "Islam and Secularism." It began by noting that "today, Turkey appears to be passing through a deep crisis tied to the axes of religion and secularism. As a group of Turkish intellectuals, we came together at Abant and concluded . . . [an] agreement regarding the following points."[105] Ten points are listed in this declaration, but the ones that are significant for this discussion are those that refer to secularism.:

> Article 6: Within a legal framework, the state should be unbiased regarding religious beliefs and philosophical views. It should protect the citizens' rights to believe or not believe and remove obstacles to the implementation of beliefs. *Secularism is essentially an attitude of the state, and a secular state cannot define religion or pursue a religious policy.* Secularism should not be used as a restricting principle in the definition and enumeration of basic rights and freedoms.
>
> Article 7: Interference in the lifestyle of citizens and sensitive points in this issue lie at the source of a number of current difficulties in Turkey. *Secularism is not in opposition to religion* and it should not be understood as interference in people's lifestyles. Secularism should broaden the field of individual freedom. Especially it should not lead to discrimination against women, and shouldn't deprive them of rights in public.[106]

In short, both at the level of state and society, mainstream Muslim political and civil society groups have reconciled their belief in Islam with political secularism. Whether this was for instrumental reasons or principled ones is superfluous—the outcome remains the same.[107] The reality in Turkey today is that a de facto Muslim theory of secularism exists that enjoys broad support throughout the country. This Muslim form of Islamic secularism has allowed Muslim intellectuals, Muslim-based parties, and Muslim civil society groups to make an important and unique contribution to a process of democratic consolidation that has few parallels in other Muslim-majority societies. In Indonesia a similar trend is visible.

Soft Muslim Secularism in Indonesia

Similar to other Muslim societies, Indonesia experienced an Islamic resurgence in the final two decades of the twentieth century. This resurgence played a central (and often neglected) role in opposing the authoritarianism of the Suharto regime (1966–1998) and in the democratic transition that followed his ouster. In 1999, a Muslim cleric, Abdurrahman Wahid, became the first democratically elected president of post-Suharto Indonesia while Amien Rais, former chairman of one of the largest Muslim civil society organizations, became the new chairperson of the People's Consultative Assembly. Muslim intellectuals, religious-based political parties, and Islamic civil society organizations have continued to play an active and constructive role in the process of democratic consolidation in Indonesia.

One of the distinguishing features of religious politics in Indonesia—in contrast with other parts of the Muslim world—has been its tolerant, democratic, pluralist, and secular orientation. Robert Hefner describes mainstream Islam in Indonesia as "civil pluralist Islam" that comes "in a variety of forms" yet whose main features are "denying the wisdom of a monolithic 'Islamic' state and instead affirming democracy, voluntarism, and a balance of countervailing powers in a state and society."[108] Greg Barton adds that it is easy to see the social welfare role that Muslim civil society organizations play in providing health care, schools, and orphanages. What is less visible is how organizations such as the thirty-five-million-strong Muhammadiyah movement and the fifty-million-strong Nahdlatul Ulama organization—two mainstream Muslim civil society groups—play a critical role in "moderat[ing] public opinion, dampening inter-communal conflict and promoting tolerance, socializing democracy and giving voice, and weight of numbers, to reformist aspirations."[109] In recent years, both of these Muslim organizations have worked together for the public campaign against corruption, collusion, and nepotism while promoting a moderate, tolerant, and progressive version of Islam.

The roots of Muslim secularism in Indonesia can be traced back to the period of Dutch colonialism and the struggle for independence. From the outset, the question of the philosophical basis of the new Indonesian state was a hotly contested issue. One group of Indonesian religious nationalists, claiming that the overwhelming majority of Indonesians were Muslims, insisted that Islam be declared the official state religion. At one point in the constitutional debates they managed to include a phrase in an early draft that made reference to Shariah law.[110] They were opposed by a group of secular nationalists who wanted a separation of religion and state. This group was concerned, among other things, with the unification of the Indonesian archipelago and its possible breakup if one religion was given special recognition. The other broad political current at the time consisted of left-wing parties, the Community Party in particular, that envisioned a socialist state. To bridge these perspectives, Ahmad Sukarno (1901–1970), the champion of Indonesia's independence struggle and its first president, developed the idea of Pancasila (five principles): (1) belief in one supreme God or monotheism, (2) a just and civilized humanism, (3) the unity of Indonesia, (4) democracy, and (5) social justice.[111] Since its proclamation in 1945, this framework has come to define Indonesian nationalism. Muslim parties were initially sympathetic to this compromise, but increasingly throughout the 1950s and into the 1960s they fought for greater explicit constitutional recognition of Islam and the merger of religion and state.[112]

In 1955, Muhammadiyah and Nahdlatul Ulama, the two largest Muslim civil society organizations, supported the inclusion of Shariah law in the Indonesian constitution. By 1999, however, after the ouster of Suharto and the transition to democracy, they opposed this measure. An important sea change had taken place in the interim.[113] While this transformation was initially theological, its political consequences for the struggle for democracy in Indonesia were profound. Gradually, during the latter half of the twentieth century, a reorientation of mainstream political Islam had occurred that included among its features the cultivation of a de facto theory of Muslim secularism.

By the late 1960s, General Suharto had strengthened his authoritarian control over the country. With the doors on independent political activity closed, Muslim groups were forced to channel their energies inward. The focus of Muslim engagement shifted during this period from political Islam to what Azyumardi Azra has called "cultural Islam."[114] This consisted of a broad rethinking of the relationship between tradition and modernity, Islam and politics, and religion and state. Bahtiar Effendy writes that a new intellectual discourse emerged that focused on three specific areas: "(1) a reexamination of the theological or philosophical underpinnings of political Islam; (2) a redefinition of the political objectives of Islam; and (3) reassessment of the ways by which those political ideals can be effectively realized."[115] This also coincided with the reform and modernization of Islamic educational schools, the rise of a new middle class, and the sending of Indonesian students both to modern state universities and abroad for higher education, many of whom would return and make important contributions to the reformation of Indonesian Islam. At the forefront of this intellectual transition were a group of Muslim intellectuals who were educated in both traditional Islamic schools and in modern secular institutions. The most articulate and prominent member of this new intellectual class was Nurcholish Madjid (1939–2005).

If the measure of a man's influence can be obtained from the reaction to his death, then Madjid was a tremendously influential man. When he died in 2005, he was given a state funeral and buried in the Kalibata Heroes Cemetery in south Jakarta. The president, the vice-president, the speaker of the People's Consultative Assembly, ministers, foreign diplomats, and hundreds of officials from different religious, political, and civil organizations attended the ceremony. Thousands of citizens also participated. The newspapers were filled with glowing obituaries, some noting that he had been "ahead of his time" and that rather than enriching himself or his family, he had educated "the nation with his intellectuality and honesty."[116] President Susilo Bambang Yudhoyono issued a statement: "Today we are in mourning. One of our nation's best sons and a great Muslim intellectual, who has enlightened the nation, has passed away. . . . He gave me strength to push for reform, to create good governance and eradicate corruption."[117] Most studies on the intellectual history of Indonesian Islam make reference to Nurcholish Madjid's landmark "secularization" speech on 2 January 1970.[118] It marked a turning point in Madjid's career, where he went from a student leader to a nationally recognized and controversial public intellectual. It also marked an important milestone in the development of a new Islamic liberalism that was to significantly contribute to the transformation of Muslim thinking in Indonesia.

At the invitation of several student organizations, Madjid was asked to prepare a working paper for discussion and debate. The occasion was an Eid ul-Fitr party, marking the end of Ramadan. As he recalled later, such occasions were regular occurrences and in the past had often involved "lengthy boring speeches containing nothing other than political demagoguery." This time, the student organizers wanted to conduct a "free discussion about matters concerning contemporary Islam in Indonesia."[119]

Madjid prepared a presentation entitled "The Necessity of Renewal of Islamic Thought and the Problem of Integration of the Islamic Community."[120] He was under the impression this was to be a closed meeting for students, yet hundreds of people attended, and his paper was later leaked to the press and published. It sparked a huge debate, initially among student groups and later throughout the country. Numerous essays, speeches, sermons, and two books were written offering a refutation of Madjid's thesis. According to one account, "during the course of the 1970s no less than 100 polemical articles were published in newspapers and journals" in response to Madjid's lecture.[121]

The speech began by pointing to a dilemma facing Indonesian Muslims: how can the reformation of Muslim thought be pursued while simultaneously preserving Muslim unity? A critique and reform of Islamic thought would undoubtedly provoke disagreement and disunity, when one group of reformers broke off from the rest. Nonetheless, this was a risk worth taking, Madjid argued, because Muslim thinking in Indonesia had become "fossilized and obsolete, devoid of dynamism."[122]

There was a growing and new-found interest in Islam in Indonesian society, Madjid observed. He quickly qualified this observation, however, by saying that this should not be a cause for celebration among Muslims because what really mattered was not the quantity but the quality of believers. He ended the first part of his speech by calling for a "renovation of ideas" and affirming that a "renewal has to start with two closely related actions, that is, freeing oneself from traditional values and seeking values which are oriented toward the future."[123]

According to Madjid, one measure of the intellectual lethargy afflicting Muslims was their inability to differentiate between values that were "transcendental from those that were temporal." The core problem as he saw it was that "everything becomes transcendental and valued as *ukhrawi* [pertaining to the hereafter] without exception," thus excluding it from critical scrutiny due to its alleged sacredness. The results of this general Muslim attitude "are most injurious," he noted, because "Islam assumes the same value as tradition, and to be [normatively] Islamic is the same . . . as being traditionalist." Developing his critique further, he observed that the "glasses through which Muslims see the scale of values have made them unable to respond properly to the development of thought in the world today." The "hierarchy of values is often the reverse," he noted. Muslims, in other words, were intellectually unprepared for meeting the challenges of the modern world because they could not distinguish between issues that were sacred (and off limits to excessive critical scrutiny) and those that were not. The solution he offered was the "'temporalizing', of values which are in fact worldly, and the freeing of the *umma* [Muslim community] from the tendency to spiritualize them." He called for new creative thinking and the cultivation of a "mental readiness to always test and retest the truth of a value in the face of material, moral or historical facts [so this may] become a characteristic of Muslims."[124]

In the next part of his speech, Madjid issued a clarion call for freedom of thought. He encouraged Muslims to develop the confidence to engage with new ideas, however unconventional and controversial, and to support a general freedom of expression. Echoing John Stuart Mill, Madjid noted that "in the confrontation of ideas and thoughts, even error can be of considerable benefit, because it will induce truth to express itself and grow as a strong force."[125] He called on Indonesian Muslims to link the "idea of progress" with "an open mental attitude, in the form of a readiness to accept and to take (temporal) values from whatever source as long as they contain truth."[126]

Madjid's lecture was grounded in a radical reinterpretation of two fundamental Islamic principles: *tauhid* (the oneness of God) and *khalifat al-Allah fi al-ardh* (the notion that humans are God's vicegerents on earth). From this he extracted the idea that only God is transcendent and divine and as a consequence everything in the earthly realm should be viewed as temporal and subject to criticism. To confuse the temporal with the transcendental or, worse yet, to assign divine attributes to the sphere of worldly activity is a theological contradiction. "For to sacralize anything other than God, is, in reality, *shirk* [polytheism]," Madjid argued which according to the Koran is "the highest wrong-doing" (31:13). Madjid thus called for an "an attitude of 'desacralization' towards that which is other than God, namely, the world, its problems and values which are related to it."[127]

One of the reasons this speech generated such controversy was because of the controversial terminology Madjid employed. Much of the polemics and criticism that followed his lecture centered on his usage of the term *sekularisasi* (secularization), which he referred to as a "liberating process."[128] He was borrowing the concept from modern social science theory and specifically from the work of Harvey Cox, Talcott Parsons, and Robert Bellah.[129] Even though Madjid clearly distinguished secularization (as a sociological process that assists in a rational understanding of the world) from secularism (an ideology that is antireligious) in his landmark speech, this distinction and his broader intellectual point about the need for Islamic reform was lost on his critics. In his own words:

> By "secularization" is not meant the application of secularism, because "secularism" is the name for an ideology, a new closed worldview which functions very much like a new religion. What is meant here [by secularization] are all forms of "liberating development."... So, by "secularization" one does not mean the application of secularism and the transformation of Muslims into secularists. What is intended is the "temporalizing" of values which are in fact worldly, and the freeing of the *umma* [Muslim community] from the tendency to spiritualize them.[130]

What Madjid was trying to convey was that secularization is a *process* that leads to liberation of the mind from ideological constraints and thus allows for a reevaluation of religious thought and practice. In this sense, it was a liberating development. Secularism on the other hand was an alien ideology that was hostile to religion and should be avoided.[131]

The implications of Madjid's theological reformulations were profound. His call for the "temporalizing of values" and the "desacralization" of worldly problems had clear implications for the question of religion-state relations. It effectively suggested that there was nothing sacred with respect to the concept of an Islamic state, Islamic political parties, or political ideologies that invoked the name of religion. All were subject to criticism and debate, and there was nothing divine or sacred about them. Both in his famous 1970 speech and in a follow-up lecture in 1972 in which he sought to clarify his earlier remarks, he criticized Islamic political parties and the notion of an "Islamic state," denying that there was anything sacred about them and claiming instead that they were simply human constructs. With respect to Muslim political parties, Madjid invoked a set of words that have since become a catchphrase in Indonesia that embodies his political philosophy: "Islam Yes, Islamic Party No!"[132]

The other important implication that flowed from Madjid's thesis was that normatively Muslims should direct their commitments to Islamic principles and values, *not* to Muslim political parties or politicians. In other words, in the realm of politics, "the most important thing [is] not the form but the substance of the state."[133] M. Syafi'i Anwar credits Madjid with contributing to the cultivation of a "substantive-inclusive approach to political Islam" that is in marked contrast to the "legal-exclusive approach" championed by Islamic fundamentalists. The legal-exclusivist approach is philosophically scripturalist and believes in the integration of religion and state, the state application of Islamic law, and the necessity for Muslims to establish an Islamic state. The "substantive-inclusive approach," by contrast, believes there is no clear political model that can be extracted from Islamic teachings. Moreover, the Qur'an is viewed as a book of "ethical and moral guidance for governing a polity, including how to achieve ethical justice, freedom, equality, democracy and other injunctions," not a text that deals with the minutiae of political or social life.[134] In addition, the "substantive-inclusive" approach firmly rejects the ideas that Islam can be diminished to a single political ideology; that Islamic authenticity necessitates the creation of an "Islamic state" or that there should be an established state religion. In short, Madjid was articulating a vision of an Islamic humanism that emphasized ethics over the acquisition of political power.[135]

While Nurcholish Madjid was the most articulate proponent of these ideas, he was not the only one championing them. He was joined by a new generation of younger Islamic thinkers who came from similar backgrounds and were concerned with the same set of social and political questions. Prominent names were Syafii Maarif, Dawam Rahardjo, Djohan Effendi, Harun Nasution, and Abdurrahman Wahid.[136] They all possessed solid religious credentials and had organic ties to civil society, which both contributed to the success of their ideas and gave their reformist political theology a broad exposure. According to Hefner, these Muslim intellectuals were successful in Indonesia partly because of the strategy they employed.

> Rejecting the scholasticism of classical jurisprudence, these writers kept Qur'anic knowledge at the center of their arguments. But they struggled to contextualize this knowledge through an eclectic exploration of other traditions and new intellectual paradigms. Western social science, classical Islamic scholarship, Indonesian history—these and other sources were drawn into the effort to create a new Muslim discourse of civility and pluralism.[137]

While these reformist Islamic ideas remain popular today in Indonesia and have taken strong hold within its political culture, they continue to meet opposition from radical jihadist and some Islamic fundamentalist groups. Furthermore, opinion polls consistently reveal that at the local level there is strong and arguably growing support for the application of Shariah law.[138] These developments undoubtedly pose serious challenges to Indonesia's democratic consolidation.

What explains these contrasting political trends? While the roots of Islamic fundamentalism were examined in Chapter 1 in terms of the rise of Shariah consciousness, Farish Noor has situated it in the context of the failure of the existing civil legal system to combat corruption and injustice and to hold politicians accountable. As a result, people are starting to look for alternatives. For some, Islamic law serves as a panacea for solving social problems. He notes that "one of the main reasons Shariah . . . [has] become so popular . . . is [because of] the failure of the secular option itself."[139] Azyumardi Azra, a leading Indonesian scholar and public intellectual, agrees. He similarly attributes this phenomenon to the "failure of the government to enforce the law," adding that "as long as the government is . . . weak and indecisive, these groups will hold sway." His recommendations are to strengthen the secular option as an alternative to Shariah law. Specifically, "strengthen the state and good governance; secondly, enhancement of democracy and civil society; thirdly, reinforcement of law and order; and lastly, speeding up economic recovery."[140] In the coming years the failure of good governance will pose a serious challenge to the future of political secularism in Indonesia. This observation applies to other Muslim-majority societies where the failure of secular governments is directly related to the popularity of an Islamist alternative.

At the moment, however, at the national level, support for political secularism remains strong in Indonesia.[141] One reason is because of the nature of Pancasila, which has helped reconcile the tension between religion and state and enjoys the support of mainstream Muslim groups in Indonesia. Azyumardi Azra calls Pancasila "religious-friendly secularism."[142] While it clearly recognizes the importance of religion in public life, it does not single out one religion for special recognition. There are distinct parallels here with the Indian version of secularism, which Amartya Sen has described as a form of "secularism [which] demands that the state be equidistant from all religions—refusing to take sides and having a neutral attitude towards them."[143]

The variant of secularism supported by Muslim political parties in Indonesia is a mild version of secularism, but it is strong enough to support liberal democracy.[144] While it recognizes a functional separation between religion and state, it also rejects the privatization of religion and instead encourages the participation of religious parties in the public sphere. The tolerant and inclusive orientation of mainstream political Islam in Indonesia prevents it from trying to impose one religious interpretation on society, and thus in a genuine Tocquevillian sense, religion both nurtures and sustains democracy and secularism in Indonesia today.

In conclusion, the process of liberalization and democratization in Indonesia is incontrovertibly linked to the activities of Muslim intellectuals, Muslim political parties, and religion-based civil society groups. Like their counterparts in Turkey, they have developed a de facto theory of Muslim secularism while maintaining a commitment to the principles and rituals of their religion. This indigenization of secularism and the embrace of human rights is a key factor in explaining the contributions Muslim groups have made to the political development of their societies. In the process, an important political constituency, with extensive grassroots support, has been brought on board the liberal-democratic train, thus propelling these two societies forward in significant ways that have few parallels in other parts of the Muslim world. While the discussion to this point has been limited to the case of Muslim-majority societies, parallel developments involving other religious traditions lend support to the political relationship between a religious reformulation, secularism, and democratization that I am considering in this chapter.

An Islamic *Aggiornamento*? Parallels with Catholicism

In Samuel Huntington's influential study on the "third wave" of democratization, he noted that one distinguishing feature was that it was "overwhelmingly a Catholic wave." According to Huntington, "roughly three-quarters of the countries that transited to democracy between 1974 and 1989 were Catholic countries."[145] This fact raises important questions about the relationship between Catholicism and democracy and the factors that contributed to the Catholic wave of democratization in the late twentieth century.

While the variables that contribute to democratization are always multiple and often have important socioeconomic origins, in keeping with this book's emphasis on transformations in political culture and their effect on democratic development, a critical theoretical question emerges: did any significant change take place within Catholicism around the time of the third wave that affected the process of democratization in Catholic countries?

In José Casanova's retrospective reflections on this topic, he identifies a critical series of events that contributed to the third wave of democratization. These events were fundamentally related to the "official reformulation or *aggiornamento* of the Catholic tradition connected with the Second Vatican Council" in the 1960s.[146] This transformation of religious doctrine reconciled Catholicism with core aspects of modernity such as religious liberty, human rights, and democracy. A concomitant of this development was that it allowed the church to contribute to emancipatory struggles in Catholic-majority societies for arguably the first time in history.

Casanova reminds us that the Catholic Church's contribution to democratization during the 1970s was a "historical first." In the long struggle for democracy in Europe and Latin America, the Church was often allied with the authoritarian status quo, a point Tocqueville recognized in the early nineteenth century. "Catholic groups in general had been almost consistently on the other side of the democratic barricades,"[147] Casanova forcibly observes. The reformulation of Catholic doctrine in the 1960s, he suggests, had a direct bearing on the struggle for liberal democracy because the forces for democracy and the Catholic Church were now marching in the same direction for the first time in history.

Casanova identifies two key developments during this period: (1) the Second Vatican Council's Declaration on Religious Freedom, *Dignitatis Humanea*, and (2) the Church's appropriation of the modern discourse of universal human rights, beginning with Pope John XXIII's encyclical *Mater et Magistra* (1961).[148] This marked a shift in Catholic doctrine with respect to modern concepts of human rights dating back to at least the eighteenth century, when Pope Pius VI condemned the French National Assembly's Declaration of the Rights of Man. Throughout the nineteenth and twentieth centuries, the Catholic Church consistently opposed the advent of liberal democracy. In 1832, Pope Gregory XVI referred to freedom of conscience as "an absurd and erroneous opinion" while Pope Pius IX's *Syllabus of Errors* (1864) condemned the separation of church and state, religious freedom, "progress, liberalism and recent civilization."[149]

Much of the theoretical groundwork for the doctrinal shift of the 1960s was undertaken earlier by Catholic intellectuals such as Jacques Maritain and John Courtney Murray.[150] One of the critical theological shifts that redirected the moral compass of Catholicism was the "transference of the principle of *libertas ecclesiae* that the church had guarded so zealously through the ages to the individual human, from *libertas ecclesiae* to *libertas personae*." After this change, "the discourse on human rights [became]...central to the papal encyclicals and to the pastoral letters of national Conferences of Bishops throughout the world." Casanova suggests that this doctrinal shift was a necessary precondition to a Catholic contribution to political development. Only "now could the church play a truly positive role in the constitution of civil societies and in the process of democratization throughout the Catholic world."[151]

The second major development that influenced democratization during this period in Catholic societies was a shift in church-state relations. Two related events were observable: a "voluntary disestablishment from the state" by the Church and a general Catholic "disengagement from political society proper." Despite the prominent role played by many Catholics during the third wave of democratization, this did not translate into calls for the establishment of Catholicism as the official state religion or spawn Catholic political parties.[152] A de facto secularization (of the weak variety described in chapter 3) of Catholic political thought can be observed during this time period. This realignment of church-state relations approximates Stepan's concept of the "twin tolerations," such that both religious groups and the state recognize the limits of their political reach and respect the minimum boundaries of freedom of action for both state actors and civil society that are required to sustain a liberal democracy.[153]

Casanova is quick to point out, however, that this voluntary de facto secularization of Catholic political thought did "not necessarily mean the privatization of Catholicism." What it does suggest is that "this relocation [away from the state] is the very condition for the possibility of a modern public religion, for a modern form of public Catholicism."[154] Casanova is suggesting that the theological reconciliation of Church doctrine with the minimum core requirements of liberal democracy has enabled Catholic groups to play a more constructive role in the strengthening of liberal democracy and subsequent creation of a more just society. By virtue of their participation in efforts to shape public opinion on hotly contested moral questions, Catholic groups force "modern societies to reflect publicly and collectively on their normative structures."[155] In this process, society is shaped by Catholics' democratic participation in public debate, while at the same time Catholics are forced to confront and come to terms with the difficult and complex questions modernity poses to religious groups living in a globalized and plural world.

Returning to the link between religious reformation, secularism, and democratization, Casanova concludes that a comparison between Islam and Catholicism is instructive for understanding contemporary Muslim politics. Reminding us of the importance of a historical perspective when thinking about the relationship between religion and democracy, Casanova observes that Catholicism, like Islam today,

> was viewed for a long time as the paradigmatic antimodern fundamentalist religion. Catholicism served as the central focus of the Enlightenment critique of religion. It offered for centuries the most spirited, principled, and seemingly futile resistance to modern processes of secularization and modernization. It resisted capitalism, liberalism, the modern secular state, the democratic revolutions, socialism, and continues to resist the sexual revolution and feminism. . . . Every incrimination of Islam as a fundamentalist, antimodern and anti-Western religion could have been directed even more justifiably against Catholicism not so long ago.[156]

To speak, therefore, of a Catholic "essence" that was decidedly and forever antidemocratic and illiberal would be both historically false and analytically unhelpful. The same general analytical principle applies to the case of Muslim societies where "essentialist interpretations of Islam tend to preclude the possibility that contemporary Muslims may find their own models of Muslim *aggiornamentos* (they are likely to be plural), which like the Catholic one would offer viable responses attuned both to their religious tradition and to modern requirements."[157]

From the perspective of democratic theory, two critical questions emerge: (1) what changed inside Catholicism that had positive consequences for the development of liberal democracy? and (2) are similar developments occurring anywhere in the world of Islam today? Consolidating a core component of his argument, Casanova concludes:

> The swift democratization of Catholic countries following the Vatican *aggiornamento* demonstrates not so much the fact that at long last the Catholic Church gave up its traditional resistance to modernity, allowing democratization to proceed and thus, the final triumph of modernity over tradition, but rather the practical advantages that accrue when actors are able to offer traditional religious legitimation

for modern developments. *The sacralization of the modern discourse of human rights by the church was the single most important factor in the mobilization of Catholic resources for democratization.*[158]

Similarly, Casanova suggests, comparable trends are observable in Turkey, Iran, and Indonesia today. The sequence of religious transformation leading to a changed relationship between religion and liberal democracy is worth noting: a religious reformulation leads to a religious accommodation and reconciliation with political secularism and universal human rights, thus lending critical support to democratization efforts on the part of religious groups who have previously bolstered authoritarianism. The same general process and sequence of events that occurred in the Catholic tradition during the 1960s and 1970s, seems to be repeating itself, approximately thirty years later, in several key Muslim societies.[159]

Conclusion

This chapter was devoted to exploring the obstacles and challenges of secularism in Muslim societies. Rejecting an analytical framework that focuses exclusively on the inner political theology of Islam and early Islamic history, the crisis of secularism in Muslim societies today was attributed to several historical, political, and psychological factors. Most of them are a derivative of the colonial and imperial encounter between Europe (and later the United States) and the Muslim world in the previous two centuries. Secularism's demise was also attributed to the failure of modernization paradigms that were imposed on Muslim societies by the elites who controlled the post-colonial state. Unlike in Europe, where the emergence of political secularism was tied to pluralism, religious toleration and political development, in the Muslim world, secularism has been associated with repressive regimes, failed development strategies, and foreign intervention. A central paradox confronts the democratic theorist: liberal democracy demands a form of secularism, yet secularism suffers from ill repute in Muslim societies. What is the way forward? The answer to this question shaped the last part of this chapter.

New thinking on how political secularism can be advanced in Muslim societies can occur by 1) by studying the process of modernization in Europe with special focus on the symbiotic relationship between a religious reformation and secularization and 2) learning the lessons from recent political gains for liberal democracy in Turkey and Indonesia.

A contributing factor to the emergence and acceptance of political secularism, on a mass level, is the reformation of religious thought.[160] This is one reason why secularism was successful in Europe. In other words, the connection between the separation of church and state and the creation of a just society gradually came to be accepted for political reasons that were intimately tied to the Wars of Religion. In the Muslim world, by contrast, its political history has been significantly different. The colonial and post-colonial state imposed secularism on their religious societies from above, *without* the concomitant emergence of a political culture that could sustain and support such a separation. Getting this sequence right (i.e. a religious reformation prior to the spread of secularization) will help to revive the prospects for political secularism in Muslim societies, with potential positive consequences for the development of liberal democracy as well.

Recent developments in Turkey and Indonesia, which stand separate from the rest of the Muslim world in terms of recent gains for liberal democracy, provide evidence that this is possible. The advances in these two countries are directly attributable to the construction of an indigenous theory of Muslim secularism. Islamic intellectuals and mass-based Muslim political parties have played a leading role in advancing democratization and liberalization of these societies by engaging in reconciliation and embracing a home-grown version of Muslim secularism. This process of the growth and cultivation of Muslim secularism provides a potential model for other Muslim societies grappling with the difficult and emotionally charged relationship between religion, secularism, and liberal democracy.

Conclusion

This book has attempted to rethink the historical, theoretical and practical relationship between religion, secularism, and liberal democracy. The contemporary politics of three countries in the Muslim world, Iran, Turkey, and Indonesia were briefly discussed to illuminate this relationship. The central problematic that flows from this inquiry and that this book has sought to explicate is that liberal democracy, as a modern political regime, requires a form of secularism to sustain itself, yet simultaneously the primary intellectual, political, and cultural resources that Muslim democrats can draw on are largely religious. A paradox thus confronts the social scientist. Unraveling this paradox had been the objective of the preceding chapters.

Critically, this book has sought to undermine a long-standing and unexamined assumption in the social sciences that religious politics is structurally incompatible with democratization and liberalization. In the course of doing so, the following three broad but interrelated arguments were advanced.

First, in societies where religion is the principal marker of identity, the road to liberal democracy, whatever other twists and turns it makes, cannot avoid passing through the gates of religious politics. This claim runs counter to many of the core assumptions of mainstream social science theory, where the relationship between religion and liberal democracy is usually discussed pejoratively. A critical reexamination of the historical record, however, suggests different

lessons can be learned from the relationship between religion and democratization, especially when viewed from what Fernand Braudel has called the
longue durée (the study of history as a long duration). The prominence of
religious politics in the public sphere, I have argued, forms an important and
often neglected part of the history and struggle for liberal democracy that has
been underappreciated by social scientists. Fundamentally, this is a problem of
historical amnesia that needs to be overcome by those seeking a deeper
understanding of both the relationship between religion and politics in general
and the complicated politics of contemporary Muslim societies in particular.

Second, I have not challenged the formula that liberal democracy requires
a form of secularism. However, I have advanced two qualifications. First,
religious traditions are not born with an inherent liberal, democratic or secular
orientation; these ideas must be socially constructed. In Akeel Bilgrami's
succinct formulation secularism "has to be earned, not assumed."[1] Second,
how secularism is earned and then indigenized as part of the political culture
in an emerging democracy is a critical and often ignored part of the debate that
deserves greater attention and research focus. I have argued that an emerging
secular consensus is linked to a subtle transformation of religious ideas about
politics that is often a by-product of an existential political crisis in which
religion is deemed to be a source of political conflict. In order for secularism
to survive over the long term as a key political principle and value of liberal-
democratic politics, it must develop strong intellectual roots from within
society in order to survive. In this context, religious groups can play an
important role in the advancement of liberal democracy. In order for them to
do so, however, they must develop a political theory of secularism that is
compatible both with the core functional requirements of liberal democracy
and their own political theologies.

Furthermore, I have argued that there are different models of secularism
that liberal democracy can accommodate. The literature on democratic theory
is particularly weak in clarifying these various models, along with the precise
relationship and parameters of coexistence between religious groups and state
institutions in a liberal democracy. How secularism is defined is critical to
expanding our understanding of this topic. I have argued that there is greater
theoretical room and flexibility when discussing this subject than is generally
assumed. What is fundamentally required is a critical reexamination of the
relationship between political secularism and liberal democracy that is rooted
in a critical study of history, comparative political theory, comparative religion,
and political sociology. This reexamination is especially important in the
context of advancing a democratic theory for Muslim societies, given the
salience of religious parties and actors in the Islamic world today.

Finally, I have argued that a symbiotic relationship exists between a religious reformation and liberal-democratic development. While the first typically proceeds the second, they are deeply interwoven and interrelated processes. Understanding the connection between reformed religious ideas and democratization is especially important in societies dominated by an illiberal and undemocratic religiopolitical doctrine, in that it suggests a way forward. I have argued that political development does not require the privatization or marginalization of religion from the public sphere, but in order for religious groups to make a lasting contribution to democratic consolidation, a reinterpretation of religious ideas with respect to individual rights and the moral bases of legitimate political authority is needed. In short, the contribution religious groups can make to the development of democracy is often a function of their ability to undertake some form of doctrinal reformulation in this direction. I have presented evidence to support this argument from the historical development of liberal democracy in the West (i.e. the Catholic tradition) and from emerging trends in the Muslim world today.

Overall, I have argued that democratic theorists need to reexamine the role of religion in the social construction and development of liberal democracy. Doing so requires a rethinking of the concept of secularism more broadly, but this is especially required in the context of advancing a democratic theory for Muslim societies today.

Chapter 1 established the relevant theoretical and historical background needed to contemplate this subject. Three separate but interrelated arguments were advanced. First, liberal political philosophers and modernization theorists have generally discussed the connection between religion and liberal democracy in ahistorical terms. Liberal philosophers have forgotten that religious discourse was often a precondition to the rise of an early modern public sphere and that in subsequent years the role of religion in politics was a major theme of public debate in many long-standing liberal democracies. More important, liberal political theorists have generally not pursued the question of *how* emerging democracies have agreed to democratically negotiate and bargain over the normative relationship between religion and government. Doing so would shed considerable light on the contemporary struggle for democracy in the Muslim world, where debates on democratization cannot be separated from debates on religion's status in the polis.

Development theory from its early inception suffered from a Eurocentric and secular bias, in both the mainstream modernization and neo-Marxist dependency schools of thought. In retrospect, part of the problem can be explained by an overdependence on nineteenth- and early-twentieth-century European thinkers such as Marx and Weber whose intellectual influence on the nature and process of political development has been profound in the social sciences. By the early twentieth century, the high culture in Europe was thoroughly secularized, and thus a discussion of religion and political development was not central to developmental theorizing. It was assumed, mistakenly, that because religion's normative relationship with government had been largely resolved in the West, this must also be true universally. This assumption has led to a deep structural bias in thinking about political development in non-Western societies, Muslim societies in particular.

If one wanted to look to Europe for insight on this topic, a more appropriate place to turn is the seventeenth century, when the role of religion was more prominent in public life and philosophers such as Hobbes, Spinoza, Locke, and others wrote extensively on the theologico-political problem facing their societies. Development theorists and political philosophers interested in the relationship between religion and democracy are advised to focus on the early modern period of European history for insight and lessons to be learned that might have applicability in non-Western parts of the developing world, especially in those societies that are in the early phases of modernization where religion remains a key marker of identity and a reference point for debates about religion-state relations.

The second argument advanced in Chapter 1 pertained to the relationship between Islamic fundamentalism and modernity. I argued that political Islam is a far more complicated social phenomenon than is generally appreciated by social scientists. I focused on mainstream political Islam, not the extreme ends of the Islamist spectrum where Osama Bin Laden, the Taliban, and Al Qaeda are properly located.

I have shown that radical religious politics has emerged in the Muslim world in the context of a rapid modernization process and the social upheaval that accompanied the breakdown and transformation of old religious and political orders. History has shown that the anxiety and psychological uncertainty that is unleashed during such a period often produces mass-based religious movements whose popularity is tied to the period of social breakdown and its reconstruction. During more tranquil times, the ideology of religious militancy loses it appeal in the face of more liberal interpretations of state-society relations. I suggested parallels between Islamic fundamentalism and English Puritanism, drawing on Michael Walzer's *Revolution of the Saints*, a study of radical religious politics in early modern England. By analyzing the topic of Islamic fundamentalism historically and sociologically, rather than focusing exclusively on its doctrinal content, the links between radical religious protest movements and democratization over the long term were highlighted.

The political theology of John Locke was the main theme of Chapter Two. Locke was deliberately chosen because he is widely credited with laying out the blueprint for our modern conceptions of liberal democracy. What is generally not appreciated, however, in contemporary discussions of Locke, is the relationship between the religious underpinnings of his political philosophy and democratization. Investigating these underpinnings reveals that Locke's *reinterpretation* of religious ideas with respect to government, along with a competition of "dueling scriptures" between himself and his more conservative critics were pivotal to advancing a new theory of state-society relations that today forms the bedrock of our modern understanding of liberal democracy. Parallels were drawn between Locke and Iranian reformist intellectuals' use of a common strategy for advancing religious reform and reshaping political norms in deeply religious societies. Here I demonstrated how quasi-liberal-democratic ideas can be articulated among religious adherents in both Christianity and Islam. Highlighting the philosophical underpinnings of this position was the main point of Chapter 2. For this reason, the political theology of John Locke merited extended examination.

Chapter 3 was devoted to an examination of secularism and its relationship to liberal democracy. I argued that secularism is an ambiguous concept that is open to several different interpretations. Politically, secularism suggests some form of separation between the realm of politics and the domain of religion, and this can lead to more than one political model that may be compatible with liberal democracy, I identified two secular liberal democratic models in the Western world: a religion-hostile French model and a religion-tolerant Anglo-American one. Both models, I argued, emerged as by-products of the unique political histories of these countries and their unique experiences with nation-building, particularly the evolving set of relations between church and state that were socially constructed over a long period of time, after often bitter, acrimonious, and violent conflict.

Alexis de Tocqueville and Richard Rorty have both written influentially on the relationship between religion and democracy, yet they have arrived at contrasting positions on a potential religious contribution to liberal-democratic development. In seeking a deeper understanding of the precise connection between secularism and liberal democracy, I then investigated the work of Alfred Stepan and his concept of what he calls the "twin tolerations."

Stepan's contribution is unique, in that he focuses on the precise institutional and constitutional relationship between secularism and liberal democracy. Agreeing with his analytical framework, I argued that there is considerable flexibility and versatility in a liberal democracy with respect to the boundaries between religion and government. Two lines, however, that cannot be crossed are that a liberal-democratic constitution cannot give religious organizations veto power over decisions adopted by democratic legislatures and the state cannot ban religious groups from political activity simply because they are religious. These "minimum boundaries of freedom," which Stepan employs as a substitute for the term "secularism," and which both the state and religious group must respect, are required for a healthy coexistence of religion and liberal democracy. I argued that due to the theoretical depth of his argument and the new terminology he employs (i.e. the "twin tolerations"), Stepan's thesis has a unique saliency in both illuminating the theoretical debate on Islam and democracy and arming Muslim democrats with arguments and a strategy to advance the cause of democracy in their own societies where the question of secularism is a deeply contested one.

Finally, Chapter 4 explored the current crisis of secularism in Muslim societies. It was attributed to several factors, the most salient being the actual "lived experiences" of Muslim communities during the twentieth century. During this period, secularism became identified with the oppressive policies of the postcolonial state and the interventions of leading Western powers, both of whom have invoked secularism to varying degrees to justify their political behavior. The result has been a reaction and a rejection of secularism on the part of key constituencies in Muslim societies. Connecting secularism with the challenge of Muslim identity construction in the era of globalization, I argued that the debate on Islam and secularism has been further complicated by this process of identity construction, which rejects secularism as being, allegedly, inherently alien to notions of Muslim authenticity. Finally, and most critically, drawing on the work of Abdou Filaly-Ansary and Marshall Hodgson I identified the weak intellectual roots of secularism within the Muslim world as a key factor in explaining the weak receptivity to secular political principles among the masses.

Lessons from recent political events in two Muslim-majority countries, Indonesia and Turkey, suggest a way out of the core paradox that sets the framework for this book: liberal democracy requires a form of secularism, yet Muslim democrats have to work within and draw on a political tradition that is rooted in religion. Events in Turkey and Indonesia reveal how Muslim political parties and Islamic intellectuals can contribute to liberal-democratic development. In both cases, democratic contributions have been achieved by Muslim political parties and intellectuals who have undergone a doctrinal shift and gradually developed an indigenous Islamic understanding of secularism that has embraced political pluralism, human rights, and the rules of democratic governance. This indigenization of secularism is a key feature of Muslim political movements in Turkey and Indonesia that sets them apart from the rest of the Muslim world.

The larger theoretical point to be learned from events in Turkey and Indonesia is that shifts in religious doctrine can contribute to political development. Such shifts do not require the privatization of religion; rather, recent empirical evidence has demonstrated that the use of religion in the public sphere, subject to constraints that Stepan has outlined, can significantly contribute to the development and consolidation of liberal democracy, especially in polities where religion is a marker of identity.

In short, religion is a key and often ignored variable in the long and torturous struggle for liberal democracy that social scientists ignore at their own analytical peril. This book has attempted to highlight this critical interpretive point.

In today's polarized world, where religion has increasingly become part of the domestic and international debate, a rethinking of long-standing premises, assumptions, and theories about the relationship between religion and democracy is needed. While these assumptions do not need to be entirely jettisoned, they do need to be critically reassessed and updated, in response to both the global rise of religious consciousness and new empirical evidence that demonstrates the positive contributions *some* religious groups have made to the development and consolidation of liberal democracy.

Such a rethinking of old premises, assumptions, and theories is especially needed to help observers comprehend the vertiginous and seemingly incomprehensible politics of Muslim societies today. A frequent obstacle one encounters in seeking a deeper grasp of this topic is the problem of what I call "false universalisms." What I mean by this term are misconceptions that arise from the tendency to assume that our historical experience in the West with social and political development is the universal norm and has been identical for the entire world. This is a special problem when considering the topic of secularism and religion-state relations more broadly. While crosscultural parallels do exist, it is important to bear in mind that other religious traditions have had a different historical experience and memory with respect to the role of religion in public life, and it is precisely this memory and experience that shapes contemporary attitudes.

Familiarizing ourselves with these different histories, memories, and experiences is vitally important in today's increasingly plural and globalized world. That said, however, a new history of religion-state relations is currently being written in several key Muslim countries that is markedly different from the past. This will undoubtedly shape the view of future generations who choose to investigate this topic and who might perhaps one day read this book.

Notes

PREFACE TO PAPERBACK EDITION

1. John Esposito, "Tunisia after its first free elections," *Washington Post* guest blog, http://www.washingtonpost.com/blogs/guest-voices/post/tunisia-after-its-first-free-elections/2011/10/24/gIQAsuYgCM_blog.html, accessed November 1, 2011.

2. This book, 123–130.

3. See Bashar al-Assad's interview with Charlie Rose, May 27, 2010.

4. Amnesty International, *Crackdown in Syria: Terror in Tell Kalakh* (London: Amnesty International, July 6, 2011), Human Rights Watch, *"By All Means Necessary: Individual and Command Responsibility for Crimes Against Humanity in Syria* (New York: Human Rights Watch, December 15, 2011) and U.N. General Assembly, *Report of the International Independent Commission of Inquiry on the Syrian Arab Republic* (A/HRC/S-17/2/Add.1), November 23, 2011.

5. Marc Champion and Ayla AlBayrak, "Erdoğan Gets Warm Welcome in Cairo," *Wall Street Journal*, September 13, 2011.

6. Marc Champion and Matt Bradley, "Islamists Criticize Turkish Premier's 'Secularist' Remarks, *Wall Street Journal*, September 15, 2011 and "[Analysis] Erdoğan presents Turkey as model for Arabs," *Today's Zaman*, September 14, 2011.

7. "Egypt's Muslim Brotherhood criticizes Erdoğan's call for a secular state," *Al Arabiya News*, September 14, 2011 and "Egypt's Islamists warn Erdoğan: Don't seek Middle East domination," *Haaretz*, September 14, 2011.

8. Ipek Yazdani, "No need for secularism in Tunisia: Ghannouchi," *Hurriyet Daily News*, December 24, 2011.

9. Interview with *Euronews*, "Post revolution politics in Tunisia," January 13, 2012, http://www.euronews.com/2012/01/13/post-revolution-politics-in-tunisia/, accessed April 24, 2012.

10. Rached Ghannouchi, "Secularism and Relation between Religion and the State from the Perspective of the Nahdha Party," March 2, 2012, transcript available at website for the Center for the Study of Islam and Democracy, www. csidonline.org.

11. Shmuel Eisenstadt, "Multiple Modernities," *Daedalus* 129 (Winter 2000), 1–29.

PREFACE

1. Fred Dallmayr, "Beyond Monologue: For a Comparative Political Theory," *Perspectives on Politics* 2 (June 2004), 254.

2. The one lonely voice was Hamid Algar, "The Oppositional Role of the Ulama in Twentieth-Century Iran," in Nikki Keddie, ed., *Scholars, Saints and Sufis: Muslim Religious Institutions since 1500* (Berkeley: University of California Press, 1972), 231–255. On the left, scholars such as Fred Halliday, *Iran: Dictatorship and Development* (New York: Penguin Books, 1979), 211–248, and Maxime Rodinson, *Marxism and the Muslim World* (London: Monthly Review Press, 1981), 290–306, had little to say about the religious opposition in Iran. Similarly, modernization theorists such as James Bill, *The Politics of Iran: Groups, Classes and Modernization* (Columbus, Ohio: Merrill, 1972), and Marvin Zonis, *The Political Elite of Iran* (Princeton, N.J.: Princeton University Press, 1971), failed in this regard as well. The best general critique of development paradigms with respect to Muslim politics is Sami Zubaida, *Islam, the People and the State: Political Ideas and Movements in the Middle East* (London: Tauris, 1993), 121–182.

3. Bernard Lewis, "Islamic Revolution," *New York Review of Books* 34 (21 January 1988), 46–49, reprinted in Bernard Lewis, *From Babel to Dragomans: Interpreting the Middle East* (New York: Oxford University Press, 2004), 300, 303. Bernard Lewis wrote extensively on the Iranian revolution. He located the revolutionary character of Iranian politics, for example, in the deep annals of Shi'a history. See his "The Shi'a," *New York Review of Books* 32 (15 August 1985), 7–10. Also see his "The Revolt of Islam," *New York Review of Books* 30 (30 June 1983), 35–38; "How Khomeini Made It," *New York Review of Books* 31 (17 January 1985), 10–13; and *The Political Language of Islam* (Chicago: University of Chicago, 1988). Elie Kedourie wrote along similar lines. See his *Islam in the Modern World* (New York: Holt, Rinehart and Winston, 1980), 43–52, and *Politics in the Middle East* (New York: Oxford University Press, 1992), 337–346.

4. Ernest Gellner, *Postmodernism, Reason and Religion* (New York: Routledge, 1992), 4–22.

5. For the text of Gellner's last lecture see Ernest Gellner, "Religion and the Profane," *Eurozine* (28 August 2000), www.eurozine.com/articles/2000-08-28-gellner-en.html.

6. Abdelwahab El-Affendi, "On the State, Democracy and Pluralism," in Suha Taji-Farouki and Basheer Nafi, eds., *Islamic Thought in the Twentieth Century* (New York: Tauris, 2004), 180.

7. C. Wright Mills, *The Sociological Imagination* (New York: Oxford University Press, 1959), 20.

8. Theda Skocpol, George Ross, Tony Smith, and Judith Eisenberg Vichniac, summarizing C. Wright Mills in "Barrington Moore's Social Origins and Beyond: Historical Social Analysis since the 1960s," in Theda Skocpol, ed., *Democracy, Revolution and History* (Ithaca, N.Y.: Cornell University Press, 1998), 5. The authors also note that Barrington Moore chose his research questions based on the same moral considerations. Also see Mills, *Sociological Imagination*, 21.

INTRODUCTION

1. By "religious politics" I mean political behavior that draws on religion as a key reference point in political debate, moral argumentation, and political mobilization. It is similar to Stathis Kalyvas's definition of "unsecular politics," which refers to "a political context in which religious ideas, symbols and rituals are used as the primary (though not exclusive) instrument of mobilization by at least one major political party (i.e. a credible contender for power)." See his "Unsecular Politics and Religious Mobilization," in Thomas Kselman and Joseph Buttigieg, eds., *European Christian Democracy* (Notre Dame, Ind.: University of Notre Dame Press, 2003), 293–294.

2. See Shibley Telhami, "A Growing Muslim Identity," *Los Angeles Times*, 11 July 2004 and Telhami's 2006 Annual Arab Public Opinion Survey. Available online at www.brookings.edu/views/speeches/telhami20070208.pdf, where 45% said that "Muslim" was the most important aspect of their identity, compared to 29% who said "citizen of my country" and 20% who said "Arab." Also, see John Esposito and Dalia Mogahed, *Who Speaks for Islam?: What a Billion Muslims Really Think* (New York: Gallup Press, 2007), 5–6, 85–87. On secularism's troubled legacy in Muslim societies see Chapter 4.

3. Although I use the terms "Islamic fundamentalism," "Islamism," and "political Islam" interchangeably in this book, I am in broad agreement with the reservations of those scholars who note that the term "Islamic fundamentalism" is more accusatory than descriptive. In my utilization, the term refers to any group that makes Islam the centerpiece of its political platform. In his deconstruction of the concept, Juan Eduardo Campo writes: "rather than referring to an objective set of phenomena . . . [Islamic fundamentalism] has been created to serve as a key element in European and American hegemonic discourses about these societies in order to subordinate and control them. This means that it is of little explanatory value; does not facilitate rendering modern amalgamations of religion and politics more intelligible—unless it is seen first in reference to the scholars and institutions who have actually invented and used it" ("The Ends of Islamic Fundamentalism: Hegemonic Discourse and the Islamic Question in Egypt," *Contention* 4 [Spring 1995], 168). John Esposito discusses the etymology of the word "fundamentalism" and makes a case for its nonuse in reference to Muslim societies. See Esposito, *The Islamic Threat: Myth or Reality?* (New York: Oxford University Press, 1992), 7–8, for a brief discussion. Similarly, Joe Stork and Joel Beinin prefer the term "political Islam" to "Islamic fundamentalism." See their insightful essay "On the Modernity, Historical Specificity and International Context of Political Islam," in Joel Beinin and Joe Stork, eds., *Political Islam: Essays from Middle East Report* (Berkeley: University of California Press, 1997), 3–25. For a general introduction to the topic, arguably the best book available is Mohammed Ayoob,

The Many Faces of Political Islam: Religion and Politics in the Muslim World (Ann Arbor: University of Michigan Press, 2008).

4. For a representative sample of elite opinion during this period, consider the remarks of Willy Claes, then secretary-general of the North Atlantic Treaty Organization (NATO). In 1995 he told the German newspaper *Suddeutsche Zeitung*: "NATO is much more than a military alliance. It has committed itself to defending the basic principles of civilization that bind North America and Europe." Against whom are these principles of Western civilization to be defended against? "[Islamic] fundamentalism," which "is as dangerous as Communism was. Please do not underestimate this risk" (cited in "NATO Chief Warns of Islamic Extremists," *Globe and Mail*, 3 February 1995). I explore this issue in "From the Red Menace to the Green Peril: The Enduring Legacy of the Cold War and its Links to Political Islam," *Middle East Affairs Journal* 3 (summer-fall 1997), 47–60.

5. John Zogby Group International, Inc., "American Attitudes towards Islam: A Nationwide Poll," *American Journal of Islamic Social Sciences* 10 (fall 1993), 403–407. A March 2006 Washington Post-ABC poll found that "a growing proportion of Americans are expressing unfavorable views of Islam, and a majority now say that Muslims are disproportionately prone to violence," and "the proportion of Americans who believe that Islam helps to stoke violence against non-Muslims has more than doubled since the [September 11] attacks, from 14 percent in January 2002 to 33 percent today. The survey also found that one in three Americans have heard prejudiced comments about Muslims lately. In a separate question, slightly more (43 percent) reported having heard negative remarks about Arabs" (Claudia Deane and Darryl Fears, "Negative Perception of Islam Increasing," *Washington Post*, 9 March 2006). For a recent study of these trends see Peter Gottschalk and Gabriel Greenberg, *Islamophobia: Making Muslims the Enemy* (Lanham, Md.: Rowman and Littlefield, 2008), 1–12, 143–151.

6. A more comprehensive answer on pejorative Western attitudes toward Islam and Muslims demands an engagement with the history of Islam-West relations. Two exceptional studies stand out in this genre: Thierry Hentsch, *Imagining the Middle East* (Montreal: Black Rose Books, 1992), 1–21, 119–158, and Emran Qureshi and Michael Sells, eds., *The New Crusades: Constructing the Muslim Enemy* (New York: Columbia University Press, 2003), 1–47.

7. All of the authors listed here wrote about Islam in their post-Cold War writings. They first published their arguments in essays that were subsequently turned into widely discussed books. Francis Fukuyama, *The End of History and the Last Man* (New York: Free Press, 1992), 217, 235–237. On a side note, Fukuyama suggested as early as 1991 that following the Cold War, "the world will henceforth be divided along different lines, with the Third World and Islamic world defining the main axis of conflict" (quoted in Martin Walker, "American Eagle Cheated of Its Prey," *Guardian Weekly*, 8 September 1991). Benjamin Barber, *Jihad vs. McWorld: How Globalism and Tribalism Are Reshaping the World* (New York: Ballantine Books, 1996), 205–216; Robert Kaplan, *The Coming Anarchy: Shattering the Dreams of the Post Cold War* (New York: Vintage Books, 2000), 59–98, and *Eastward to Tartary: Travels to the Balkans, the Middle East and the Caucasus* (New York: Vintage Books, 2001), 96–99, 115–121; Samuel

Huntington, *The Clash of Civilizations and the Remaking of World Order* (New York: Simon and Schuster, 1996), 56–78, 207–218. During this period, other prominent Western intellectuals who warned of a coming Islamic threat were Bernard Lewis, "The Roots of Muslim Rage," *Atlantic Monthly* 266 (September 1990), 47–60, and "Islam and Liberal Democracy," *Atlantic Monthly* 271 (February 1993), 89–98; Giovanni Sartori, "Rethinking Democracy: Bad Polity and Bad Politics," *International Social Science Journal* 43 (August 1991), 437–450, and Conor Cruise O'Brien, *On the Eve of the Millennium* (Concord, Ontario: Anansi, 1994), 12–28, 139. Conor Cruise O'Brien, the famous Irish man of letters, at the end of the Cold War made the following observation about Islam and Muslims: "Muslim society looks profoundly repulsive. . . . It looks repulsive because it is repulsive. . . . A Westerner who claims to admire Muslim society, while still adhering to Western values, is either a hypocrite or an ignoramus or a bit of both. At the heart of the matter is the Muslim family, an abominable institution. . . . Arab and Muslim society is sick, and has been sick for a long time. In the last century, the Arab [*sic*] thinker Jamal al-Afghani wrote: 'Every Muslim is sick, and his only remedy is in the Koran.' Unfortunately the sickness gets worse the more the remedy is taken" ("Sick Man of the World," *Times* [London], 11 May 1989).

8. Francis Fukuyama, "History Is Still Going Our Way," *Wall Street Journal*, 5 October 2001.

9. Some of the intellectuals who have written on this issue since 9/11 with considerable influence include Michael Ignatieff, "The Attack on Human Rights," *Foreign Affairs* 80 (November–December 2001), 102–116; Francis Fukuyama, "Their Target: The Modern World," *Newsweek* 138 (17 December 2001), 42–48; Bernard Lewis, "The Revolt of Islam," *New Yorker* 77 (19 November 2001), 51–63; Christopher Hitchens, "9/11, Islamic Fascism and The Secular Intellectual: An Evening with Christopher Hitchens," *Salmagundi* 133–134 (winter–spring 2002), 3–30. For Ignatieff's views on Islam and Muslims after 9/11 see Tom Blackwell, "Canada Needs 'Lethal Power,' Ignatieff Says," *National Post*, 7 November 2002.

10. I partially borrow these questions from three essays: Giovanni Sartori, "How Far Can Free Government Travel?" *Journal of Democracy* 6 (July 1995), 101–111; Alfred Stepan, "Religion, Democracy and the 'Twin Tolerations,'" *Journal of Democracy* 11 (October 2000), 37–57, and Robert Hefner, "On the History and Cross-cultural Possibility of a Democratic Ideal," in Hefner, ed., *Democratic Civility: The History and Cross-cultural Possibility of a Modern Political Ideal* (New Brunswick, N.J.: Transaction, 1998), 3–49.

11. Alexis de Tocqueville, *Democracy in America*, translated by Henry Reeve (New York: Vintage Books, 1990), 1:325.

12. Robert Dahl, Ian Shapiro, and Jose Antonio Cheibub, eds., *The Democracy Sourcebook* (Cambridge, Mass.: MIT Press, 2003); Ricardo Blaug and John Schwarzmantel, eds., *Democracy: A Reader* (New York: Columbia University Press, 2001); Ronald Terchek and Thomas Conte, eds., *Theories of Democracy: A Reader* (Lanham, Md.: Rowman and Littlefield, 2001). The Dahl, Shapiro, and Cheibub reader includes two essays that deal with the topic of culture and democracy, but not systematically highlighting the tension between religion and democracy in the sense that Tocqueville was referring to. Also see Kenneth Wald and Clyde Wilcox, "Getting Religion: Has

Political Science Rediscovered the Faith Factor?" *American Political Science Review* 100 (November 2006), 523–529, whose authors write that apart "from economics and geography, it is hard to find a social science that has given less attention to religion than political science."

13. Mikaela A. McDermott and Brian Katulis, "Even the Word 'Democracy' Now Repels Mideast Reformers," *Christain Science Monitor*, 20 May 2004; "Broader Middle East and North Africa Initiative: Imperilled at Birth," *International Crisis Group Report*, 7 June 2004. Also see the interview with Nader Fergany (coordinator of the UNDP Arab Development Reports), "The USA Has Given Democracy a Bad Name," www. qantara.de/webcom/show_article.php/_c-476/_nr-189/_p-1/i.html. For a concise overview of the debate on democracy in the Muslim world during the twentieth century see Abdelwahab El-Affendi, "On the State, Democracy and Pluralism," in Basheer Nafi and Suha Taji-Farouki, eds., *Islamic Thought in the Twentieth Century* (New York: Tauris, 2004), 180–203.

14. In Clifford Geertz's famous social scientific definition, religion is part of "a cultural system." He defines religion as "(1) a system of symbols which acts to (2) establish powerful, pervasive, and long-lasting moods and motivations in men by (3) formulating conceptions of a general order of existence and (4) clothing these conceptions with such an aura of factuality that (5) the moods and motivations seem uniquely realistic" (*The Interpretation of Cultures: Selected Essays* [New York: Basic Books, 1973], 90).

15. Bernard Lewis, "Islam and Liberal Democracy," *Atlantic Monthly* 271 (February 1993), 92.

16. John Locke, *Two Treatises of Government*, edited by Peter Laslett (Cambridge: Cambridge University Press, 1988); Jean-Jacques Rousseau, *On the Social Contract*, translated by Donald Cress (Indianapolis: Hackett, 1987), and John Stuart Mill, *On Liberty*, edited by Gertrude Himmelfarb (New York: Penguin Books, 1974). The relationship between "liberalism" and "democracy" is very complex and beyond the scope of this book. Suffice to note, however, that understanding the history of both and their interrelationship is useful in comprehending the problems and obstacles to liberal-democratic development in non-Western societies. One of the first modern thinkers to insightfully reflect on the relationship between liberalism and democracy was Benjamin Constant (1767–1830). See his famous address to the Royal Academy in Paris in 1819, "De la Liberté des Anciens Comparée à celle des Modernes," reprinted in Benjamin Constant, *Constant: Political Writings*, edited by Biancamaria Fontana (Cambridge: Cambridge University Press, 1988), 307–328.

17. On Schumpeterian democracy see Joseph Schumpeter, "Another Theory of Democracy," in Joseph Schumpeter, *Capitalism, Socialism and Democracy* (New York: Harper, 1950), 269–283. For deliberative democracy see Joshua Cohen, "Deliberative Democracy and Democratic Legitimacy," in James Bohman and William Rehg, eds., *Deliberative Democracy: Essays on Reason and Politics* (Cambridge, Mass.: MIT Press, 1997), 67–92.

18. I am mindful of the important reservations raised by Bhikhu Parekh on "The Cultural Particularity of Liberal Democracy," in David Held, ed., *Prospects for*

Democracy: North, South, East, West (Stanford, Calif.: Stanford University Press, 1993), 156–175. Notwithstanding his important insights, to which I am sympathetic, my understanding of the prospects for liberal democracy in the non-Western world is closer to the position of Amartya Sen as articulated in the following three essays: "Democracy as a Universal Value," *Journal of Democracy* 10 (July 1999), 3–17, "Human Rights and Asian Values," *New Republic* 217 (14–21 July 1997), 33–40, and "Why Democratization Is Not the Same as Westernization," *New Republic* 229 (6 October 2003), 28–33. Some maintain that among political theorists, only John Stuart Mill was a liberal democrat (properly understood) in contrast to Jean Jacques Rousseau, who was more of a participationist, and John Locke, whose conception of democracy was more limited in scope than Mill's. I am agreeing, however, with those who think that Locke's joint emphasis on individual rights, representative democracy, and legitimacy via consent makes him a prototypical, albeit an early, liberal democrat. As for Rousseau, his emphasis on popular sovereignty was endorsed by all liberal democrats (at least until the "realist" revisionists in the twentieth century).

19. The caveat pertains to the constitutional protection of basic rights and liberties. For a comprehensive discussion of liberal democracy and its problems see Frank Cunningham, *Theories of Democracy: A Critical Introduction* (New York: Routledge, 2002), 27–72.

20. Robert Dahl, *Democracy and Its Critics* (New Haven, Conn.: Yale University Press, 1989), 220.

21. Robert Dahl, *Polyarchy: Participation and Opposition* (New Haven, Conn.: Yale University Press, 1971), 3.

22. Alfred Stepan, *Arguing Comparative Politics* (New York: Oxford University Press, 2001), 226–227.

23. Ibid.

24. Ibid.

25. Samuel Huntington,The *Clash of Civilizations and the Remaking of the Modern World* (New York: Simon & Schuster, 1996), 70.

26. Ibid., 70.

27. Ibid., 71, 69.

28. Ibid.

29. Ibid., 151.

30. Ibid., 238.

31. Stepan, in his critique of Huntington, points out how the decidedly Western origins of the Marxist-Leninist party structure in China go completely unmentioned in Huntington's analysis of democracy in China (*Arguing Comparative Politics*, 215).

32. I. F. Stone, *The Trial of Socrates* (Boston: Little Brown, 1988), 135–139, 174–180, focuses on his alleged political violations, while James Colaiaco, *Socrates against Athens: Philosophy on Trial* (New York: Routledge, 2001), 105–130, highlights his alleged religious ones. For background see Mark McPherran, *The Religion of Socrates* (University Park: Penn State University Press, 1996), 1–28.

33. Roger Strauss, "The Relations of Religion to Democracy," *Public Opinion Quarterly* 2 (January 1938), 37–38.

34. John Rawls, *Political Liberalism* (New York: Columbia University Press, 1996), 10–11.

35. James Reichley, "Democracy and Religion," *PS* 19 (Autumn 1986), 801–806.

36. Charles Taylor, "The Politics of Recognition," in Amy Gutmann, ed. *Multiculturalism: Examining the Politics of Recognition* (Princeton, N.J.: Princeton University Press, 1994), 25–73.

37. I am indebted to Stathis Kalyvas's entire corpus of scholarship on religion and politics for shaping my thinking on this topic. See the bibliography for specific references.

38. In other words, I am disagreeing with scholars such as Samuel Huntington who argue that "a sense of individualism and a tradition of rights and liberties" is unique to Western civilization and thus "The West was West long before it was modern" (Huntington, *Clash of Civilizations*, 71, 69).

39. The academic literature on Islam and secularism tends to be polarized. On one side are scholars such as Bernard Lewis, Ernest Gellner, Samuel Huntington, Elie Kedourie, and John Waterbury, who make an argument, for various reasons, in defense of "Islamic exceptionalism." On the other side, scholars such as James Piscatori, Dale Eickelman, Sadiq Al Azm, Abdou Filali-Ansary, and Ira Lapidus argue, for various reasons, in favor of a potential accommodation between Islam and secularism. See Bernard Lewis, *What Went Wrong? The Clash between Islam and Modernity in the Middle East* (New York: Harper Collins, 2003), 96–116; Ernest Gellner, *Conditions of Liberty: Civil Society and Its Rivals* (New York: Penguin Books, 1996), 15–29; Huntington, *Clash of Civilizations*, 56–78, 207–218; Elie Kedourie, *Democracy and Arab Political Culture* (Washington, D.C.: Washington Institute for Near East Policy, 1992), 1–11; John Waterbury, "Democracy without Democrats? The Potential for Political Liberalization in the Middle East," in Ghassan Salamé, ed., *Democracy without Democrats? The Renewal of Politics in the Muslim World* (New York: Tauris, 1994), 23–47; James Piscatori and Dale Eickelman, *Muslim Politics* (Princeton, N.J.: Princeton University Press, 1996), 46–79; Sadiq Al Azm, "Is Islam Secularizable?" in Elisabeth Ozdalga and Sune Persson, eds., *Civil Society, Democracy and The Muslim World* (Istanbul: Swedish Research Institute, 1997), 17–22; Abdou Filali-Ansary, "Muslims and Democracy," and "The Challenge of Secularization," in Larry Diamond, Marc F. Plattner, and Daniel Brumberg, eds., *Islam and Democracy in the Middle East* (Baltimore: Johns Hopkins University Press, 2003), 193–207, 232–236; Ira Lapidus, "The Separation of State and Religion in the Development of Early Islamic Society," *International Journal of Middle Eastern Studies* 6 (1975), 363–385. Always insightful are the work of Wilfred Cantwell Smith, *Islam in Modern History* (Princeton, N.J.: Princeton University Press, 1957), 107–109, 172–183, and the scholarship of Sami Zubaida, "Islam and Secularization," *Asian Journal of Social Science* 33 (September 2005), 438–448.

40. Tocqueville gives us an indication of this when he observes that the "religious atmosphere of the country was the first thing that struck me on arrival in the United States" and that "for the Americans the ideas of Christianity and liberty are so completely mingled that it is almost impossible to get them to conceive of the one without the other" (*Democracy in America*, 295, 293). In the case of Europe, Christian democratic

parties played a critical—and often neglected role—in the construction
and consolidation of liberal democracy in Belgium, the Netherlands, Austria, Germany,
and Italy. See Strathis Kalyvas, *The Rise of Christian Democracy in Europe* (Ithaca,
N.Y.: Cornell University Press, 1996).

41. Democratic theorists unfamiliar with the Islamic world often rely on the work
of Bernard Lewis as the main source of scholarly authority on this topic. In an article in
the *Journal of Democracy* aimed at providing a comparative historical overview of the
relationship between Islam and liberal democracy, Lewis steadfastly avoided any mention
of the role of religion in the political development of the West. See Bernard Lewis, "Islam
and Liberal Democracy: A Historical Overview," *Journal of Democracy* 7 (April 1996),
52–63. Both Jean Elshtain (who quotes from Lewis explicitly), and Roger Scruton
acknowledge the role of religion in the political development of the West yet argue that
Christianity's inner creed is essentially different from that of Islam with respect to politics.
See Jean Elshtain, *Just War against Terror: The Burden of American Power in a Violent World*
(New York: Basic Books, 2003), 28–34, 139–144; Roger Scruton, *The West and the Rest:
Globalization and the Terrorist Threat* (Wilmington, Del.: ISI Books, 2002), 3–4, 47–51,
132–144. For echoes of Bernard Lewis's views on Islam and secularism among left-of-
center political philosophers see Charles Taylor, "The Politics of Recognition," in Amy
Gutmann, ed., *Multiculturalism: Examining the Politics of Recognition* (Princeton, N.J.:
Princeton University Press, 1994), 62, and Chantal Mouffe, *The Return of the Political*
(New York: Verso, 1993), 132. In the field of the comparative politics of the Middle East,
debates on political culture and democracy have gone beyond the work of Bernard
Lewis, who no longer represents the field. For a more nuanced perspective, albeit one
that still adheres to many of the modernization theory assumptions on the role of
religion in political development of Muslim societies, see Waterbury, "Democracy
without Democrats."

42. For a brief summary see Howard Handleman, *The Challenge of Third World
Development*, 3rd ed. (Uppper Saddle River, N.J.: Prentice Hall, 2003), 35–42.

43. Rex Brynen, Bahgat Korany, and Paul Noble, eds., *Political Liberalization and
Democratization in the Arab World*, vol. 1 (Boulder, Colo.: Lynne Rienner, 1995), 7.

44. Larry Diamond, "Three Paradoxes of Democracy," in Larry Diamond and
Marc Plattner, eds., *The Global Resurgence of Democracy*, 2nd ed. (Baltimore: Johns
Hopkins University Press, 1996), 120.

45. On the merits of such a crosscultural comparison see Richard Bulliet, *The Case
for Islamo-Christian Civilization* (New York: Columbia University Press, 2004), 1–45.

46. In the growing literature on Islam and democracy, rarely is a comparative-
historical approach employed that draws on insights from Western political theory. This
approach is absent in most of the leading scholarly investigations of this subject, including Diamond et al., *Islam and Democracy in the Middle East* ; Brynen et al., *Political
Liberalization and Democratization*, vols. 1 and 2; John Esposito and John Voll, *Islam and
Democracy* (New York: Oxford University Press, 1996); Noah Feldman, *After Jihad:
America and the Struggle for Islamic Democracy* (New York: Farrar, Straus and Giroux,
2003); Waterbury, "Democracy without Democrats"; Lewis, "Islam and Liberal
Democracy"; Bernard Lewis, "Why Turkey Is the Only Muslim Democracy," *Middle East*

Quarterly 1 (March 1994), 41–49; I. William Zartman, "Democracy and Islam: The Cultural Dialectic," *The Annals of the American Academy of Political and Social Science* 524 (November 1992), 181–191; Bassam Tibi, "Democracy and Democratization in Islam," in Michele Schmiegelow, *Democracy in Asia* (New York: Palgrave, 1997), 127–146; Gudrun Kramer, "Islamist Notions of Democracy," in Beinin and Stork, *Political Islam*, 71–82; Martin Kramer, "Islam vs. Democracy," in Martin Kramer, *Arab Awakening and Islamic Revival* (New Brunswick, N.J.: Transaction, 1996), 265–78; Abdelwahab El-Affendi, "Democracy and the Islamist Paradox," in Roland Axtmann, ed., *Understanding Democratic Politics* (London: Sage, 2003), 311–320; Khaled Abou El Fadl, *Islam and the Challenge of Democracy*, edited by Joshua Cohen and Deborah Chasman (Princeton, N.J.: Princeton University Press, 2004); Abdulaziz Sachedina, *The Islamic Roots of Democratic Pluralism* (New York: Oxford University Press, 2001); Ahmad Moussalli, *The Islamic Quest for Democracy, Pluralism and Human Rights* (Gainesville: University Press of Florida, 2001); M. Steven Fish, "Islam and Authoritarianism," *World Politics* 55 (October 2002), 4–37; S. V. R. Nasr, "Democracy and Islamic Revivalism," *Political Science Quarterly* 110 (summer 1995), 261–285; Adrian Karatnychy, "Muslim Countries and the Democracy Gap," *Journal of Democracy* 13 (January 2002), 99–112; Fatima Mernissi, *Islam and Democracy: Fear of the Modern World*, translated by Mary Jo Lakeland (Cambridge: Perseus, 2002); Timothy Sisk, ed., *Islam and Democracy: Religion, Politics and Power in the Middle East* (Washington, D.C.: United States Institute of Peace, 1992); Nazih Ayubi, "Islam and Democracy," in David Potter, David Goldblatt, Margaret Kiloh, and Paul Lewis, eds., *Democratization* (Cambridge: Polity Press, 1997), 345–366; Asef Bayat, *Making Islam Democratic: Social Movements and the Post-Islamist Turn* (Palo Alto, Calif.: Stanford University Press, 2007). While not dealing explicitly with the question of Islam and democracy, the following authors have written insightfully from a comparative political theory-historical perspective: Roxanne Euben, *Enemy in the Mirror: Islamic Fundamentalism and the Limits of Modern Rationalism* (Princeton, N.J.: Princeton University Press, 1999); L. Carl Brown, *Religion and State: The Muslim Approach to Politics* (New York: Columbia University Press, 2000); Fred Dallmayr, *Dialogue among Civilizations: Some Exemplary Voices* (New York: Palgrave, 2002); Charles Butterworth, "State and Authority in Arabic Political Thought," in Ghassan Salamé, ed., *The Foundations of the Arab State* (London: Croom Helm, 1987), 91–111; Bjorn Olav Utvik, "The Modernizing Force of Islam," in John Esposito and Francois Burgat, eds., *Modernizing Islam: Religion in the Public Sphere in Europe and the Middle East* (New Brunswick, N.J.: Rutgers University Press, 2003), 43–67, and Ellis Goldberg, "Smashing Idols and the State: The Protestant Ethic and Egyptian Sunni Radicalism," in Juan R.I. Cole, ed., *Comparing Muslim Societies: Knowledge and the State in a World Civilization* (Ann Arbor: University of Michigan Press, 1992), 195–236.

47. Peter Waldman, "A Historian's Take on Islam Steers U.S. in Terrorism Fight," *Wall Street Journal*, 3 February 2004.

48. For some glaring examples of a misreading of trends in Muslim politics, consider the following two examples. On 23 June 1980, at a colloquium at Tel Aviv University, Bernard Lewis predicted that "the Islamic resurgence has reached its peak, and that from now onwards it will probably decline rather than ascend" (quoted in Gabriel Ben Dor, *State and Conflict in the Middle East* [New York: Praeger, 1983], 35. More recently, the two

principal U.S. Middle East scholars advising the Bush administration on Iraq policy in the lead-up to the 2003 invasion predicted "scenes of rejoicing in their cities would exceed those that followed the liberation of Kabul" (Bernard Lewis), and "precious few among them dream of a Shi'a state. The majority of them are secularists" (Fouad Ajami). Bernard Lewis, "Time for Toppling," *Wall Street Journal*, 27 September 2002, and Fouad Ajami, "Iraq and the Arabs' Future," *Foreign Affairs* 82 (January–February 2003), 12.

49. Sheri Berman, "Lessons from Europe," *Journal of Democracy* 18 (January 2007), 38.

50. Fred Dallmayr, "Toward a Comparative Political Theory," in Fred Dallmayr, ed., *Border Crossings: Toward a Comparative Political Theory* (Lanham, Md.: Lexington Books, 1999), 1–2. Also see Fred Dallmayr, "Beyond Monologue: For a Comparative Political Theory," *Perspectives on Politics* 2 (June 2004), 249–257.

51. Dallmayr, "Toward a Comparative Political Theory," 2.

52. Sudipta Kaviraj, "In Search of Civil Society," in Sudipta Kaviraj and Sunil Khilnani, eds., *Civil Society: History and Possibilities* (Cambridge: Cambridge University Press, 2001), 287.

53. Ibid. Fred Dallmayr adds that comparative political theorists "need to steer a middle course between narrow area specialists and abstract generalists: while the former slight the 'theoretical,' the latter miss the 'comparative' component of comparative political theory. Among prominent contemporary approaches, comparative theory clearly departs from what is commonly called 'formal theory,' which imposes a general, universal 'form' on diverse phenomena, thereby revealing its debt to the universalist claims of the European Enlightenment." Dallmayr also suggests that comparative political theorists should be familiar with at least one major non-European language (Dallmayr, "Beyond Monologue," 249).

54. Bernard Lewis, *What Went Wrong? The Clash between Islam and Modernity in the Middle East* (New York: Perennial, 2003).

55. For a representative example of this problematic approach see Bernard Lewis's comparative treatment of the role of religion in politics in the West and in the Muslim world in *The Crisis of Islam: Holy War and Unholy Terror* (New York: Random House, 2003), 13–20.

56. Fukuyama, *End of History*, 49–50. I borrow this point from Anthony Arblaster.

57. *Arab Development Report 2002: Creating Opportunities for Future Generations* (New York: United Nations Development Program, 2002), and *Freedom in the World 2001–2002: The Democracy Gap* (New York: Freedom House, 2001). The second report highlighted the "Islamic World's Democracy Deficit." See their press release, www.freedomhouse.org/media/pressrel/121801.htm. I summarize the findings of these reports in Nader A. Hashemi, "Inching towards Democracy: Religion and Politics in the Muslim World," *Third World Quarterly* 24 (June 2003), 563–564.

58. Correspondence with Ian Shapiro, 21 July 2004.

59. David Wooton, ed., *Divine Right and Democracy: An Anthology of Political Writings in Stuart England* (New York: Penguin Books, 1986).

60. Alfred Stepan, "World Religious Systems and Democracy: Crafting the 'Twin Tolerations,' " in Stepan, *Arguing Comparative Politics* (New York: Oxford University Press, 2001), 213–253.

61. Bernard Lewis, *Islam and the West* (New York: Oxford University Press, 1993), 174–186.

62. Peter Iver Kaufman, *Redeeming Politics* (Princeton, N.J.: Princeton University Press, 1990). In addition, Thomas Hobbes in the *Leviathan* called for the institutional union of state and church, or as the subtitle of his famous book reads: "The Matter, Forme and Power of a Common Wealth Ecclesiasticall *and* Civil (emphasis added). See chaps. 13, 26, 39.

63. Filali-Ansary, "Challenge of Secularization," 235.

64. Marshall Hodgson, "Modernity and the Islamic Heritage," in Hodgson, *Rethinking World History: Essays on Europe, Islam, and World History* (Cambridge: Cambridge University Press, 1993), 220. He discusses this theme also in *The Venture of Islam: The Gunpower Empires and Modern Times* (Chicago: University of Chicago Press, 1974), 3:417–436.

65. See the special issue of *Daedalus* on religion and secularism, especially S. V. R. Nasr, "Lessons from the Muslim World," *Daedalus* 132 (Summer 2003), 67–72, for a cogent summary.

66. See Munir Shafiq, "Secularism and the Arab-Muslim Condition," and Abdelwahab Elmessiri, "Secularism, Immanence and Deconstruction," in John Esposito and Azzam Tamimi, eds., *Islam and Secularism in the Middle East* (New York: New York University Press, 2000), 139–50 and 52–80.

67. Akeel Bilgrami, "Secularism, Nationalism and Modernity," in Rajeev Bhargava, ed., *Secularism and Its Critics* (New Delhi: Oxford University Press, 1998), 393.

68. Wilfred Cantwell Smith, *Islam in Modern History* (Princeton, N.J.: Princeton University Press, 1997), 304. I thank Karen Armstrong for this reference.

69. David Held, "Democracy: From City-States to a Cosmopolitan Order?," in David Held, ed., *Prospects for Democracy: North, South, East, West* (Stanford, Calif.: Stanford University Press, 1993), 14.

70. I borrow these observations from Robert Hefner, *Civil Islam: Muslims and Democratization in Indonesia* (Princeton, N.J.: Princeton University Press, 2000), 3, and Russell Arben Fox, "Confucianism and Communitarianism in a Liberal-democratic World," in Fred Dallmayr, ed., *Border Crossings: Toward a Comparative Political Theory* (Lanham, Md.: Lexington Books, 1999), 185–186.

71. For a representative sample see Giovanni Sartori's comments on events in Algeria in the early 1990s with respect to the Front islamique du Salut (FIS), and democracy in "How Far Can Free Government Travel?" in Larry Diamond and Marc Plattner, eds., *The Global Divergence of Democracies* (Baltimore: Johns Hopkins University Press, 2001), 55–56.

CHAPTER 1

1. "World Religious Systems and Democracy: Crafting the 'Twin Tolerations,'" in Alfred Stepan, *Arguing Comparative Politics* (New York: Oxford University Press, 2001), 213–253.

2. Ibid., 227–229. John Rawls, *Political Liberalism* (New York: Columbia University Press, 1993); Bruce Ackerman, *Social Justice in the Liberal State* (New Haven, Conn.: Yale University Press, 1980).

3. The epigraph is from "Maxime Rodinson on Islamic 'Fundamentalism,' " an unpublished interview with Gilbert Achar, *Middle East Report* 34 (Winter 2004), 4.

4. Robert Kaplan has written that the "terrorist attacks on the World Trade Center and the Pentagon highlight the tragic relevance not just of [Samuel] Huntington's ideas about a clash of civilizations but of his entire life's work." Huntington's "sharp opinions," Kaplan adds, "about the collision of Islam and the West, about the role of the military in a liberal society, about what separates countries that work from countries that don't—have proved to be as prescient as they have been controversial. Huntington has been ridiculed and vilified, but in the decades ahead his view of the world will be the way it really looks." Robert Kaplan, "Looking the World in the Eye," *Atlantic Monthly* 288 (December 2001), 68–82.

5. Rawls, *Political Liberalism*, 133–172. Discussed by Stepan, "World Religious Systems and Democracy," 227. An "overlapping consensus" refers to how supporters of different religious, political or philosophical views can agree on a specific form of political organization based on shared moral values.

6. Rawls, *Political Liberalism*, 12.

7. Ibid., 151.

8. "Freestanding conceptions of political justice" refers to noncomprehensive religious or philosophical doctrines that may have validity in the private sphere but not the public sphere. See Rawls, *Political Liberalism*, 10–11.

9. Stepan, "World Religious Systems and Democracy," 228.

10. Ibid., n. 39.

11. Adam Przeworski, "Democracy as a Contingent Outcome of Conflicts," in Jon Elster and Rune Slagstad, eds., *Constitutionalism and Democracy* (Cambridge: Cambridge University Press, 1988), 59–80.

12. Stepan, "World Religious Systems and Democracy," 228. Stepan discusses, for example, the case of Holland, where in 1917 religion was "taken off the political agenda of majority decision making only as a result of an extensive bargaining process that ended up in a democratic—but not liberal—consociational agreement." The bargain that was struck allocated money, space, and mutual vetoes to religious communities "with competing comprehensive doctrines concerning many aspects of the educational process, the media, civil society, political society, and indeed, virtually the entire ensemble of Dutch democratic political procedures and practices."

13. Ibid., 229. For the case of Belgium see Stathis S. Kalyvas, "Democracy and Religious Politics: Evidence from Belgium," *Comparative Political Studies* 31 (June 1998), 292–320.

14. Ibid.

15. Irene Gendzier, *Development against Democracy: Manipulating Political Change in the Third World* (Hampton, Conn.: Tyrone Press, 1995), 109, 12.

16. For the ongoing relevance of modernization theory, with significant adjustments based on recent findings, see Ronald Inglehart and Wayne Baker, "Modernization,

Cultural Change, and the Persistence of Traditional Values," *American Sociological Review* 65 (February 2000), 19–51. My definition of modernization theory is partly drawn from their definition. For a discussion and critique see Jonathan Fox, *Ethnoreligious Conflict in the Late Twentieth Century* (Lanham, Md.: Lexington Books, 2002), 31–63.

17. B. C. Smith, *Understanding Third World Politics: Theories of Political Change and Development*, 2nd ed.(New York: Palgrave, 2003), 44–74; John Martinussen, *Society, State and Market: Competing Theories of Development* (London: Zed Books, 1997), 25–31, 167–176.

18. Some of the important works in this area are: Samuel P. Huntington, *Political Order in Changing Societies* (New Haven, Conn.: Yale University Press, 1968); Gabriel Almond and James Coleman, eds., *The Politics of Developing Areas* (Princeton, N.J.: Princeton University Press, 1960); Lucian Pye and Sidney Verba, *Political Culture and Political Development* (Princeton, N.J.: Princeton University Press, 1965); David Apter, *The Politics of Modernization* (Chicago: University of Chicago Press, 1965); Cyril E. Black, ed., *Comparative Modernization: A Reader* (New York: Free Press, 1976); and Myron Weiner and Samuel P. Huntington, eds., *Understanding Political Development* (Prospect Heights, Ill.: Waveland Press, 1987).

19. Daniel Lerner, "Modernization: Social Aspects," in David L. Sills, ed., *International Encyclopedia of the Social Sciences* (New York: Crowell Collier and Macmillan, 1968), 10:386–395.

20. Emphasis added. Gabriel Almond and G. Bingham Powell, *Comparative Politics: A Development Approach* (Boston: Little Brown, 1966), 105.

21. Donald Smith, ed., *Religion and Modernization* (New Haven, Conn.: Yale University Press, 1974), 4.

22. Fred R. Von der Mehden, *Religion and Modernization in Southeast Asia* (Syracuse, N.Y.: Syracuse University Press, 1986), 13.

23. Lisa Anderson, "Arab Democracy: Dismal Prospects," *World Policy Journal* 28 (Fall 2001), 53–60.

24. Samuel P. Huntington, "Will Countries Become More Democratic?" *Political Science Quarterly* 99 (Summer 1984), 193–218; Dankwart A. Rustow, "Transitions to Democracy: Toward a Dynamic Model," *Comparative Politics* 2 (April 1970), reprinted in Lisa Anderson, ed., *Transitions to Democracy* (New York: Columbia University Press, 1999), 14–41.

25. Anderson, "Arab Democracy," 53.

26. Huntington, "Will Countries Become More Democratic," 216. Seymour Martin Lipset makes a similar argument in "The Social Requisites of Democracy Revisited," *American Sociological Review* 59 (February 1994), 6.

27. See the draft party platform of the Egyptian Muslim Brotherhood, released in October 2007, which calls for the creation of a council of religious experts to oversee government. For details see Maggie Michael, "Egypt's Brotherhood Party Details Platform Akin to That of Iran," *Boston Globe*, 11 October 2007, and Amr Hamzawy, "Egypt: Regression in the Muslim Brotherhood's Party Platform?" *Arab Reform Bulletin* 5 (October 2007), http://www.carnegieendowment.org/publications/index.cfm?fa=view&id=19648&prog=zgp&proj=zdrl,zme#hamzawy. For background see Gudrun

Kramer, "Islamist Notions of Democracy," in Joel Beinin and Joe Stork, eds., *Political Islam: Essays from Middle East Report* (Berkeley: University of California Press, 1997), 71–82. On human rights see Ann Elizabeth Mayer, *Islam and Human Rights: Tradition and Politics*, 4th ed. (Boulder, Colo.: Westview Press, 2007), 9–97.

28. To give just one mainstream example, consider Princeton University Middle East scholar John Waterbury. In his discussion of democracy and its challenges in the Middle East, he seems to share many of Huntington's assumptions and biases with respect to political Islam and its connection to democratization. His discussion of political Islam is both ahistorical and neo-Orientalist. He observes that "political Islam must enter the equation as a unique force. It is not like any other religion in that its very heart lies in its sacred texts." While he does make a passing reference to the long view of history and the possibility of a reconciliation between religious politics and political development, he remains "profoundly sceptical" that this may happen, in part because of the sui generis nature of the Muslim faith. Where "the scriptures are both holy and explicit," he affirms, "as is the case in Islam, pragmatic compromise will be very difficult" ("Democracy Without Democrats?: the potential for political liberalization in the Middle East," in Ghassan Salamé, ed., *Democracy without Democrats? The Renewal of Politics in the Muslim World* [New York: Tauris, 1994], 45, 40, 39). This book seeks to challenge these widely held assumptions.

29. The reference to the "latent benefits" of Islamic fundamentalism might seem shocking to the reader. This will be explicated in this chapter in the context of Michael Walzer's thesis on the revolutionary Puritan "saint" as a modernizing agent in a traditional society. I will argue that mainstream Islamic fundamentalists are performing a similar role today in the Middle East. For a recent contribution to this debate see Francis Fukuyama and Nadav Samin, "Can Any Good Come of Radical Islam?" *Commentary* 114 (September 2002), 34–38.

30. In making this observation, I am reminded of Karl Marx's observation that it "is not the consciousness of men that determine their being, but, on the contrary, their social being that determines their consciousness." Quoted in Robert Tucker, ed., *The Marx-Engels Reader*, 2nd ed. (New York: Norton, 1978), 4.

31. Gregg Easterbrook, "Death and Dogma: Behind the Moslem Fury at 'Satanic Verses'—The West's Enduring Ignorance of Islam," *Washington Post*, 19 February 1989.

32. One of the critical differences is that radical protest movements in the Muslim world are significantly shaped by the impact of Western intervention both past and present. See Khaled Abou El Fadl, "9/11 and the Muslim Transformation," in Mary Dudziak, ed., *September 11 in History: A Watershed Moment ?* (Durham, N.C.: Duke University Press, 2003), 70–111. On the merits of civilizational comparison see Richard Bulliet, *The Case for Islamo-Christian Civilization* (New York: Columbia University Press, 2004), 1–45.

33. I am borrowing some of these ideas from Hazem Ghobarah's unpublished essay "Gateways to Modernity: Puritanism and Islamism?" December 1995, rev. 1997, www.la.utexas.edu/chenry/civil/archives97/csdefs/0007.html.

34. Arend Lijphart, "Comparative Politics and the Comparative Method," *American Political Science Review* 65 (September 1971), 682–693, and Arend Lijphart, "The

Comparable-Cases Strategy in Comparative Research," *Comparative Political Studies* 8 (July 1975), 158–177. Also see Gary King, Robert Keohane, and Sidney Verba, *Designing Social Inquiry* (Princeton, N.J.: Princeton University Press, 1994).

35. Ghobarah, "Gateways to Modernity."

36. Ibid.

37. Fred Dallmayr, "An Islamic Reformation? Some Afterthoughts," in Charles Kurzman and Michaelle Browers, eds., *An Islamic Reformation?* (Lanham, Md.: Lexington Books, 2004), 178–184. Also see L. Carl Brown, *Religion and State: The Muslim Approach to Politics* (New York: Columbia University Press, 2000), 136–139, who endorses this approach.

38. Dallmayr cites "the process of globalization" as particularly salient in its transformative impact on traditional societies, both Christian and Muslim.

39. The details of this event come from three sources: Rodney Stark and Williams Bainbridge, *The Future of Religion: Secularization, Revival and Cult Formation* (Berkeley: University of California Press, 1985), 506–507; Tal Howard, "Charisma and History: The Case of Münster, Westphalia, 1534–1535," *Essays in History* 35 (1993), 49–65; and George Huntston Williams, *The Radical Reformation*, 3rd ed. (Kirksville, Mo.: Sixteenth Century Journal, 1992), 553–588.

40. Williams, *Radical Reformation*, 571.

41. My first exposure to the Münster uprising and its relationship to social change in the Muslim world was via a lecture by Saad Eddin Ibrahim in Cairo, Egypt, in February 1997. Ibrahim's conference paper, on which I draw, is "From Taliban to Erbakan: The Case of Islam, Civil Society and Democracy," in Elisabeth Özdalga and Sune Persson, eds., *Civil Islam, Democracy and the Muslim World: Papers Read at a Conference Held at the Swedish Research Institute in Istanbul, 28–30 October 1996* (Istanbul: Swedish Research Institute in Istanbul, 1997), 33–44.

42. Refers to a specific event in Muslim history: Muhammad's migration from Mecca to Medina in September 622, which coincides with the first year of the Islamic era.

43. Thomas Hobbes, *Behemoth or the Long Parliament* (Chicago: University of Chicago Press, 1990), 21–22.

44. Much of this discussion draws on Ibrahim, "From Taliban to Erbakan."

45. A recent World Bank study on poverty in the Middle East and North Africa noted: "very little progress was made on the poverty front. The region's average poverty rate fluctuated between 20, and 25 percent during the entire decade of the 1990s. By 2001, approximately 52 million people were poor, an *increase* in absolute numbers of approximately 11.5 million people, compared with the situation in 1987." (Farrukh Iqbal, *Sustaining Gains in Poverty Reduction and Human Development in the Middle East and North Africa* [Washington, D.C.: World Bank, 2006], xix; emphasis added.).

46. Stark and Bainbridge, *Future of Religion*, 507.

47. Personal correspondence, 2 May 2003.

48. (London: Secker and Warburg, 1958), 291–292. I am indebted to John Trumpbour for this quotation and for drawing my attention to the link between Anabaptism in Germany in the sixteenth century and Puritanism in England in the seventeenth century.

49. Ernest Tucker, "Primitivism as a Radical Response to Religious Crisis: The Anabaptists of Munster in the 1530s and the Taliban of Afghanistan in the 1990s," in Charles Kurzman and Michaelle Browers, eds., *An Islamic Reformation?* (Lanham, Md.: Lexington Books, 2004), 147–158.

50. Fouad Ajami, "Nowhere Man," *New York Times Magazine* (7 October 2001).

51. Thomas Friedman, "The Saudi Challenge," *New York Times*, 20 February 2002; emphasis added.

52. Lewis Spitz, *The Renaissance and Reformation Movements* (Chicago: Rand McNally, 1971), 399.

53. Mark Mazower, *Dark Continent: Europe's Twentieth Century* (New York: Knopf, 1999), ix–xvi, 395–403. Also see Charles Tilly, *Contention and Democracy in Europe, 1650–2000* (Cambridge: Cambridge University Press, 2004), 168–205.

54. Ibid.

55. Daniel Pipes, *In the Path of God: Islam and Political Power* (New York: Basic Books, 1983), 29–93; Elie Kedourie, *Democracy and Arab Political Culture* (Portland, Ore: Frank Cass, 1994), 1–11, and David Pryce Jones, *The Closed Circle* (London: Paladin, 1990), 1–33.

56. This thinking is echoed by prominent Islamist theoreticians such as Sayyid Qutb and Abu al-A'la Mawdudi. In his discussion of Islamic political theory, for example, Qutb refers to Islam as "a comprehensive philosophy and a homogeneous unity," while arguing that "to introduce into it any foreign element would mean ruining it" (Sayyid Qutb, *Social Justice in Islam*, translated by John B. Hardie and Hamid Algar, rev. ed. [Oneonta, N.Y.: Islamic Publications International, 2000], 117).

57. Bernard Lewis, *The Middle East and the West* (New York: Harper Torchbooks, 1964), 48; emphasis added; quoted in Yahya Sadowski, "The New Orientalism and Democracy Debate," in Beinin and Stork, *Political Islam*, 35.

58. Ibid.

59. Ernest Gellner, *Postmodernism, Reason and Religion* (London: Routledge, 1992), 1–22. For a succinct summary see Ernest Gellner, *Conditions of Liberty: Civil Society and Its Rivals* (New York: Penguin Books, 1994), 15–29, and his *Muslim Society* (Cambridge: Cambridge University Press, 1981), 1–16, 99–113.

60. Sami Zubaida summarizing Gellner in *Islam, the People and the State: Political Ideas and Movements in the Middle East* (New York: Tauris, 1993), xiv–xv. For a concise overview and critique of Gellner on this topic see, Dale Eickelman, "From Here to Modernity: Ernest Gellner on Nationalism and Islamic Fundamentalism," in John A. Hall, *The State of the Nation: Ernest Gellner and the Theory of Nationalism* (Cambridge: Cambridge University Press, 1998), 258–271, and Sami Zubaida, "Is There a Muslim Society? Ernest Gellner's Sociology of Islam," *Economy and Society* 24 (May 1995), 151–188.

61. Martin Kramer, "Hizbullah: The Calculus of Jihad," in Martin E. Marty and R. Scott Appleby, eds., *Fundamentalisms and the State: Remaking Politics, Economics, and Militance* (Chicago: University of Chicago Press, 1993), 539.

62. Ibid.

63. Juan Eduardo Campo, "The Ends of Islamic Fundamentalism: Hegemonic Discourse and the Islamic Question in Egypt," *Contention* 4 (spring 1995), 174–175.

Campo, while praising Kramer for including some valuable information about Hizbullah in his article notes that "it unfortunately neglects to discuss in any meaningful way the most immediate cause for the rise of the organization: the 1982 Israeli invasion and American complicity with it." This is typical of many Orientalist scholars and political modernization theorists. The role of West in the internal affairs of the Third World is always considered helpful at best, benign at worst.

64. For a lengthy response to the essentialist interpretation of Muslim politics by Orientalist scholars see Zubaida, *Islam, the People and the State*, 121–182. Recently, there has been an attempt to link the behavior of the Barbary pirates in North Africa in the early nineteenth century to the activities of Al Qaeda, as if to suggest that America has always faced a threat from radical Islam dating back to the origins of the republic. See Michael Oren, *Power, Faith and Fantasy: America in the Middle East, 1776 to the Present* (New York: Norton, 2007), 17–40. For a riposte see Nader Hashemi, "Misreading America's Past in the Middle East," *Chicago Tribune*, 18 February 2007.

65. Hindu fundamentalism has largely escaped critical scrutiny by Western intellectuals. Martha Nussbaum is one notable exception. See her *The Clash Within: Democracy, Religious Violence and India's Future* (Cambridge, Mass.: Harvard University Press, 2007), 152–185. For example, V. S. Naipaul suffered no negative press after he endorsed the destruction of the Babri Mosque in Ayodhya, India, while describing Hindu fundamentalism as a "mighty creative process" (see his interview with Dilip Padgoankar, *Times of India*, 18 July 1993). For an exhaustive treatment of the subject see the five volumes of the Fundamentalism Project, edited by Martin E. Marty and R. Scott Appleby and published by the University of Chicago Press: *Fundamentalisms Observed* (1991), *Fundamentalisms and the State: Remaking Polities, Economies and Militance* (1993), *Fundamentalisms and Society: Reclaiming the Sciences, the Family and Education* (1993), *Accounting for Fundamentalism: The Dynamic Character of Movements* (1994), and *Fundamentalisms Comprehended* (1995).

66. Charles Taylor, *The Malaise of Modernity* (Concord, Ontario: Anansi, 1991), 1–12. For an excellent scholarly treatment of comparative fundamentalisms see Nikki Keddie, "The New Religious Politics: Where, When and Why Do 'Fundamentalisms' Appear?" *Comparative Studies in Society and History* 40 (October 1998), 696–723.

67. Charles J. Halperin, *Russia and the Golden Horde: The Mongol Impact on Russian History* (Bloomington: Indiana University Press, 1985), 129.

68. After the attack on the World Trade Center on 11 September 2001, it was widely reported in the press that church attendance in the United States had significantly increased. See Laurie Goodstein, "As Attacks' Impact Recedes, a Return to Religion as Usual," *New York Times*, 21 November 2001.

69. James Piscatori, *Islam in a World of Nation-States* (Cambridge: Cambridge University Press, 1986), 31.

70. Karen Armstrong, "Is a Holy War Inevitable?" *GQ* (January 2002), 98. For Armstrong's thoughtful treatment of and elaboration on this subject see *The Battle for God* (New York: Knopf, 2001), 135–364.

71. John Sigler, "Understanding the Resurgence of Islam: The Case of Political Islam," *Middle East Affairs Journal* 2 (Summer-Fall 1996), 86. I am indebted to John

Sigler for shaping my thoughts on the relationship between religion, modernity, and fundamentalism. I draw heavily on his insights for this section of the book.

72. Roland Robertson and JoAnn Chirico, "Humanity, Globalization, and Worldwide Religion Resurgence: A Theoretical Exploration," *Sociological Analysis* 46 (1985), 233, quoted by John Voll, *Islam: Continuity and Change in the Modern World*, 2nd ed. (Syracuse, N.Y.: Syracuse University Press, 1994), 376.

73. Benjamin Barber, *Jihad vs. McWorld* (New York: Ballantine Books, 1995). I am indebted to John Sigler for this insight.

74. Also helpful in this regard is the concept of historical and political trajectories employed by Perry Anderson and Jean-Francois Bayart. For a short summary of their views as they apply to the developing world see John Martinussen, *Society, State and Market: A Guide to Competing Theories of Development* (London: Zed Books, 1997), 179–180. For a more detailed discussion see Perry Anderson, *Lineages of the Absolute State* (London: Verso, 1979), and Jean-Francois Bayart, "Finishing with the Idea of the Third World: The Concept of the Political Trajectory," in James Manor, ed., *Rethinking Third World Politics* (London: Longman, 1991), 51–71.

75. Fernand Braudel, "La Longue Durée," in *Écrits sur l'histoire* (Paris: Flammarion, 1985), 41–83.

76. Ibid., 50.

77. Ibid., 54.

78. L. Carl Brown, *Religion and State: The Muslim Approach to Politics*, 137.

79. Şerif Mardin, *Religion, Society, and Modernity in Turkey* (Syracuse, N.Y.: Syracuse University Press, 2006), 206–297, and M. Hakan Yavuz, *Islamic Political Identity in Turkey* (New York: Oxford University Press, 2003), 207–238.

80. Michael Walzer, *Revolution of the Saints: A Study in the Origins of Radical Politics* (Cambridge, Mass.: Harvard University Press, 1965). I am indebted to John Sigler for bringing this book to my attention.

81. J. A. Sharpe, *Early Modern England: A Social History, 1550–1760* (London: Edward Arnold, 1987), 77–98, 198–224, 227–253.

82. Walzer, *Revolution of the Saints*, 200–201.

83. Ibid., 201.

84. Ibid., 201–202.

85. Ibid., 202.

86. Ibid., 202–203.

87. Ibid., 302.

88. Ibid., 300.

89. Ibid., 310. In this context Walzer draws a comparison between Lenin and Oliver Cromwell. See page 310 n. 14.

90. Ibid., 311.

91. Ibid., 312; emphasis in original.

92. Ibid., 316.

93. Ibid., 317.

94. Ibid., 317–320.

95. For the ideas and the title of this section I am heavily indebted to Ghobarah, "Gateways to Modernity."

96. Lawrence Stone, *Social Change and Revolution in England, 1540–1640* (London: Longmans, 1980), and *Causes of the English Revolution, 1529–1642* (London: Routledge and Kegan Paul, 1972); Michael Mullet, *Radical Religious Movements in Early Modern Europe* (London: Allen and Unwin, 1980); Christopher Hill, *Puritanism and Revolution: Studies in Interpretation of the English Revolution of the Seventeenth Century* (London: Secker and Warburg, 1958); Perez Zagorin, *The English Revolution: Politics, Events and Ideas* (Brookfield, Vt.: Ashgate, 1998). David Hume made a similar argument that certain strands of Protestantism (especially Quakers), when viewed over the long term, had contributed to liberalism. He also suggested that a certain strand of Catholicism (Jansenism) was playing a similar role in France. See Hume, "Of Superstition and Enthusiasm," in *Essays and Treatises on Several Subjects: Essays, Moral, Political and Literary* (Bristol, England: Thoemmes Press, 2002), 1:175–81.

97. Ghobarah, "Gateways to Modernity."

98. Max Weber, *The Protestant Ethic and the Spirit of Capitalism*, translated by Talcott Parsons (New York: Routledge, 2001).

99. Walzer, *The Revolution of the Saints*, 1.

100. Ibid., 1–2.

101. Ibid., 10–11.

102. On the contribution of religious radicalism to English democracy see A. S. P. Woodhouse, "Religion and Some Foundations of English Democracy," *Philosophical Review* 61 (October 1952), 503–531. Robert Dahl suggests that early democratic theory has it roots in radical Protestantism. See his *Democracy and Its Critics* (New Haven, Conn.: Yale University Press, 1989), 32.

103. Nazih Ayubi, *Political Islam: Religion and Politics in the Arab World* (New York: Routledge, 1991), 120–157; Olivier Roy, *The Failure of Political Islam*, translated by Carol Volk (Cambridge, Mass.: Harvard University Press, 1994), 1–47, and *Globalized Islam: The Search for a New Ummah* (New York: Columbia University Press, 2004), 1–99; L. Carl Brown, *Religion and State: The Muslim Approach to Politics* (New York: Columbia University Press, 2000), 79–86; James Piscatori and Dale Eickelman, *Muslim Politics* (Princeton, N.J.: Princeton University Press, 1996), 22–45; John Esposito and Francois Burgat, eds., *Modernizing Islam: Religion in the Public Sphere in Europe and the Middle East* (New Brunswick, N.J.: Rutgers University Press, 2003), 1–14; Beinin and Stork, "On the Modernity, Historical Specificity, and International Context of Political Islam," in *Political Islam*, 3–25; Seyyed Vali Reza Nasr, *The Vanguard of the Islamic Revolution: The Jama'at-I Islami of Pakistan* (New York: Oxford University Press, 1994), 3–43; Mohammed Ayoob, *The Many Faces of Political Islam: Religion and Politics in the Muslim World* (Ann Arbor: University of Michigan Press, 2008), 1–22, and Charles Kurzman, "Bin Laden and Other Thoroughly Modern Muslims," *Contexts* 1 (Fall-Winter 2002), 13–20.

104. Zubaida, *Islam, the People and the State*, 3.

105. Ibid., 59. Ervand Abrahamian makes a similar point in *Khomeinism: Essays on the Islamic Republic* (Berkeley: University of California Press, 1993), 13–38. Also see Sami Zubaida, "Is Iran an Islamic State?" in Beinin and Stork, *Political Islam*, 103–119.

106. Abdulaziz Sachedina, *The Just Ruler in Shi'ite Islam: The Comprehensive Authority of the Jurist in Imamite Jurisprudence* (New York: Oxford University Press,

1988); Said Amir Arjomand, "Ideological Revolution in Shi'ism," in Arjomand, ed., *Authority and Political Culture in Shi'ism* (Albany: State University of New York Press, 1988), 179–209, and Arjomand, *The Shadow of God and the Hidden Imam: Religion, Political Order, and Societal Change in Shi'ite Iran from the Beginning to 1890* (Chicago: University of Chicago Press, 1984); Hamid Enayat, "Iran: Khumayni's Concept of the 'Guardianship of the Jurisconsult,' " in James Piscatori, ed., *Islam in the Political Process* (Cambridge: Cambridge University Press, 1983), 160–180; Hamid Mavani, "The Basis of Leadership: Khumayni's Claims and the Classic Tradition" (Master's Thesis, Institute for Islamic Studies, McGill University, 1992). In a series of influential books in the late 1990s, Mohsen Kadivar provided an exhaustive critique of Khomeini's doctrine of *velayat-e faqih* (guardianship of the Islamic jurist) that garnered him publicity and eventually landed him in jail. Relying exclusively on Shia sources, he launched a solid theological and scholarly refutation of the ruling ethos of conservative clergy in Iran while simultaneously remaining within the bounds of Shia jurisprudence. Kadivar's basic argument in *Nazariyaha-ye dawlat dar fiqh-e Shia* (Theses on the State in Shia Jurisprudence) was that Khomeini's thesis on the guardianship of the Islamic jurist was simply one thesis among many that Shia theologians have expounded over the years, ranging from a religious justification of monarchy to democracy, and thus can in no way be considered *the* definitive or authoritative political model for the Shia school of jurisprudence. Kadivar discusses nine different theories on government that Shia theologians have produced over the years. Mohsen Kadivar, *Nazariyaha-ye dawlat dar fiqh-e Shia* (Theses on the State in Shi'i Jurisprudence) (Tehran: Nashr-e Ney, 1997), 58, 80, 97, 108, 112, 127, 141, 154, 175.

107. Zubaida, *Islam, the People and the State*, 155. The classic study in English on the Muslim Brotherhood is Richard Mitchell, *The Society of the Muslim Brothers* (New York: Oxford University Press, 1993), 209–259.

108. Zubaida, *Islam, the People and the State*, 155.

109. John Sigler, "Understanding the Resurgence of Islam," 82.

110. Gilles Kepel, *Jihad: The Trail of Political Islam* (Cambridge, Mass.: Harvard University Press, 2002), 34. For discussion of the political thought of Sayyid Qutb see Roxanne Euben, *Enemy in the Mirror: Islamic Fundamentalism and the Limits of Modern Rationalism* (Princeton, N.J.: Princeton University Press, 1999), 49–92, and the two volumes by Sayed Khatab *The Political Thought of Sayyid Qutb: The Theory of Jahiliyyah* (New York: Routledge, 2006), and *The Power of Sovereignty: The Political and Ideological Philosophy of Sayyid Qutb* (New York: Routledge, 2006). For a discussion of the political ideas of Mawlana Mawdudi see Seyyed Vali Reza Nasr, *Mawdudi and the Making of Islamic Revivalism* (New York: Oxford University Press, 1996). In the introduction to his influential book *Ma'lim fi al-tariq* (Milestones on the Road), Qutb invokes the term "vanguard" (*tali'a*) on a number of occasions. See Qutb, *Milestones*, translated by M. M. Siddiqui (Indianapolis: American Trust, 1990), 5.

111. Saad Eddin Ibrahim, *Egypt, Islam and Democracy: Critical Essays* (Cairo: American University of Cairo Press, 2002), 17, 75. Confirming these trends is Ayubi, *Political Islam*, 158–177.

112. Carrie Rosefsky Wickham, *Mobilizing Islam: Religion, Activism and Political Change in Egypt* (New York: Columbia University Press, 2002), 36–62. Francois Burgat's writings confirm these findings too. See Francois Burgat and William Dowell, *The Islamist Movement in North Africa* (Austin: Center for Middle East Studies, University of Texas, 1993), 99, and Burgat, *Face to Face with Political Islam* (New York: Tauris, 2003), 10–23.

113. Population figures of 1950 are from *World Population Prospects: The 2002 Revision*, vol. 1 (New York: United Nations Department of Economic and Social Affairs, Population Division, 2002), 210; 2002 population figures are from *World Statistics Pocketbook* (New York: United Nations Department of Economic and Social Affairs, 2002), 60; 1951–52 education figures are from *World Survey on Education* (New York: UNESCO, 1955), 221; 2001–2002 education figures are from *The Statistical Yearbook, 1995–2002* (Cairo: Central Agency for Public Mobilization and Statistics, 2003), 83.

114. Lawrence Stone, *Causes of the English Revolution, 1529–164* 2 (London: Routledge and Kegan Paul, 1972), 113.

115. Ghobarah, "Gateways to Modernity." Figures for Oxford from Lawrence Stone, ed., *The University in Society*, vol. 1, *Oxford and Cambridge from the Fourteenth to the Early Nineteenth Century* (Princeton, N.J.: Princeton University Press, 1974), 3–110. Especially see app. 4, table 1A, "Estimated Annual Freshman Admissions to Oxford (Decennial Averages) 1500–1909" (91). For Cambridge see Victor Morgan et al., *A History of the University of Cambridge*, vol. 2, *1546–1750* (Cambridge: Cambridge University Press, 2004), and table 24, "Annual Matriculations in the University of Cambridge," in David Cressy, "Education and Literacy in London and East Anglia, 1580–1700" (Ph.D. diss., Cambridge University, 1973), 222.

116. Stone, *Causes of the English Revolution*, 113.

117. Ibid., 114.

118. Ghobarah, "Gateways to Modernity."

119. Ellis Goldberg, "Smashing Idols and the State: The Protestant Ethic and Egyptian Sunni Radicalism," in Juan R. I. Cole, ed., *Comparing Muslim Societies: Knowledge and the State in a World Civilization* (Ann Arbor: University of Michigan Press, 1992), 195.

120. Bjorn Olav Utvik, "The Modernizing Force of Islam," in John Esposito and Francois Burgat, eds., *Modernizing Islam: Religion in the Public Sphere in Europe and the Middle East* (New Brunswick, N.J.: Rutgers University Press, 2003), 43, 44.

121. Bjorn Olav Utvik, "Religious Revivalism in Nineteenth-Century Norway and in Twentieth-Century Egypt: A Critique of Fundamentalism Studies," unpublished paper, 4.

122. Utvik, "Modernizing Force of Islam," 52.

123. Ibid., 52–53.

124. Juan Cole, "Shiite Religious Parties Fill Vacuum in Southern Iraq," *Middle East Report Online* (22 April 2003), and David Patel, "Religious Authority and Politics in Post-Saddam Iraq," *Arab Reform Bulletin* 2 (May 2004). Available online at: http://www.carnegieendowment.org/publications/index.cfm?fa=view&id=1536#authority.

125. To explain the proto-modern character of mainstream political Islam, Utvik discusses their attitude toward modern technology and economics, an aspect of religious politics that is not emphasized by the other authors. See Utvik, "The Modernizing Force of Islam," 45–50. Because this point was briefly mentioned above in the subsection on "The Malaise of Modernity and Political Islam" it will not be repeated here.

126. Andrea Rugh, "Reshaping Personal Relationships in Egypt," in Martin Marty and R. Scott Appleby, ed., *Fundamentalisms and Society: Reclaiming the Sciences, the Family, and Education* (Chicago: University of Chicago Press, 1993), 176, quoted in Utvik, "The Modernizing Force of Islam," 57.

127. Saad Eddin Ibrahim, *Egypt, Islam and Democracy,* 12–13.

128. Quoted in Ellis Goldberg, "Smashing Idols and the State: The Protestant Ethic and Egyptian Sunni Radicalism," 220.

129. Utvik, "The Modernizing Force of Islam," 57–58.

130. James Piscatori and Dale Eickelman, *Muslim Politics* (Princeton, N.J.: Princeton University Press, 1996), 38.

131. Ibid., 39, 41–42.

132. Ibid., 43.

133. Utvik, "The Modernizing Force of Islam," 58.

134. Jose Casanova, "Civil Society and Religion: Restrospective Reflections on Catholicism and Prospective Reflections on Islam," *Social Research* 68 (Winter 2001), 1059.

135. Utvik, "Religious Revivalism," 7.

136. Ibid., 58–59.

137. Ibid., 59. Olivier Roy suggests there is also a link between Islamism and secularization. He writes: "neofundamentalism is a paradoxical agent of secularization, as Protestantism was in its time [although this is far from obvious in reading Calvin], because it individualizes and desocializes religious observance. It addresses the individual who explicitly decides to place his life exclusively under the sign of religion and who for that reason breaks with the majority environment" (*Secularism Confronts Islam,* translated by George Holoch [New York: Columbia University Press, 2007], 76). He explains this point in greater detail in *Globalized Islam: The Search for a New Ummah* (New York: Columbia University Press, 2004), 88–92.

138. I borrow this idea from Ghobarah, "Gateways to Modernity." The theory of a mass society is discussed by Daniel Bell, *The End of Ideology: On the Exhaustion of Political Ideas in the Fifties* (Boston: Harvard University Press, 1988), 21–38.

139. Utvik, "The Modernizing Force of Islam," 61–62.

140. Lisa Anderson, "Fulfilling Prophecies: State Policy and Islamist Radicalism," in John Esposito, ed., *Political Islam: Revolution, Radicalism or Reform?* (Boulder, Colo.: Lynne Rienner, 1997), 25–26.

141. Sami Zubaida concurs with this analysis. See his "Trajectories of Political Islam," *Index on Censorship* 25 (July–August 1996), 150–157.

142. Barrington Moore, *Social Origins of Dictatorship and Democracy: Lord and Peasant in the Making of the Modern World* (Boston: Beacon Press, 1993), 413–414.

There is an emerging body of literature, post-September 11, that likens mainstream political Islam to European fascism. Deconstructing this claim is the subject of a future research project of mine.

143. Utvik, "The Modernizing Force of Islam," 62. See Anthony Marx, *Faith in Nation: Exclusionary Origins of Nationalism* (New York: Oxford University Press, 2003), 191–206.

144. Michael McFaul, "Chinese Dreams, Persian Realities," *Journal of Democracy* 16 (October 2005), 74–82 and Mehran Kamrava, *Iran's Intellectual Revolution* (Cambridge: Cambridge University Press, 2008), 214–226.

145. Ali Mirsepassi, *Intellectual Discourse and the Politics of Modernization: Negotiating Modernity in Iran* (Cambridge: Cambridge University Press, 2000), 73.

146. Said Amir Arjomand, "Iran's Revolution in Comparative Perspective," *World Politics* 38 (April 1986), 390.

CHAPTER 2

This chapter is a revised and updated version of my article "The Relevance of John Locke to Social Change in the Muslim World: A Comparison with Iran," *Journal of Church and State* 46 (winter 2004), 39–53. I am indebted to Duncan Ivison both for the title of this chapter and for deepening my understanding of Locke's political philosophy.

1. Ian Shapiro, "John Locke's Democratic Theory," in John Locke, *Two Treatises of Government and A Letter Concerning Toleration*, edited by Ian Shapiro (New Haven, Conn.: Yale University Press, 2003), 309.

2. Anthony Arblaster, *Democracy*, 2nd ed. (Minneapolis: University of Minnesota Press, 1994), 32. Mark Goldie observes that "there is no mystery about the type of polity that Locke thought it prudent to adopt. It was Old England's 'Ancient Constitution,' comprising monarch, nobility and representatives of the commonality." Goldie reminds us that this polity was discussed by Locke in *The Fundamental Constitutions of Carolina* (1669). At the start of this work, Locke justifies aristocracy so "that we may avoid erecting a numerous democracy" (*Locke: Political Essays*, edited by Mark Goldie [Cambridge: Cambridge University Press, 1997], xxiv, 161–162). His political views evolved, however, as he grew older.

3. Shapiro, "John Locke's Democratic Theory," 310; emphasis added.

4. For a rigorous assessment of his argument and contribution see James Tully, "Locke," in J. H. Burns, ed., *The Cambridge History of Political Thought 1450–1700* (Cambridge: Cambridge University Press, 1991), 616–652. For a more succinct overview see Maurice Cranston, "John Locke and Government by Consent," in David Thomson, ed., *Political Ideas* (New York: Penguin Books, 1966), 67–80.

5. Ignoring the relationship between religion and political development is to some extent a feature of the way Western political theory is taught. Generally, a student enrolled in a first-year political philosophy course rarely reads parts 3 and 4 of Hobbes's *Leviathan* or Locke's *First Treatise on Government*, let alone anything from Augustine or Aquinas. There is an almost 1800-year gap between Aristotle and Machiavelli, both standard authors in the Western political theory canon, thus eclipsing a huge part of Western political history where religious politics was dominant. It is

my contention that this approach to the study of Western political theory prevents students from appreciating struggles over the relationship between religion and politics in non-Western societies today.

6. Sheldon Wolin, *Politics and Vision: Continuity and Innovation in Western Political Thought*, expanded ed. (Princeton, N.J.: Princeton University Press, 2004), 87.

7. Graham Maddox, *Religion and the Rise of Democracy* (New York: Routledge, 1996), 92–94.

8. David Held, *Models of Democracy*, 2nd ed. (Stanford, Calif.: Stanford University Press, 1996), 37. For background see Mark Lilla, *The Stillborn God: Religion, Politics and the Modern West* (New York: Knopf, 2007), 17–103.

9. In making this point, I draw on Alfred Stepan's insightful argument about the relationship between religion and democracy. He observes: "one can expect, therefore, that in polities where a significant component of one of the world's major religions may be under the sway of a nondemocratic doctrinally based religious discourse, one of the major tasks of political and spiritual leaders who would like . . . to revalue democratic norms in their own religious community will be to continually mount theologically convincing public arguments about the legitimate multivocality of their religion. Such arguments may violate Rawls's requirement for freestanding public reasoning—but they may be vital to the success of the democratization process in a country in the midst of a contestation over the meaning and the appropriateness of democracy" (Alfred Stepan, *Arguing Comparative Politics* [New York: Oxford University Press, 2001], 229).

10. Abdou Filali-Ansary, "The Challenge of Secularization," in Larry Diamond, Marc Plattner, and Daniel Brumberg, eds., *Islam and Democracy in the Middle East* (Baltimore: Johns Hopkins University Press, 2003), 235.

11. Perez Zagorin, *How the Idea of Religious Toleration Came to the West* (Princeton, N.J.: Princeton University Press, 2003), 72–92.

12. The Exclusion Crisis was the attempt to exclude Charles II's Catholic brother (James II) from succession to the English throne.

13. Zagorin, *How the Idea of Toleration Came to the West*, 290.

14. Emphasis added (1.4). John Locke, *Two Treatises of Government*, edited by Peter Laslett (Cambridge: Cambridge University Press, 1988), 285–286. (All citations from the *Two Treatises of Government* are from this edition.) Likewise, in his famous chapter on property, Locke begins by affirming that "whether we consider *natural Reason*, which tells us, that Men, being once born, have a right to their Preservation. . . . Or *Revelation*, which gives us an account of those Grants God made of the World to Adam . . . 'tis very clear, that God . . . has given the Earth to the Children of Men, given it to Mankind in common" (2.25; emphasis added).

15. John Locke, *A Letter Concerning Toleration*, edited by James Tully (Indianapolis: Hackett, 1983), 31; emphasis added.

16. For a succinct overview see John Dunn, *Locke: A Very Short Introduction* (New York: Oxford University Press, 2003), 1–26.

17. On Locke's early years and his support for authoritarianism and opposition to religious pluralism see John Dunn, *Locke* (Oxford: Oxford University Press, 1984), 22–27.

18. John Locke, "'Preface to the Reader' from the *First Tract on Government* (1661)," in *Locke: Political Essays*, Goldie ed., 7–8.

19. Voltaire, *The Philosophical Dictionary*, translated by H. I. Wolf (New York: Knopf, 1924), 24. Also in this genre see Shadia Drury, *Terror and Civilization: Christianity, Politics and the Western Psyche* (New York: Palgrave, 2003), 45–74.

20. Zagorin, *How the Idea of Toleration Came to the West*, 314. Also see R. I. Moore, *The Formation of a Persecuting Society: Power and Deviance in Western Europe, 950–1250* (Oxford: Blackwell, 1987), 172–196.

21. Zagorin, *How the Idea of Toleration Came to the West*, 249.

22. John Locke, *First Tract on Government* (1661), in *Locke: Political Essays*, Goldie ed., 40–41.

23. Ibid., 8.

24. Dunn, *Locke*, 24.

25. The writings of Richard Hooker (1554–1600), an Anglican priest and influential theologian, are a reference work for this period, especially his eight-volume treatise *Of the Lawes of Ecclesiasticall Politie.* See his fifth book and his discussion of "True Religion is the roote of all true virtues and the stay of all well ordered common-wealthes," in *The Folger Library Edition of The Works of Richard Hooker*, edited by W. Speed Hill (Cambridge, Mass.: Harvard University Press, 1977), 2:16–22.

26. Thomas Hobbes, *Leviathan*, edited by Richard Tuck (Cambridge: Cambridge University Press, 1996), 199. For similar views by Spinoza and Grotius see Zagorin, *How the Idea*, 186–187, 172, 174.

27. John Locke, "An Essay on Toleration" (1667), in *Locke: Political Essays*, Goldie ed., 159.

28. James Tully, introduction to John Locke, *A Letter Concerning Toleration*, edited by Tully (Indianapolis: Hackett, 1983), 6.

29. Ibid., 11.

30. Ibid.

31. Locke was not the sole author of this new interpretation of Christianity. The reformist ideas he was promoting were being discussed in various forms in Europe at the time. For the immediate English background see Zagorin, *How the Idea of Toleration Came to the West*, 188–239. For a more precise account of Locke's views of Christianity see Locke, *The Reasonableness of Christianity: As delivered in the Scriptures*, edited by John Higgins-Biddle (New York: Clarendon Press, 1999).

32. Locke, *Letter Concerning Toleration*, Tully ed., "true religion," 23, 25, 26, 27, 36, 39; "true Christian/Christianity," 23, 58; "true Church," 23, 29 (three times), 30; "truly Christian Church," 25.

33. Revealingly, many reformist Muslims make an identical argument. At the end of his *Letter*, Locke poses the question whether "Factions, Tumults, and Civil War . . . [are] the fault of the Christian Religion?" and answers: "It is not the diversity of Opinions . . . but the refusal of Toleration to those that are of different Opinions . . . that has produced all the Bustles and Wars, that have been in the Christian World" (pp. 54–55). In other words, Locke is arguing, the problem is tolerant Christianity versus intolerant Christianity, not Christianity itself.

34. Locke, *Letter Concerning Toleration*, Tully ed., 23; emphasis added.

35. Ibid.

36. Ibid.; emphasis added.

37. Ibid.

38. Ibid.; emphasis in original.

39. Ibid., 24–25; emphasis in original.

40. Ibid., 25.

41. Zagorin, *How the Idea of Toleration Came to the West*, xiii. Also see W. K. Jordan, *The Development of Religious Toleration in England: From the Beginning of the English Reformation to the Death of Queen Elizabeth* (London: Allen and Unwin, 1932); Joseph Lecler, *Toleration and Reformation*, translated by T. L. Westow (London: Longmans, 1960); and Henry Kamen, *The Rise of Toleration* (New York: Longman, 1967).

42. The execution of Algernon Sidney is a case in point. A prominent Whig leader and revolutionary radical, he was arrested and executed for plotting against the English monarchy. Among the charges at his trial was his authoring of seditious manuscripts. For background, in particular his relationship to Locke, see Jonathan Scott, *Algernon Sidney and the English Republic 1623–1677* (Cambridge: Cambridge University Press, 1988), 207–221.

43. I borrow this idea from Shapiro, "Locke's Democratic Theory," 321–322.

44. John Locke, *Letter Concerning Toleration*, Tully ed., 28.

45. Ibid.

46. Ibid., 32.

47. Ibid. Similarly, Locke affirms that "these Religious Societies I call Churches: and these, I say the Magistrate ought to tolerate. For the business of these Assemblies of the People is nothing but what is lawful for every man in particular to take care of; I mean the Salvation of their Souls: nor in this case is there any difference between the National Church, and other separated Congregations" (39).

48. Ibid., 36.

49. Ibid., 29.

50. Ibid., 26, 27

51. Jeremy Waldron, *God, Locke and Equality: Christian Foundations in Locke's Political Thought* (Cambridge: Cambridge University Press 2002), 210.

52. The outlines of twentieth-century Christian liberation theology and the Social Gospel Movement can be detected in Locke's reinterpretation of Christianity, as is evidenced by his emphasis on "Charity, Meekness and Good-will in general towards all Mankind" (*Letter Concerning Toleration*, Tully ed., 23), and his criticism of people who argue over "frivolous things" while ignoring "the Substantial and truly Fundamental part of religion" (36).

53. Sir Robert Filmer, *Patriarcha and Other Writings*, edited by Johann Sommerville (Cambridge: Cambridge University Press, 1991), 1–68. For a short but authoritative summary of Filmer see John Dunn, *The Political Thought of John Locke: An Historical Account of the Argument of the "Two Treatises of Government"* (Cambridge: Cambridge University Press, 1969), 58–76.

54. Locke quoting Filmer (1.104); emphasis in original.

55. Locke quoting Filmer (1.44); emphasis in original.

56. This point is not sufficiently appreciated by students who solely read the *Second Treatise*. Furthermore, prior to Peter Laslett's 1960 edition of *Two Treatises*, many writers thought Locke was writing against Hobbes, thus downplaying the religious underpinnings of Locke's political philosophy.

57. Locke, *Two Treatises of Government*, Laslett ed., 135.

58. Ibid., 138.

59. Ibid.

60. Dunn, *Political Thought of John Locke*, 60, and Richard Ashcraft, *Locke's Two Treatises of Government* (London: Allen and Unwin, 1987), 62.

61. Dunn, *Political Thought of John Locke*, 99; Waldron, *God, Locke and Equality*, 189.

62. For the case of the Sunni Muslim world, primarily Egyptian Islamists, see Gudrun Kramer, "Islamist Notions of Democracy," in Joel Beinin and Joe Stork, eds., *Political Islam: Essays from Middle East Report* (Berkeley: University of California Press, 1997), 71–82.

63. Filmer, *Patriarcha or The Natural Power of Kings*, Sommerville ed., 133.

64. *First Treatise of Government* 1.107. This passage was brought to my attention by Waldron, *God, Locke and Equality*, 17.

65. *First Treatise of Government*, 1.13; emphasis added. Also see Locke, *A Letter Concerning Toleration*, Tully ed., 27, 44, where Locke acknowledges the final moral authority of scripture in matters political, properly understood.

66. *First Treatise of Government*, 1.81.

67. Ibid. 1.20. Similarly, Locke observes that "having placed such a mighty Power in *Adam*, and upon that supposition, founded all Government, and all Power of Princes, it is reasonable to expect, that he should have proved this with Arguments clear and evident, suitable to the weightiness of the Cause." Locke adds: "For it is scare credible, that in a Discourse where he pretends to confute the *Erroneous Principle* of Man's *Natural Freedom*, he should doe it by a bare supposition of *Adam's Authority*, without offering any Proof for that Authority" (1.10–11).

68. Ibid. 1.60.

69. Ibid. 1.16.

70. Ibid. 1.44; Locke quoting Filmer. The other key verse Filmer relies on from the Book of Genesis is "And God blessed them, and God said unto them, Be fruitful, and multiply, and replenish the earth, and subdue it: and have dominion over the fish of the sea, and over the fowl of the air, and over every living thing that moveth upon the earth" (1:28). See chapter 4 of the *First Treatise* for Locke's critique.

71. "Should I have desired any sober Man only to have read the Text, and considered to whom, and on what occasion it was spoken, he would no doubt have wondered how our . . . [Filmer] found out Monarchical absolute Power in it, had he not had an exceeding good Faculty to find it himself, where he could not shew it [to] others" (1.49).

72. Locke, *A Letter Concerning Toleration*, Tully ed., 44.

73. Locke, *First Tract on Government*, 1.44.

74. Ibid. 1.44.

75. Ibid. 1.45; emphasis in original.

76. Ibid. 1.47.

77. Ibid.; emphasis in original.

78. Ibid. 1.48.

79. Ibid. 1.49; emphasis in original.

80. Ibid.

81. Ibid. 1.49.

82. Locke, *Two Treatises of Government*, 2.8, 2.13.

83. Ibid. 2.95. Dunn is correct to observe that at the core of the dispute between Locke and Filmer was a deeper philosophical point: do men make their own history or is it largely predetermined for them? (*Political Thought of John Locke*, 68).

84. Jeremy Waldron, *God, Locke and Equality*, 189; emphasis added.

85. Richard Ashcraft notes that although "Locke had good political reasons for citing the words of one of the architects of Anglican thought against his Anglican opponents, this fact should not be allowed to obscure the Aristotelian dimensions of Locke's political thought." Ashcraft is suggesting that because Hooker himself was an Aristotelian thinker, Locke actually does rely on Aristotle but only indirectly through the filter of Hooker's writings (Ashcraft, *Locke's Two Treatises of Government*, 68).

86. Waldron, *God, Locke and Equality*, 5.

87. Leo Strauss, *Natural Right and History* (Chicago: University of Chicago Press, 1999), 202–251. Thomas Pangle, *Spirit of Modern Republicanism: The Moral Vision of American Founders and the Philosophy of Locke* (Chicago: University of Chicago Press, 1990), 131–140.

88. I borrow this idea from James Piscatori and Dale Eickelman, who have written: "although it has been argued that Islam does not aid the process of modernization . . . to construct a claim that changes are Islamic is to render them legitimate and acceptable" (*Muslim Politics* [Princeton, N.J.: Princeton University Press, 1996], 25).

89. Marc Bloch, "Towards a Comparative History of European Societies," in Frederic C. Lane and Jelle C. Riemersma, eds., *Enterprise and Secular Change: Reading in Economic History* (Homewood, Ill.: R. D. Irwin, 1953), 494–521. I borrow this citation from Norman Finkelstein, *Image and Reality of the Israel-Palestine Conflict* (New York: Verso, 1995), 89.

90. See chapter 1 for a discussion of the merits of comparing the political development of Islam with that of Christianity.

91. There is very important democratic tradition in Iran, dating back to the 1906 constitutional revolution that is largely unknown in the West. For background see Janef Afary, *The Iranian Constitutional Revolution, 1906–1911* (New York: Columbia University Press, 1996), 63–208; Vali Nasr and Ali Gheissari, *Democracy in Iran: History and the Quest for Liberty* (New York: Oxford University Press, 2006), 23–43; Fakhreddin Azimi, *The Quest for Democracy in Iran: A Century of Struggle against Authoritarian Rule* (Cambridge, Mass.: Harvard University Press), 19–68, and R. K. Ramazani, "Iran, Democracy and the United States," in Robert Fatton Jr. and R. K. Ramazani, eds., *The Future of Liberal Democracy: Thomas Jefferson and the Contemporary World* (New York: Palgrave, 2004), 185–201.

92. One of the key differences between Iran in the late twentieth century and England in the late seventeenth century that influenced the process of democratization has been the role of the modern twentieth-century authoritarian state in Iran with its powers of surveillance, intrusion in the lives of citizens, and ability to project its power and enforce its political will across a wide swathe of territory in a manner that King Charles II of England could only dream of. Similarly, one could point to the different international and economic contexts that affected the process of democratization. Notwithstanding these differences and in keeping with the caveats I mentioned on political culture and causality in the introduction, I believe that a comparison between Iran and England is appropriate due to distinct parallels on how political transformations can occur within deeply religious societies.

93. For background on how they arrived at this position and consolidated their control of the Iranian state see Mehdi Moslem, *Factional Politics in Post-Khomeini Iran* (Syracuse, N.Y.: Syracuse University Press, 2002), 11–46; Mohsen Milani, *The Making of Iran's Islamic Revolution: From Monarchy to Islamic Republic*, 2nd ed. (Boulder, Colo.: Westview, 1994), 171–217.

94. See Asef Bayat, *Making Islam Democratic: Social Movements and the Post-Islamist Turn* (Palo Alto, Calif.: Stanford University Press, 2007), 49–135; Daniel Brumberg, *Reinventing Khomeini: The Struggle for Reform in Iran* (Chicago: University of Chicago Press, 2001), 185–229, Ahmad Ashraf and Ali Banuazizi, eds., special issue, *International Journal of Politics, Culture and Society* 15 (Winter 2001), especially their lead essay, "Iran's Torturous Path to 'Islamic Liberalism,' " 237–256; and Kamrava, *Iran's Intellectual Revolution*, 10–43, 214–226.

95. Hassan Yousefi Eshkevari, *Kherad dar ziyafat-e Din* [Reason in the House of Religion] (Tehran: Qasideh, 2000), Akbar Ganji, *Talaqqi-yi fashisti az din va hukumat: Asibshinasi-yi guzar bi-dawlat-i dimukratik- i tawsiih-gira* [The Fascist Interpretation of Religion and Government: The Pathology of Transition to a Democratic and Development-oriented state] (Tehran: Tarh-e No, 2000), Mohammed Mujtahid-Shabistari, *Naqdi bar qiraat-i rasmi-yi din* [A Critique of the Official Reading of Religion] (Tehran: Tarh-e No, 2000), Mohsen Kadivar, *Daghdaghe ha-yi Hukumat-i-dini* (Crises of Religious Government)(Tehran: Nashr-e Ney, 2000), Emadeddin Baghi, *Terajediy-i Democracy dar Iran: Baz-khan Ghatl-hayi Zanjeereh-i* [The Tragedy of Democracy in Iran: Revisiting the Serial Murders] (Tehran: Nashr-e Ney, 1999), and Saeed Hajjarian, *Az Shahed-i Qodsi to Shahed-i Bazari: Orfi-shodan-i Din dar Sepehr-i Siyasat* (From the Sacred Witness to the Profane Witness: The Secularization of Religion in the Sphere of Politics) (Tehran: Tarh-e No, 1999). Also see Afshin Matin-Asgari, "The Intellectual Best-sellers of Post-revolutionary Iran: On Backwardness, Elite-killing and Western Rationality," *Iranian Studies* 37 (March 2004), 73–88, and Farhad Khosrokhavar, "The New Intellectuals of Iran," *Social Compass* 51 (June 2004), 191–202. Hassan Yousefi Eshkevari and Akbar Ganji's writings have been translated into English in book format. See Eshkevari, *Islam and Democracy in Iran: Eshkevari and the Quest for Reform*, edited and translated by Ziba Mir Hosseini and Richard Tapper (New York: Tauris, 2006) and Akbar Ganji, *The Road to Democracy in Iran* (Cambridge, MA: MIT Press, 2008) Also see Farhang Rajaee, *Islamism and Modernism: The Changing Discourse in Iran* (Austin: University of Texas Press, 2007), 193–236.

96. Akbar Ganji, "30 Million People and Six Individuals," *Sobh-e Emrooz* (Tehran), 27 May 1999. A leading theoretician of the radical right—and religious mentor to Mahmoud Ahmadinejad—is Ayatollah Muhammad Taqi Mesbah Yazdi. For similar paternalistic attitudes see his "Hukumat va Mashru'iyyat" [Government and Legitimacy], *Kitab-i Naqd* (Summer 1998), no. 7, 42–77. Also relevant are his books, *Nazarriyeh-i Siyassi Islam* [A political theory of Islam] (Qum: Mo'asseseh-i Amoozeshi ra Pezhohesh-i Imam Khomeini, 2001), vols. 1 and 2, and *Negahi Guzrah be Velayat e Faqih* [A quick glance at the theory of Velayat e Faqih] (Qum: Mo'asseseh-i Imam Khomeini, 2000).

97. Editorial, *Jahan-e-Islam* (Tehran), 1 February 1999.

98. Eric Rouleau, "Un Enjeu Pour Le Monde Musalman: En Iran, islam contre islam," *Le Monde Diplomatique* (June 1999).

99. Yousef Saanei, "The Women's Mufti: Interview with Grand Ayatollah Yousef Saanei," by Manal Lutfi, *Asharq Al-Awsat* (English ed.), 6 April 2007.

100. Robin Wright, *Sacred Rage: The Wrath of Militant Islam* (New York: Touchstone Books, 2001), 280. In September 2008, when Iran's conservative-dominated 8th Majlis sought to pass legislation in favor of polygamy, Saanei weighed in on the debate by issuing a statement on his website that taking a second wife without the permission of the first is "a moral sin and a crime under Shariah law." He added: "I pray that such a decision that is oppressive to women will not be made into law . . . God forbid that the Majlis should add another problem to the existing problems of women." See his website: http://www.saanei.org/page.php?pg=showzanan&i-d=12&lang=fa. For more on Ayatollah Saanei see Geneive Abdo and Jonathan Lyons, *Answering Only to God: Faith and Freedom in Twenty-first-century Iran* (New York: Holt, 2003), 18–25.

101. Ayatollah Yusuf Saanei, *Ahkam-e Banavon* (Rulings on women) (Qum: Maysam Tammar, 2007), 80–81. Also see Nazila Fathi, "Ayatollah Tugs at Ties Constricting Iran's Women," *New York Times*, 29 July 2001. In his interview with *Asharq Al-Awsat* he qualified his support for gender equality by noting that "in Islam women's rights differ from men's in only two matters: the first is inheritance, the Quran clearly states that a man is entitled to double the woman's share, and the second is in the case of divorce; men can divorce their wives while women cannot divorce their husbands. These two cases are clearly stated, however in all other rights they are equal."

102. Saanei, "The Women's Mufti."

103. Navid Kermani, "Religious Reformist Thinkers in Iran: Intellectually Victorious, but Politically Defeated," www.Qantara.de (1 February 2005). For Saanei's views on democracy in Iran see his interview with Linden MacIntyre, wherein he stated: "The Supreme Leader has only one vote and he should not be able to impose his ideas on anyone else. He is not infallible. He is capable of making mistakes just like everyone else. To err is human"; www.pbs.org/wgbh/pages/frontline/shows/tehran/interviews/saanei.html.

104. Nazila Fathi, "Ayatollah Tugs at Ties Constricting Iran's Women," *New York Times*, 29 July 2001.

105. Quoted in Christopher de Ballaigue, *The Struggle for Iran* (New York: New York Review of Books, 2007), 3, 8.

106. Ali Raiss-Tousi, "Iran Demonstrators Denounce Israel, Khatami Allies," Reuters, 31 December 1999.

107. Nazila Fathi, "Iranian Leader Bars Press Bill of Reform Bloc," *New York Times*, 7 August 2000.

108. *Keyhan* (Tehran), 16 August 2000.

109. *Khordad* (Tehran), and *Iran* (Tehran), 2 November 1999.

110. Islamic Republic News Agency (IRNA), 28 November 2002.

111. News conference, Vision of the Islamic Republic of Iran Network 1, Tehran (in Persian), 28 August 2004.

112. "Khatami Vows to Struggle for Establishment of Real Islam in Iran," IRNA, 27 November 2002.

113. "Iran Reformist Leader Warns of 'Religious Dictatorship,' " Agence France Presse, 13 December 2002.

114. Robert Filmer, *Patriarcha and Other Political Works of Sir Robert Filmer*, edited by Peter Laslett (Oxford: Blackwell, 1949), 232, quoted in Dunn, *Political Thought of John Locke*, 70.

115. Safa Haeri, "Conservative Clerics Rally in Support of Khameneh'i," *Iran Press Service*, 27 December 1997.

116. Quoted in Moslem, *Factional Politics in Post-Khomeini Iran*, 100–101.

117. Ayatollah Ruhullah Khomeini, "Islamic Government," in *Islam and Revolution: Writings and Declarations of Imam Khomeini*, translated by Hamid Algar (Berkley: Mizan Press, 1981), 63.

118. Quoted in Dunn, *Political Thought of John Locke*, 63.

119. Emphasis added. Vision of the Islamic Republic of Iran Network 1, Tehran, in Persian, 21 March 1998. Following the 2004 parliamentary elections, whose results were predetermined after hundreds of reformist candidates were banned from running, thus ensuring a conservative victory, Ayatollah Ali Meshikini announced that the conservative candidates who were elected to the new Parliament were all divinely approved. "Seven months ago . . . God's angels supplied the list of [conservative] candidate's names and their addresses" to the hidden Shia imam. This representative of God "endorsed all of their names," Meshkini announced in his Friday prayer sermon. (Jamsheed Barzegar, "Parliamentary Representatives: Elected by the People or Appointed by the Hidden [Shia] Imam?" BBC Persian Service, 13 June 2004).

120. Abdol Karim Soroush, *Qabz va Bast-i tiorik-i Shari'at* [Theory on the contraction and expansion of the Shari'a] (Tehran: Mu'assassah-yi Farhangi-yi Sirat, 1990). In English the standard reference is *Reason, Freedom and Democracy in Islam*, translated and edited by Ahmad Sadri and Mahmoud Sadri (New York: Oxford University Press, 1999). For a thoughtful treatment see Fred Dallmayr's discussion of Soroush's thesis on Islam and democracy in *Dialogue among Civilizations: Some Exemplary Voices* (New York: Palgrave, 2002), 167–184.

121. De Ballaigue, *Struggle for Iran*, 76.

122. Shirin Ebadi, "Islam, Democracy and Human Rights," lecture, Syracuse University, 10 May 2004, published in *Syracuse University News*, 12 May 2004; emphasis added. For an elaboration on these remarks see Ebadi, *Iran Awakening: One Woman's Journey to Reclaim Her Life and Country* (New York: Random House, 2007), 121–122.

123. Ian Shapiro, "Introduction: Reading Locke Today," in Locke, *Two Treatises of Government and A Letter Concerning Toleration*, Shapiro ed., xiv.

124. 1.49.

125. "Re-elected Iran Leader Vows 'Freedom, Justice,' " *Associated Press*, 11 June 2001; emphasis added.

126. Emran Qureshi, unpublished interview with Eqbal Ahmad, 21 December 1994.

CHAPTER 3

1. Charles Taylor, "Modes of Secularism," in Rajeev Bhargava, ed., *Secularism and Its Critics* (New Delhi: Oxford University Press, 1998), 31. For background see Emmet Kennedy, *Secularism and Its Opponents from Augustine to Solzhenitsyn* (New York: Palgrave, 2006), 10–180; Steve Bruce, *God Is Dead: Secularization in the West* (Oxford: Blackwell, 2002), 1–44; Steve Bruce, ed., *Religion and Modernization: Sociologists and Historians Debate the Secularization Thesis* (New York: Oxford University Press, 1992), 1–7; David Martin, *A General Theory of Secularization* (Oxford: Blackwell, 1978), 12–99; Robert Bellah, *Beyond Belief: Essays on Religion in a Post-traditionalist World* (Berkeley: University of California Press, 1991), 20–50; Pippa Norris and Ronald Inglehart, *Sacred and Secular: Religion and Politics Worldwide* (Cambridge: Cambridge University Press, 2004), 3–32, and Talal Asad, *Formations of the Secular: Christianity, Islam, Modernity* (Stanford, Calif.: Stanford University Press, 2003), 21–66.

2. Nikki Keddie, "Secularism and Its Discontents," *Daedalus* 132 (summer 2003), 14.

3. John Keane, "Secularism?" in David Marquand and Ronald Nettler, eds., *Religion and Democracy* (Oxford: Blackwell, 2000), 6.

4. Ibid.

5. Ibid. For more documentation on the evolving use of the term "secularism" see Keddie, "Secularism and Its Discontents," 15, and Taylor, "Modes of Secularism," 31–35.

6. Asad, *Formations of the Secular*, 23–24.

7. George Jacob Holyoake, *The Principles of Secularism*, 3rd ed. rev. (London: Austin,1870), 11.

8. Keddie, "Secularism and Its Discontents," 16.

9. Harvey Cox, *The Secular City: Secularization and Urbanization in Theological Perspective* (New York: MacMillan, 1966), 17.

10. Peter Berger, *The Sacred Canopy: Elements of a Sociological Theory of Religion* (New York: Anchor Books, 1967), 107.

11. I borrow this simple way of thinking about secularism from Lutfhi Assyaukanie's unpublished paper "Islam and Secularism in Indonesia."

12. Notes from Charles Taylor intensive half course "Secularization," University of Toronto, Department of Political Science, 8–18 November 2004. A discussion of this can be found in the introduction of Charles Taylor, *A Secular Age* (Cambridge, Mass.: Harvard University Press, 2007), 1–22.

13. Taylor, *Secular Age*, 3.

14. John Wycliffe, *Tractatus de civili dominio*, edited by Reginald Lane Poole (New York: John Reprint, 1966); William of Ockham, *A Short Discourse on the Tyrannical Government*, translated by John Kilcullen and edited by Arthur Stephen McGrade (Cambridge: Cambridge University Press, 1992); Marsilius of Padua, *The Defender of Peace*, edited and translated by Annabel Brett (Cambridge: Cambridge University Press, 2005).

15. Keane, "Secularism?" 6, 10. Drawing on the work of Karl Jaspers, John Pottenger discusses three axial periods that gave shape to the Western worldview with a focus on church-state relations and the struggle for liberal democracy. See his scholarly treatment of the topic in *Reaping the Whirlwind: Liberal Democracy and the Religion Axis* (Washington, D.C.: Georgetown University Press, 2007), 47–91.

16. The scope of this book does not allow for a comprehensive investigation of the history of secularism. Anyone wanting to undertake this task would be advised to follow José Casanova's observation that four mutually reinforcing, interrelated, and complementary processes contributed to the development of secularization in the West: the Protestant Reformation, the formation of modern nation-states, the rise of capitalism, and the scientific revolution. See his important study *Public Religions in the Modern World* (Chicago: Chicago University Press, 1994), 19–39.

17. Taylor, "Modes of Secularism," 32.

18. Perez Zagorin, *How the Idea of Religious Toleration Came to the West* (Princeton, N.J.: Princeton University Press, 2003). Zagorin highlights the writings of Sebastian Castellio, whom he calls "the first champion of religious toleration." Zagorin views Castellio as a pioneer in trying to demarcate the moral boundary between civil order and religion, of which the latter should be off limits to the judgments of magistrates. This early division between the realm of politics and religion can be viewed as an early form of secularism. See Zagorin, *How the Idea*, 128–132. Kennedy goes back even further to Augustine's distinction between the City of Man and the City of God to find the early roots of secularism. See his discussion in *Secularism and Its Opponents*, 13–22.

19. Thomas Hobbes, *Leviathan*, edited by Richard Tuck (Cambridge: Cambridge University Press, 1996), 2; emphasis added.

20. Ibid., 83; emphasis added. Edwin Curley's statement is more accurate when he notes that Hobbes did not advocate a "separation of church and state, but a subordination of the church to the state" ("Hobbes and the Cause of Religious Toleration," in Patricia Springborg, ed., *The Cambridge Campanion to Hobbes's Leviathan* [Cambridge: Cambridge University Press, 2007]), 309.

21. Hobbes, chap. 43, "*Of what is* Necessary for *a Mans Reception into the Kingdome of Heaven*," in *Leviathan*, Tuck ed., 402.

22. Ibid., 403; emphasis added.

23. I draw on Edwin Curley's discussion of Hobbes and religion here, in particular his introduction to Hobbes, *Leviathan*, edited by Edwin Curley (Indianapolis: Hackett, 1994), xlii. In chap. 26, Hobbes speaks directly to this point when he observes: "I conclude therefore, that in all things not contrary to the Morall Law . . . all Subjects are bound to obey that for divine Law, which is declared to be so, by the Lawes of the Commonwealth."

24. Ibid., 413.

25. Taylor, "Modes of Secularism," 34–35. Mark Lilla suggests another very important secularizing consequence that flows from Hobbes's political philosophy. Hobbes's analysis of the condition of man in the state of nature and the role of religion in human affairs revolutionized thinking in the West on the relationship between religion and politics. The reference here is to the early chapters of the *Leviathan* in which Hobbes discusses human psychology, physiology, and social relations in a unique way that has had a lasting influence. See Mark Lilla, *The Stillborn God: Religion, Politics and the Modern West* (New York: Knopf, 2007), 75–92.

26. Martin Luther, "On Secular Authority," in Harro Hopfl, ed., *Luther and Calvin: On Secular Authority* (Cambridge: Cambridge University Press, 1991), 10–11. Roger Williams (1603–1683) preceded Locke by a generation and deserves credit for both an earlier argument on church-state separation and religious toleration. Why he has not been recognized for this groundbreaking contribution is a matter of speculation. For background see Martha Nussbaum, *Liberty of Conscience: In Defense of America's Tradition of Religious Equality* (New York: Basic Books, 2008), 34–71.

27. Zagorin provides an excellent background discussion of these events in *How the Idea of Toleration Came to the West*, 188–288.

28. John Locke, *A Letter Concerning Toleration*, edited by James Tully (Indiana: Hackett, 1983), 26.

29. John Stuart Mill, *Three Essays on Religion* (New York: Greenwood Press, 1969), 3–122. For background reading see Owen Chadwick, *The Secularization of the European Mind in the Nineteenth Century* (Cambridge: Cambridge University Press, 1975), 21–37; Berger, *Sacred Canopy*, 105–125, and Taylor, *Secular Age*, 352–419.

30. John Stuart Mill, *Autobiography* (New York: Penguin Books, 1989), 180.

31. John Stuart Mill, *On Liberty*, edited with an introduction by Gertrude Himmelfarb (New York: Penguin Books, 1985), 66–67; emphasis added.

32. William Doyle, *The French Revolution: A Very Short Introduction* (New York: Oxford University Press, 2001), 76. For background reading see John McManners, *The French Revolution and the Church* (London: S.P.C.K., 1969), 140–150, and Nigel Aston, *Religion and Revolution in France, 1780–1804* (Washington, D.C.: Catholic University of America, 2000), 279–335.

33. Bhikhu Parekh, *Rethinking Multiculturalism: Cultural Diversity and Political Theory* (Cambridge, Mass.: Harvard University Press, 2000), 322. Parekh is here entering an ongoing debate on the relation between religion and democracy, between those who see no place for religion in democratic deliberation about public policy issues and those who reject this stance. As noted earlier, John Rawls is a prominent theorist in the former camp, as is Robert Audi, while those standing against them include Nicholas Wolterstorff, Veit Bader, Nancy Rosenblum, and Lucas Swaine, among others. The main source in Rawls is lectures 5 and 6, in Rawls, *Political Liberalism* (New York: Columbia University Press, 1996). A debate between Wolterstorff and Audi appears in their jointly authored *Religion in the Political Sphere* (Lanham, Md.: Rowman and Littlefield, 1997). Relevant articles by Veit Bader, "Religions and States: A New Typology and Plea for Non-Constitutional Pluralism," 55–91; Nancy Rosenblum, "Religious Parties, Religious

Political Identity and the Cold Should of Liberal Democratic Thought," 23–53; and Lucas Swaine, "Institutions of Conscience: Politics and Principle in a World of Religious Pluralism," 93–118 appeared in "Religious Pluralism, Politics and the State," special issue, *Ethical Theory and Moral Practice* 6 (March 2003). Most of those in the anti-Rawls/Audi camp see potential harmony between religion and democracy. An exception is Frank Cunningham, who argues that notwithstanding the necessity and the possibility of crossfertilization, there remains an insurmountable core conflict between democracy and religion, "The Conflicting Truths of Religion and Democracy," *Social Philosophy Today* 21 (July 2005), 65–80.

34. Taylor, "Modes of Secularism," 31.

35. One model of secularism that is relevant to Muslim societies is the successful non-Western model of secularism that exists in India. See the volume put together by Bhargava, *Secularism and Its Critics*, especially the debate between Ashis Nandy and Akeel Bilgrami, 321–344, 380–417. On the relevance of Indian secularism for Muslim societies see Amartya Sen, "East and West: The Reach of Reason," *New York Review of Books* 47 (20 July 2000), 33–38, and Amartya Sen, *Identity and Violence: The Illusion of Destiny* (New York: Norton, 2006), 59–83.

36. Ahmet Kuru describes these two traditions as "passive" and "assertive" forms of secularism. See his insightful essay, "Passive and Assertive Secularism: Historical Conditions, Ideological Struggles and State Policies toward Religion," *World Politics* 59 (July 2007), 568–594, and his forthcoming book, *Secularism and State Policies toward Religion: The United States, France, and Turkey* (Cambridge: Cambridge University Press, 2009).

37. The case of the contemporary United States is somewhat different from that of France and Britain. Obviously, the role of religion in public life is more visible and contentious in the United States, but I would still argue that a broad consensus exists on the role of religion and its limits in U.S. politics and that the overwhelming majority of Americans, even those on the evangelical right, remain committed to upholding the First Amendment to the U.S. Constitution.

38. T. Jeremy Gunn, "Under God but Not the Scarf: The Founding Myths of Religious Freedom in the United States and *Laïcité* in France," *Journal of Church and State* 46 (Winter 2004), 9.

39. Blandine Kriegel, *The State and the Rule of Law*, translated by Jeffrey Cohen and Marc LePain (Princeton, N.J.: Princeton University Press, 1995), 3–14.

40. John Bowen, *Why the French Don't Like Headscarves: Islam, the State and the Public Space* (Princeton, N.J.: Princeton University Press, 2007), 14.

41. Ibid., 15.

42. For further discussion see "After Secularization," special issue, *Hedgehog Review* 8 (Spring–Summer 2006). For a succinct overview and analysis of *laïcité* with special reference to the case of Islam see Olivier Roy, *Secularism Confronts Islam*, translated by George Holoch (New York: Columbia University Press, 2007), 13–35.

43. Patrice Higonnet, "An Overview of the Separation of Church and State," paper presented at the conference "Comparing Separations: State and Religion in

France and the United States," Center for European Studies, Harvard University, 9–10 December 2005,; emphasis in original.

44. Robert Woodberry and Timothy Shah, "Christianity and Democracy: Pioneering Protestants," *Journal of Democracy* 15 (April 2004), 47–61.

45. John Ruedy, ed., *Islamism and Secularism in North Africa* (London: Macmillan, 1994), xiv.

46. The same broad generalizations can be applied to certain secular political ideologies. The twentieth century is replete with examples of intolerance and blood spilled in the name of secular political doctrines such as nationalism, National Socialism, and Communism, to name a few.

47. Hobbes, *Leviathan*, Tuck ed., 225. Hobbes, it should be recalled, did not believe in the rule of popular sovereignty, except in that brief moment when the commonwealth is established.

48. Olivier Zunz and Alan Kahan, eds., *The Tocqueville Reader: A Life in Letters and Politics* (Oxford: Blackwell, 2002), 1–30.

49. Alexis de Tocqueville, *Democracy in America*, translated by Henry Reeve (New York: Vintage Books, 1990), 1:308. I am indebted to Hillel Fradkin, "Does Democracy Need Religion?" *Journal of Democracy* 11 (January 2000), 87–94, for stimulating my thinking on this topic.

50. Tocqueville, *Democracy in America*, Reeve trans. 1:305.

51. Ibid., 1:306.

52. Ibid., 1:6–7.

53. Ibid., 1:7–8.

54. Ibid., 1:10.

55. Ibid., 1:4.

56. Ibid., 1:12; emphasis added. I'm relying on Gerald Bevin's translation of the last part of this passage, which can be found in Alexis de Tocqueville, *Democracy in America*, translated by Gerald Bevin (New York: Penguin Books, 2003), 21.

57. Tocqueville, *Democracy in America*, Reeve trans., 12–13.

58. Ibid., 1:325.

59. Ibid., 1:308.

60. Ibid., 1:325.

61. Ibid., 1:308.

62. Ibid., 1:309.

63. Ibid., 2:23. For his "Notes on the Koran" see Alexis de Tocqueville, *Writings on Empire and Slavery*, edited and translated by Jennifer Pitts (Baltimore: Johns Hopkins University Press, 2001), 27–35. For a thoughtful treatment on the relevance of Tocqueville to the debate on Islam and democracy see Arun Venkataraman, "Islam and Democracy: A Tocquevillian Approach," *Critique* (Spring 2007), http://lilt.ilstu.edu/critique/spring07docs/Venkataraman2.pdf.

64. Richard Rorty, "Trotsky and the Wild Orchids," in Mark Edmundson, ed., *Wild Orchids and Trotsky: Messages from American Universities* (New York: Viking, 1993), reprinted in Richard Rorty, *Philosophy and Social Hope* (New York: Penguin Books, 1999), 5.

65. Ibid., 6.

66. Rorty, *Philosophy and Social Hope*, 4.

67. Richard Rorty, "The Moral Purposes of the University: An Exchange," *Hedgehog Review* 2 (Fall 2000), 107.

68. Quoted in Jason Boffetti, "How Richard Rorty Found Religion," *First Things* 143 (May 2004), 24.

69. Richard Rorty, "On September 11, 2001," in *Take Care of Freedom and Truth Will Take Care of Itself*, edited and introduced by Eduardo Mendieta (Stanford, Calif.: Stanford University Press, 2006), 118.

70. See the first four essays under the heading "Religion and Morality from a Pragmatist Point of View," in Richard Rorty, *Philosophy as Cultural Politics: Philosophical Papers* (Cambridge: Cambridge University Press, 2007), 1–70, and Richard Rorty and Gianni Vattimo, *The Future of Religion*, edited by Santiago Zabala (New York: Columbia University Press, 2005). For a good summary and analysis of Rorty's views on religion see G. Elijah Dann, *After Rorty: The Possibilities for Ethics and Religious Belief* (New York: Continuum International, 2006), 42–157.

71. New York: Anchor Books, 1994.

72. Richard Rorty, *Philosophy and Social Hope* (New York: Penguin Books, 1999), 169. The original essay appeared in Richard Rorty, "Religion as a Conversation Stopper," *Common Knowledge* 3 (Spring 1994), 1–6.

73. Rorty, *Philosophy and Social Hope*, 170–171.

74. Richard Rorty, "The Priority of Democracy to Philosophy," in *Objectivity, Relativism and Truth* (Cambridge: Cambridge University Press, 1991), 175.

75. Rorty, *Philosophy and Social Hope*, 173.

76. Richard Rorty, "Religion in the Public Square: A Reconsideration," *Journal of Religious Ethics* 31 (March 2003), 141.

77. Ibid., 141.

78. Ibid., 142.

79. Richard Rorty, "Anticlericalism and Atheism," in Rorty and Vattimo, *The Future of Religion*, 33.

80. Rorty, "Religion in the Public Square," 142, 147, 148.

81. Ibid., 147, 148–149. Rorty credits two pieces of scholarship with helping him reconsider his views on the relationship between religion and democracy: Jeffery Stout, *Democracy and Tradition* (Princeton, N.J.: Princeton University Press, 2004) and Nicholas Wolterstorff, "Why We Should Reject What Liberalism Tells Us about Speaking and Acting for Religious Reasons," in Paul J. Weithman, ed., *Religion and Contemporary Liberalism* (Notre Dame, Ind.: University of Notre Dame Press, 1997), 162–181.

82. Perhaps a better comparison would have been between Richard Rorty and Bhikhu Parekh rather than Rorty and Tocqueville, given that Tocqueville was writing when the United States was an emerging liberal democracy, while Parekh's views are more contemporaneous. For Parekh's views that counterbalance those of Rorty, see his discussion of "religion and public life" in *Rethinking Multiculturalism: Cultural Diversity and Political Theory* (Cambridge, Mass.: Harvard University Press, 2000), 321–335.

83. Alfred Stepan, *Arguing Comparative Politics* (New York: Oxford University Press, 2001), 213–253. An earlier version appeared as "Religion, Democracy, and the

'Twin Tolerations,'" *Journal of Democracy* 11 (October 2000), 27–57. All page references will be from his book.

84. Ibid., 213.

85. Ibid.

86. Robert Dahl, *Polyarchy: Participation and Opposition* (New Haven, Conn.: Yale University Press, 1971), 1–3. Quoted in Stepan, *Arguing Comparative Politics*, 216.

87. Stepan, *Arguing Comparative Politics*, 216.

88. Ibid., 216.

89. Ibid., 217.

90. Ibid., 218.

91. Ibid., 219.

92. At www.royal.gov.uk; emphasis added. For background see I. Naamani Tarkow, "The Significance of the Act of Settlement in the Evolution of English Democracy," *Political Science Quarterly* 58 (December 1943), 537–561.

93. See the International Constitutional Law Project website, www.oefre.unibe. ch/law/icl/index.html. Also see Robert Maddex, *Constitutions of the World*, 2nd ed. (Washington, D.C.: Congressional Quarterly, 2001), 137–141, 314–318.

94. Maddex, *Constitutions of the World*, 221. For background see Stathis Kalyvas, *The Rise of Christian Democracy in Europe* (Ithaca, N.Y.: Cornell University Press, 1996), 1–20 and Thomas Kselman and Joseph A. Buttigieg, eds., *European Christian Democracy: Historical Legacies and Comparative Perspectives* (Notre Dame, Ind.: University of Notre Dame Press, 2003), 1–10.

95. Jonathan Fox, "World Separation of Religion and State into the Twenty-first Century," *Comparative Political Studies* 39 (June 2006), 561. Fox also concludes that modernization is associated with higher government involvement in religion and that Muslim majority states have the lowest levels of separation of religion and state.

96. Jonathan Fox, "Do Democracies Have Separation of Religion and State?" *Canadian Journal of Political Science* 40 (March 2007), 19.

97. Ibid., 19–20. Also see Jonathan Fox and Shmuel Sandler, "Separation of Religion and State in the Twenty-first Century: Comparing the Middle East and Western Democracies," *Comparative Politics* 37 (April 2005), 317–335 and Jonathan Fox, *A World Survey of Religion and State* (Cambridge: Cambridge University Press, 2008).

98. Stepan, *Arguing Comparative Politics*, 222; emphasis in original.

99. Ibid.

100. Stepan, *Arguing Comparative Politics*, 223.

101. Ibid., 222; emphasis in original.

102. Ibid., 216.

103. Ibid., 216–217.

104. Ibid., 217. As reformists in Iran will attest, this problem is at the core of the Iranian constitution. It effectively blocked President Muhammad Khatami's democratization efforts during his tenure as president (1997–2005). For background see William Samii, "Dissent and Iranian Elections: Reasons and Implications." *Middle East Journal* 58 (Summer 2004), 403–423.

105. Stepan provides two tables that demonstrate the versatility of his approach, *Arguing Comparative Politics*, 224–225.

CHAPTER 4

1. Seyyed Hossein Nasr, *Islamic Life and Thought* (Albany: State University of New York Press, 1981), 14.

2. Ignácz Goldziher, "Dahriyya," in *Encyclopaedia of Islam*, new ed., vol. 2 (Leiden: Brill, 1960), 95–97. In a personal conversation with Nikki Keddie she observed that the term *dahr* and the early origins of the term "secular" both have the same meaning. The etymological roots of the word secular can be traced back to the Latin *saeculum*, which refers to "age" or "generations" in the sense of the passage of temporal time. The Qur'anic term *dahr* has the same original meaning. I am indebted to Professor Keddie for drawing my attention to this fact and for her close reading and comments on an early draft of this chapter.

3. The Persian title was *Haqiqat-i mazhabi-i naichiri va bayan-i hal-i naichiriyyan* (The Truth of the Naichiri Sect and an Explanation of the Condition of the Naichiris). For a summary of the debate between Renan and Afghani and a translation of Afghani's rejoinder see Nikki Keddie, *An Islamic Response to Imperialism: Political and Religious Writings of Sayyid Jamal ad-Din "al-Afghani"* (Berkeley: University of California Press, 1983), 84–95, 181–187.

4. For background see Nikki Keddie, *Sayyid Jamal ad-Din "al-Afghani"* (Berkeley: University of California Press, 1972), 143–170.

5. Goldziher, "Dahriyya," 97.

6. Albert Hourani, *Arabic Thought in the Liberal Age 1798–1939* (Cambridge: Cambridge University Press, 1983), 108.

7. Personal correspondence, 26 November 2007. Afghani's work still resonates among Muslims in part because several of the central tropes of his thought—anti-imperialism, Muslim unity, and independence from foreign intervention—are still relevant for Muslim politics today. To cite just one example, on the centennial of his death the following book appeared in Iran: Hasan Yousefi Eshkevari, *Dara-ye Qafeleh* (The Caravan Bell: Seven articles on the Work and Thought of Seyyed Jamal Eddin Asadabadi) (Tehran: Chapakhsh, 1997).

8. Abou Filali-Ansary, "Muslims and Democracy," in Larry Diamond, Marc Plattner, and Daniel Brumberg, eds., *Islam and Democracy in the Middle East* (Baltimore: Johns Hopkins University Press, 2003), 194–195.

9. Ibid., 195. Also see Bernard Lewis, *The Political Language of Islam* (Chicago: University of Chicago Press, 1988), 117.

10. John Keane, "Secularism?" in David Marquand and Ronald L. Nettler, eds., *Religion and Democracy* (Oxford: Blackwell, 2000), 15. The term *madaniyya* is also commonly used for secularism, especially in Egypt. Also see Talal Asad, *Formations of the Secular: Christianity, Islam and Modernity* (Palo Alto, Calif.: Stanford University Press, 2003), 206–207.

11. Filali-Ansary, "Muslims and Democracy," 195. For a thoughtful treatment of the topic see Kate Zebiri, "Muslim Anti-secularist Discourse in the Context of Muslim-Christian Relations," *Islam and Christian-Muslim Relations* 9 (1998), 47–64.

12. William Shepard, "The Diversity of Islamic Thought: Towards a Typology," in Suha Taji-Faroukhi and Basheer Nafi, eds., *Islamic Thought in the Twentieth Century* (New York: Tauris, 2004), 61; emphasis added.

13. See Juan Cole, *Napolean's Egypt: Invading the Middle East* (New York: Palgrave, 2007), 245–248, and Juan Cole, "Bush's Napoleonic Folly," *Nation* 285 (10 September 2007).

14. Muhammad Khalid Masud, "The Construction and Deconstruction of Secularism as an Ideology of Contemporary Muslim Thought," *Asian Journal of Social Science* 33 (September 2005), 364.

15. John Pottenger provides an excellent historical overview that highlights the long history of debate and contestation on religion-state relations in the context of the development of Western liberal democracy. See his *Reaping the Whirlwind: Liberal Democracy and the Religious Axis* (Washington, D.C.: Georgetown University Press), 47–121.

16. Vali Nasr, "Secularism: Lessons from the Muslim World," *Daedalus* 132 (Summer 2003), 68. Also see S. V. R. Nasr, "European Colonialism and the Emergence of Modern Muslim States," in John Esposito, ed., *The Oxford History of Islam* (New York: Oxford University Press, 1999), 549–599, and Francois Burgat, *Face to Face with Political Islam* (New York: Tauris, 2003), 43–46.

17. Shahrough Akhavi notes that at the start of the twentieth century Iran was a semi-colony, in the sense that the "Belgians administer[ed] the customs service.... Swedish officers command[ed] the state police.... Russian officers staff[ed] and command[ed] the [gendarmerie].... Hungarians ... administer[ed] the Treasury.... The Dutch own[ed] and operate[d] the only telegraph line ... and large industrial operations (textiles)." See his insightful essay, "Iran: Implementation of an Islamic State," in John Esposito, ed., *Islam in Asia: Religion, Politics and Society* (New York: Oxford University Press, 1987), 29. Nikki Keddie and Mehrdad Amanat also use the term. See "Iran under the Later Qajars, 1848–1922," in Peter Avery, Gavin Hambly, and Charles Melville, eds., *The Cambridge History of Iran: From Nadir Shah to the Islamic Republic* (Cambridge: Cambridge University Press, 1991), 181.

18. Keddie and Amanat, "Iran under the Later Qajars," 174, 181.

19. Cyrus Ghani covers this period in *Iran and the Rise of Reza Shah: From Qajar Collapse to Pahlavi Power* (New York: Tauris, 2000), 325–412.

20. For a succinct overview see Ervand Abrahamian, *A History of Modern Iran* (Cambridge: Cambridge University Press, 2008), and Ali Ansari, *Modern Iran since 1921: The Pahlavis and After* (London: Pearson Education, 2003), 40–74.

21. Karen Armstrong, *The Battle for God* (New York: Knopf, 2000), 198.

22. Gavin Hambly, "The Pahlavi Autocracy: Riza Shah, 1921–1941," in Avery, Hambly and Melville, *Cambridge History of Iran*, 7:232–233. On Reza Pahlavi's 1934 visit to Turkey see Afshin Marashi, "Performing the Nation: The Shah's Official State Visit to Kemalist Turkey, June to July 1934," in Stephanie Cronin, ed., *The Making of Modern Iran: State and Society under Riza Shah, 1921–1941* (London: Routledge/Curzon, 2003), 99–119. Also see Jean-Francois Bayart, "Republican Trajectories in Iran and Turkey: A Tocquevillian Reading," in Ghassan Salamé, ed., *Democracy without Democrats?*

The Renewal of Politics in the Muslim World (London: Tauris, 1994), 282–299 and
Shahrough Akhavi, *Religion and Politics in Contemporary Iran* (Albany: State University
of New York Press, 1980), 28–59.

23. Mosaddeq was a firm believer in the non-aligned movement. Had he not been
toppled he likely would have joined Nehru, Sukarno, and Tito in the creation of the Non-
Aligned Movement. For background see Homa Katouzian, *Musaddiq and the Struggle for
Power in Iran* (New York: Tauris, 1999), 95–112, and Homa Katouzian, "Mosaddeq's
Government in Iranian History: Arbitrary Rule, Democracy, and the 1953 Coup," in
Malcolm Bryne and Mark Gasiorowski, eds., *Mohammad Mosaddeq and the 1953 Coup in
Iran* (Syracuse, N.Y.: Syracuse University Press, 2004), 1–26.

24. Lest one think otherwise, in his interpretation and recollection of Iranian
history, the Shah's references to Islam were always polite and very respectful. He
writes that Iran "developed the Shiah branch of the Moslem faith, in which
I fervently believe." For his references to Islam see Mohammed Reza Shah Pahlavi,
Mission for My Country (New York: Hutchinson, 1961), 21, 23–24.

25. Hambly, "Pahlavi Autocracy," 267.

26. Ali Mirsepassi, *Intellectual Discourse and the Politics of Modernization: Negotiating
Modernity in Iran* (Cambridge: Cambridge University Press, 2000), 65–95 provides an
excellent overview of this development in Iran on which I have drawn. Also see Mansoor
Moaddel, *Jordanian Exceptionalism: A Comparative Analysis of State-Religion Relationships in
Egypt, Iran, Jordan, and Syria* (New York: Palgrave, 2002), 46–55.

27. Azadeh Kian-Thiébaut, *Secularization of Iran: A Doomed Failure? The New
Middle Class and the Making of Modern Iran* (Paris: Peeters, 1998), 211–226. Nikki
Keddie covers this period of uneven development in *Modern Iran: Roots and Results of
Revolution* (New Haven, Conn.: Yale University Press, 2003), 132–169. Also see Vali
Nasr, "Religion and Global Affairs: Secular States and Religious Oppositions," *SAIS
Review* 18 (Summer-Fall 1998), 32–37.

28. I am indebted to Richard Bulliet for drawing my attention to this point.

29. John Waterbury, "Democracy without Democrats? The Potential for Political
Liberalization in the Middle East," in Salamé, *Democracy without Democrats*, 41.

30. Nilüfer Göle, "Authoritarian Secularism and Islamist Politics: The Case of
Turkey," in Augustus Richard Norton, ed., *Civil Society in the Middle East* (Leiden: Brill,
1996), 1:20.

31. Ibid.

32. Armstrong, *Battle for God*, 192.

33. Nasr, "Secularism," 69.

34. In discussing these events, the U.S. ambassador Dennis Ross wrote: "We must
keep our eye on the essential prize. The key question now is whether the Palestinians will
have a secular future or an Islamist future. Our stake in a national, secular future for the
Palestinians is very clear. Without that, there will be no prospect of peace, and Islamists will
control the most evocative issue in the region. We should quietly be making that point with
the Saudis" ("Can Fatah Compete with Hamas?" *New Republic*, 16 July 2007). The policy,
therefore, of supporting Fatah, in part because they are secular, while downplaying their
rampant corruption, nepotism, and authoritarianism, and boycotting Hamas, despite their

legitimate parliamentary victory in January 2006, and the broad legitimacy they enjoy in the Muslim world, does not bode well for either democracy or secularism in Muslim societies. This is especially true given that the Palestine question is a key "identity issue" for Muslims today, due to its perceived connection with the legacy of colonialism and imperialism. For analysis and background see Henry Siegman, "Those Who Do Not Want Hamas Will Get al Qaida," *Al Hayat*, 24 June 2007; Alastair Crooke, "Our Second Biggest Mistake in the Middle East," *London Review of Books* 29 (5 July 2007); and the report by the United Nations Under-Secretary-General, Alvaro de Soto, "End of Mission Report," May 2007, which was leaked to the *Guardian* and is available at http://image.guardian.co.uk/sys-files/Guardian/documents/2007/06/12/DeSotoReport.pdf.

35. Pew Charitable Trust, *Trends 2005* (Washington, D.C.: Pew Research Center, 2005), 105–119.

36. Mikaela McDermott and Brian Katulis, "Even the Word 'Democracy' Now Repels Mideast Reformers," *Christian Science Monitor*, 20 May 2004.

37. Abdallah Al-Jarrar and Cedric Cullingford, "The Concept of Democracy: Muslim Views," *Politics* 27 (February 2007), 16–23.

38. Generally speaking, due to their lower socioeconomic status, French Muslims cannot afford to send their children to private schools, unlike the more affluent Christians and Jews in France. More significantly, this debate is being driven by racist French views toward Muslims, a point most objective observers concede. Anyone not persuaded that French racism is a salient factor in this debate should consider the speech Jacques Chirac delivered in June 1991 during "une soirée mondaine." He observed: "It is clear that having Spanish, Polish or Portuguese people . . . poses fewer problems than having Muslims or blacks. How do you think a French worker feels when he sees on the landing a family with a man who has maybe three or four wives, about 20 kids, who receives around 50,000 francs in social services, of course without working . . . and if you add the noise and smell . . . no wonder the French worker across the land goes mad" (Naima Bouteldja, "The Reality of l'affaire du foulard," *Guardian*, 25 February 2005). For background see John Bowen, *Why the French Don't Like Headscarves: Islam, the State, and Public Space* (Princeton, N.J.: Princeton University Press, 2006), 63–152, and Jonathan Lawrence and Justine Vaisse, *Integrating Islam: Political and Religious Challenges in Contemporary France* (Washington, D.C.: Brookings Institution Press, 2006), 163–174.

39. "Headscarf ban sparks new Protests," 17 January 2004: http://news.bbc.co.uk/2/hi/europe/3405453.stm. The widely influential Sunni Muslim leader Yusuf Qaradawi penned a letter to President Chirac protesting French secularism, as did the Chief Mufti of Syria, Ahmad Kaftaro. Ayatollah Muhammad Hussein Fadlallah, often referred to as the spiritual leader of Hezbullah, also wrote an open letter to Chirac in which he complained of a "stripping of liberties from Muslims, even when they have not disobeyed the law," and warned of an emerging climate "hostile to religion and to Muslim citizens" in Europe. See "Lettre ouverte menaçante de Fadlallah, fondateur et guide spirituel du Hezbollah, à Jacques Chirac," posted on the website of the Conseil Régional du culte musulman Champagne Ardenne at http://www.crcm-cha.org/modules.php?name=News&file=article&sid=63. The letter was dated 20 December 2003.

40. For background on these events see Joan Wallach Scott, *Politics of the Veil* (Princeton, N.J.: Princeton University Press, 2007), 1–89; Neil MacMaster, "Islamophobia in France and the 'Algerian Problem,'" in Emran Qureshi and Michael Sells, eds., *The New Crusades: Constructing the Muslim Enemy* (New York: Columbia University Press, 2003), 288–313, and Talal Asad, "Reflections on Laïcité and the Public Sphere," *Items and Issues* 5, no. 3 (2005), 1–11.

41. "A Conversation on the Theme 'An Islamic Reformation,' between Bernard Lewis and Khaled Abou El Fadl," organized by the Global Policy Exchange, 18 October 2002, www.gpexchange.org/pages/details.html. North American and European identity is being shaped in a similar way, but in reverse.

42. Khaled Abou El Fadl, "Orphans of Modernity and the Clash of Civilizations," *Global Dialogue* 4 (spring 2002), 10. He makes a similar argument in "9/11 and the Muslim Transformation," in Mary L. Dudziak ed., *September 11 in History: A Watershed Moment?* (Durham, N.C.: Duke University Press, 2003), 70–111.

43. Khaled Abou El Fadl, "Islam and the Theology of Power," *Middle East Report* 221 (winter 2001), 28–33.

44. Abou El Fadl, "Orphans of Modernity," 11.

45. Quoted in William Fisher, "Muslim Scholar Urges Halt to Extreme Punishments," Inter Press Service, 28 April 2005; emphasis added. Muhammad Khalid Masud picks up on this point in the context of the Muslim debate on secularism. He accurately writes that one reason secularism has few supporters in the Muslim world is that "secularism has been perceived essentially as a politico-religious ideology," not as an important political principle needed to sustain a functioning liberal democracy. His survey of five Muslim thinkers makes this point abundantly clear. Due to the perception of secularism as an alien ideology, Islamic identity and authenticity is constructed in relationship to, and in the rejection of, secularism. See his well-researched article "The Construction and Deconstruction of Secularism as an Ideology of Contemporary Muslim Thought," *Asian Journal of Social Science* 33 (September 2005), 363–383.

46. Much of this topic is subsumed under the theme of authenticity, which Robert Lee has explored in *Overcoming Tradition and Modernity: the Search for Islamic Authenticity* (Boulder, Colo.: Westview Press, 1997), 1–24, 191–195. Also see Sami Zubaida, *The Search for Authenticity in Middle East Cultures: Religion, Community and Nation*, occasional paper (Washington, D.C.: Center for Contemporary Arab Studies, 2004), 3–12.

47. Ayatollah Ruhullah Khomeini, "Islamic Government," in *Islam and Revolution: Writings and Declarations of Imam Khomeini*, translated by Hamid Algar (Berkley: Mizan Press, 1981), 38. Khomeini makes the same point, linking the separation of religion and politics to an imperialist plot to weaken the Muslim world. See his lecture on 19 February 1978 in Najaf, "In Commemoration of the First Martyrs of the Revolution," in ibid., 219. While political Islam is widely believed to have started with Iran's 1979 Islamic Revolution and then spread to the rest of the Muslim world, Bassam Tibi notes that the "rise of political Islam has clearly started in the Arab part of the Middle East. . . . The prominent contemporary Islamic revivalist Yusuf al-Qaradawi published

his call for the 'Islamic solution' (*al-hall al-Islami*) in the early 1970s, a time when Khomayni's name was completely unknown in the Arab part of the Middle East" ("Major Themes in the Arabic Political Literature of Islamic Revivalism, 1970–1985: The Islamic System of Government (*al-nizam al-islami*), *Shura* Democracy and the Implementation of the Shari'a as opposed to Secularism (*'ilmaniyya*)," *Islam and Christian-Muslim Relations* 3 (December 1992), 187.

48. "Khamenei: Integration of Religion, Politics, Iran's Strong Point," Islamic Republic of Iran News Agency (IRNA), 10 September 2002. His linking of secularism to colonialism and to the U.S.-backed Pahlavi monarchy is worth noting here. This is a common theme one encounters in the internal Muslim debate on secularism: secularism is to be rejected because of its "otherness," especially its association with colonialism and imperialism.

49. Munir Shafiq, "Secularism and the Arab-Muslim Condition," in Azzam Tamimi and John L. Esposito, eds., *Islam and Secularism in the Middle East* (New York: New York University Press, 2000), 147.

50. Abdelwahab Elmessiri, "Secularism, Immanence and Deconstruction," in Tamimi and Esposito, *Islam and Secularism in the Middle East*, 57.

51. Tarik Jan, "Mawdudi's Critique of the Secular Mind," *Muslim World* 93 (July–October 2003), 503–519; Seyyed Vali Reza Nasr, *Mawdudi and the Making of Islamic Revivalism* (New York: Oxford University Press, 1995), 80–106; Ahmad Moussalli, *Moderate and Radical Islamic Fundamentalism: The Quest for Modernity, Legitimacy and the Islamic State* (Gainesville: University of Florida Press), 132–154, and Adnan Musallam, *From Secularism to Jihad: Sayyid Qutb and the Foundations of Radical Islamism* (Westport, Conn.: Praeger, 2005). In his discussion of Islamic political theory, Sayyid Qutb notes that "we must be careful when we describe Islam not to relate it to other principles and theories in order to explain it by means of them or to relate it to them. Islam is a comprehensive philosophy and a homogeneous unity, and to introduce into it any foreign element would mean ruining it. It is like a delicate and perfect piece of machinery that may be completely ruined by the presence of an alien component" (Sayyid Qutb, *Social Justice in Islam*, translated by John B. Hardie and Hamid Algar, rev. ed. [Oneonta, N.Y.: Islamic Publications International, 2000], 117).

52. Yusuf Qaradawi, *'Al-Hulul al Mustawradah wa Kayfa Jaat 'alaa Ummatina'* [How the Imported Solutions Disastrously Affected Our Ummah] (Cairo: Maktabat Wahbah, 1977), 113–114. Also see Yusuf Qaradawi, *al-Islam wa-al- Ilmaniyah* [Islam and Secularism] (Beirut: Mo'assassat al-Rissalah, 2000). For background see Alexander Flores, "Secularism, Integralism and Political Islam: The Egyptian Debate," *Middle East Report* 23 (July–August 1993), 32–38, and Fouad Zakariyya, *Myth and Reality in the Contemporary Islamist Movement*, translated by Ibrahim M. Abu-Rabi' (London: Pluto Press, 2005), 23–33. For similar views from a leading Islamist thinker and political leader in Morocco, see Abdessalam Yassine, *Winning the Modern World for Islam*, translated by Martin Jenni (Iowa City, Iowa: Justice and Spirituality, 2000), 19–30, 156–168. For a more nuanced interpretation on secularism from Rachid Ghannouchi, a leading Tunisian Islamist, see Azzam Tamimi, *Rachid*

Ghannouchi: A Democrat within Islamism (New York: Oxford University Press, 2001), 105–124.

53. Quoted in Bassam Tibi, "Major Themes in the Arabic Political Literature of Islamic Revivalism, 1970–1985: The Islamic System of Government (*al-nizam al-islami*), *Shura* Democracy and the Implementation of the Shari'a as Opposed to Secularism (*'ilmaniyya*)," *Islam and Christian-Muslim Relations* 4 (June 1993), 93.

54. Muhammad Imarah, *al-Almaniyya wa Nahdatuna al-Haditha* [Secularism and Our Modern Renaissance] (Cairo: Dar al Shorouq, 1986), 12–18. I am relying on Fauzi Najjar's summary of Imarah's views in "The Debate on Islam and Secularism in Egypt," *Arab Studies Quarterly* 18 (spring 1996), 7–8.

55. For analysis and background see Piers Gillespie, "Current Issues in Indonesian Islam: Analyzing the 2005 Council on Indonesian Ulama Fatwa No. 7 Opposing Pluralism, Liberalism and Secularism," *Journal of Islamic Studies* 18 (May 2007), 202–240. In August 2007, the head of the Indonesia branch of the radical Islamist organization Hizb ut-Tahrir described secularism as "the mother of all destruction" (Tom Peter, "At a Massive Rally, Hizb ut-Tahrir Calls for a Global Muslim state," *Christian Science Monitor*, 14 August 2007).

56. Syed Naquib al-Attas, *Islam, Secularism and the Philosophy of the Future* (London: Mansell, 1985), 23.

57. Ibid., 24–29.

58. "Malaysia Not a Secular State, Says Najib," Malaysia National News Agency (Bernama), 17 July 2007, and "Malaysia an Islamic State but Minority Rights Protected, Says Deputy PM," Associated Press, 17 July 2007.

59. "Iraqi Sunnis against Secular Constitution," Islamonline.net, 11 February 2005.

60. Michael Jansen, "Shia Clerics Insist on the Adoption of Islamic Law," *Irish Times*, 7 February 2005.

61. "*Iraqi President Rules Out Islamic Regime in His Country,*" *Agence France Presse*, 25 April 2005.

62. Wan Hamidi Hamid, "I Am Not a Secularist, Says Abbas," *New Strait Times*, 23 October 2007. The revealing question here is why did Abbas go out of his way in Malaysia to insist that he was "not a secularist"?

63. "Community Party Sees the Light, Adopts Politics of Religion," Reuters, 22 November 2003.

64. As mentioned earlier, a comprehensive analysis on the history of secularism and its discontents in the Muslim world remains to be written. In this chapter I have only been able to scratch the surface. Fundamentally, however, the different histories of religion-state relations in Muslim societies, in contrast to the West, needs to be examined. I briefly discuss this issue in "Political Islam versus Secularism," *Literary Review of Canada* 16 (September 2008), http://lrc.reviewcanada.ca/index.php?page= Political-Islam-Versus-Secularism. One final observation is in order. Kate Zebiri, in her survey and analysis of Muslim antisecularist discourses, provides the following useful summary of Muslim attitudes toward secularism: "In recent decades a fairly elaborate Muslim anti-secularist discourse has evolved. This discourse holds that secularism cannot form a proper societal basis because, unlike divine law, it is subject to the

limitations of human reason; that it results in the exclusion of morality from the political arena since it places no restraints on rulers; and that this in turn results in a breakdown in moral values as witnessed in contemporary Western societies. Secularism is associated with the denial of spirituality or religiosity, with materialism, hedonism and often atheism. Secularism is sometimes seen as diametrically opposed to authenticity; anti-secularists may assert, for example, that Muslim societies were robbed of their true essence in the colonialist onslaught, and that this essence is now being restored by the Islamic 'awakening.' ... The promotion of secularism is often described as part of a plan to weaken and undermine Islam, so that to accuse anyone of being secularist is to accuse them of being anti-Islamic, co-opted by foreign governments, etc." (see Zebiri, "Muslim Anti-secularist Discourse," 50). Any comprehensive analysis of secularism and its discontents in Muslim societies will have to take these observations into account.

65. Abdou Filali-Ansary, "The Challenge of Secularization," in Diamond et al., *Islam and Democracy in the Middle East*, 235.

66. For a succinct overview of the debate on democracy in the Muslim world during the twentieth century see Abdelwahab El-Affendi, "On the State, Democracy and Pluralism," in Basheer Nafi and Suha Taji-Farouki, eds., *Islamic Thought in the Twentieth Century* (New York: Tauris, 2004), 180–203. El-Effendi notes at the start of his essay that "the tension between democracy and secularism ... remains the dominant feature of Muslim politics to this day."

67. Wolfhart Pannenberg, "How to Think about Secularism," *First Things* 64 (June–July 1996), 27–32. See also John McManners, ed., *The Oxford History of Christianity* (New York: Oxford University Press, 1993), 243–309.

68. Roger Williams (1603–1683) preceded Locke and deserves credit for an earlier argument on church-state separation (albeit a mild one). See Edwin Gaustad, *Roger Williams* (New York: Oxford University Press, 2005), 74–84.

69. Noel Malcolm, *Aspects of Hobbes* (New York: Oxford University Press, 2002), 23.

70. Thomas Hobbes, *Leviathan*, edited by Richard Tuck (Cambridge: Cambridge University Press, 1996), 3.

71. Patricia Springborg, in an authoritative overview of Hobbes's attitude toward religion, writes that "Hobbes' religious views, which he stated over and over in various places, show a remarkable consistency—which is not to say that they are coherent. ... Hobbes both professed official conformity to the doctrines of the Anglican Church and a vehement anticlericalism throughout his long life" ("Hobbes on Religion," in Tom Sorell, ed., *The Cambridge Companion to Hobbes* [Cambridge: Cambridge University Press, 1996], 346–380). For background see A. P. Martinich, *Two Gods of Leviathan: Thomas Hobbes on Religion and Politics* (Cambridge: Cambridge University Press, 1992), 1–16, 40–67, and Johann Sommerville, "*Leviathan* and Its Anglican Context," in Patricia Springborg, ed., *The Cambridge Companion to Hobbes's Leviathan* (Cambridge: Cambridge University Press, 2007), 358–374.

72. John Locke, *A Letter Concerning Toleration*, edited by James Tully (Indianapolis: Hackett, 1983), 26.

73. For background see Owen Chadwick, *The Reformation* (New York: Penguin Books, 1972), 11–247; Alister McGrath, *Reformation Thought: An Introduction*, 2nd

ed. (Oxford: Blackwell, 1993), 218–235; Diarmaid MacCulloch, *The Reformation* (New York: Viking, 2004), 645–683, and Patrick Collinson, *The Reformation: A History* (New York: Random House, 2004), 1–14.

74. Nasr, "Secularism: Lessons from the Muslim World," 68.

75. Ibid.

76. Afaf Lutfi al-Sayyid Marsot, *Egypt in the Reign of Muhammad Ali* (Cambridge: Cambridge University Press, 1984), 162–195.

77. Marshall Hodgson, "Modernity and the Islamic Heritage," in Hodgson, *Rethinking World History: Essays on Europe, Islam, and World History* (Cambridge: Cambridge University Press, 1993), 220; emphasis added.

78. Ibid., 222.

79. Ibid., 222.

80. Ibid., 222.; emphasis added.

81. Ibid., 223.

82. L. Carl Brown, *Religion and State: The Muslim Approach to Politics* (New York: Columbia University Press, 2000), 137, refers to the "vertiginous convulsions" brought on by the situation Hodgson describes. Charles Issawi in his comparative treatment of modernization in Egypt and Japan makes a similar point: the Japanese embrace of modernity was more integrated and harmonious with Japan's traditional culture, in contrast to that of Egypt. See Charles Issawi, "Why Japan?" in Ibrahim Ibrahim, ed., *Arab Resources: The Transformation of a Society* (London: Croom Helm, 1983), 283–300. Marshall Hodgson briefly explores this theme in the epilogue of *The Venture of Islam: The Gunpowder Empires and Modern Times*, vol. 3 (Chicago: University of Chicago Press, 1974), 417–436, and Wilfred Cantwell Smith touches on this point at the beginning of his *Islam in Modern History* (Princeton, N.J.: Princeton University Press, 1957), 3–7.

83. Nikki Keddie's discussion of secularism in the Muslim world conforms to this assessment. While writing more broadly about secularism in the non-Western world, she observes: "There were relatively few intellectual figures with relatively little influence espousing secularism before it became a major political or governmental cause. As for popular belief, there is no doubt but that non-Western modernizing governments greatly preceded their populations in secularist beliefs and practices. This primacy of governments in secularization has been somewhat obscured by the fact that not only Western but also indigenous scholars often prefer to discuss the achievements of intellectuals rather than those of governments. While more intellectuals preceded governments in secularism in the West, even in this field scholarship often overstates the role of intellectuals" ("Secularism and the State: Towards Clarity and Global Comparison," *New Left Review* 226 [November–December 1997], 27]).

84. Ibid., 35.

85. Of course there is infinitely more to this story. Richard Bulliet has pointed out that unlike the West, where religion was a source of conflict and was tied to the breakdown of social order in the case of many Muslim societies, religion was used to limit political tyranny, not bolster it. See his discussion in *The Case for Islamo-Christian Civilization* (New York: Columbia University Press, 2004), 68–75. For a more recent, thoughtful, and insightful discussion along similar lines that emphasizes the role of

Islamic law and legal scholars, see Noah Feldman, *The Fall and Rise of the Islamic State* (Princeton: Princeton University Press, 2008), 19–55.

86. According to the 2007 Freedom House rankings, on a scale of 1 (most free) to 7 (least free), Indonesia received a 2 for political rights and a 3 for civil liberties, while Turkey's score was 3 for political rights and 3 for civil liberties. These were some of the highest rankings among the members of the Organization of Islamic Conference. Other member countries which received high scores were Mali, Benin, Suriname, and Senegal; www.freedomhouse.org/template.cfm?page=372&year=2007.

87. A 2007 Gallup Poll noted that "Turks' attitudes regarding Shariah (Islamic religious law) are different from those in many other predominately Muslim countries." When asked "whether Shariah should be the only source of legislation, a source, but not the only source, or not a source of legislation, 41% chose the latter option; by comparison, in no other predominantly Muslim country . . . was this figure nearly as high. Slightly more than one in four Turks (26%) say Shariah should be one source of legislation, but not the sole source, while just 7% say it should be the only source" (Steve Crabtree, "Turks at Odds Over Islamic Law," 10 December 2007, www.gallup.com/poll/103129/Turks-Odds-Over-Islamic-Law.aspx). The case of Indonesia and Shariah law is more complex and I will discuss it later. Suffice it to say, however, that since the transition to democracy following the ouster of Suharto, political parties at the national level that have explicit Islamist agendas have faired poorly in recent national elections. See R. William Liddle and Saiful Mujani, "The Real Face of Indonesian Islam," *New York Times*, 11 October 2003, and Angus Reid Global Monitor, "Indonesians Endorse Secular Politics," 11 October 2007, www.angus-reid.com/polls/view/indonesians_endorse_secular_politics.

88. M. Hakan Yavuz, *Islamic Political Identity in Turkey* (New York: Oxford University Press, 2003), 207–264. Also see M. Hakan Yavuz, *Secularism and Muslim Democracy in Turkey* (Cambridge: Cambridge University Press, forthcoming).

89. During a campaign speech in 1997, Erdoğan recited a poem based on a work written in the 1920s by the nationalist hero Ziya Gökalp: "The mosques are our barracks, the minarets are our spears, their domes and our helmets and the faithful are our army." He was charged with provoking religious hatred and sentenced to a jail term of ten months, of which he served four. For a short biography of Erdoğan see Jenny White, *Islamist Mobilization in Turkey: A Study in Vernacular Politics* (Seattle: University of Washington Press, 2002), 137–142. For a succinct profile of Erdoğan see Vincent Boland, "Eastern Premise," *Financial Times*, 3 December 2004; and for a longer discussion of him consult Mertin Heper and Şule Toktaş, "Islam, Modernity, and Democracy in Contemporary Turkey: The Case of Recep Tayyip Erdoğan," *Muslim World* 93 (April 2003), 157–185.

90. For background see Niyazi Berkes, *The Development of Secularism in Turkey* (Montreal: McGill University Press, 1964), 3–18, 479–503; Bernard Lewis, *The Emergence of Modern Turkey*, 3rd ed. (New York: Oxford University Press, 2002), 175–209, 401–442, and Eric Zürcher, *Turkey: A Modern History*, 3rd ed. (New York: Tauris, 2004), 93–205. Şerif Mardin notes that the roots of secularism in Turkey precede the rise of Atatürk and can be located in the mid-nineteenth-century Tanzimat reform period

of the Ottoman Empire. See his "Religion and Secularism in Turkey," in Ali Kazancigil and Ergun Özbudun, eds., *Atatürk: Founder of a Modern State* (London: Hurst, 1997), 191–219, and Serif Mardin, *Religion, Society, and Modernity in Turkey* (Syracuse, N.Y.: Syracuse University Press, 2006), 225–242, 260–297.

91. Selcan Hacaoglu, "Turkey's President Says Islamist Threat to Secular Establishment at Highest Level," *Independent*, 14 April 2007. He hinted that a foreign conspiracy was trying to turn Turkey into an Islamic fundamentalist state. These views were echoed by some in the West who similarly accused the AK Party of trying to secretly construct an Islamist state. Ayaan Hirsi Ali, for example, accused Erdoğan and Gül of deception. She affirmed that they were pursuing a secret plan of "gradual-ism" to create a fundamentalist state by using "democratic means to erode democracy." She then went on to criticize "well-meaning but naive European leaders [who] were manipulated by the ruling Islamists into saying that Turkey's army should be placed under civil control, like all armies in EU member states." ("Can Secular Turkey Survive Democracy?" *Los Angeles Times*, 9 May 2007).

92. Sabrina Tavernise, "Turkish Military Issues Threat as Voting Is Derailed," *New York Times*, 28 April 2007. "Military Steps in Presidential Election Debate," *Zaman*, 28 April 2007.

93. Türkan Saylan, "Open Letter to the European Union," 30 April 2007; obtained via personal correspondence.

94. Günter Seufert, "Kemalists versus Liberal Intellectuals in Turkey: Promoting the Kemalist Personality Cult and Keeping Rank," www.qantara.de (25 May 2007), www.qantara.de/webcom/show_article.php/_c-476/_nr-791/i.html?PHPSESSID= baa1d508ffe20efobfbo4a5550739e48. Many of these demonstrations were marked by a strong sense of paternalism and subtle racism toward Turks who dressed differently and came from rural areas. See Sabrina Tavernise, "In Turkey, Fear about Religious Lifestyle," *New York Times*, 30 April 2007.

95. For background on these events in 2007 see M. Hakan Yavuz and Michael Gunter, "Turkish Paradox: Progressive Islamists versus Reactionary Secularists," *Critique* 16 (fall 2007), 289–301.

96. Yavuz, *Islamic Political Identity in Turkey*, 184. The "internal secularization of religion" is described by Yavuz as the "rationalization of religious practices and exclu-sion of magical elements and the acceptance of a universal conception of the sacred. Moreover, secular thinking has been incorporated into mainstream Islamic thought. 'Internal secularization' is the process by which Muslims focus all their energy and activism increasingly on this world and decreasingly on a postulated otherworld" (5). For differences in how secularism is defined and understood by the AK Party versus the Kemalist establishment see Ahmet Kuru, "Reinterpretation of Secularism in Turkey: The Case of the Justice and Development Party," in M. Hakan Yavuz, ed., *The Emergence of a New Turkey: Democracy and the AK Party* (Salt Lake City: University of Utah Press, 2006), 139–146. For background on how Turkish Muslim intellectuals such as Ali Bulac underwent an ideological transformation see Ihsan Dagi, "Rethinking Human Rights, Democracy, and the West: Post-Islamist Intellectuals in Turkey," *Critique* 13 (summer 2004), 135–151. More broadly on the transformation of key political

actors who emerged out of the Refah and Virtue parties and came to form the AK Party see Ihsan Dagi, "The Justice and Development Party: Identity, Politics and Human Rights Discourse in the Search for Security and Legitimacy," in Yavuz, *Emergence of a New Turkey*, 88–106. One way to take the measure of this transformation within Turkish political Islam is to compare and contrast the political views today of Recep Tayip Erdoğan with that of Necmettin Erbakan. See Erbakan's interview with *Asharq Al-Awsat* in which he described Erdoğan as a "failure" and an insincere Muslim. He also blamed a Jewish and Zionist conspiracy for the demise of his political ambitions in Turkey (Necmettin Erbakan, "Turkey: Q & A with Necmettin Erbakan," by Manal Lutfi, *Asharq Al-Awsat* [English ed.], 16 November 2007).

97. Ersin Kalaycioglu, "State and Civil Society in Turkey: Democracy, Development and Protest," in Amyn Sajoo, ed., *Civil Society in the Muslim World: Contemporary Perspectives* (New York: Tauris, 2002), 247–272. For my comparative analysis of Turkey and Indonesia I have drawn on Greg Barton, "Turkey's Gülen hizmet and Indonesia's Neo-modernist NGOs: Remarkable Examples of Progressive Islamic Thought and Civil Society Activism in the Muslim World," in Fethi Mansouri and Shahram Akbarzadeh, eds., *Political Islam and Human Security* (Newcastle, England: Cambridge Scholars Press, 2006), 140–160.

98. Thomas Michel, "Sufism and Modernity in the Thought of Fethullah Gülen," *Muslim World* 95 (July 2005), 341–358.

99. Yavuz, *Islamic Political Identity in Turkey*, 180.

100. Elizabeth Özdalga, "Secularizing Trends in Fethullah Gülen's Movement: Impass or Opportunity for Further Revival?" *Critique* 12 (spring 2003), 72. Also of relevance is Bulent Aras and Omer Caha, "Fethullah Gülen and his Liberal 'Turkish Islam' Movement," *Middle East Review of International Affairs Journal* (December 2000), www.biu.ac.il/SOC/besa/meria/journal/2000/issue4/jv4n4a4.html, and M. Hakan Yavuz and John Esposito, *Turkish Islam and the Secular State: The Gülen Movement* (Syracuse, N.Y.: Syracuse University Press, 2003), xiii–xxxiii. The most comprehensive and scholarly overview of the Gülen movement can be obtained in Yavuz, *Islamic Political Identity in Turkey*, 178–205.

101. In August 2000, Fethullah Gülen was indicted for trying to overthrow the Turkish state. The state prosecutor asked for a ten-year sentence. Gülen never faced trial because ostensibly he had left Turkey for medical treatment in the United States. He was acquitted in 2006.

102. Yavuz, *Islamic Political Identity in Turkey*, 179.

103. Fethullah Gülen, "A Comparative Approach to Islam and Democracy," *SAIS Review* 21 (Summer-Fall 2001), 134.

104. Ibid., 134–135. For more of his views on government see Fethullah Gülen, *Pearls of Wisdom*, translated by Ali Unal (Somerset, N.J.: Light, 2005), 85–92.

105. The declarations appear in the appendices of Yavuz and Esposito, *Turkish Islam and the Secular State*, 251–256. For further information see the Abant Platform website, www.abantplatform.org.

106. Yavuz and Esposito, *Turkish Islam and the Secular State*, 252; emphasis added.

107. Hard-line secularists often accuse Muslim parties with having a "secret agenda," implying that they cannot be trusted. But how does one measure political "intention" in social science research? I submit that it cannot be measured empirically. What fundamentally matters is the track record of politicians and political parties after they assume public office.

108. Robert Hefner, *Civil Islam: Muslims and Democratization in Indonesia* (Princeton, N.J.: Princeton University Press, 2000), 12–13. For an overview of different approaches to political Islam in Indonesia see Bahtiar Effendy, "What Is Political Islam? An Examination of Its Theoretical Mapping in Modern Indonesia," in Chaider Bamualim, ed., *A Portrait of Contemporary Indonesia* (Jakarta: Pusat Bahasa dan Budaya and Konrad Adenauer Stiflung, 2005), 1–38.

109. Greg Barton, "Turkey's Gülen hizmet and Indonesia's Neo-modernist NGOs," 146.

110. This became known as the 1945 Jakarta Charter. Its removal from the constitution has been a frequent bone of contention among Muslim groups throughout the post-independence period. When political space opened up after the ouster of Suharto, for example, there were new calls for the recognition of Shariah law in the Indonesian constitution. For background see Nadirsyah Hosen, *Shari'a and Constitutional Reform in Indonesia* (Singapore: Institute of Southeast Asian Studies, 2007), 60–70; Bahtiar Effendy, *Islam and the State in Indonesia* (Singapore: Institute for Southeast Asian Studies, 2003), 15–44, and Martin van Bruinessen, "Islamic State or State Islam? Fifty Years of State-Islam Relations in Indonesia," in Ingrid Wessel, ed., *Indonesien am Ende des 20. Jahrhunderts: Analysen zu 50 Jahren unabhängiger Entwicklung* (Hamburg: Abera-Verlag, 1996), 19–34.

111. George McTurnan Kahin, *Nationalism and Revolution in Indonesia* (Ithaca, N.Y.: Cornell University Press, 1952), 122–126.

112. In a 1952 in visit to Pakistan, Mohammad Natsir (1907–1993), a prominent Muslim leader of the postindependence period, praised Pancasila as a philosophy that met the needs of Indonesian Muslims. He cited the first principle of Pancasila, recognition of monotheism, as proof. By 1957, however, he was saying the exact opposite. Compare his lecture at the Pakistan Institute for World Affairs (1952) with his remarks on 12 November 1957 before the Constitutional Assembly in which he stated that "the basis of our nation should be religion, and not an idea that is unlikely to be accepted by all people, namely Pancasila." For his statement in praise of Pancasila see Bahtiar Effendy, *Islam and the State in Indonesia*, 38. For his opposition to Pancasila see Luthfi Assyaukanie, "Islam and Secularism in Indonesia," unpublished paper, 5. For analysis see Herbert Feith, *The Decline of Constitutional Democracy in Indonesia* (Ithaca, N.Y.: Cornell University Press, 1962), 273–285.

113. Robin Bush, "Redefining 'Political Islam' in Indonesia: Nahdlatul Ulama and Khttah '26," *Studia Islamika* 7 (2000), 59–86.

114. Personal Interview, Jakarta, 15 March 2007.

115. Bahtiar Effendy, *Islam and the State in Indonesia*, 66.

116. The *New York Times* obituary noted that he was "known as the conscience of his nation." (Jane Perlez, "Nurcholish Madjid, 66, Advocate of Moderate Islam, Dies," 1 September 2005).

117. Ann Kull, *Piety and Politics: Nurcholish Madjid and His Interpretation of Islam in Modern Indonesia* (Lund, Sweden: Department of History and Anthropology of Religions, Lund University, 2005), 87–88.

118. For a succinct summary see Hefner, *Civil Islam*, 116–119. For a longer treatment see Greg Barton, "Neo-Modernism: A Vital Synthesis of Traditionalist and Modernist Islamic Thought in Indonesia," *Studia Islamika* 2 (1995), 13–24; Chaider Bamualim, "Transforming the Ideal Transcendental into the Historical Humanistic: Nurcholish Madjid's Islamic Thinking in Indonesia (1970–1995)," (Master's Thesis, Faculty of Letters and Theology, University of Leiden 1998), 22–32, and Effendy, *Islam and the State in Indonesia*, 71–75.

119. Kull, *Piety and Politics*, 59.

120. An English translation appears in Nurcholish Madjid, "The Necessity of Renewing Islamic Thought and the Problem of the Integration of the Ummat," in M. Kamal Hassan, *Muslim Intellectual Responses to 'New Order' Modernisation in Indonesia* (Kuala Lumpur: Dewan Bahasa dan Pustaka, 1980), 187–197; reprinted in Charles Kurzman, ed., *Liberal Islam: A Sourcebook* (New York: Oxford University Press, 1998), 284–289. All citations are from the Kurzman edition.

121. Siti Fathimah, "Modernism and the Contextualization of Islamic Doctrines: The Reform of Indonesian Islam Proposed by Nurcholish Madjid" (Master's Thesis, McGill University), 34, quoted in Kull, *Piety and Politics*, 60. Looking back, Madjid never came to regret the substance of his remarks, which he continued to defend throughout his life. His only regrets were with his choice of terminology and the boldness with which he articulated his thoughts. In his own words: "I wish I had never made such a tactical blunder as that manifest in my speech on January 2, 1970. It was socially too expensive, and we suffered irreparable damage to our reputation within the Muslim community. If I were able to go back in time, I would follow my previous methods, i.e. *penetration pacifique*, the 'smuggling method' of introducing new ideas" (ibid., 61).

122. Madjid, "Necessity of Renewing Islamic Thought," 285.

123. Ibid., 286.

124. Ibid., 286.

125. Ibid., 287. Compare this statement by Nurcholish Madjid with John Stuart Mill's observation that the "peculiar evil of silencing the expression of an opinion is, that it is robbing the human race; posterity as well as the existing generation—those who dissent from the opinion, still more than those who hold it. If the opinion is right, they are deprived of the opportunity of exchanging error for truth; if wrong, they lose, what is almost as great a benefit, the clearer perception and livelier impression of truth, produced by its collision with error" (*On Liberty*, edited by Gertrude Himmelfarb [New York: Penguin Books, 1985], 76).

126. Ibid.

127. Nurcholish Madjid, "Necessity of Renewing Islamic Thought," 286.

128. For criticism of Nurcholish Madjid see Kull, *Piety and Politics*, 227–240.

129. Harvey Cox, *The Secular City: Secularization and Urbanization in Theological Perspective* (New York: MacMillan, 1966), 1–32; Talcott Parsons et al., eds., *Theories of*

Society: Foundations of Modern Sociological Theory (New York: Free Press of Glencoe, 1961), 249–251, 256–263; Robert Bellah, *Beyond Belief: Essays on Religion in a Post-traditionalist World* (Berkeley: University of California Press, 1991), 146–167.

130. Madjid, "Necessity of Renewing Islamic Thought," 286.

131. It is critical to note that the term "secularism" in Indonesia is understood as synonymous with atheism or irreligiosity, hence Madjid's attempt to distance himself from it. For the dominant view of how secularism was understood among Indonesian Muslims see "The Dangers of Secularism," Mohammad Natsir's speech in 1957 in the Constitutent Assembly, in Herbert Feith and Lance Castles, eds., *Indonesian Political Thinking 1945–1965* (Ithaca, N.Y.: Cornell University Press, 1970), 215–219. For background see Assyaukanie, "Islam and Secularism in Indonesia," unpublished manuscript, 5.

132. Madjid's 1972 speech was entitled "Reinvigorating Religious Understanding in the Indonesian Muslim Community" (reproduced in Kurzman, *Liberal Islam*, 289–294). In this lecture, he criticizes the notion of an "Islamic state," noting that its genesis is due to an inferiority complex that Muslims suffer from in relation to Western civilization. At the end of his lecture he states: "the concept of 'Islamic state' is a distortion of the [properly] proportioned relationship between religion and state. The state is one of the aspects of worldly life whose dimension is rational and collective, while religion is an aspect of another kind of life whose dimension is spiritual and personal." He goes on to say, however, "of course, it is not possible . . . to separate state and religion."

133. M. Syafi'i Anwar, "The Clash of Religio-political Thought: The Contest between Radical-Conservative Islam and Progressive-Liberal Islam in Post-Soheharto Indonesia," in T.N. Srinivasan, ed., *The Future of Secularism* (New Delhi: Oxford University Press, 2007), 213, summarizing Nurcholish Madjid.

134. Ibid., 189–190.

135. Bahtiar Effendy captures this new Muslim approach to politics with the following summary: "The changing nature of the bases of support for contemporary Indonesian Islam has served as one of the primary causes of the emergence of a novel perception in which political Islam no longer has to be conceived in a formalistic/legalistic and scripturalistic way. Many of its actors have come to envision politics more as a mundane, secular affair, rather than as an extension of the sacred religion. It operates not necessarily on the basis of a dry, fixed pattern of religious scriptures, but on moral and ethical standards such as justice, equality, and freedom, which are essential to Islamic precepts" ("What Is Political Islam," 21). Also see Amien Rais, "An Interview with Amien Rais," by Alfred Stepan and Mirjam Künkler, *Journal of International Affairs* 61 (Fall-Winter 2007), 205–216.

136. For background see Greg Barton, "Islamic Liberalism and the Prospects for Democracy in Indonesia," in Michele Schmiegelow, ed., *Democracy in Asia* (New York: St. Martin's Press, 1997), 427–451; Greg Barton, *Abdurrahman Wahid: Muslim Democrat, Indonesian President* (Honolulu: University of Hawai'i Press, 2002), 119–131; Greg Barton, "Indonesia's Nurcholish Madjid and Abdurrahman Wahid as Intellectual Ulama: The Meeting of Islamic Traditionalism and Modernism in Neo-modernist Thought," *Islam and Christian-Muslim Relations* 8 (October 1997), 323–350; Howard Federspiel, *Indonesian*

Muslim Intellectuals of the Twentieth Century (Singapore: Institute for Southeast Asian Studies, 2006), 61–90, and Kamaruzzaman Bustamam-Ahmad, "Tracing the Roots of Indonesian Muslim Intellectuals: A Bibliographical Survey," *Kyoto Review of Southeast Asia* 8 (March 2007), http://kyotoreviewsea.org/ kamaruzaman.htm.

137. Hefner, *Civil Islam,* 118–119.

138. On the views of Muslim educators in Indonesia and Shariah law see Robert Hefner, "Making Democracy Work Islamically," *Inside Indonesia* 90 (October–December 2007), http://insideindonesia.org/content/view/1016/47/.

139. While these comments were specifically referring to the situation in Malaysia, where support for political secularism is weaker, they are believed to be applicable across most Muslim societies. See Farish Noor, "Why Hudud? (Why Not?)" in Greg Fealy and Virginia Hooker, eds., *Voices of Islam in Southeast Asia: A Contemporary Sourcebook* (Singapore: Institute for Southeast Asian Studies, 2006), 175.

140. Azyumardi Azra, *Indonesia, Islam and Democracy: Dynamics in a Global Context* (Jakarta: Solstice, 2006), 24. Greg Fealy makes the important observation that Indonesians understand the concept of Shariah differently from Americans. For Indonesians, it is synonymous with the way Americans view the Ten Commandments: as a basic statement of morality. In other words, it is a "symbol of one's Islamic-ness," not an endorsement of human suffering. Moreover, he notes there is no consensus in Indonesia on what constitutes Shariah. Polls also indicate that support for Shariah drops when specific corporeal punishments are mentioned (Greg Fealy, "In Fear of Radical Islam: A Critical Examination of the Evidence," unpublished paper [November 2005]). There is undoubtedly more to this phenomenon but space does not allow for a comprehensive explanation. Another critical factor is historical memory. In contrast with the West, religion has not been a divisive force in Muslim societies (until recently). Thus Muslims look back historically on the role of religion in the polis with more sympathy than people in the West. For background, see Noah Feldman, *The Fall and Rise of the Islamic* State, 19–55.

141. Saful Mujani and R. William Liddle compare the electoral results of Indonesia's first free election in 1955 with those of the second one in 1999. They observe that one "important indicator of the political moderation of Indonesian Muslims today is the decline in popular support for pro-*shari'a* parties since 1955. In the 1999 election, seven parties won significant percentages of the vote. Only three of the seven are based on Islam: Hamzah Haz's PPP, with 11 percent; the Crescent Moon and Star Party (PBB), with 2 percent; and the Justice Party (PK), with just 1 percent. The remaining four, which together took a resounding 76 percent of the vote, are all committed to the secular state. They include Megawati's PDI-P, with 34 percent; the Joint Secretariat of Functional Groups (Golkar), with 22 percent; the National Awakening Party (PKB), with 13 percent; and the National Mandate Party (PAN), with 7 percent. Golkar was the military-backed state party that regularly won well over half the vote in the tightly controlled elections of the Suharto period, but it now competes on equal terms with the other parties. PKB, headed by former president Abdurrahman Wahid, is the party of NU but opposes implementation of the *shari'a.* PAN was founded by Amien Rais, national chair of Muhammadiyah for much of

the 1990s, and seems to have received much of its 1999 vote from Muhammadiyah members. Its national board includes several non-Muslims, and it also opposes implementation of the *shari'a*" ("Politics, Islam and Public Opinion," *Journal of Democracy* 15 [January 2004], 112).

142. Azyumardi Azra, personal interview, Jakarta, 15 March 2007.

143. Amartya Sen, *The Argumentative Indian: Writings on Indian Culture, History and Identity* (New York: Penguin Books, 2006), 295–296. For more on the debate on Indian secularism see Rajeev Bhargava, ed., *Secularism and its Critics* (New Delhi: Oxford University Press, 1998), 1–28.

144. Abdurrahman Wahid, "Indonesia's Mild Secularism," *SAIS Review* 21 (Summer-Fall 2001), 25–28.

145. Samuel Huntington, *The Third Wave: Democratization in the Late Twentieth Century* (Norman: Oklahoma University Press, 1991), 76.

146. José Casanova, "Civil Society and Religion: Retrospective Reflections on Catholicism and Prospective Reflections on Islam," *Social Research* 68 (Winter 2001), 1043.

147. Ibid., 1042.

148. Ibid., 1046.

149. Quoted in Daniel Philpott, "The Catholic Wave," *Journal of Democracy* 15 (April 2004), 34. For background see John McGreevy, *Catholicism and American Freedom: A History* (New York: Norton, 2003), 250–281.

150. J. Leon Hooper, ed., *Bridging the Sacred and the Secular: Selected Writings of John Courtney Murray* (Washington, D.C.: Georgetown University Press, 1994), 187–199 and Jacques Maritain, *Christianity and Democracy: The Rights of Man and Natural Law*, translated by Doris Anson (San Francisco: Ignatius Press, 1986), 11–84.

151. Casanova, "Civil Society and Religion," 1046–1047.

152. Ibid.

153. Philpott, "The Catholic Wave," 32.

154. Casanova, "Civil Society and Religion," 1047. José Casanova, *Public Religions in the Modern World* (Chicago: University of Chicago Press, 1994), 40–66, 211–235.

155. Casanova, "Civil Society and Religion," 1049.

156. Ibid., 1054, 1074.

157. Ibid., 1054.

158. Ibid., 1075; emphasis added.

159. Two leading authorities on Muslim politics, in their recent writings, seem to challenge this argument. In an important essay on Muslim democracy, Vali Nasr writes that the "depth of commitment to liberal and secular values that democratic consolidation requires is a condition for Muslim Democracy's final success, not for its first emergence. As with the case with Christian Democracy in Europe, it is the imperative of competition inherent in democracy that will transform the unsecular tendencies of Muslim Democracy into long-term commitment to democratic values. . . . The shifts that Muslim Democracy will spark in Muslims' attitudes toward society and politics will come not from theoretical suppositions but from political imperatives. The rise of Muslim Democracy suggests *that political change will precede religious change*. . . . It has not been intellectuals who have given

shape to Muslim Democracy, but rather politicians such as Turkey's Recep Tayyip Erdoğan, Pakistan's Nawaz Sharif, and Malaysia's Anwar Ibrahim and Mahatir bin Mohamad. They are the ones grappling with key questions surrounding the interaction of Muslim values with democratic institutions, the nature of Muslims' voting behavior, the shape and location of an 'Islamic' voter base, and the like." In the end, Nasr concludes that the "answers will not come from the realm of theory and ideology, but from that of pragmatism and politics" (Vali Nasr, "The Rise of Muslim Democracy," *Journal of Democracy* 16 [April 2005], 15–16, 25; emphasis added.). While I am in broad agreement with these observations, I am not as categorical as Nasr when he claims progress toward liberal democracy in Muslim societies "will come not from theoretical suppositions but from political imperatives." In the case of Turkey, for example, while he is right to highlight the seminal contributions to liberal democracy from politicians such as Abdullah Gül and Recep Tayyip Erdoğan, I would argue that influential ideas of public intellectuals, religious leaders, and organizations such as Fethullah Gülen and Ali Bulac have been very important as well. Similarly, in the case of Iran one could argue that work of nonpoliticians such as Abdolkarim Soroush, Mohsen Kadivar, and Akbar Ganji has been, arguably, more influential and significant than the contributions of reformist politicians such as Mohammad Khatami and Mostafa Moin in advancing democratization. This applies to the case of Indonesia as well, as I discuss in this chapter. Finally, my analysis is more concerned with questions of democratic consolidation than democratic transition (which is the focus of Nasr's analysis), and in particular with the question of political secularism, a topic Nasr does not deal with in his essay on Muslim democracy cited earlier. Nonetheless, there is a tension here between my argument and that of Vali Nasr, especially given that we are both drawing on the lessons from Catholicism and democracy that shed light on the politics of the Muslim world. Olivier Roy, in a more recent contribution, while focusing on the debate within France and its Muslim community, makes similar arguments about sequencing and the primacy of political change over theological change. See his *Secularism Confronts Islam*, translated by George Holoch (New York: Columbia University Press, 2007), 39, 91, 98–99. I hope to write more about this specific topic in the near future in an attempt to reconcile my argument with that of Vali Nasr and Olivier Roy.

160. William Shepard writes: "[a] very major reinterpretation of Islam will be necessary before it can be congenial to secularism. A step in this direction is a reinterpretation of Islamic history that puts the relatively secular Umayyads [661–750] in a much better light than pious Muslims have usually seen them, that emphasizes the secular elements of the Abbasid [750–1258] period of glory, and deemphasizes the cultural (as distinct from more strictly 'religious') significance of the early Medinan state and the Rightly Guided Caliphate; but I doubt if this is sufficient." He also recommends the development of a "secularist interpretation of the basic Islamic symbol system as found in the Qur'an and the Sunna, both of which have a lot to say about public life." See his insightful essay "Islam and Ideology: Towards a Typology," *International Journal of Middle East Studies* 19 (August 1987), 324. Muhammad Khalid Masud suggests that the distinction in the Islamic scholarly tradition between *ibadaat* (the worship of God), and *mu'amalaat* (social interaction between people) could be developed further in the construction of a Muslim secularism ("Construction and Deconstruction of

Secularism," 375–376). Finally, reviving the type of "Muslim secularism" exemplified by the political theology of Ali Abd al-Raziq (1888–1966) in his controversial 1925 book *al-Islam wa usul al-hukm* (Islam and the Principles of Governance) is needed. For background see Albert Hourani, *Arabic Thought in the Liberal Age, 1798–1939* (Cambridge: Cambridge University Press, 1983), 183–192. A French translation of this important book is available: Ali Abderraziq, *L'Islam et les fondements du pouvoir,* translated by Abdou Filali-Ansary (Paris: La Découverte, 1994).

CONCLUSION

1. Akeel Bilgrami, "Secularism, Nationalism and Modernity," in Rajeev Bhargava, ed., *Secularism and Its Critics* (New Delhi: Oxford University Press, 1998), 393.

Bibliography

BOOKS AND CHAPTERS IN EDITED BOOKS

Abdo, Geneive, and Jonathan Lyons. *Answering Only to God: Faith and Freedom in Twenty-first-century Iran*. New York: Holt, 2003.

Abou El Fadl, Khaled. "9/11 and the Muslim Transformation." In Mary Dudziak, ed.,*September 11 in History: A Watershed Moment?* Durham, N.C.: Duke University Press, 2003, 70–111.

Abou El Fadl, Khaled. *Islam and the Challenge of Democracy*. Edited by Joshua Cohen and Deborah Chasman. Princeton, N.J.: Princeton University Press, 2004.

Abrahamian, Ervand. *A History of Modern Iran*. Cambridge: Cambridge University Press, 2008.

Abrahamian, Ervand. *Khomeinism: Essays on the Islamic Republic*. Berkeley: University of California Press, 1993.

Ackerman, Bruce. *Social Justice in the Liberal State*. New Haven, Conn.: Yale University Press, 1980.

Afary, Janet. *The Iranian Constitutional Revolution, 1906–1911*. New York: Columbia University Press, 1996.

Akhavi, Shahrough. *Religion and Politics in Contemporary Iran*. Albany: State University of New York Press, 1980.

Akhavi, Shahrough. "Iran: Implementation of an Islamic State." In John Esposito, ed., *Islam in Asia: Religion, Politics and Society*. New York: Oxford University Press, 1987, 27–52.

Al Azm, Sadiq. "Is Islam Secularizable?" In Elisabeth Ozdalga and Sune Persson, eds.,*Civil Society, Democracy and The Muslim World*. Istanbul: Swedish Research Institute, 1997, 17–22.

Al-Attas, Syed Naquib. *Islam, Secularism and the Philosophy of the Future.* London: Mansell, 1985.

Algar, Hamid. "The Oppositional Role of the Ulama in Twentieth-Century Iran." In Nikki Keddie, ed., *Scholars, Saints, and Sufis: Muslim Religious Institutions since 1500.* Berkeley: University of California Press, 1972, 231–255.

Almond, Gabriel, and James Coleman, eds. *The Politics of Developing Areas.* Princeton, N.J.: Princeton University Press, 1960.

Almond, Gabriel, and G. Bingham Powell. *Comparative Politics: A Development Approach.* Boston: Little Brown, 1966.

Anderson, Lisa. "Fulfilling Prophecies: State Policy and Islamist Radicalism." In John Esposito, ed., *Political Islam: Revolution, Radicalism or Reform?* Boulder, Colo.: Lynne Rienner, 1997, 17–31.

Anderson, Perry. *Lineages of the Absolute State.* London: Verso, 1979.

Andrews, George Reid, and Herrick Chapman, eds. *The Social Construction of Democracy: 1870–1990.* New York: New York University Press, 1995.

Ansari, Ali. *Modern Iran since 1921: The Pahlavis and After.* London: Pearson Education, 2003.

Anwar, M. Syafi'i Anwar. "The Clash of Religio-political Thought: The Contest between Radical Conservative Islam and Progressive-Liberal Islam in Post-Soheharto Indonesia." In T.N. Srinivasan, ed., *The Future of Secularism.* New Delhi: Oxford University Press, 2007, 186–254.

Apter, David. *The Politics of Modernization.* Chicago: University of Chicago Press, 1965.

Arab Development Report 2002: Creating Opportunities for Future Generations. New York: United Nations Development Program, 2002.

Arab Development Report 2004: Towards Freedom in the Arab World. New York: United Nations Development Program, 2005.

Arblaster, Anthony. *Democracy.* 2nd ed. Minneapolis: University of Minnesota Press, 1994.

Arjomand, Said Amir. *The Shadow of God and the Hidden Imam: Religion, Political Order, and Societal Change in Shi'ite Iran from the Beginning to 1890.* Chicago: University of Chicago Press, 1984.

Arjomand, Said Amir. *The Turban for the Crown: The Islamic Revolution in Iran.* New York: Oxford University Press, 1988.

Arjomand, Said Amir. "Ideological Revolution in Shi'ism." In Said Amir Arjomand, ed., *Authority and Political Culture in Shi'ism.* Albany: State University of New York Press, 1988, 179–209.

Arjomand, Said Amir, ed. *Authority and Political Culture in Shi'ism.* Albany: State University of New York Press, 1988.

Armstrong, Karen. *The Battle for God.* New York: Knopf, 2001.

Armstrong, Karen. *Islam: A Short History.* New York: Random House, 2002.

Asad, Talal. *Formations of the Secular: Christianity, Islam, Modernity.* Palo Alto, Calif.: Stanford University Press, 2003.

Ashcraft, Richard. *Locke's Two Treatises of Government.* London: Allen and Unwin, 1987.

Aston, Nigel. *Religion and Revolution in France 1780–1804.* Washington, D.C.: Catholic University of America, 2000.

Audi, Robert, and Nicholas Wolterstorff. *Religion in the Public Sphere: The Place of Religious Convictions in Public Debate*. Lanham, Md.: Rowman and Littlefield, 1997.

Ayoob, Mohammed. *The Many Faces of Political Islam*. Ann Arbor: University of Michigan Press, 2008.

Ayubi, Nazih. *Political Islam: Religion and Politics in the Arab World*. New York: Routledge, 1991.

Ayubi, Nazih. "Islam and Democracy." In David Potter, David Goldblatt, Margaret Kiloh, and Paul Lewis, eds. *Democratization*. Cambridge: Polity Press, 1997, 345–366.

Azimi, Fakhreddin. *The Quest for Democracy in Iran: A Century of Struggle against Authoritarian Rule*. Cambridge, Mass.: Harvard University Press, 2008.

Azyumardi Azra. *Indonesia, Islam and Democracy: Dynamics in a Global Context* Jakarta: Solstice, 2006.

Ballaigue, Christopher de. *The Struggle for Iran*. New York: New York Review of Books, 2007.

Bamualim, Chaider. "Transforming the Ideal Transcendental into the Historical Humanistic: Nurcholish Madjid's Islamic Thinking in Indonesia (1970–1995)." Master' thesis, University of Leiden, 1998.

Barber, Benjamin. *Strong Democracy: Participatory Politics for a New Age*. Berkeley: University of California Press, 1984.

Barber, Benjamin. *Jihad vs. McWorld: How Globalism and Tribalism are Reshaping the World*. New York: Ballantine Books, 1996.

Barton, Greg. "Islamic Liberalism and the Prospects for Democracy in Indonesia." In Michele Schmiegelow, ed., *Democracy in Asia*. New York: St. Martin' Press, 1997, 427–451.

Barton, Greg. *Abdurrahman Wahid: Muslim Democrat, Indonesian President*. Honolulu: University of Hawai'i Press, 2002.

Barton, Greg. "Turkey' Gülen hizmet and Indonesia' Neo-modernist NGOs: Remarkable Examples of Progressive Islamic Thought and Civil Society Activism in the Muslim world." In Fethi Mansouri and Shahram Akbarzadeh, eds., *Political Islam and Human Security*. Newcastle, UK: Cambridge Scholars Press, 2006, 140–160.

Bayart, Jean-Francois. "Finishing with the Idea of the Third World: The Concept of the Political Trajectory." In James Manor, ed., *Rethinking Third World Politics*. London: Longman, 1991, 51–71.

Bayart, Jean-Francois. "Republican Trajectories in Iran and Turkey: a Tocquevillian Reading." In Ghassan Salamé, ed., *Democracy without Democrats: The Renewal of Politics in the Muslim World*. London: Tauris, 1994, 282–299.

Bayat, Asef. *Making Islam Democratic: Social Movements and the Post-Islamist Turn*. Palo Alto, Calif.: Stanford University Press, 2007.

Beinin, Joel, and Joe Stork, eds. *Political Islam: Essays from Middle East Report*. Berkeley: University of California Press, 1997.

Bell, Daniel. *The End of Ideology: On the Exhaustion of Political Ideas in the Fifties*. Cambridge, Mass.: Harvard University Press, 1988.

Bellah, Robert. *Beyond Belief: Essays on Religion in a Post-Traditionalist World*. Berkeley: University of California Press, 1991.

Ben Dor, Gabriel. *State and Conflict in the Middle East*. New York: Praeger, 1983.

Benhabib, Seyla. *Situating the Self: Gender, Community and Postmodernism in Contemporary Ethics*. New York: Routledge, 1992.

Benhabib, Seyla. *The Claims of Culture: Equality and Diversity in the Global Era*. Princeton, N.J.: Princeton University Press, 2002.

Berger, Peter. *The Sacred Canopy: Elements of a Sociological Theory of Religion*. New York: Anchor Books, 1967.

Berger, Peter. "Desecularization of the World: A Global Overview." In Peter Berger, ed., *The Desecularization of the World: Resurgent Religion and World Politics*. Washington, D.C.: Ethics and Public Policy Center, 1999.

Berkes, Niyazi. *The Development of Secularism in Turkey*. Montreal: McGill University Press, 1964.

Bhargava, Rajeev, ed. *Secularism and Its Critics*. New Delhi: Oxford University Press, 1998.

Bilgrami, Akeel. "Secularism, Nationalism and Modernity." In Rajeev Bhargava, ed., *Secularism and Its Critics*. New Delhi: Oxford University Press, 1998, 380–417.

Bill, James. *The Politics of Iran: Groups, Classes and Modernization*. Columbus, Ohio: Merrill, 1972.

Black, Cyril, ed. *Comparative Modernization: A Reader*. New York: Free Press, 1976.

Blaug, Ricardo, and John Schwarzmantel, eds. *Democracy: A Reader*. New York: Columbia University Press, 2001.

Bloch, Marc. "Towards a Comparative History of European Societies." In Frederic C. Lane and Jelle C. Riemersma, eds., *Enterprise and Secular Change: Reading in Economic History*. Homewood, Ill.: R. D. Irwin, 1953, 494–521.

Bowen, John. *Why the French Don't Like Headscarves: Islam, the State and the Public Space*. Princeton, N.J.: Princeton University Press, 2007.

Brown, L. Carl. *Religion and State: The Muslim Approach to Politics* New York: Columbia University Press, 2000.

Bruce, Steve, ed. *Religion and Modernization: Sociologists and Historians Debate the Secularization Thesis*. New York: Oxford University Press, 1992.

Bruce, Steve. *God is Dead: Secularization in the West*. Oxford: Blackwell, 2002.

Brumberg, Daniel. *Reinventing Khomeini: The Struggle for Reform in Iran*. Chicago: University of Chicago Press, 2001.

Brynen, Rex, Baghat Korany, and Paul Noble, eds. *Political Liberalization and Democratization in the Arab World*. 2 vols. Boulder, Colo.: Lynne Rienner, 1995–98.

Bulliet, Richard. *The Case for Islamo-Christian Civilization*. New York: Columbia University Press, 2004.

Burgat, Francois. *Face to Face with Political Islam*. New York: Tauris, 2003.

Burgat, Francois, and William Dowell. *The Islamist Movement in North Africa*. Austin: Center for Middle East Studies, University of Texas, 1993.

Butterworth, Charles. "State and Authority in Arabic Political Thought." In Ghassan Salamé, ed., *The Foundations of the Arab State*. London: Croom Helm, 1987, 91–111.

Carter, Stephen. *The Culture of Disbelief: How American Law and Politics Trivialize Religious Devotion.* New York: Anchor Books, 1994.

Casanova, José. *Public Religions in the Modern World.* Chicago: University of Chicago Press, 1994.

Casanova, José. "Secularization Revisited: A Reply to Talal Asad." In David Scott and Charles Hirschkind, eds., *Powers of the Secular Modern: Talal Asad and His Interlocutors.* Stanford, Calif.: Stanford University Press, 2006, 12–30.

Chadwick, Owen. *The Reformation.* New York: Penguin Books, 1972.

Chadwick, Owen. *The Secularization of the European Mind in the Nineteenth Century.* Cambridge: Cambridge University Press, 1975.

Chehabi, Houchang. *Iranian Politics and Religious Modernism: The Liberation Movement of Iran under the Shah and Khomeini.* Ithaca, N.Y.: Cornell University Press, 1990.

Cohen, Joshua. "Deliberative Democracy and Democratic Legitimacy." In James Bohman and William Rehg, eds., *Deliberative Democracy: Essays on Reason and Politics.* Cambridge, Mass.: MIT Press, 1997, 67–92.

Colaiaco, James. *Socrates against Athens: Philosophy on Trial.* New York: Routledge, 2001.

Cole, Juan. *Napolean' Egypt: Invading the Middle East.* New York: Palgrave, 2007.

Collinson, Patrick. *The Reformation: A History.* New York: Random House, 2004.

Constant, Benjamin. *Constant: Political Writings.* Edited by Biancamaria Fontana. Cambridge: Cambridge University Press, 1988.

Cox, Harvey. *The Secular City: Secularization and the Urbanization in Theological Perspective.* New York: MacMillan, 1966.

Cranston, Maurice. "John Locke and Government by Consent." In David Thomson, ed., *Political Ideas.* New York: Penguin Books, 1966, 67–80.

Cressy, David. "Education and Literacy in London and East Anglia, 1580–1700." Ph.D. diss., Cambridge University, 1973.

Crick, Bernard. *Democracy: A Very Short Introduction.* New York: Oxford UniversityPress, 2002.

Cunningham, Frank. *Theories of Democracy: A Critical Introduction.* New York: Routledge, 2002.

Curley, Edwin. "Hobbes and the Cause of Religious Toleration." In Patricia Springborg, ed., *The Cambridge Campanion to Hobbes' Leviathan.* Cambridge: Cambridge University Press, 2007, 309–334.

Dagi, Ihsan. "The Justice and Development Party: Identity, Politics and Human Rights Discourse in the Search for Security and Legitimacy." In M. Hakan Yavuz, ed., *The Emergence of a New Turkey: Democracy and the AK Party.* Salt Lake City: University of Utah Press, 2006, 88–106.

Dahl, Robert. *Polyarchy: Participation and Opposition.* New Haven, Conn.: Yale University Press, 1971.

Dahl, Robert. *Democracy and Its Critics.* New Haven, Conn.: Yale University Press, 1989.

Dahl, Robert. *On Democracy*. New Haven, Conn.: Yale University Press, 1998.

Dahl, Robert. "Political Culture and Economic Development." In Fredrik Engelstad and Ragnvald Kalleberg, eds., *Social Time and Social Change: Perspectives on Sociology and History*. Oslo: Scandinavian University Press, 1999, 87–108.

Dahl, Robert, Ian Shapiro, and Jose Antonio Cheibub, eds. *The Democracy Sourcebook*. Cambridge, Mass.: MIT Press, 2003.

Dallmayr, Fred, ed. *Border Crossings: Toward a Comparative Political Theory*. Lanham, Md.: LexingtonBooks, 1999.

Dallmayr, Fred. *Dialogue among Civilization: Some Exemplary Voices*. New York: Palgrave, 2003.

Dallmayr, Fred. "An Islamic Reformation? Some Afterthoughts." In Charles Kurzman and Michaelle Browers, eds., *An Islamic Reformation?* Lanham, Md.: Lexington Books, 2004, 178–184.

Dann, G. Elijah. *After Rorty: The Possibilities for Ethics and Religious Belief*. New York: Continuum International, 2006.

Dekmejian, R. Hrair. "Islamic Revival: Catalysts, Categories and Consequences." In Shireen Hunter, *The Politics of Islamic Revivalism*. Indianapolis: Indiana University Press, 1988, 3–19.

Diamond, Larry. "Three Paradoxes of Democracy." In Larry Diamond and Marc Plattner, eds., *The Global Resurgence of Democracy*, 2nd ed. Baltimore: Johns Hopkins University Press, 1996, 111–123.

Diamond, Larry, and Marc F. Plattner, eds. *The Global Resurgence of Democracy*. 2nd ed. Baltimore: Johns Hopkins University Press, 1996.

Diamond, Larry, and Marc F. Plattner, eds. *The Global Divergence of Democracies*. Baltimore: Johns Hopkins University Press, 2001.

Diamond, Larry, Marc F. Plattner, and Daniel Brumberg, eds. *Islam and Democracy in the Middle East*. Baltimore: Johns Hopkins University Press, 2003.

Doyle, William. *The French Revolution: A Very Short Introduction*. New York: Oxford University Press, 2001.

Dunn, John. *The Political Thought of John Locke: An Historical Account of the Argument of the "Two Treatises of Government."* Cambridge: Cambridge University Press, 1969.

Dunn, John. *Locke*. Oxford: Oxford University Press, 1984.

Dunn, John, ed. *Democracy: The Unfinished Journey 508 BC to AD 1993*. New York: Oxford University Press, 1992.

Dunn, John. *Locke: A Very Short Introduction*. New York: Oxford University Press, 2003.

Drury, Shadia. *Terror and Civilization: Christianity, Politics and the Western Psyche*. New York: Palgrave, 2003.

Ebadi, Shirin. *Iran Awakening: One Woman' Journey to Reclaim Her Life and Country*. New York: Random House, 2007.

Effendy, Bahtiar. *Islam and State in Indonesia*. Singapore: Institute for Southeast Asian Studies, 2003.

Effendy, Bahtiar. "What Is Political Islam? An Examination of Its Theoretical Mapping in Modern Indonesia." In Chaider Bamualim, ed., *A Portrait of Contemporary*

*Indonesia.*Jakarta: Pusat Bahasa dan Budaya and Konrad Adenauer Stiflung, 2005, 1–38.

Eickelman, Dale. "From Here to Modernity: Ernest Gellner on Nationalism and Islamic Fundamentalism." In John A. Hall, ed., *The State of the Nation: Ernest Gellner and the Theory of Nationalism.* Cambridge: Cambridge University Press, 1998, 258–271.

El-Affendi, Abdelwahab. *Who Needs an Islamic State?* London: Grey Seal, 1991.

El-Affendi, Abdelwahab. "Democracy and the Islamist Paradox." In Roland Axtmann, ed., *Understanding Democratic Politics.* London: Sage, 2003, 311–320.

El-Affendi, Abdelwahab. "On the State, Democracy and Pluralism." In Basheer Nafi and Suha Taji-Farouki, eds., *Islamic Thought in the Twentieth Century.* New York: Tauris, 2004, 180–203.

Elmessiri, Abdelwahab. "Secularism, Immanence and Deconstruction." In Azzam Tamimi and John L. Esposito, eds., *Islam and Secularism in the Middle East.* New York: New York University Press, 2000, 52–80.

Elshtain, Jean. *Democracy on Trial.* Concord, Ontario: Anansi, 1993.

Elshtain, Jean. *Just War against Terror: The Burden of American Power in a Violent World.* New York: Basic Books, 2003.

Enayat, Hamid. *Modern Islamic Political Thought.* Austin: University of Texas Press, 1982.

Enayat, Hamid. "Iran: Khumayni's Concept of the 'Guardianship of the Jurisconsult.'" In James Piscatori, ed., *Islam in the Political Process.* Cambridge: Cambridge University Press, 1983, 160–180.

Eskhevari, Hassan Yousefi. *Islam and Democracy in Iran: Eshkevari and the Quest for Reform.* Edited and translated by Ziba Mir Hosseini and Richard Tapper. New York: Tauris, 2006.

Esposito, John, ed. *Islam and Development: Religion and Socio-political Change.* Syracuse, N.Y.: Syracuse University Press, 1980.

Esposito, John. *The Islamic Threat: Myth or Reality?* New York: Oxford University Press, 1992.

Esposito, John, and Francois Burgat, eds. *Modernizing Islam: Religion in the Public Sphere in Europe and the Middle East.* New Brunswick, N.J.: Rutgers University Press, 2003.

Esposito John, and Azzam Tamimi, eds. *Islam and Secularism in the Middle East.* New York: New York University Press, 2000.

Esposito, John, and John Voll. *Islam and Democracy.* New York: Oxford University Press, 1996.

Esposito, John, and Dalia Mogahed. *Who Speaks for Islam?: What a Billion Muslims Really Think.* New York: Gallup Press, 2007.

Euben, Roxanne. *Enemy in the Mirror: Islamic Fundamentalism and the Limits of Modern Rationalism.* Princeton, N.J.: Princeton University Press, 1999.

Falk, Richard. "Can Political Democracy Survive the Religious Resurgence?" In Jean Allain, ed., *Unlocking the Middle East: The Writings of Richard Falk.* Northhampton, Mass.: Olive Branch Press, 2003, 34–46.

Feith, Herbert. *The Decline of Constitutional Democracy in Indonesia.* Ithaca, N.Y.: Cornell University Press, 1962.

Federspiel, Howard. *Indonesian Muslim Intellectuals of the Twentieth Century.* Singapore: Institute for Southeast Asian Studies, 2006.

Feldman, Noah. *After Jihad: America and the Struggle for Islamic Democracy.* New York: Farrar, Straus and Giroux, 2003.

Feldman, Noah. *Divided by God: America's Church-State Problem and What We Should Do about It.* New York. Farrar, Straus and Giroux, 2006.

Feldman, Noah. *The Fall and Rise of the Islamic State.* Princeton, N.J.: Princeton University Press, 2008.

Filali-Ansary, Abdou. "Muslims and Democracy." In Larry Diamond, Marc Plattner, and Daniel Brumberg, eds., *Islam and Democracy in the Middle East.* Baltimore: Johns Hopkins University Press, 2003, 193–207.

Filali-Ansary, Abdou. "The Challenge of Secularization." In Larry Diamond, Marc Plattner, and Daniel Brumberg, eds., *Islam and Democracy in the Middle East.* Baltimore: Johns Hopkins University Press, 2003, 232–236.

Filmer, Robert. *Patriarcha or The Natural Power of Kings.* Edited by Johann Sommerville. Cambridge: Cambridge University Press, 1991.

Finkelstein, Norman. *Image and Reality of the Israel-Palestine Conflict.* New York: Verso, 1995.

Fox, Jonathan. *Ethnoreligious Conflict in the Late Twentieth Century.* Lanham, Md.: Lexington Books, 2002.

Fox, Russel Arben. "Confucianism and Communitarianism in a Liberal-democratic World." In Fred Dallmayr, ed., *Border Crossings: Toward a Comparative Political Theory.* Lanham, Md.: Lexington Books, 1999, 185–211.

Freedom in the World 2001–2002: The Democracy Gap. New York: Freedom House, 2001.

Fukuyama, Francis. *The End of History and the Last Man.* New York: Free Press, 1992.

Ganji, Akbar. *The Road to Democracy in Iran.* Cambridge, MA: MIT Press, 2008.

Gaustad, Edwin. *Roger Williams.* New York: Oxford University Press, 2005.

Geertz, Clifford. *The Interpretation of Cultures: Selected Essays by Clifford Geertz.* New York: Basic Books, 1973.

Gellner, Ernest. *Muslim Society.* Cambridge: Cambridge University Press, 1983.

Gellner, Ernest. *Postmodernism, Reason and Religion.* London: Routledge, 1992.

Gellner, Ernest. *Conditions of Liberty: Civil Society and Its Rivals.* New York: Penguin Books, 1994.

Gendzier, Irene. *Development against Democracy: Manipulating Political Change in the Third World.* Hampton, Conn.: Tyrone Press, 1995.

Ghani, Cyrus. *Iran and the Rise of Reza Shah: From Qajar Collapse to Pahlavi Power.* New York: Tauris, 2000.

Goldberg, Ellis. "Smashing Idols and the State: The Protestant Ethic and Egyptian Sunni Radicalism." In Juan Cole, ed., *Comparing Muslim Societies: Knowledge and the State in a World Civilization.* Ann Arbor: University of Michigan Press, 1992, 195–236.

Goldie, Mark, ed. *Locke: Political Essays.* Cambridge: Cambridge University Press, 1997.

Goldziher, Ignácz. "Dahriyya." In *Encyclopaedia of Islam.* New ed. Vol. 2. Leiden: Brill, 1960, 95–97.

Gottschalk, Peter and Gabriel Greenberg. *Islamophobia: Making Muslims the Enemy.* Lanham, Md.: Rowman and Littlefield, 2008.

Göle, Nilüfer. "Authoritarian Secularism and Islamist Politics: The Case of Turkey." In Augustus Richard Norton, ed., *Civil Society in the Middle East.* Leiden: Brill, 1996, 1:17–43.

Gülen, Fethullah. *Pearls of Wisdom.* Translated by Ali Unal. Somerset, N.J.: Light, 2005.

Halliday, Fred. *Iran: Dictatorship and Development.* New York: Penguin Books, 1979.

Halperin, Charles. *Russia and the Golden Horde: The Mongol Impact on Russian History.* Bloomington: Indiana University Press, 1985.

Hambly, Gavin. "The Pahlavi Autocracy: Riza Shah, 1921–1941." In Peter Avery, Gavin Hambly, and Charles Melville, eds., *The Cambridge History of Iran: From Nadir Shah to the Islamic Republic,* vol. 7. Cambridge: Cambridge University Press, 1991, 244–293.

Handleman, Howard. *The Challenge of Third World Development.* 3rd ed. Upper Saddle River, N.J.: Prentice Hall, 2003.

Hashemi, Nader. "Islamic Fundamentalism and the Trauma of Modernization: Reflections on Religion and Radical Politics." In Charles Kurzman and Michelle Browers, eds., *An Islamic Reformation?* Lanham, Md.: Lexington Books, 2004, 159–177.

Haynes, Jeff. *Democracy in the Developing World: Africa, Asia, Latin America and the Middle East.* Oxford: Blackwell, 2001.

Hefner, Robert. "On the History and Cross-cultural Possibility of a Democratic Ideal." In Robert Hefner, ed., *Democratic Civility: The History and Cross-cultural Possibility of a Modern Political Ideal.* New Brunswick, N.J.: Transaction, 1998, 3–49.

Hefner, Robert. *Civil Islam: Muslims and Democratization in Indonesia.* Princeton, N.J.: Princeton University Press, 2000.

Held, David, ed. *Prospects for Democracy: North, South, East, West.* Palo Alto, Calif.: Stanford University Press, 1993.

Held, David. *Models of Democracy.* 2nd ed. Palo Alto, Calif.: Stanford University Press, 1996.

Hentsch, Thierry. *Imagining the Middle East.* Montreal: Black Rose Books, 1992.

Hill, W. Speed, ed. *The Folger Library Edition of The Works of Richard Hooker.* Vol. 2. Cambridge, Mass.: Harvard University Press, 1977.

Hill, Christopher. *Puritanism and Revolution: Studies in Interpretation of the English Revolution of the Seventeenth Century.* London: Secker and Warburg, 1958.

Hobbes, Thomas. *Behemoth or the Long Parliament.* Chicago: University of Chicago Press, 1990.

Hobbes, Thomas. *Leviathan.* Edited by Edwin Curley. Indianapolis: Hackett, 1994.

Hobbes, Thomas. *Leviathan.* Edited by Richard Tuck. Cambridge: Cambridge University Press, 1996.

Hodgson, Marshall. "Modernity and the Islamic Heritage." In Marshall Hodgson, *Rethinking World History: Essays on Europe, Islam, and World History.* Cambridge: Cambridge University Press, 1993, 207–243.

Hodgson, Marshall. *The Venture of Islam: The Gunpower Empires and Modern Times.* Vol. 3. Chicago: University of Chicago Press, 1974.

Holyoake, George Jacob. *The Principles of Secularism.* 3rd rev. ed. London: Austin, 1870.

Hooper, J. Leon, ed. *Bridging the Sacred and the Secular: Selected Writings of John Courtney Murray.* Washington, D.C.: Georgetown University Press, 1994.

Hosen, Nadirsyah. *Shari'a and Constitutional Reform in Indonesia.* Singapore: Institute of Southeast Asian Studies, 2007.

Hourani, Albert. *Arabic Thought in a Liberal Age 1798–1939.* Cambridge: Cambridge University Press, 1983.

Hume, David. "Of Superstition and Enthusiasm." In David Hume, *Essays and Treatises on Several Subjects: Essays, Moral, Political and Literary.* Bristol, England: Thoemmes Press, 2002, 1: 75–81.

Huntington, Samuel. *Political Order in Changing Societies.* New Haven, Conn.: Yale University Press, 1968.

Huntington, Samuel. *The Third Wave: Democratization in the Late Twentieth Century.* Norman, Okla.: Oklahoma University Press, 1991.

Huntington, Samuel. *The Clash of Civilizations and the Remarking of World Order.* New York: Simon and Schuster, 1996.

Ibrahim, Saad Eddin. "From Taliban to Erbakan: The Case of Islam, Civil Society and Democracy." In Elisabeth Ozdalga and Sune Persson, eds. *Civil Islam, Democracy and the Muslim World: Papers Read at a Conference Held at the Swedish Research Institute in Istanbul, 28–30 October 1996.* Istanbul: Swedish Research Institute in Istanbul, 1997, 33–44.

Ibrahim, Saad Eddin. *Egypt, Islam and Democracy: Critical Essays.* Cairo: American University of Cairo Press, 2002.

Inglehart, Ronald, and Pippa Norris. *Sacred and Secular: Religion and Politics Worldwide.* Cambridge: Cambridge University Press, 2004.

Iqbal, Farrukh. *Sustaining Gains in Poverty Reduction and Human Development in the Middle East and North Africa.* Washington, D.C.: World Bank, 2006.

Issawi, Charles. "Why Japan?" In Ibrahim Ibrahim, ed., *Arab Resources: The Transformation of a Society.* London: Croom Helm, 1983, 283–300.

Jordan, W. K. *The Development of Religious Toleration in England: From the Beginning of the English Reformation to the Death of Queen Elizabeth.* London: Allen and Unwin, 1932.

Kahin, George McTurnan. *Nationalism and Revolution in Indonesia.* Ithaca, N.Y.: Cornell University Press, 1952.

Kalaycioglu, Ersin. "State and Civil Society in Turkey: Democracy, Development and Protest." In Amyn Sajoo, ed., *Civil Society in the Muslim World: Contemporary Perspectives.* New York: Tauris, 2002, 247–272.

Kalyvas, Stathis. *The Rise of Christian Democracy in Europe.* Ithaca, N.Y.: Cornell University Press, 1996.

Kalyvas, Stathis. "Unsecular Politics and Religious Mobilization: Beyond Christian Democracy." In Thomas Kselman and Joseph Buttigieg, eds., *European Christian Democracy: Historical Legacies and Comparative Perspectives.* Notre Dame, Ind.: University of Notre Dame Press, 2003, 293–320.

Kamen, Harry. *The Rise of Toleration*. New York: Longman, 1967.

Kamrava, Mehran. *Iran's Intellectual Revolution*. Cambridge: Cambridge University Press, 2008.

Kaplan, Robert. *The Coming Anarchy: Shattering the Dreams of the Post Cold War*. New York: Vintage Books, 2000.

Kaplan, Robert. *Eastward to Tartary: Travels to the Balkans, the Middle East and the Caucasus*. New York: Vintage Books, 2001.

Katouzian, Homa. *Musaddiq and the Struggle for Power in Iran*. New York: Tauris, 1999.

Katouzian, Homa. "Mosaddeq's Government in Iranian History: Arbitrary Rule, Democracy, and the 1953 Coup." In Malcolm Bryne and Mark Gasiorowski, eds., *Mohammad Mosaddeq and the 1953 Coup in Iran*. Syracuse, N.Y.: Syracuse University Press, 2004, 1–26.

Kaufman, Peter Iver. *Redeeming Politics*. Princeton, N.J.: Princeton University Press, 1990.

Kaviraj, Sudipta. "In Search of Civil Society." In Sudipta Kaviraj and Sunil Khilnani, eds., *Civil Society: History and Possibilities*. Cambridge: Cambridge University Press, 2001, 287–323.

Keane, John. "The Limits of Secularism." In John L. Esposito and Azzam Tamimi, eds., *Islam and Secularism in the Middle East*. New York: New York University Press, 2000, 29–37.

Keane, John. "Secularism?" In David Marquand and Ronald Nettler, eds., *Religion and Democracy*. Oxford: Blackwell, 2000, 5–19.

Keddie, Nikki. *Sayyid Jamal ad-Din "al-Afghani."* Berkeley: University of California Press, 1972.

Keddie, Nikki. *An Islamic Response to Imperialism: Political and Religious Writings of Sayyid Jamal ad-Din "al-Afghani."* Berkeley: University of California Press, 1983.

Keddie, Nikki, and Mehrdad Amanat. "Iran under the Later Qajars, 1848–1922." In Peter Avery, Gavin Hambly, and Charles Melville, eds., *The Cambridge History of Iran: From Nadir Shah to the Islamic Republic*. Cambridge: Cambridge University Press, 1991, 7:174–212.

Keddie, Nikki. *Modern Iran: Roots and Results of Revolution*. New Haven, Conn.: Yale University Press, 2003.

Kedourie, Elie. Islam in the Modern World. New York: Holt, Rinehart and Winston, 1980.

Kedourie, Elie. Politics in the Middle East. New York: Oxford University Press, 1992.

Kedourie, Elie. *Democracy and Arab Political Culture*. Portland, Ore.: Frank Cass, 1994.

Kennedy, Emmet. *Secularism and Its Opponents from Augustine to Solzhenitsyn*. New York: Palgrave, 2006.

Kepel, Gilles. *Jihad: The Trail of Political Islam*. Cambridge, Mass.: Harvard University Press, 2002.

Khatab, Sayed. *The Political Thought of Sayyid Qutb: The Theory of Jahiliyyah*. New York: Routledge, 2006.

Khatab, Sayed. *The Power of Sovereignty: The Political and Ideological Philosophy of Sayyid Qutb*. New York: Routledge, 2006.

Khomeini, Ruhollah. "Islamic Government." *Islam and Revolution: Writings and Declarations of Imam Khomeini*. Translated and annotated by Hamid Algar. Berkeley: Mizan Press, 1981, 25–166.

Khomein, Ruhollah. "In Commemoration of the First Martyrs of the Revolution." *Islam and Revolution: Writings and Declarations of Imam Khomeini*. Translated and annotated by Hamid Algar. Berkeley: Mizan Press, 1981, 212–227.

Kian-Thiébaut, Azadeh. *Secularization of Iran: A Doomed Failure? The New Middle Class and the Making of Modern Iran*. Paris: Peeters, 1998.

King, Gary, Robert Keohane, and Sidney Verba, *Designing Social Inquiry*. Princeton, N.J.: Princeton University Press, 1994.

Kramer, Gudrun. "Islam and Pluralism." In Rex Brynen, Bahgat Korany, and Paul Noble, eds., Political Liberalization and Democratization in the Arab World, vol. 1, Theoretical Perspectives. Boulder, Colo.: Lynne Rienner, 1995, 113–128.

Kramer, Gudrun. "Islamist Notions of Democracy." In Joel Beinin and Joe Stork, eds., Political Islam: Essays from Middle East Report. Berkeley: University of California Press, 1997, 71–82.

Kramer, Martin. "Hizbullah: The Calculus of Jihad." In Martin E. Marty and R. Scott Appleby, eds., *Fundamentalisms and the State: Remaking Politics, Economics, and Militance*. Chicago: University of Chicago Press, 1993, 539–556.

Kramer, Martin. "Islam vs. Democracy." In Martin Kramer, *Arab Awakening and Islamic Revival*. New Brunswick, N.J.: Transaction, 1996, 265–78.

Kriegel, Blandine. *The State and the Rule of Law*. Translated by Jeffrey Cohen and Marc LePain. Princeton, N.J.: Princeton University Press, 1995.

Kselman, Thomas, and Joseph A. Buttigieg, eds. *European Christian Democracy: Historical Legacies and Comparative Perspectives*. Notre Dame, Ind.: University of Notre Dame Press, 2003.

Kull, Ann. *Piety and Politics: Nurcholish Madjid and His Interpretation of Islam in Modern Indonesia*. Lund, Sweden: Department of History and Anthropology of Religions, Lund University, 2005.

Kurer, Oskar. *The Political Foundations of Development Policies*. Lanham, Md.: University Press of America, 1997.

Kuru, Ahmet. "Reinterpretation of Secularism in Turkey: The Case of the Justice and Development Party." In M. Hakan Yavuz, ed., *The Emergence of a New Turkey: Democracy and the AK Party*. Salt Lake City: University of Utah Press, 2006, 136–159.

Kurzman, Charles. *Liberal Islam: A Sourcebook*. New York: Oxford University Press, 1998.

Kurzman, Charles. *Modernist Islam 1840–1940: A Sourcebook*. New York: Oxford University Press, 2002.

Kurzman, Charles. "Critics Within: Islamic Scholars' Protests against the Islamic State in Iran." In Charles Kurzman and Michaelle Browers, eds., *An Islamic Reformation?* Lanham, Md.: Lexington Books, 2004, 79–100.

Lawerence, Jonathan, and Justine Vaisse. *Integrating Islam: Political and Religious Challenges in Contemporary France*. Washington, D.C.: Brookings Institution Press, 2006.

Lecler, Joseph. *Toleration and Reformation.* Translated by T. L. Westow. London: Longmans, 1960.

Lee, Robert. *Overcoming Tradition and Modernity: The Search for Islamic Authenticity.* Boulder, Colo.: Westview Press, 1997.

Lerner, Daniel. "Modernization: Social Aspects." In David L. Sills, ed., *International Encyclopaedia of the Social Sciences.* New York: Crowell Collier and Macmillan, 1968, 386–395.

Lewis, Bernard. *The Political Language of Islam.* Chicago: University of Chicago, 1988.

Lewis, Bernard. *Islam and the West.* New York: Oxford University Press, 1993.

Lewis, Bernard. *The Emergence of Modern Turkey.* 3rd ed. New York: Oxford University Press, 2002.

Lewis, Bernard. *What Went Wrong? The Clash between Islam and Modernity in the Middle East.* New York: Perennial, 2003.

Lewis, Bernard. *The Crisis of Islam: Holy War and Unholy Terror.* New York: Random House, 2003.

Lewis, Bernard. "A Historical Overview." In Larry Diamond, Marc F. Plattner, and Daniel Brumberg, eds., *Islam and Democracy in the Middle East.* Baltimore: Johns Hopkins University Press, 2003, 208–219.

Lilla, Mark. *The Stillborn God: Religion, Politics and the Modern West.* New York: Knopf, 2007.

Linz, Juan, and Alfred Stepan. *Problems of Democratic Transition and Consolidations: Southern Europe, South America, and Post-communist Europe.* Baltimore: Johns Hopkins University Press, 1996.

Linz, Juan. *Totalitarian and Authoritarian Regimes.* Boulder, Colo.: Lynne Rienner, 2000.

Lijphart, Arend. *Patterns of Democracy: Government Forms and Performance in Thirty-six Countries.* New Haven, Conn.: Yale University Press, 1999.

Locke, John. *A Letter Concerning Toleration.* Edited by James Tully. Indiana: Hackett, 1983.

Locke, John. *Two Treatises of Government.* Edited by Peter Laslett. Cambridge: Cambridge University Press, 1988.

Locke, John. *First Tract on Government* (1661). In *Locke: Political Essays,* edited by Mark Goldie. Cambridge: Cambridge University Press, 1997, 3–53.

Locke, John. "An Essay on Toleration (1667)". In *Locke: Political Essays,* edited by Mark Goldie. Cambridge: Cambridge University Press, 1997, 134–159.

Locke, John. *The Reasonableness of Christianity: As Delivered in the Scriptures.* Edited by John Higgins-Biddle. New York: Clarendon Press, 1999.

Luther, Martin. "On Secular Authority." In Harro Hopfl, ed., *Luther and Calvin: On Secular Authority.* Cambridge: Cambridge University Press, 1991.

MacCulloch, Diarmaid. *The Reformation.* New York: Viking, 2004.

MacMaster, Neil. "Islamophobia in France and the 'Algerian Problem.'" In Emran Qureshi and Michael Sells, eds., *The New Crusades: Constructing the Muslim Enemy.* New York: Columbia University Press, 2003, 288–313.

Maddex, Robert. *Constitutions of the World,* 2nd ed. Washington, D.C.: Congressional Quarterly, 2001.

Maddox, Graham. *Religion and the Rise of Democracy*. New York: Routledge, 1996.

Madjid, Nurcholish. "The Necessity of Renewing Islamic Thought and the Problem of the Integration of the Ummat." In M. Kamal Hassan, *Muslim Intellectual Responses to 'New Order' Modernisation in Indonesia*. Kuala Lumpur: Dewan Bahasa dan Pustaka, 1980, 187–197.

Madjid, Nurcholish. "Reinvigorating Religious Understanding in the Indonesian Muslim Community." In Charles Kurzman, ed., *Liberal Islam: A Sourcebook*. New York: Oxford University Press, 1998, 289–294.

Madjid, Nurcholish. "The Necessity of Renewing Islamic Thought and Reinvigorating Religious Understanding." In Charles Kurzman, ed., *Liberal Islam: A Sourcebook*. New York: Oxford University Press, 1998, 284–294.

Madjid, Nurcholish. "In Search of Islamic Roots for Modern Pluralism: The Indonesian Experiences." In Mark Woodward, ed., *Toward a New Paradigm: Recent Developments in Indonesian Islamic Thought*. Tempe: Arizona State University, 1996, 89–116.

Madjid, Nurcholish. "Indonesian Muslims Enter a New Age." In Virginia Hooker and Amin Saikal, eds., *Islamic Perspectives on the New Millennium*. Singapore: Institute for Southeast Asian Studies, 2004, 74–88.

Malcolm, Noel. *Aspects of Hobbes*. New York: Oxford University Press, 2002.

Marashi, Afshin. "Performing the Nation: The Shah's Official State Visit to Kemalist Turkey, June to July 1934." In Stephanie Cronin, ed., *The Making of Modern Iran: State and Society under Riza Shah, 1921–1941*. London: Routledge/Curzon, 2003, 99–119.

Mardin, Şerif. "Religion and Secularism in Turkey." In Ali Kazancigil and Ergun Özbudun, eds., *Atatürk: Founder of a Modern State*. London: Hurst, 1997, 191–219.

Mardin, Şerif. *Religion, Society, and Modernity in Turkey*. Syracuse, N.Y.: Syracuse University Press, 2006.

Maritain, Jacques. *Christianity and Democracy: The Rights of Man and Natural Law*. Translated by Doris Anson. San Francisco: Ignatius Press, 1986.

Marquand, David, and Ronald L. Nettler, eds. *Religion and Democracy*. Oxford: Blackwell, 2000.

Marsilius, of Padua. *The Defender of Peace*. Edited and translated by Annabel Brett. Cambridge: Cambridge University Press, 2005.

Marsot, Afaf Lutfi al-Sayyid. *Egypt in the Reign of Muhammad Ali*. Cambridge: Cambridge University Press, 1984.

Martin, David. *A General Theory of Secularization*. Oxford: Blackwell, 1978.

Martin, Vanessa. *Islam and Modernism: The Iranian Revolution of 1906*. London: Tauris, 1989.

Martinich, A. P. *Two Gods of Leviathan: Thomas Hobbes on Religion and Politics*. Cambridge: Cambridge University Press, 1992.

Martinussen, John. *Society, State and Market: Competing Theories of Development*. London: Zed Books, 1997.

Marty, Martin, and R. Scott Appleby, eds. *Fundamentalisms Observed*. Chicago: University of Chicago Press, 1991.

Marty, Martin, and R. Scott Appleby, eds. *Fundamentalisms and Society: Reclaiming the Sciences, the Family and Education*. Chicago: University of Chicago Press, 1993.

Marty, Martin, and R. Scott Appleby, eds. *Fundamentalisms and the State: Remaking Polities, Economies and Militance*. Chicago: University of Chicago Press, 1993.

Marty, Martin, and R. Scott Appleby, eds. *Accounting for Fundamentalism: The Dynamic Character of Movements*. Chicago: University of Chicago Press, 1994.

Marty, Martin, and R. Scott Appleby, eds. *Fundamentalisms Comprehended*. Chicago: University of Chicago Press, 1995.

Marx, Anthony. *Faith in Nation: Exclusionary Origins of Nationalism*. New York: Oxford University Press, 2003.

Mavani, Hamid. "The Basis of Leadership: Khumayni's Claims and the Classic Tradition." Master's thesis, Institue for Islamic Studies, McGill University, 1992.

Mawdudi, Abu al-A'la. *Islamic Law and Consitution*. Translated and edited by Khurshid Ahmad. Lahore: Islamic Publications, 1986.

Mayer, Ann Elizabeth. Islam and Human Rights: Tradition and Politics. 4th ed. Boulder, Colo.: Westview Press, 1995.

Mayo, Henry B. *An Introduction to Democratic Theory*. New York: Oxford University Press, 1960.

Mazower, Mark. *Dark Continent: Europe's Twentieth Century*. New York: Knopf, 1999.

McGrath, Alister. *Reformation Thought: An Introduction*. 2nd ed. Oxford: Blackwell, 1993.

McGreevy, John. *Catholicism and American Freedom: A History*. New York: Norton, 2003.

McManners, John. *The French Revolution and the Church*. London: S.P.C.K., 1969.

McManners, John, ed. *The Oxford History of Christianity*. New York: Oxford University Press, 1993.

McPherran, Mark. *The Religion of Socrates*. University Park: Penn State University Press, 1996.

Menashri, David. *Post-revolutionary Politics in Iran: Religion, State and Power*. Portland, Ore.: Frank Cass, 2001.

Mernissi, Fatima. *Islam and Democracy: Fear of the Modern World*. Translated by Mary Jo Lakeland. Cambridge: Perseus, 2002.

Migdal, Joel. *Strong Societies and Weak States: State-society Relations and State Capabilities in the Third World*. Princeton, N.J.: Princeton University Press, 1988.

Milani, Mohsen. *The Making of Iran's Islamic Revolution: From Monarchy to Islamic Republic*. 2nd ed. Boulder, Colo.: Westview, 1994.

Mill, John Stuart. *Three Essays on Religion*. New York: Greenwood Press, 1969.

Mill, John Stuart. *On Liberty*. Edited by Gertrude Himmelfarb. New York: Penguin Books, 1985.

Mill, John Stuart. *Autobiography*. New York: Penguin Books, 1989.

Miller, David. *Political Philosophy: A Very Short Introduction*. New York: Oxford University Press, 2003.

Mills, C. Wright. *The Sociological Imagination*. New York: Oxford University Press, 1959.

Mirsepassi, Ali. *Intellectual Discourse and the Politics of Modernization: Negotiating Modernity in Iran*. Cambridge: Cambridge University Press, 2000.

Mitchell, Richard. *The Society of the Muslim Brothers*. New York: Oxford University Press, 1993.

Moaddel, Mansoor. *Jordanian Exceptionalism: A Comparative Analysis of State-Religion Relationships in Egypt, Iran, Jordan, and Syria*. New York: Palgrave, 2002.

Moore, Barrington. *Social Origins of Dictatorship and Democracy: Lord and Peasant in the Making of the Modern World*. Boston: Beacon Press, 1993.

Moore, R. I. *The Formation of a Persecuting Society: Power and Deviance in Western Europe*. Oxford: Blackwell, 1987.

Morgan, Victor, et al. A *History of the University of Cambridge*. Vol. 2. *1546–1750*. Cambridge University Press, 2004.

Moslem, Mehdi. *Factional Politics in Post-Khomeini Iran*. Syracuse, N.Y.: Syracuse University Press, 2002.

Mouffe, Chantal. *The Return of the Political*. New York: Verso, 1993.

Moussalli, Ahmad. *The Islamic Quest for Democracy, Pluralism and Human Rights* Gainesville: University Press of Florida, 2001.

Moussalli, Ahmad. *Moderate and Radical Islamic Fundamentalism: The Quest for Modernity, Legitimacy and the Islamic State*. Gainesville: University of Florida Press, 1999.

Mullet, Michael. *Radical Religious Movements in Early Modern Europe*. London: Allen and Unwin, 1980.

Musallam, Adnan. *From Secularism to Jihad: Sayyid Qutb and the Foundations of Radical Islamism*. Westport, Conn.: Praeger, 2005.

Nandy, Ashis. "The Politics of Secularism and the Recovery of Religious Tolerance." In R .B. J. Walker and Saul Mendlovitz, eds., *Contending Sovereignties: Redefining Political Community*. Boulder, Colo.: Lynne Rienner, 1990, 125–144.

Nasr, Seyyed Hossein. *Islamic Life and Thought*. Albany: State University of New York Press, 1981.

Nasr, Seyyed Vali Reza. *The Vanguard of the Islamic Revolution: The Jama'at-i Islami of Pakistan*. Berkeley: University of California Press, 1994.

Nasr, Seyyed Vali Reza. *Mawdudi and the Making of Islamic Revivalism*. New York: Oxford University Press, 1995.

Nasr, Seyyed Vali Reza. "European Colonialism and the Emergence of Modern Muslim States." In John Esposito, ed., *The Oxford History of Islam*. New York: Oxford University Press, 1999, 549–599.

Nasr, Vali, and Ali Gheissari. *Democracy in Iran: History and the Quest for Liberty*. New York: Oxford University Press, 2006.

Natsir, Mohammad. "The Dangers of Secularism." In Herbert Feith and Lance Castles, eds., *Indonesian Political Thinking 1945–1965*. Ithaca, N.Y.: Cornell University Press, 1970, 215–219.

Noor, Farish. "Why Hudud? (Why Not?)" In Greg Fealy and Virginia Hooker, eds., *Voices of Islam in Southeast Asia: A Contemporary Sourcebook*. Singapore: Institute for Southeast Asian Studies, 2006, 174–175.

Norton, Augustus Richard, ed. *Civil Society in the Middle East*. Vol. 2. Leiden: Brill, 1996.

Nussbaum, Martha. *The Clash Within: Democracy, Religious Violence and India's Future*. Cambridge, Mass.: Harvard University Press, 2007.

Nussbaum, Martha. *Liberty of Conscience: In Defense of America's Tradition of Religious Equality.* New York: Basic Books, 2008.

O'Brien, Conor Cruise. *On the Eve of the Millennium.* Concord, Ontario: Anansi, 1994.

Ockham, William. *A Short Discourse on the Tyrannical Government.* Translated by John Kilcullen and edited by Arthur Stephen McGrade. Cambridge: Cambridge University Press, 1992.

Oren, Michael. *Power, Faith and Fantasy: America in the Middle East, 1776 to the Present.* New York: Norton, 2007.

Pahlavi, Mohammed Reza Shah. *Mission for My Country.* New York: Hutchinson, 1961.

Pangle, Thomas. *Spirit of Modern Republicanism: The Moral Vision of American Founders and the Philosophy of Locke.* Chicago: University of Chicago Press, 1990.

Parekh, Bhiku. *Rethinking Multiculturalism: Cultural Diversity and Political Theory.* Cambridge, Mass.: Harvard University Press, 2000.

Parekh, Bhikhu. "The Cultural Particularity of Liberal Democracy." In David Held, ed., *Prospects for Democracy: North, South, East, West.* Stanford, Calif.: Stanford University Press, 1993, 156–175.

Parsons, Talcott, et al., eds. *Theories of Society: Foundations of Modern Sociological Theory.* New York: Free Press of Glencoe, 1961.

Pew Charitable Trust. *Trends 2005.* Washington, D.C.: Pew Research Center, 2005.

Pipes, Daniel. *In the Path of God: Islam and Political Power.* New York: Basic Books, 1983.

Piscatori, James. *Islam in a World of Nation-States.* Cambridge: Cambridge University Press, 1986.

Piscatori, James, and Dale Eickelman. *Muslim Politics.* Princeton, N.J.: Princeton University Press, 1996.

Pottenger, John. *Reaping the Whirlwind: Liberal Democracy and the Religion Axis.* Washington, D.C.: Georgetown University Press, 2007.

Pryce Jones, David. *The Closed Circle.* London: Paladin, 1990.

Przeworski, Adam. "Democracy as a Contingent Outcome of Conflicts." In Jon Elster and Rune Slagstad, eds., *Constitutionalism and Democracy.* Cambridge: Cambridge University Press, 1988, 59–80.

Pye, Lucian, and Sydney Verba. *Political Culture and Political Development.* Princeton, N.J.: Princeton University Press, 1965.

Qureshi, Emran, and Michael Sells, eds. *The New Crusades: Constructing the Muslim Enemy.* New York: Columbia University Press, 2003.

Qutb, Sayyid. *Milestones.* Translated by M. M. Siddiqui. Indianapolis: American Trust, 1990.

Qutb, Sayyid. *Social Justice in Islam.* Translated by John B. Hardie and Hamid Algar. Rev. ed. Oneonta, N.Y.: Islamic Publications International, 2000.

Rajaee, Farhang. *Islamism and Modernism: The Changing Discourse in Iran.* Austin: University of Texas Press, 2007.

Ramazani, R. K. "Iran, Democracy and the United States." In Robert Fatton Jr. and R. K. Ramazani, eds., *The Future of Liberal Democracy: Thomas Jefferson and the Contemporary World.* New York: Palgrave, 2004, 185–201.

Rawls, John. *Political Liberalism.* New York: Columbia University Press, 1993.

Reudy, John, ed. *Islamism and Secularism in North Africa.* London: Macmillan, 1994.

Richard, Alan, and John Waterbury. *A Political Economy of the Middle East: State, Class, and Economic Development.* Boulder, Colo.: Westview Press, 1990.

Roberts, J. M. *The Penguin History of the World.* New York: Penguin Books, 1990.

Rodinson, Maxime. *Marxism and the Muslim World.* London: Monthly Review Press, 1981.

Rorty, Richard. "The Priority of Democracy to Philosophy." In Richard Rorty, *Objectivity, Relativism and Truth.* Cambridge: Cambridge University Press, 1991, 1:175–196.

Rorty, Richard. *Philosophy and Social Hope.* New York: Penguin Books, 1999.

Rorty, Richard. "Anticlericalism and Atheism." In Rorty and Vattimo, *Future of Religion.* Edited by Santiago Zabala. New York: Columbia University Press, 2005, 29–42.

Rorty, Richard, and Gianni Vattimo. *The Future of Religion.* Edited by Santiago Zabala. New York: Columbia University Press, 2005.

Rorty, Richard. "On September 11, 2001." In Eduardo Mendieta, ed., *Take Care of Freedom and Truth Will Take Care of Itself.* Palo Alto, Calif.: Stanford University Press, 2006, 114–119.

Rorty, Richard. *Philosophy as Cultural Politics: Philosophical Papers.* Cambridge: Cambridge University Press, 2007.

Rousseau, Jean-Jacques. *On the Social Contract.* Translated by Donald Cress. Indianapolis: Hackett, 1987.

Roy, Olivier. *The Failure of Political Islam.* Translated by Carol Volk. Cambridge, Mass.: Harvard University Press, 1994.

Roy, Olivier. *Globalized Islam: The Search for a New Ummah.* New York: Columbia University Press, 2004.

Roy, Olivier. *Secularism Confronts Islam.* Translated by George Holoch. New York: Columbia University Press, 2007.

Rugh, Andrea. "Reshaping Personal Relationships in Egypt." In Martin Marty and R. Scott Appleby, eds., *Fundamentalisms and Society: Reclaiming the Sciences, the Family, and Education.* Chicago: University of Chicago Press, 1993, 151–180.

Rustow, Dankwart. "Transitions to Democracy: Toward a Dynamic Model." In Lisa Anderson, ed., *Transitions to Democracy.* New York: Columbia University Press, 1999, 14–41.

Sachedina, Abdulaziz. *The Just Ruler in Shi'ite Islam: The Comprehensive Authority of the Jurist in Imamite Jurisprudence.* New York: Oxford University Press, 1988.

Sachedina, Abdulaziz. *The Islamic Roots of Democratic Pluralism.* New York: Oxford University Press, 2001.

Sadowski, Yahya. "The New Orientalism and the Democracy Debate." In Joel Beinin and Joe Stork, eds., *Political Islam: Essays from Middle East Report.* Berkeley: University of California Press, 1997, 33–50.

Salamé, Ghassan, ed. *Democracy without Democrats? The Renewal of Politics in the Muslim World.* New York: Tauris, 1994.

Sartori, Giovanni. "How Far Can Free Government Travel?" In Larry Diamond and Marc Plattner, eds., *The Global Divergence of Democracies.* Baltimore: Johns Hopkins University Press, 2001, 52–62.

Schumpeter, Joseph. "Another Theory of Democracy." In Joseph Schumpeter, *Capitalism, Socialism and Democracy.* New York: Harper, 1950, 269–283.

Scott, Jonathan. *Algernon Sidney and the English Republic 1623–1677.* Cambridge: Cambridge University Press, 1988.

Scott, Joan Wallach. *Politics of the Veil.* Princeton, N.J.: Princeton University Press, 2007.

Scruton, Roger. *The West and the Rest: Globalization and the Terrorist Threat.* Wilmington, Del.: ISI Books, 2002.

Sen, Amartya. *Identity and Violence: The Illusion of Destiny.* New York: Norton, 2006.

Sen, Amartya. *The Argumentative Indian: Writings on Indian Culture, History and Identity.* New York: Penguin Books, 2006.

Shafiq, Munir. "Secularism and the Arab-Muslim Condition." In Azzam Tamimi and John L. Esposito, eds., *Islam and Secularism in the Middle East.* New York: New York University Press, 2000, 139–150.

Shapiro, Ian. "John Locke's Democratic Theory." In John Locke, *Two Treatises of Government and A Letter Concerning Toleration*, edited by Ian Shapiro. New Haven, Conn.: Yale University Press, 2003, 309–340.

Sharpe, J. A. *Early Modern England: A Social History, 1550–1760.* London: Edward Arnold, 1987.

Shepard, William. "The Diversity of Islamic Thought: Towards a Typology." In Suha Taji-Faroukhi and Basheer Nafi, eds., *Islamic Thought in the Twentieth Century.* New York: Tauris, 2004, 61–104.

Sisk, Timothy, ed. *Islam and Democracy: Religion, Politics and Power in the Middle East.* Washington, D.C.: United States Institute of Peace, 1992.

Skocpol, Theda and George Ross, Tony Smith, and Judith Eisenberg Vichniac. "Barrington Moore's Social Origins and Beyond: Historical Social Analysis since the 1960s." In Theda Skocpol, ed., *Democracy, Revolution and History.* Ithaca, N.Y.: Cornell University Press, 1998, 1–24.

Smith, B. C. *Understanding Third World Politics: Theories of Political Change and Development.* 2nd ed. New York: Palgrave, 2003.

Smith, Donald, ed. *Religion and Modernization.* New Haven, Conn.: Yale University Press, 1974.

Smith, Wilfred Cantwell. *Islam in Modern History.* Princeton, N.J.: Princeton University Press, 1997.

Sommerville, Johann. "*Leviathan* and Its Anglican Context." In Patricia Springborg, ed., *The Cambridge Companion to Hobbes's Leviathan.* Cambridge: Cambridge University Press, 2007, 358–374.

Sorensen, Georg. *Democracy and Democratization: Processes and Prospects in a Changing World.* 2nd ed. Boulder, Colo.: Westview, 1993.

Soroush, Abdol Karim. *Reason, Freedom and Democracy in Islam.* Translated and edited by Ahmad Sadri and Mahmoud Sadri. New York: Oxford University Press, 1999.

Spitz, Lewis. *The Renaissance and Reformation Movements.* Chicago: Rand McNally, 1971.

Springborg, Patricia. "Hobbes on Religion." In Tom Sorell, ed., *The Cambridge Companion to Hobbes.* Cambridge: Cambridge University Press, 1996, 346–380.

Stark, Rodney, and William Bainbridge. *The Future of Religion: Secularization, Revival and Cult Formation.* Berkeley: University of California Press, 1985.

Statistical Yearbook, 1995–2002. Cairo: Central Agency for Public Mobilization and Statistics, 2003.

Stepan, Alfred. "World Religious Systems and Democracy: Crafting the 'Twin Tolerations.'" In Alfred Stepan, *Arguing Comparative Politics.* New York: Oxford University Press, 2001, 213–253.

Stone, I. F. *The Trial of Socrates.* Boston: Little Brown, 1988.

Stone, Lawrence. *Causes of the English Revolution, 1529–1642.* London: Routledge and Kegan Paul, 1972.

Stone, Lawrence, ed. *The University in Society.* Vol. 1. *Oxford and Cambridge from the Fourteenth to the Early Nineteenth Century.* Princeton, N.J.: Princeton University Press, 1974.

Stone, Lawrence. *Social Change and Revolution in England, 1540–1640.* London: Longmans, 1980.

Stork, Joe. "Oil, Islam and Israel: U.S. Policy and Democratic Change in the Middle East." In Jochen Hippler, ed., *The Democratisation of Disempowerment: The Problem of Democracy in the Third World.* London: Pluto Press, 1995, 153–172.

Stork, Joe, and Joel Beinin. "On the Modernity, Historical Specificity and International Context of Political Islam." In Joel Beinin and Joe Stork, eds., *Political Islam: Essays from Middle East Report.* Berkeley: University of California Press, 1997, 3–25.

Stout, Jeffrey. *Democracy and Tradition.* Princeton, N.J.: Princeton University Press, 2004.

Strauss, Leo. *Natural Right and History.* Chicago: University of Chicago Press, 1999.

Tamimi, Azzam. *Rachid Ghannouchi: A Democrat within Islamism.* New York: Oxford University Press, 2001.

Taylor, Charles. *The Malaise of Modernity.* Concord, Ontario: Anansi, 1991.

Taylor, Charles. "Modes of Secularism." In Rajeev Bhargava, ed., *Secularism and Its Critics.* New Delhi: Oxford University Press, 1998, 31–51.

Taylor, Charles. "The Politics of Recognition." In Amy Gutmann, ed., *Multiculturalism: Examining the Politics of Recognition.* Princeton, N.J.: Princeton University Press, 1994, 25–73.

Taylor, Charles. *A Secular Age.* Cambridge, Mass.: Harvard University Press, 2007.

Terchek, Ronald, and Thomas Conte, eds. *Theories of Democracy: A Reader.* Lanham, Md.: Roman and Littlefield, 2001.

Tibi, Bassam. "Democracy and Democratization in Islam." In Michele Schmiegelow, *Democracy in Asia.* New York: Palgrave, 1997, 127–146.

Tocqueville, Alexis de. *Democracy in America.* Translated by George Lawrence. New York: HarperCollins, 1988.

Tocqueville, Alexis de. *Democracy in America.* Translated by Henry Reeve. 2 vols. New York: Vintage Books, 1990.

Tocqueville, Alexis de. *Writings on Empire and Slavery.* Edited and translated by Jennifer Pitts. Baltimore: Johns Hopkins University Press, 2001.

Tocqueville, Alexis de. *Democracy in America and Two Essays on America.* Translated by Gerald Bevin. New York: Penguin Books, 2003.

Tilly, Charles. *Contention and Democracy in Europe, 1650–2000.* Cambridge: Cambridge University Press, 2004.

Tucker, Ernest. "Primitivism as a Radical Response to Religious Crisis: The Anabaptists of Munster in the 1530s and the Taliban of Afghanistan in the 1990s." In Charles Kurzman and Michaelle Browers, eds., *An Islamic Reformation?* Lanham, Md.: Lexington Books, 2004, 147–158.

Tucker, Robert, ed. *The Marx-Engels Reader.* 2nd ed. New York: Norton, 1978.

Tully, James. Introduction to John Locke, *A Letter Concerning Toleration,* edited by James Tully. Indianapolis: Hackett, 1983, 1–18.

Tully, James. "Locke." In J. H. Burns, ed., *The Cambridge History of Political Thought 1450–1700.* Cambridge: Cambridge University Press, 1991, 616–652.

Turabi, Hassan. "The Islamic State." In John Esposito, ed., *Voices of Resurgent Islam.* New York: Oxford University Press, 1983, 241–251.

Utvik, Bjorn Olav. "The Modernizing Force of Islam." In John Esposito and Francois Burgat, eds., *Modernizing Islam: Religion in the Public Sphere in Europe and the Middle East.* New Brunswick, N.J.: Rutgers University Press, 2003, 43–67.

van Bruinessen, Martin. "Islamic State or State Islam? Fifty Years of State-Islam Relations in Indonesia." In Ingrid Wessel, ed., *Indonesien am Ende des 20. Jahrhunderts: Analysen zu 50 Jahren unabhängiger Entwicklung.* Hamburg: Abera-Verlag, 1996, 19–34.

Vanhanen, Tatu. *Prospects of Democracy: A Study of 172 Countries.* New York: Routledge, 1997.

Voll, John. *Islam: Continuity and Change in the Modern World.* 2nd ed. Syracuse, N.Y.: Syracuse University Press, 1994.

Voltaire. *The Philosophical Dictionary.* Translated by H. I. Wolf. New York: Knopf, 1924.

Von der Mehden, Fred. *Religion and Modernization in Southeast Asia.* Syracuse, N.Y.: Syracuse University Press, 1986.

Waldron, Jeremy. *God, Locke and Equality: Christian Foundations in Locke's Political Thought.* Cambridge: Cambridge University Press 2002.

Walzer, Michael. *Revolution of the Saints: A Study in the Origins of Radical Politics.* Cambridge, Mass.: Harvard University Press, 1965.

Waterbury, John. "Democracy without Democrats? The Potential for Political Liberalization in the Middle East." In Ghassan Salamé, ed., *Democracy without Democrats? The Renewal of Politics in the Muslim World.* New York: Tauris, 1994, 23–47.

Weber, Max. *The Sociology of Religion.* Boston: Beacon Press, 1963.

Weber, Max. *The Protestant Ethic and the Spirit of Capitalism.* Translated by Talcott Parsons. New York: Routledge, 2001.

Weiner, Myron, and Samuel Huntington, eds. *Understanding Political Development.* Prospect Heights, Ill.: Waveland Press, 1987.

White, Jenny. *Islamist Mobilization in Turkey: A Study in Vernacular Politics.* Seattle: University of Washington Press, 2002.

Wickham, Carrie Rosefsky. *Mobilizing Islam: Religion, Activism and Political Change in Egypt.* New York: Columbia University Press, 2002.

Williams, George Huntston. *The Radical Reformation.* 3rd ed. Kirksville, Mo.: Sixteenth Century Journal, 1992.

Wiktorowicz, Quintan, ed. *Islamic Activism: A Social Movement Theory Approach.* Bloomington: Indiana University Press, 2004.

Wolin, Sheldon. *Politics and Vision: Continuity and Innovation in Western Political Thought.* expanded ed. Princeton, N.J.: Princeton University Press, 2004.

Wolterstorff, Nicholas. "Why We Should Reject What Liberalism Tells Us about Speaking and Acting for Religious Reasons." In Paul J. Weithman, ed., *Religion and Contemporary Liberalism.* Notre Dame, Ind.: University of Notre Dame Press, 162–181.

Wooton, David, ed. *Divine Right and Democracy: An Anthology of Political Writings in Stuart England.* New York: Penguin Books, 1986.

World Population Prospects: The 2002 Revision. Vol. 1. New York: United Nations Department of Economic and Social Affairs, Population Division, 2002.

World Statistics Pocketbook. New York: United Nations Department of Economic and Social Affairs, 2002.

World Survey on Education. New York: UNESCO, 1955.

Wright, Robin. *Sacred Rage: The Wrath of Militant Islam.* New York: Touchstone Books, 2001.

Wycliffe, John. *Tractatus de civili dominio.* Edited by Reginald Lane Poole. New York: John Reprint, 1966.

Yassine, Abdessalam. *Winning the Modern World for Islam.* Translated by Martin Jenni. Iowa City, Iowa: Justice and Spirituality, 2000.

Yavuz, M. Hakan. *Islamic Political Identity in Turkey.* New York: Oxford University Press, 2003.

Yavuz, M. Hakan, and John Esposito, eds. *Turkish Islam and the Secular State: The Gülen Movement.* Syracuse, N.Y.: Syracuse University Press, 2003.

Zagorin, Perez. *The English Revolution: Politics, Events and Ideas.* Brookfield, Vt.: Ashgate, 1998.

Zagorin, Perez. *How the Idea of Religious Toleration Came to the West.* Princeton, N.J.: Princeton University Press, 2003.

Zakariyya, Fouad. *Myth and Reality in the Contemporary Islamist Movement.* Translated by Ibrahim M. Abu-Rabi'. London: Pluto Press, 2005.

Zonis, Marvin. *The Political Elite of Iran.* Princeton, N.J.: Princeton University Press, 1971.

Zubaida, Sami. *Islam, the People and the State: Political Ideas and Movements in the Middle East.* New York: Tauris, 1993.

Zubaida, Sami. "Is Iran an Islamic State?" In Joel Beinin and Joe Stork, eds., *Political Islam: Essays from Middle East Report.* Berkeley: University of California Press, 1997, 103–119.

Zubaida, Sami. *Law and Power in the Islamic World.* New York: Tauris, 2003.

Zubaida, Sami. *The Search for Authenticity in Middle East Cultures: Religion, Community and Nation.* Occasional paper. Washington, D.C.: Center for Contemporary Arab Studies, 2004.

Zunz, Olivier, and Alan Kahan, eds. *The Tocqueville Reader: A Life in Letters and Politics*. Oxford: Blackwell, 2002.

Zürcher, Erik. *Turkey: A Modern History*. 3rd ed. New York: Tauris, 2004.

PERIODICAL ARTICLES

Abdallah, Al-Jarrar, and Cedric Cullingford. "The Concept of Democracy: Muslim Views," *Politics* 27 (February 2007), 16–23.

Abou El Fadl, Khaled. "Islam and the Theology of Power." *Middle East Report* 221 (Winter 2001), 28–33.

Abou El Fadl, Khaled. "Constitutionalism and the Islamic Sunni Legacy." *UCLA Journal of Islamic and Near Eastern Law* 1 (Fall-Winter 2001–2002), 67–101.

Abou El Fadl, Khaled. "Orphans of Modernity and the Clash of Civilizations." *Global Dialogue* 4 (Spring 2002), 1–16.

Abou El Fadl, Khaled. "Islam and the Challenge of Democratic Commitment." *Fordham International Law Journal* 27 (December 2003), 4–71.

Achar, Gilbert. "Maxime Rodinson on Islamic "Fundamentalism." *Middle East Report* 34 (Winter 2004), 2–4.

Ajami, Fouad. "Iraq and the Arabs' Future." *Foreign Affairs* 82 (January-February 2003), 2–18.

Anderson, Lisa. "Arab Democracy: Dismal Prospects." *World Policy Journal* 28 (Fall 2001), 53–60.

Aras, Bulent, and Omer Caha. "Fethullah Gulen and His Liberal 'Turkish Islam' Movement." *Middle East Review of International Affairs* (December 2000); www.biu.ac.il/SOC/besa/meria/journal/2000/issue4/jv4n4a4.html.

Arjomand, Said Amir. "Iran's Revolution in Comparative Perspective." *World Politics* 38 (April 1986), 383–414.

Arjomand, Said Amir. "The Reform Movement and the Debate on Modernity and Tradition in Contemporary Iran." *International Journal of Middle East Studies* 34 (November 2002), 719–731.

Armstrong, Karen. "Is a Holy War Inevitable?" *GQ* (January 2002), 96–101, 122–123.

Asad, Talal. "Reflections on Laïcité and the Public Sphere." *Items and Issues* 5, no. 3 (2005), 1–11.

Ashraf, Ahmed, and Ali Banuazizi. "Iran's Tortuous Path toward 'Islamic Liberalism.'" *International Journal of Politics, Culture and Society* 15 (Winter 2001), 237–256.

Bader, Veit. "Religions and States: A New Typology and Plea for Non-Constitutional Pluralism." *Ethical Theory and Moral Practice* 6 (March 2003), 55–91.

Baker, Wayne, and Ronald Inglehart. "Modernization, Cultural Change, and the Persistence of Traditional Values." *American Sociological Review* 65 (February 2000), 19–51.

Barton, Greg. "Neo-Modernism: A Vital Synthesis of Traditionalist and Modernist Islamic Thought in Indonesia." *Studia Islamika* 2 (1995), 5–75.

Barton, Greg. "Indonesia's Nurcholish Madjid and Abdurrahman Wahid as Intellectual Ulama: The Meeting of Islamic Traditionalism and Modernism in Neo-modernist Thought." *Islam and Christian-Muslim Relations* 8 (October 1997), 323–350.

Berman, Sheri. "Lessons from Europe." *Journal of Democracy* 18 (January 2007), 28–41.

Boffetti, Jason. "How Richard Rorty Found Religion." *First Things* 143 (May 2004), 24–29.

Bush, Robin. "Redefining 'Political Islam' in Indonesia: Nahdlatul Ulama and Khittah '26." *Studia Islamika* 7 (2000), 59–86.

Bustamam-Ahmad, Kamaruzzaman. "Tracing the Roots of Indonesian Muslim Intellectuals: A Bibliographical Survey." *Kyoto Review of Southeast Asia* 8 (March 2007); http://kyotoreviewsea.org/kamaruzaman.htm.

Campo, Juan Eduardo. "The Ends of Islamic Fundamentalism: Hegemonic Discourse and the Islamic Question in Egypt." *Contention* 4 (Spring 1995), 167–194.

Carroll, James. "Why Religion Still Matters." *Daedalus* 132 (Summer 2003), 9–13.

Casanova, José. "Civil Society and Religion: Retrospective Reflections on Catholicism and Prospective Reflections on Islam." *Social Research* 68 (Winter 2001), 1041–1080.

Cole, Juan. "Bush's Napoleonic Folly." *Nation* 285 (10 September 2007); www.thenation.com/doc/20070910/cole.

Cole, Juan. "Shiite Religious Parties Fill Vacuum in Southern Iraq." *Middle East Report Online*, 22 April 2003; www.merip.org/mero/mero042203.html.

Crooke, Alastair. "Our Second Biggest Mistake in the Middle East." *London Review of Books* 29 (5 July 2007).

Cunningham, Frank. "The Conflicting Truths of Religion and Democracy." *Social Philosophy Today* 21 (July 2005), 65–80.

Dagi, Ihsan. "Rethinking Human Rights, Democracy, and the West: Post-Islamist Intellectuals in Turkey." *Critique* 13 (summer 2004), 135–151.

Dallmayr, Fred. "Beyond Monologue: For a Comparative Political Theory." *Perspectives on Politics* 2 (June 2004), 249–257.

Davis, Derek. "Thomas Jefferson and the 'Wall of Separation.'" *Journal of Church and State* 45 (Winter 2003), 5–13.

Fish, M. Steven. "Islam and Authoritarianism." *World Politics* 55 (October 2002), 4–37.

Flores, Alexander. "Secularism, Integralism and Political Islam: The Egyptian Debate." *Middle East Report* 23 (July–August 1993), 32–38.

Fox, Jonathan, and Shmuel Sandler. "Separation of Religion and State in the Twenty-first Century: Comparing the Middle East and Western Democracies." *Comparative Politics* 37 (April 2005), 317–335.

Fox, Jonathan. "World Separation of Religion and State into the Twenty-First Century." *Comparative Political Studies* 39 (June 2006), 537–569.

Fox, Jonathan. "Do Democracies Have Separation of Religion and State?" *Canadian Journal of Political Science* 40 (March 2007), 1–25.

Fradkin, Hillel. "Does Democracy Need Religion?" *Journal of Democracy* 11 (January 2000), 87–94.

Fukuyama, Francis. "Their Target: The Modern World." *Newsweek* 138 (17 December 2001), 42–48.

Fukuyama, Francis, and Nadav Samin. "Can Any Good Come of Radical Islam?" *Commentary* 114 (September 2002), 34–38.

Gellner, Ernest. "Religion and the Profane." *Eurozine* (28 August 2000); www.eurozine .com/articles/2000–08–28-gellner-en.html.

Gillespie, Piers. "Current Issues in Indonesian Islam: Analyzing the 2005 Council on Indonesian Ulama Fatwa No. 7 Opposing Pluralism, Liberalism and Secularism." *Journal of Islamic Studies* 18 (May 2007), 202–240.

Gülen, Fethullah. "A Comparative Approach to Islam and Democracy." *SAIS Review* 21 (Summer–Fall 2001), 133–138.

Gunn, T. Jeremy. "Under God but Not the Scarf: The Founding Myths of Religious Freedom in the United States and *Laïcité* in France." *Journal of Church and State* 46 (Winter 2004), 7–24.

Hashemi, Nader. "How Dangerous Are the Islamists?" *Middle East Affairs Journal* 2 (Summer–Fall 1996), 12–23.

Hashemi, Nader. "From the Red Menace to the Green Peril: The Enduring Legacy of the Cold War and Its Linkage to Political Islam." *Middle East Affairs Journal* 3 (Winter 1997), 47–60.

Hashemi, Nader. "Islam, Democracy and Alexis de Tocqueville." *Queen's Quarterly* 110 (Spring 2003), 21–29.

Hashemi, Nader. "Inching toward Democracy: Religion and Politics in the Muslim World." *Third World Quarterly* 24 (June 2003), 563–578.

Hashemi, Nader. "The Relevance of John Locke to Social Change in the Muslim World: A Comparison with Iran." *Journal of Church and State* 46 (Winter 2004), 39–53.

Hashemi, Nader. "Rethinking Religion, Secularism and Democracy in the Muslim World: Reflections on the Stepan Thesis." *Global Dialogue* 6 (Winter–Spring 2004), 34–43.

Hefner, Robert. "Making Democracy Work, Islamically." *Inside Indonesia* 90 (October–December 2007); http://insideindonesia.org/content/view/1016/47/.

Heper, Metin and şEule Toktaş. "Islam, Modernity, and Democracy in Contemporary Turkey: The Case of Recep Tayyip Erdoğan." *Muslim World* 93 (April 2003), 157–185.

Hitchens, Christopher. "9/11, Islamic Fascism and the Secular Intellectual: An Evening with Christopher Hitchens." *Salmagundi* 133–134 (Winter-Spring 2002), 3–30.

Howard, Tal. "Charisma and History: The Case of Münster, Westphalia, 1534–1535." *Essays in History* 35 (1993), 49–65.

Huntington, Samuel. "Will Countries Become More Democratic?" *Political Science Quarterly* 99 (Summer 1984), 193–218.

Ibrahim, Saad Eddin. "Reviving Middle Eastern Liberalism." *Journal of Democracy* 14 (October 2003), 5–10.

Ignatieff, Michael. "The Attack on Human Rights." *Foreign Affairs* 80 (November–December 2001), 102–116.

Jan, Tarik. "Mawdudi's Critique of the Secular Mind." *Muslim World* 93 (July–October 2003), 503–519.

John Zogby Group International, Inc. "American Attitudes towards Islam: A Nationwide Poll." *American Journal of Islamic Social Sciences* 10 (Fall 1993), 403–407.

Kalyvas, Stathis. "Democracy and Religious Politics: Evidence from Belgium." *Comparative Political Studies* 31 (June 1998), 292–320.

Kaplan, Robert. "Looking the World in the Eye." *Atlantic Monthly* 288 (December 2001), 68–82.

Karatnychy, Adrian. "Muslim Countries and the Democracy Gap." *Journal of Democracy* 13 (January 2002), 99–112.

Keddie, Nikki. "Secularism and the State: Towards Clarity and Global Comparison." *New Left Review* 226 (November–December 1997), 21–40.

Keddie, Nikki. "The New Religious Politics: Where, When and Why Do 'Fundamentalisms' Appear?" *Comparative Studies in Society and History* 40 (October 1998), 696–723.

Keddie, Nikki. "Secularism and Its Discontents." *Daedalus* 132 (Summer 2003), 14–30.

Khosrokhavar, Farhad. "The New Intellectuals of Iran." *Social Compass* 51 (June 2004), 191–202.

Kuru, Ahmet. "Passive and Assertive Secularism: Historical Conditions, Ideological Struggles and State Policies toward Religion." *World Politics* 59 (July 2007), 568–594.

Kurzman, Charles. "Bin Laden and Other Thoroughly Modern Muslims." *Contexts* 1 (Fall–Winter 2002), 13–20.

Lapidus, Ira. "The Separation of State and Religion in the Development of Early Islamic Society." *International Journal of Middle Eastern Studies* 6 (1975), 363–385.

Lewis, Bernard. "Islam and Liberal Democracy: A Historical Overview." *Journal of Democracy* 7 (April 1996), 52–63.

Lewis, Bernard. "Islam and Liberal Democracy." *Atlantic Monthly* 271 (February 1993), 89–98.

Lewis, Bernard. "The Revolt of Islam." *New York Review of Books* 30 (30 June 1983), 35–38.

Lewis, Bernard. "How Khomeini Made It." *New York Review of Books* 31 (17 January 1985), 10–13.

Lewis, Bernard. "The Shi'a." *New York Review of Books* 32 (15 August 1985), 7–10.

Lewis, Bernard. "Islamic Revolution." *New York Review of Books* 34 (21 January 1988), 46–49. Reprinted in Bernard Lewis, *From Babel to Dragomans: Interpreting the Middle East.* New York: Oxford University Press, 2004.

Lewis, Bernard. "The Revolt of Islam." *New Yorker* 77 (19 November 2001), 51–63.

Lewis, Bernard. "The Roots of Muslim Rage." *Atlantic Monthly* 266 (September 1990), 47–60.

Lewis, Bernard. "Why Turkey Is the Only Muslim Democracy." *Middle East Quarterly* 1 (March 1994), 41–49.

Lijphart, Arend. "Comparative Politics and the Comparative Method." *American Political Science Review* 65 (September 1971), 682–693.

Lijphart, Arend. "The Comparable-cases Strategy in Comparative Research."
    Comparative Political Studies 8 (July 1975), 158–177.
Lipset, Seymour Martin. "The Social Requisites of Democracy Revisited." *American
    Sociological Review* 59 (February 1994), 1–22.
Masud, Muhammad Khalid. "The Construction and Deconstruction of Secularism as an
    Ideology of Contemporary Muslim Thought." *Asian Journal of Social Science* 33
    (September 2005), 363–383.
Matin-Asgari, Afshin. "The Intellectual Best-sellers of Post-revolutionary Iran: On
    Backwardness, Elite-killing and Western Rationality." *Iranian Studies* 37 (March
    2004), 73–88.
McFaul, Michael. "Chinese Dreams, Persian Realities." *Journal of Democracy* 16
    (October 2005), 74–82.
Michel, Thomas. "Sufism and Modernity in the Thought of Fethullah Gülen." *Muslim
    World* 95 (July 2005), 341–358.
Milani, Mohsen. "Iran's Reform Movement and Khatami's Domestic Political Agenda."
    Journal of South Asian and Middle Eastern Studies 25 (Fall 2001), 13–21.
Mujani, Saiful, and R. William Liddle. "Politics, Islam and Public Opinion." *Journal of
    Democracy* 15 (January 2004), 109–123.
Najjar, Fauzi. "The Debate on Islam and Secularism in Egypt." *Arab Studies Quarterly* 18
    (Spring 1996), 1–21.
Nasr, Seyyed Vali Reza. "Democracy and Islamic Revivalism." *Political Science Quarterly*
    110 (Summer 1995), 261–285.
Nasr, Seyyed Vali Reza. "Secularism: Lessons from the Muslim World." *Daedalus* 132
    (Summer 2003), 67–72.
Nasr, Vali. "Religion and Global Affairs: Secular States and Religious Oppositions."
    SAIS Review 18 (Summer-Fall 1998), 32–37.
Nasr, Vali, and Ali Gheissari. "Iran's Democracy Debate." *Middle East Policy* 11 (Summer
    2004), 94–106.
Nasr, Vali. "The Rise of Muslim Democracy." *Journal of Democracy* 16 (April 2005),
    13–27.
Özdalga, Elizabeth. "Secularizing Trends in Fethullah Gulen's Movement: Impass or
    Opportunity for Further Revival?" *Critique* 12 (Spring 2003), 61–73.
Pannenberg, Wolfhart. "How to Think about Secularism." *First Things* 64 (June–July
    1996), 27–32.
Philpott, Daniel. "The Catholic Wave." *Journal of Democracy* 15 (April 2004), 32–46.
Reichley, James. "Democracy and Religion." *PS* 19 (Autumn 1986), 801–806.
Rorty, Richard. "Religion as a Conversation Stopper." *Common Knowledge* 3 (Spring
    1994), 1–6.
Rorty, Richard. "The Moral Purposes of the University: An Exchange." *Hedgehog Review*
    2 (Fall 2000), 106–119.
Rorty, Richard. "Religion in the Public Square: A Reconsideration." *Journal of Religious
    Ethics* 31 (March 2003), 141–149.
Rosenblum, Nancy. "Religious Parties, Religious Political Identity and the Cold Should of
    Liberal Democratic Thought." *Ethical Theory and Moral Practice* 6 (March 2003), 23–53.

Sartori, Giovanni. "How Far Can Free Government Travel?" *Journal of Democracy* 6 (July 1995), 101–111.

Sartori, Giovanni. "Rethinking Democracy: Bad Polity and Bad Politics." *International Social Science Journal* 43 (August 1991), 437–450.

Sen, Amartya. "Democracy as a Universal Value." *Journal of Democracy* 10 (July 1999), 3–17.

Sen, Amartya. "East and West: The Reach of Reason." *New York Review of Books* 47 (20 July 2000), 33–38.

Sen, Amartya. "Human Rights and Asian Values." *New Republic* 217 (14–21 July 1997), 33–40.

Sen, Amartya "Why Democratization Is Not the Same as Westernization." *New Republic* 229 (6 October 2003), 28–33.

Shepard, William. "Islam and Ideology: Towards a Typology." *International Journal of Middle East Studies* 19 (August 1987), 307–336.

Sigler, John. "Understanding the Resurgence of Islam: The Case of Political Islam." *Middle East Affairs Journal* 2 (Summer–Fall 1996), 79–91.

Sivan, Emmanuel. "Democracy, Catholicism and Islam." *Arab Reform Bulletin* 2 (February 2004).

Stepan, Alfred. "Religion, Democracy, and the 'Twin Tolerations.'" *Journal of Democracy* 11 (October 2000), 27–57.

Swaine, Lucas. "Institutions of Conscience: Politics and Principle in a World of Religious Pluralism." *Ethical Theory and Moral Practice* 6 (March 2003), 93–118.

Rais, Amien. "An Interview with Amien Rais." By Alfred Stepan and Mirjam Künkler. *Journal of International Affairs* 61 (Fall–Winter 2007), 205–216.

Strauss, Roger. "The Relations of Religion to Democracy." *Public Opinion Quarterly* 2 (January 1938), 37–38.

Tarkow, I. Naamani. "The Significance of the Act of Settlement in the Evolution of English Democracy." *Political Science Quarterly* 58 (December 1943), 537–561.

Tibi, Bassam. "Major Themes in the Arabic Political Literature of Islamic Revivalism, 1970–1985: The Islamic System of Government (*al-nizam al-islami*), *Shura* Democracy and the Implementation of the Shari'a as Opposed to Secularism (*'ilmaniyya*)." *Islam and Christian-Muslim Relations* 3 (December 1992), 183–210.

Tibi, Bassam. "Major Themes in the Arabic Political Literature of Islamic Revivalism, 1970–1985: The Islamic System of Government (*al-nizam al-islami*), *Shura* Democracy and the Implementation of the Shari'a as Opposed to Secularism (*'ilmaniyya*)." *Islam and Christian-Muslim Relations* 4 (June 1993), 83–99.

Venkataraman, Arun. "Islam and Democracy: A Tocquevillian Approach." *Critique* (Spring 2007); http://lilt.ilstu.edu/critique/spring07docs/Venkataraman2.pdf.

Voll, John O., and John L. Esposito. "Islam's Democratic Essence." *Middle East Quarterly* 1 (September 1994), 3–11.

Wald, Kenneth, and Clyde Wilcox. "Getting Religion: Has Political Science Rediscovered the Faith Factor?" *American Political Science Review* 100 (November 2006), 523–529.

Wahid, Abdurrahman. "Indonesia's Mild Secularism." *SAIS Review* 21 (Summer–Fall 2001), 25–28.

Woodberry, Robert, and Timothy Shah. "Christianity and Democracy: Pioneering Protestants." *Journal of Democracy* 15 (April 2004), 47–61.

Woodhouse, A. S. P. "Religion and Some Foundations of English Democracy." *Philosophical Review* 61 (October 1952), 503–531.

Wuthnow, Robert. "Understanding Religion and Politics." *Daedalus* 120 (Summer 1991), 1–20.

Yavuz, M. Hakan, and Michael Gunter. "Turkish Paradox: Progressive Islamists versus Reactionary Secularists." *Critique* 16 (Fall 2007), 289–301.

Zartman, I. William. "Democracy and Islam: The Cultural Dialectic." *Annals of the American Academy of Political and Social Science* 524 (November 1992), 181–191.

Zebiri, Kate. "Muslim Anti-secularist Discourse in the Context of Muslim-Christian Relations." *Islam and Christian-Muslim Relations* 9 (1998), 47–64.

Zubaida, Sami. "Is There a Muslim Society? Ernest Gellner's Sociology of Islam." *Economy and Society* 24 (May 1995), 151–188.

Zubaida, Sami. "Trajectories of Political Islam." *Index on Censorship* 25 (July–August 1996), 150–157.

Zubaida, Sami. "Islam and Secularization." *Asian Journal of Social Science* 33 (September 2005), 438–448.

FOREIGN LANGUAGE SOURCES

Abderraziq, Ali. *L'Islam et les fondements du pouvoir.* Translated by Abdou Filali-Ansary. Paris: La Découverte, 1994.

Baghi, Emadeddin. *Tirazhidi-i dimkrasi dar Iran: bazkhvani-i qatlha-yi zanjirah'i* [The Tragedy of Democracy in Iran: Revisiting the Serial Murders]. Tehran: Nashre-Ney, 1998.

Bazegar, Jamsheed. "Parliamentary Representatives: Elected by the People or Appointed by the Hidden [Shia] Imam?" BBC Persian Service, 13 June 2004.

Braudel, Fernand. *Écrits sur l'histoire.* Paris: Flammarion, 1985.

Eskhevari, Hassan Yousefi. *Kherad dar Zeyafat Din* [Reason in the House of Religion]. Tehran: Ghaseedeh, 2000.

Fadlallah, Muhammad Hussein. "Lettre ouverte menaçante de Fadlallah, fondateur et guide spirituel du Hezbollah, à Jacques Chirac"; Posted on the website of the Conseil Régional du culte musulman Champagne Ardenne; http://www.crcm-cha.org/modules.php?name=News&file=article&sid=63.

Ganji, Akbar. *Talaqqi-yi fashisti az din va hukumat: Asibshinasi-yi guzar bi-dawlat-i dimukratik- i tawsiih-gira*[The Fascist Interpretation of Religion and Government: The Pathology of Transition to a Democratic and Development-oriented state]. Tehran: Tarh-e No, 2000.

Ganji, Akbar. "30 Million People and Six Individuals," *Sobh-e Emrooz* (Tehran), 27 May 1999.

Hajjarian, Saeed. *Az Shahed-i Qodsi ta Shahed-i Bazari: Orfi-shodan-i Din dar Sepehr-i Siyasat* (From the Sacred Witness to the Profane Witness: The Secularization of Religion in the Sphere of Politics) (Tehran: Tarh-e No, 1999).

Hajjarian, Saeed. *Jumhouriyat: Afsoon-zedaie as ghodrat* [Republic: Demystifying Political Power]. Tehran: Tarh-e No, 1999.

Imarah, Muhammad. *al-Almaniyya wa Nahdatuna al-Haditha* [Secularism and Our Modern Renaissance]. Cairo: Dar al Shorouq, 1986.

Kadivar, Mohsen. *Baha-ye Azadi: Defaiyat-e Mohsen Kadivar dar dadgah-e Vizhe-ye Ruhaniyat* [The Price of Freedom: Mohsen Kadivar's Defense before the Special Clerical Court]. Tehran: Nashr-e Ney, 1999.

Kadivar, Mohsen. *Daghdaghe ha-yi Hukumat-i-dini* (Crises of Religious Government) (Tehran: Nashr-e Ney, 2000).

Kadivar, Mohsen. *Nazariyaha-ye dawlat dar fiqh-e Shia* (These on the State in Shi'i Jurisprudence) (Tehran: Nashr-e Ney, 1997).

Mesbah Yazdi, Muhammad. *Negahi Guzrah be Velayat e Faqih* [A Quick Glance at the Theory of Velayat e Faqih]. Qum: Moasseseh-ye Imam Khomeini, 2000.

Mesbah, Yazdi, Muhammad. *Nazarriyeh Siyassi Islam* [A Political Theory of Islam]. 2 vols. Qum: Moasseseh-ye Imam Khomeini, 2001.

Mujtahid-Shabistari, Muhammad. *Naqdi bar qiraat-i rasmi-yi din* [A Critique of the Official Reading of Religion] Tehran: Tarh-e No, 2000.

Qaradawi, Yusuf. *'Al-Hulul al Mustawradah wa Kayfa Jaat 'alaa Ummatina'* [How the Imported Solutions Disastrously Affected our Ummah]. Cairo: Maktabat Wahbah, 1977.

Qaradawi, Yusuf. *al-Islam wa al-Ilmaniyah* [Islam and Secularism]. Beirut: Mo'assassat al-Rissalah, 2000.

Rouleau, Eric. "Un Enjeu Pour Le Monde Musalman: En Iran, islam contre islam." *Le Monde Diplomatique* (June 1999).

Saanei, Ayatollah Yusuf. *Ahkam-e Banavon* [Rulings on women]. Qum: Maysam Tammar, 2007.

Soroush, Abdol Karim. *Qabz va Bast-i tiorik-i Shari'at* [Theory on the Contraction and Expansion of the Shariah]. Tehran: Mu'assassah-yi Farhangi-yi Sirat, 1990.

Tocqueville, Alexis de. *De la démocratie en Amérique*. Paris: Gallimard, 1986.

NEWS SOURCES

Without Author

"Communist Party Sees the Light, Adopts Politics of Religion." Reuters, 22 November 2003.

"Headscarf Ban Sparks New Protests." *BBC News*, 17 January 2004; http://news.bbc.co.uk/2/hi/europe.3405453.stm.

"Iran Reformist leader Warns of 'Religious Dictatorship.'" Agence France Presse, 13 December 2002.

"Iraqi President Rules Out Islamic Regime in His Country." Agence France Presse, 25 April 2005.

"Iraqi Sunnis against Secular Constitution." Islamonline.net, 11 February 2005; www.islamonline.net/English/News/2005-02/11/article02.shtml.

"Islam Based on People's Rule." *Iran Daily* (Tehran), 10 August 2004.

"Khamenei: Integration of Religion, Politics, Iran's Strong Point." Islamic Republic of
 Iran News Agency, 10 September 2002.

"Malaysia Not a Secular State, Says Najib." Malaysia National News Agency (Bernama),
 17 July 2007.

"Malaysia an Islamic State but Minority Rights Protected, Says Deputy PM." Associated
 Press, 17 July 2007.

"Military Steps in Presidential Election Debate." *Zaman* (Istanbul), 28 April 2007.

"NATO Chief Warns of Islamic Extremists." *Globe and Mail* (Toronto), 3 February 1995.

"Re-elected Iran Leader Vows 'Freedom, Justice. '" Associated Press, 11 June 2001.

With Author

Ajami, Fouad. "Nowhere Man." *New York Times Magazine*, 7 October 2001.

Ali, Ayaan Hirsi. "Can Secular Turkey Survive Democracy?" *Los Angeles Times*, 9 May 2007.

Blackwell, Tom. "Canada Needs 'Lethal Power, ' Ignatieff Says." *National Post*, 7
 November 2002.

Boland, Vincent. "Eastern Premise." *Financial Times*, 3 December 2004.

Bouteldja, Naima. "The Reality of l'affaire du foulard." *Guardian*, 25 February 2005.

Deane, Claudia, and Darryl Fears. "Negative Perception of Islam Increasing."
 Washington Post, 9 March 2006.

Easterbrook, Gregg. "Death and Dogma: Behind the Moslem Fury at 'Satanic Verses'—
 The West's Enduring Ignorance of Islam." *Washington Post*, 19 February 1989.

El-Affendi, Abdelwahab. "Do Muslims Deserve Democracy." *New Internationalist* 345
 (May 2002).

Erbakan, Necmettin. "Turkey: Q & A with Necmettin Erbakan." By Manal Lutfi. *Asharq
 Al-Awsat* (English ed.), 16 November 2007.

Fassihi, Farnaz. "For Iran, a Question of Faith." *New Jersey Star-Ledger*, 16 December 2002.

Fathi, Nazila. "Ayatollah Tugs at Ties Constricting Iran's Women." *New York Times*, 29
 July 2001.

Fathi, Nazila. "Iranian Leader Bars Press Bill of Reform Bloc." *New York Times*, 7 August
 2000.

Fisher, William. "Muslim Scholar Urges Halt to Extreme Punishments." Inter Press
 Service, 28 April 2005.

Friedman, Thomas. "The Saudi Challenge." *New York Times*, 20 February 2002.

Fukuyama, Francis. "History Is Still Going Our Way." *Wall Street Journal*, 5 October 2001.

Goodstein, Laurie. "As Attacks' Impact Recedes, a Return to Religion as Usual." *New
 York Times*, 21 November 2001.

Hacaoglu, Selcan. "Turkey's President Says Islamist Threat to Secular Establishment at
 Highest Level." *Independent*, 14 April 2007.

Haeri, Safa. "Conservative Clerics Rally in Support of Khameneh'i." *Iran Press Service*, 27
 December 1997.

Hamid, Wan Hamidi. "I Am Not a Secularist, Says Abbas." *New Strait Times*, 23 October
 2007.

Hashemi, Nader. "Misreading America's Past in the Middle East." *Chicago Tribune*, 18 February 2007.

Hirst, David. "Modernists Take on Iran's Mullahs." *Guardian Weekly*, 12 April 1998.

International Crisis Group Report. "Broader Middle East and North Africa Initiative: Imperilled at Birth." 7 June 2004.

Jansen, Michael. "Shia Clerics Insist on the Adoption of Islamic Law." *Irish Times*, 7 February 2005.

Keddie, Nikki. "Don't Judge a Woman by Her Cover: Life Is Not All Bad in Iran." *Times* (London), 9 February 2004.

Liddle, R. William, and Saiful Mujani. "The Real Face of Indonesian Islam." *New York Times*, 11 October 2003.

Lyons, Jonathon. "President Says Freedom Is Vital to Islamic Iran." Reuters, 25 November 1999.

Lewis, Bernard. "Time for Toppling." *Wall Street Journal*, 27 September 2002.

McCarthy, Rory. "Secret UN Report Condemns US for Middle East Failures." *The Guardian*, 13 June 2007.

McDermott, Mikaela, and Brian Katulis. "Even the Word 'Democracy' Now Repels Mideast Reformers." *Christian Science Monitor*, 20 May 2004.

Michael, Maggie. "Egypt's Brotherhood Party Details Platform Akin to That of Iran." *Boston Globe*, 11 October 2007.

Naqvi, Jawed. "Iran Seeks Kashmir Role, Warns of U.S. Involvement." Reuters, 19 April 1995.

O'Brien, Conor Cruise. "Sick Man of the World." *Times* (London), 11 May 1989.

Perlez, Jane. "Nurcholish Madjid, 66, Advocate of Moderate Islam, Dies." *New York Times*, 1 September 2005.

Perlman, Marc. "New Front Sets Sight on Toppling Regime." *Forward*, 16 May 2003.

Peterson, Scott. "Iranian Revelations as Press Tests New Freedom." *Christian Science Monitor*, 29 June 1998.

Padgoankar, Dilip. "An Area of Awakening," *Times of India*, 18 July 1993.

Peter, Tom. "At a Massive Rally, Hizb ut-Tahrir Calls for a Global Muslim State." *Christian Science Monitor*, 14 August 2007.

Raiss-Tousi, Ali. "Iran Demonstrators Denounce Israel, Khatami Allies." Reuters, 31 December 1999.

Ross, Dennis. "Can Fatah Compete with Hamas?" *New Republic*, 16 July 2007.

Said, Edward. "Dreams and Delusions." *Al Ahram Weekly*, 21–27 August 2003.

Saanei, Yousef. "The Women's Mufti: Interview with Grand Ayatollah Yousef Saanei." By Manal Lutfi. *Asharq Al-Awsat* (English ed.), 6 April 2007.

Siegman, Henry. "Those Who Do Not Want Hamas Will Get al Qaida." *Al Hayat*, 24 June 2007.

Sekhar, Vaishnavi. "When Organizers Almost Shooed Her off the Stage." *Times of India*, 17 January 2004.

Sen, Amartya. "Why Democratization Is Not the Same as Westernization: Democracy and Its Global Roots." *New Republic*, 6 October 2003.

Slackman, Michael. "Frustrated by Deadlock, Iranians Seek New Voice." *Los Angeles Times*, 26 July 2002.

Soto, Alvaro de. "End of Mission Report." http://image.guardian.co.uk/sys-files/ Guardian/documents/2007/06/12/DeSotoReport.pdf.

Telhami, Shibley. "A Growing Muslim Identity: Increasingly, Arabs Identify Themselves in Terms of Islam." *Los Angeles Times*, 11 July 2004.

Tavernise, Sabrina. "Turkish Military Issues Threat as Voting Is Derailed." *New York Times*, 28 April 2007.

Tavernise, Sabrina. "In Turkey, Fear about Religious Lifestyle." *New York Times*, 30 April 2007.

Waldman, Peter. "A Historian's Take on Islam Steers U.S. in Terrorism Fight." *Wall Street Journal*, 3 February 2004.

Walker, Martin. "American Eagle Cheated of Its Prey." *Guardian Weekly*, 8 September 1991.

Wright, Robin. "U.S. Now Views Iran in a More Favorable Light." *Los Angeles Times*, 14 February 2003.

WEB SITES, INTERVIEWS, LECTURES, AND UNPUBLISHED PAPERS

Ahmad, Eqbal. Interview by Emran Qureshi. Unpublished. 21 December 1994.

Angus Reid Global Monitor. "Indonesians Endorse Secular Politics." 11 October 2007; www.angus-reid.com/polls/view/indonesians_endorse_secular_politics.

Assyaukanie, Lutfhi. "Islam and Secularism in Indonesia." Unpublished paper, 2007.

Crabtree, Scott. "Turks at Odds over Islamic Law," Gallup poll, 10 December 2007; www.gallup.com/poll/103129/Turks-Odds-Over-Islamic-Law.aspx.

Ebadi, Shirin. "Islam, Democracy and Human Rights." Lecture, Syracuse University, 10 May 2004. Published in *Syracuse University News*, 12 May 2004.

Fealy, Greg. "In Fear of Radical Islam: A Critical Examination of the Evidence." Unpublished paper, November 2005.

Fergany, Nader. "The USA Has Given Democracy a Bad Name." Joint Web site of Bundeszentrale für politische Bildung (Federal Center for Political Education), Deutsche Welle, the Goethe Institut and the Institut für Auslandsbeziehungen (Institute for Foreign Cultural Relations); www.qantara.de/webcom/show_article .php/_c-476/_nr-189/_p-1/i.html.

Freedom House. *Freedom in the World 2007;* www.freedomhouse.org/template.cfm? page=372&year=2007.

Ghobarah, Hazem. "Gateways to Modernity: Puritanism and Islamism?" Unpublished manuscript, December 1995. Rev. 1997; www.la.utexas.edu/chenry/civil/ archives97/csdefs/0007.html.

Hamzawy, Amr. "Egypt: Regression in the Muslim Brotherhood's Party Platform?" *Arab Reform Bulletin* 5 (October 2007); http://www.carnegieendowment.org/ publications/index.cfm?fa—view&id—19648&prog=zgp&proj=:zdrl, zme#hamzawy.

Hashemi, Nader. "Political Islam versus Secularism." *Literary Review of Canada* 16 (September 2008); http://lrc.reviewcanada.ca/index.php?page=Political-Islam-Versus-Secularism.

Hefner, Robert. "Making Democracy Work, Islamically." *Inside Indonesia* 90 (October–December 2007); http://insideindonesia.org/content/view/1016/47/.

Higonnet, Patrice. "An Overview of the Separation of Church and State." Paper presented at the conference "Comparing Separations: State and Religion in France and the United States," Center for European Studies, Harvard University, 9–10 December 2005.

Keddie, Nikki. "Better Than the Past: What Recent History Has Taught Iranians." *Iranian* (25 April 2003); www.iranian.com/Opinion/2003/April/Lesson/index.html.

Kermani, Navid. "Religious Reformist Thinkers in Iran: Intellectually Victorious, but Politically Defeated." www.qantara.de (1 February 2005); http://www.qantara.de/webcom/show_article.php/_c-476/_nr-317/i.html.

Lewis, Bernard, and Khaled Abou El Fadl. "A Conversation on the Theme: 'An Islamic Reformation. '" Organized by the Global Policy Exchange, 18 October 2002; www.gpexchange.org/pages/details.html.

Patel, David. "Religious Authority and Politics in Post-Saddam Iraq." *Arab Reform Bulletin* 2 (May 2004); http://www.carnegieendowment.org/publications/index.cfm?fa=view&id=1536#authority.

Saanei, Yousef. Interview. PBS Frontline; www.pbs.org/wgbh/pages/frontline/shows/tehran/interviews/saanei.html.

Seufert, Günter. "Kemalists versus Liberal Intellectuals in Turkey: Promoting the Kemalist Personality Cult and Keeping Rank." www.qantara.de (25 May 2007); www.qantara.de/webcom/show_article.php/_c-476/_nr-791/i.html?PHPSESSID=baa1d508ffe20ef0bfb04a5550739e48.

Telhami, Shibley. 2006 Annual Arab Public Opinion Survey; www.brookings.edu/views/speeches/telhami20070208.pdf.

Utvik, Bjorn Olav. "Religious Revivalism in Nineteenth-Century Norway and in Twentieth-Century Egypt: A Critique of Fundamentalism Studies." Unpublished paper.

Index

CPSIA information can be obtained at www.ICGtesting.com
Printed in the USA
BVOW03s1825070214

344264BV00004B/12/P